OUR FLAG

OSKAR HIPPE

... AND RED IS THE COLOUR OF OUR FLAG

MEMORIES OF SIXTY YEARS IN THE WORKERS' MOVEMENT

OSKAR HIPPE

TRANSLATED BY ANDREW DRUMMOND

Index Books
London

Originally published as '. . . und unsere Fahn' ist rot'
by Junius Verlag GmbH, Hamburg, 1979

Translation copyright 1991 Andrew Drummond
Introduction copyright 1991 Workers International to Rebuild the Fourth
   International

Published by Index Books (Indexreach) Ltd
28 Charlotte Street, London W1P 1HJ

Typeset by Sumner Type, London SE15
Printed in Great Britain by BPCC Wheatons Ltd, Exeter

London Borough
of Enfield
Public Libraries

British Library Cataloguing in Publication Data

Hippe, Oskar, *1900-1990*
   And red is the colour of our flag: memories of sixty years
   in the workers' movement.
   1. Germany Trotskyism. Biographies
   I. Title
   335.433092

ISBN 1-871518-02-4

CONTENTS

Introduction   vii

Preface to the German edition   ix

Chapter 1: Socialism or monarchy   1

Chapter 2: An apprentice during the First World War   11

Chapter 3: Revolution in Russia, upheaval in Germany   21

Chapter 4: After the November rising   37

Chapter 5: Proletarian battalions   46

Chapter 6: 1923   63

Chapter 7: On the blacklist   77

Chapter 8: Conflict within the German Communist Party   89

Chapter 9: The end of the Weimar Republic   116

Chapter 10: Imprisoned by the Nazis 138

Chapter 11: 'A free man' in the Third Reich 167

Chapter 12: Political renewal 198

Chapter 13: A communist in an East German prison 213

Chapter 14: On the left wing of the SPD 243

Chapter 15: Review and prospects 269

Glossary of parties and organisations 290

Glossary of names 295

INTRODUCTION

We in the Workers International to Rebuild the Fourth International first made contact with Oskar Hippe as a consequence of the expulsion from the British Workers Revolutionary Party, in October 1985, of its long-time leader T.G.Healy.

A crucial part of the discussion which took place inside the Workers Revolutionary Party after the removal of Healy and his anti-communist clique supporters centred around the question of the struggle for the continuity of Bolshevism. How and why had we arrived at this situation, we asked ourselves. One of the ways in which I tried to find answers to these questions was to read about the communist movement in Germany, the history and development of the Left Opposition and of Trotskyism in general. What was the background to the numerous groups and individuals who claimed adherence to the name of Leon Trotsky and the Fourth International?

One book impressed me especially. This was Oskar Hippe's *...und unsere Fahn'ist rot.*

The more we looked into the history of our own movement, the more instances we found of Healy's corrupt political method, not only in Britain but internationally. Healy's misleadership infected the international body, the International Committee of the Fourth International. We uncovered many examples of comrades whose lives had been devoted to the struggle for socialist revolution who had been destroyed or isolated from the struggle as a result of Healy's methods. Oskar Hippe's own contribution must be understood in that light, though the details are still to be explained of how a principled and heroic fighter for communism, who had for a time been in contact with the International Committee of the Fourth International, had come to be so isolated.

In the course of the many factional struggles which took place in the post-October 1985 Workers Revolutionary Party, the clarification of the role of Stalinism was decisive. The depth of its influence had never before been so fully exposed. We had to face up to the extent of its domination, even inside the Fourth International itself, which threatened to liquidate and destroy the independence of the Trotskyist movement. The WRP's insistence upon this point resulted in many bitter divisions in the party.

This unremitting struggle also brought us into contact with international cadres who recognised and in many ways embodied the correctness of this understanding. Oskar Hippe was one such comrade.

When we issued the Ten-Point Call out of which arose the Preparatory Committee for an International Conference of Trotskyists, which Oskar supported, cadres began to come towards us and participate in the further clarification of this understanding. The so-called theory of the dual nature of Stalinism, which claims that under certain conditions the Stalinist bureaucracy can play a revolutionary role, had to be exposed. Without understanding that Stalinism is counter-revolutionary through and through, the agent of imperialism in the working-class movement internationally, the Fourth International cannot be rebuilt.

We are in no doubt that the struggle we conducted and continue to carry out gave new life and inspiration to comrades such as Oskar and Gertrud Hippe. It is to our great regret that they did not live to see the publication of this English translation of Oskar's book, or to participate in the conference in Budapest, in April 1990, which founded the Workers International to Rebuild the Fourth International. That conference was but the first step in seizing the growing opportunities which open up before us with the collapse of Stalinism worldwide.

Only a few weeks before this book went to the printers, a conference was held in Moscow, under the auspices of the Workers International, to commemorate the 50th anniversary of the assassination of Leon Trotsky. In the very homeland of the first-ever proletarian revolution, new links were forged which we are confident will see the re-establishment of the Russian section of the Fourth International.

The flame of determination of true communist fighters like Oskar Hippe cannot be extinguished. His example of principled struggle throughout his political life will be kept alive by the work of our movement. Work which brings together the best elements of working-class revolutionary leadership, so nearly destroyed by Stalinism, and enables us to go forward to the world socialist revolution.

The foreword and footnotes which follow formed part of the German edition of this book when it was published in 1979. It was Oskar's wish that they be included in the present translation.

Trudi Jackson
September 1990

PREFACE TO THE GERMAN EDITION

On 12 April 1937, during the fourth session of the Dewey Commission, the inquiry called to investigate the charges laid against Trotsky in the Moscow Trials, Leon Trotsky was asked about those who attended the Copenhagen conference of 1932. Trotsky named his comrades and political supporters, including 'Hippe, a German worker . . . he has now been released from prison. He was imprisoned for two years.'[1]

This book recounts, in his own words, the political life of the man who was mentioned in this statement before the Dewey Commission. From the time when, at the age of sixteen, he joined the workers' struggle in 1916, Oskar Hippe never ceased his political activity. This is a story which stretches from the Free Trade Union Youth Movement and the Spartacus League through to the German Communist Party (KPD), a story of active participation in the Left Opposition in the KPD and the Lenin League under the leadership of Hugo Urbahns, and then in the leadership of the legal and illegal work of the Trotskyists.

It is the story of a life that was spent in the prisons of the National Socialists (from 5 January 1934 to the end of 1936) *and* in those of the East German Stalinists (from September 1948 until 26 July 1956); a story which, after 1945, led to Left Opposition work in the West Berlin SPD and then to a position of influence in the Extra-Parliamentary Opposition — especially in the SDS student movement — and in the apprentices' and school pupils' movement, in particular the Berlin 'Falken' youth group and the Trotskyist groups. Even at the age of almost 80, Oskar Hippe is not some 'veteran', alone with his memories and isolated from the left wing, but is rather a comrade who still participates in the painful experiences of the left, by giving excellent talks, by discussing, by taking part in demonstrations and struggles. Oskar Hippe tells his story from 'below' and not, like so many others, from the upper ranks of the hierarchy. But he is not restricted by the 'worm's eye view'; on the contrary, he shows how historically significant grass roots activism can be. In this way he points the way forward for every one of the 'dispossessed'.

Oskar Hippe played an active role in the militant upsurges of the German workers' movement — especially in the years between the November Revolution of 1918 and the end of the revolutionary crisis of 1923, between the outbreak of the world economic crisis of 1929 and the Prussian coup d'état by von Papen on 21 July 1932, which decided Germany's fate. During these political struggles, including those within the socialist and communist movement, he went through experiences that passed into his very flesh and blood. We, from another generation — in spite of 1968 — can learn from them only at secondhand, by reading about them.

But if Oskar Hippe had the experience of the workers' movement, then his entire life, when considered as a whole, was spent *swimming against the stream*, a struggle against the three temporarily powerful, but in essence soulless bureaucracies which have dominated our century politically: against Fascism on the one hand, and against Stalinism and Social Democracy on the other. Material success, glory and honour is certainly not accorded those who have remained true to Marxism in our country.

'We find ourselves in a tiny boat in the middle of a mighty current.' These were Trotsky's words in April 1939, shortly before the outbreak of the Second World War.[2]

In such barbarous times, it was not possible to be anything other than a minority: 'Everything which, during its normal development, society rejects as the dregs of culture now comes back to take its revenge; capitalist civilisation now vomits up its undigested and uncooked food . . . ' (Trotsky, 1932)

While the vast majority of our grandparents and parents let themselves be herded before National Socialism, Stalinism and Social Democracy and thus became historically *guilty*, Oskar Hippe — unfortunately one of only a handful — did not capitulate, and did not let himself be confused or alarmed. If democracy and socialism have any meaning at all, then they draw it from the revolutionary line of tradition of the small groups of struggle which arose during the Weimar Republic and truly defended themselves against National Socialism. In the meantime even the historians have to admit that only an active minority of socialists and communists in Germany were *intellectually and morally* equal to the occasion,[3] but not the two large tendencies in the workers' movement: Social Democrats and Stalinists not only capitulated before Fascism but also failed in the reconstruction of postwar Germany. In the meantime they have betrayed and discredited all the values of Socialism.

Justice towards the details of history is what strikes you about Oskar Hippe's memoirs. We are put to shame by the almost preternatural tenacity of his political effort.

For us, Oskar Hippe embodies all that is good and honourable in the German workers' movement and gives us a hint of what it was capable of before its defeat and corruption. To try to emulate this would simply be ridiculous. We would only cover our nakedness with 'workerism' and 'the cult of the proletariat'. This is what happened in the late 1960s with the collapse of the German Extra-Parliamentary Opposition (APO).

This is not simply a matter of some cheap imitation of the 1920s. It is just as pointless to throw oneself in a state of emotional naivety and theoretical unpreparedness into the struggles which are now being fought on the street, in the factory and trade unions and in the political organisations themselves.

We must *live in the revolutionary tradition* and make its experiences and lessons our own.[4] We must learn that:

'In every epoch we should endeavour every time to ensure that the historical record is not overwhelmed by conformism (or any sympathy with the victors);

'Those who rule at any given time are the inheritors of all those who have been victorious. On the other hand, the oppressed class should study the picture of its enslaved ancestors rather than its liberated descendants. Blanqui and the Spartacists tried to carry the work of liberation to its final conclusion in the name of the defeated generations and not to present themselves as the liberators of future generations;

'Nothing has corrupted the German workers as deeply as the idea that they are swimming with the current. They believe that their factory work sets them free, that it is what Joseph Dietzgen calls the "saviour of the new age", and that nature is freely available. They have imagined that technical development was the head of water that moved the water they were swimming in.

'Awakening the spirit of the past means embracing a memory which shines brightly in the mind in a time of danger. History teaches us that the "state of emergency" in which we live is the rule, not the exception. We must arrive at a conception of history which accords with this.

'The consciousness that the continuity of history is being smashed belongs only to the revolutionary class in the course of its action.'[5]

The left sees itself challenged on three different fronts today:

The 'classical' problems of the 'traditional' workers' movement remain: its best elements must continue the struggle internationally against social destruction and the extension of the 'strong state', against growing oppression, Bonapartism and Fascism;

The question of war and peace is as urgent now as it was in 1913 or 1938: preventing a Third World War is not only in the interests of the workers' movement, but also in the interests of its allies. The bureaucratically-deformed 'workers' states' and the national revolutionary movements in the colonial and semi-colonial countries have a special role to play in this respect.

The alternatives offered by 'Greens' and the 'Rainbow coalitions' both provoke and enrich the 'orthodox left': the rejection of the destruction of both humanity and nature, the criticism of scientific-technical complexes — not only in the West — is a common responsibility.

To unite these three areas of responsibility in a theoretical programme and in practical organisation would also mean bringing together different social tendencies. Oskar Hippe has handed down to us many valuable experiences, over several generations, on the question of hegemony in such a broad spectrum. His friends hope for the widest possible circulation of his memoirs. Here we find documented, as rarely before, the actions of a worker and comrade who did not turn into some bloodstained accomplice of the bureaucratic machinery.

Oskar Hippe, his wife Gertrud and his comrades in arms determined their own lives by defending themselves as best they could in the darkest times. It has now become even more important to keep this firmly in the collective memory today, when a young generation is taking up the fight courageously and ready for sacrifice, but without knowing what words like 'Comintern' or 'Thermidor' really mean.

'The class struggle which is plain to the eyes of an historian schooled in Marx is a struggle for basic material things without which there can be no finer or spiritual things. Nevertheless, the last-named things are really present in the class struggle, and they are there not merely as the notion of the booty that goes to the victors. They are alive in this struggle as trust, as courage, as humour, as cunning and steadfastness, and they go back into the mists of time. Again and again, they will call into question every victory which the ruling class has ever gained.'[6]

Hans Querengaesser
Berlin, 1979

[1] *The Case of Leon Trotsky*. Report of Hearings on the Charges Made Against Him in the Moscow Trials by the Preliminary Commission of Inquiry, 1937. 2nd edition, New York, 1968 (Merit Publishers), p.137.
[2] Leon Trotsky, 'Swimming Against the Stream. Discussion with Comrades in April 1939', in *Writings 1938-1939*, edited by Naomi Allen and George Breitman, 2nd edition, New York, 1974 (Pathfinder Press), p.253.
[3] Hans Mömmsen, 'Social Democracy on the Defensive', in *Social Democracy Between Class Movement and People's Party*, Frankfurt, 1974, p.132:
'During the final phase of the Republic, it was characteristic that almost all the active elements of the German workers' movement had left the SPD or KPD and gathered in the splinter groups around the main party apparatus: in the KPD, the ISK, the "Rote Kämpfer" (Red Fighters), the SAPD and a number of smaller groups, some of which made up the SDAP'.
See also: Siegfried Bahne: *The KPD and the Fall of Weimar: the failure of a policy, 1932-1935*. Frankfurt/New York, 1976.
[4] See: Leon Trotsky, *Literature and Revolution*, 1923:
'In the exaggerated futuristic rejection of the past there is a Bohemian nihilism, but there is no proletarian revolutionism. We Marxists have always lived with history and have thus truly never ceased to be revolutionaries. We took in and experienced the traditions of the Paris Commune, long before the first Russian revolution. Then came the traditions of 1905, by which we were nourished while we prepared for a second revolution. Further back, we connected the Commune with the July Days of 1848 and the great French Revolution. In the realm of theory, we stretch across Marx to Hegel and the classical English economists. We who grew up and entered the struggle in the conditions of an organic epoch, we lived in the tradition of revolutions. Before our very eyes there arose more than one literary tendency which had proclaimed a merciless war against "bourgeois art" and accused us of doing things by halves. But just as the wind blows in circles, so these literary revolutionaries and iconoclasts of tradition found themselves on the easy path back to the Academy.
'For the intellectuals, even for their literary left wing, the October Revolution meant a complete overthrow of the world they were used to, that same world which they broke away from every sooften in order to join some new "school" and to which they returned without fail. For us, on the other hand, the Revolution was the embodiment of a tradition which we had known and worked over in our minds. We stepped from one world, which we negated in theory and undermined in practice, into a new world which we had already made our own by tradition and expectation . . .'
[5] Walter Benjamin, *Theses on the Philosophy of History*, 1940; 'On the Concept of History', in *Illuminations*, edited by Siegfried Unseld, Frankfurt, 1961, pp. 268-279.
[6] Walter Benjamin, *ibid*, p.269.

1.

MONARCHY OR SOCIALISM

I was born at the turn of the century, the youngest of twelve children. Neither my father nor my mother had time to bother much about our upbringing. My mother was on her feet from half-past four in the morning right through until late evening. Her first task was to make her husband's breakfast and his sandwiches, since he was out for thirteen hours each day. At that time we still had the ten-hour working day. With breaks and journey time, that took up to thirteen hours.

The next thing my mother had to do was to attend to the cows, and only then to look after the children, make their breakfast and prepare them for school. It was not uncommon for her to say: 'Children, I can't give you any sandwiches today, I've got to see if I can get hold of some bread.' This was because she never had any money in hand, and had to plead for every penny: often she failed to get any even then, for my father believed that the family could be kept fed on the produce from our garden and our field.

When husband and children had left the house, my mother had to feed the animals, work in the field and prepare the midday meal. It was usually my job to take my father's midday meal to him at his workplace. The afternoon and evening were the times for my mother to wash and mend clothes. In spite of all this, every spare minute was used to care for us and to give us her love.

My mother was fortunate in having two or three years between each child. My eldest sister was 24 years older than myself, and since the older ones were already grown up when the youngest were born, the burden on my mother was eased.

Eight years before I was born, there had been a tragic accident: my mother lay heavily pregnant in her bed; one of her daughters, then fourteen years old, was supposed to build a fire in the stove. In those days it was common, even for adults, to set the fire with the help of paraffin. And that is what my sister did, but she did not notice that some of the cinders in the stove were still glowing.

When my sister poured the paraffin onto the wood, a flame shot out of the stove, the container exploded, and she was immediately engulfed in bright flames, without my mother being able to do anything.

My mother became an old woman on that day, with snow-white hair, although she was only 34 years old. The neighbours who rushed in to help threw water over my sister, instead of smothering the flames with blankets. She was taken to the hospital with enormous burn blisters, but all the efforts of the doctors were in vain and she died a few days later. My mother never got over this experience and the memory plagued her until her death.

Apart from two children who died in infancy, all were healthy. Among the seven who grew up with me, I had one brother who was eighteen years older than myself. During my early years, I rarely saw him. He learned the trade of a baker and confectioner, but he could find no job, although we lived in the central German industrial area. At that time there were only a few bakeries around, because many workers baked their own bread. So he had to work in Leipzig. But he sometimes managed to get back home on Sundays.

My sisters, like most other girls when they left school, had to find a place on a farm or in service, because at that time the attitude was: 'Girls don't need to learn, they'll only go and get married and have children.' But the real reason was that there was not enough money to let girls learn as well. In many cases even the boys had to go off to the big farms or into industry.

When I was born, my father was working for the German Imperial Railway. At first he was on track maintenance, earning 2.20 marks a day for ten hours' labour. Later he worked in the goods yards, and rose to become a chief loader: this led to a better income, although my mother did not receive a penny more. But even his improved wage did not stretch to feeding a family. So, often, one of us children had to go to the butcher or the grocer to get fifteen pfennig-worth of bones on tick, or to borrow peas, lentils and rice.

Like most workers' families, we were in debt to the tradesmen. And it was not uncommon for more to be chalked up than was actually bought. Sometimes we had to return home empty-handed because the grocer or butcher had said: 'Tell your mother that she should pay off her old debts first.' But even then we were not among the poorest: we always had a piece of land and a few acres of field and meadow to grow our own grain and potatoes. From November to May, sometimes until June, there was no hardship, for there were always potatoes and bread. Each year we slaughtered two pigs, which gave us some meat. But for the other six months we were on short rations.

Later, when I was eleven, it got a bit better. Two of my sisters had married and moved to Leipzig. While the elder of the two was employed as maid in the household of a sawmill owner and was heavily influenced by religion there — her husband tended in this direction as well — the other one married a carpenter, who was at that time organised in a trade union and a political party.

My brother had by then given up his trade as baker and confectioner since he could earn more as a building worker. Together with his brother-in-law, he had joined the SPD (Sozial-Demokratische Partei Deutschlands, the German Socialist Party), in the Leutzsch branch in Leipzig. Both were active party officials. Like the majority of the branch, they were on the left of the party. They often came to visit us at weekends, since Leipzig was not so far from our village. We lived in Lützkendorf in the Geisel valley, not far from Merseburg. My father, a very conservative man, was a monarchist. So there were always arguments about social problems, which interested me as well, since I had started reading the *Generalanzeiger-Presse* newspaper which my father brought home, and the *Leipziger Volkszeitung* and pamphlets which my brother brought along. Both my brother, and my sister and her husband, who was very well-read, easily outdid the *Generalanzeiger* knowledge of my father.

I quietly gloated, for my father liked to lord it over the rest of the family, and would permit no other opinions. But here he had found his master and could scarcely find a single argument against the three of them. My elder sister and I, because we were still at school, had to go to bed at a particular time; this did not please me, for the discussions only really got going at that point. Later on, I managed to eavesdrop secretly on these arguments — I hid in a niche in the room, between the stove and the wall, after we had all said goodnight. My mother supported me in this, and my brother and sister tolerated it.

There were two reasons why I agreed with my brother's arguments: at first it was only out of sympathy, but later I accepted his political evaluations and rejected those of my father, for whom the topics of monarchy and Prussia were taboo. I was convinced much more by the arguments introduced by my father's opponents, which principally defended the rights of the workers. They demanded the abolition of the 'three-class' electoral law, and wanted in its place general and equal suffrage, more rights for agricultural and industrial workers, and a better education for workers' children, which also implied the abolition of the two-class school system. All these were social-democratic demands, as was the demand for better social conditions in working-class households. My father could find nothing better to counter this than to accuse the social democrats of being unpatriotic puppets and traitors.

One other thing attracted me increasingly to the arguments of social democracy: my father did not regard my mother as an equal partner in the family, but rather as the object of his needs, and in general acted as a patriarch in the family. When he was drunk, it was not uncommon for him to treat my mother brutally. She had to accept being fearfully cursed although she was on her feet from dawn until dusk.

By contrast, my father was always decent to the children and worried about us. Despite that, all our solidarity and love was for our mother, while our father received only a measure of respect. I saw in my brother, eighteen years older than myself, the figure whom I wanted to imitate, particularly because he would offer my mother some protection.

Until 1908, the districts of Merseburg, Querfurt and Weissenfels were simply country areas, although there was some industry in Merseburg and Weissenfels. In Merseburg there were some small metal works, while Weissenfels had a few shoe factories. But the land was used only for agriculture. Apart from the small and larger peasant holdings, there were also a few estates whose owners were the Helldorf family. (One member of the Helldorf family later became a leader of Hitler's SA — Brownshirts — in Berlin and even became chief of police there under the Nazis.) There was great social misery among the agricultural workers who had to work from early morning to late evening.

In the summer months, an agricultural worker earned twelve marks a week, in winter only ten. Women took home eight marks a week throughout the year. At that time, the Geisel valley was flourishing, and was counted among the 'golden pastures'.

Industrialisation began around 1908; drilling rigs were set up to assess the coal deposits. In our village it was discovered that the coal seam was 100 metres thick, sometimes only 40 centimetres below ground. Excavators came to uncover the coal. At the same time, briquetting works were built to process the coal. Two companies competed with each other — on the one hand the Czech company Petschek, and on the other the Werschen-Weissenfels Lignite Company, which had already opened up pits in the Zeitz coalfield.

In 1911 there was a great industrial crisis, and in the towns considerable unemployment, but in the Geisel valley, workers were in demand. The Polish mowers, who brought in the harvest on the estates during the summer months and had to go off home at the end of the season, stayed on as miners in the coalfield. My brother, who, along with my brother-in-law, was unemployed in Leipzig, came to the coalfield, and later so did my brother-in-law from Berlin.

All three found work building bridges, for the relatively good wage of 28.50 marks a week — wages that were considerably above the usual income in this area. All three lived at our house. This was the start of an interesting time for me, for the discussions now took place daily. For my mother, however, it was another burden on top of all the work she already had to do. Now she had to look after not only her own family, but also the three boarders. Nevertheless, she took this work upon herself, and her working day got even longer.

On the other hand, she no longer had to ask my father for every penny, for the three paid their board and lodging. And I had a new chore as well: each day I had to take the midday meal to my brothers-in-law and brother, as their workplace was some 35 minutes away from our village. In those days, the ten-hour day was worked in bridge-building as well, with one hour's break at midday — so there was enough time for conversation. At that time, the Morocco crisis was breaking, and there was fighting in the Balkans.

The fitters who led the work were socialists. I often spent the entire hour there listening to their conversations. So in due course I broadened my horizons. In these three years — 1911 to 1913 — the basis for my later socialist beliefs was laid both in the discussions at home and at the workplace of my relatives, but more especially in my study of Marxist literature and the newspapers of the SPD. When my father caught me reading the papers and pamphlets, he always took them away, and often threatened to burn them, without ever doing so. Then he would lecture me about the wickedness of the SPD. Any doubts which arose in my mind as a result were soon banished again by talking to my brother.

My Leipzig brother-in-law was an especially good teacher, as was my sister, his wife, who could argue very well and knew how to convince me.

In order not to be caught out again by my father, I moved out of the room into the barn for my studies. There in the loft we had straw and hay, and in the gable end of the barn there was a window one foot square which let in quite enough light to read by.

Nevertheless, I did not always have the time to pursue this pleasant pastime, for my father gave me jobs to do every day. Thus, in the summer months, I had to fetch water from the village every day — except when it rained — for we had no piped water supply. The well no longer had any water, because all the wells had dried up when the coal shafts were opened; the water table sank by many metres. The coal companies were obliged to take care of the water supply. In all the villages in the Geisel valley, water pipes were laid. The water tower, which was supposed to supply water to our village and two others, did not however provide enough pressure to reach our house. So we had water pipes in the house, but no water in those pipes. Protesting to the local council brought no results. My father was simply advised that he was in no position to take the company to court. And so I always had to fetch two barrels, each with 1.5 cubic metres of water, in a handcart, and my father used them to water the plants in the garden. In any case, each day I spent several hours on the most varied tasks. But in spite of this, I still found time for the study of Marxist writings as well as my schoolwork.

On the other hand I did not neglect games with other children: according to the time of year, different games were played. One of the favourites was flying kites in the autumn — we made the kites ourselves. In winter there was sledging and skating on the village pond. We children only had one pair of shoes each, which were worn only on special occasions; the rest of the year we ran around in wooden clogs, even to school. But in order to get on with our beloved skating, an old pair of father's or brother's boots was taken, the skates were tied on to those, and off we went on to the ice. We also enjoyed cops and robbers.

None of the workers' children wanted to be a cop, for the police were notorious among the workers. So we always had to draw lots. And often we succeeded in persuading the sons of peasants to play the cops. Paradoxical though it may sound, it was not the children playing the cops who had a gun, but the 'robbers'. From friends who were apprenticed, we had managed to get hold of a length of seamless piping which had been welded closed at one end and drilled so that we could load it with powder. This weapon we mounted on a handcart, and thus we marched out against the gendarmes, four dogs pulling the cart. The gun was loaded with gunpowder and small pieces of gravel, blocked up at one end with a piece of newspaper, and then shot at the 'police'. Luckily, there was never an accident.

The game would be played out on a larger scale whenever the schoolchildren of a few villages met up with those of other villages. These 'battles' took place on a large meadow on both sides of the railway line. We were armed with wooden swords which we had made ourselves. On the 'General's Hill' stood the local notables — and the real gendarmes — who watched the events, but never interfered, even when the battle turned dangerous. The girls joined in too, and it was their job to collect the pebbles which the boys hurled at each other. And so-called 'assaults' took place,

Oskar's parents outside their house in Lützkendorf: a golden-wedding portrait in 1925

more than once resulting in bloodied heads. Once, during such an attack led by a boy on horseback — incidentally, the only time that a peasant's son was ever allowed to play 'captain' — the stone-throwing got so violent that both sides had to retreat. The 'captain' on horseback was captured by our opponents, and disappeared for three full days: the opposing army had locked him in an old pigsty on a farm on one of the estates. After a long search, the youth of the opposing force set him free again, and no one ever asked who had been responsible for the kidnapping. The following day, a dozen women from the estate were sent by the owner to pick up all the pebbles from the meadow.

Apart from his job, my father also had much to do in the house and the garden. All the work connected with brickwork, painting and carpenting was done by him. There was little time to visit the pub. So we children had to go out in the evening to fetch one, or even two, 'buffers' of Nordhausen spirits. (A 'buffer' was a flattened bottle holding an eighth of a litre of schnapps.) Sometimes when I fetched the schnapps, I had a sip and topped it up with water again. But I could only do that if it was the second 'buffer', for my father would notice it in the first one.

While he was always quite peaceful when he drank his schnapps at home, it was quite bad when he stopped off at the pub after work: my mother really suffered then. All the aggression which had built up in him at work was let out on her. As long as my brother was in the house, my mother had a certain amount of protection. And then the aggression was worked off in fearful curses which my mother had to ignore.

But for most of the time my father was busy in the garden or the field, even on Sundays. Although he had religious leanings, at the times of church services he carried on working in his garden, which lay right beside the church. The priest, who was annoyed by this, denounced him. After this first warning, my father still continued working during church services. He was fined three marks. And still he continued to work during the services, because he considered that his work disturbed no one. He justified it by pointing out that the briquetting plant, which had 24 pressing machines, worked on Sundays and made a tremendous noise.

One of those machines was driven by electricity, and when it was running it sounded like a machine-gun — but that did not disturb the good priest. I often talked to my cousin, who was also my best friend, about the discussions which took place in our house. I told him that when I was grown up I would devote myself to socialism. His father, my uncle, was a member of the 'free-thinking' party, much like today's liberals.

My cousin considered that no one could be a socialist, and that he would become a democrat. We talked about the fines which my father had to pay

AND RED IS THE COLOUR OF OUR FLAG

for working in his garden during church service. We were both enraged and wondered how we could express our protest against church and priest. We decided to smash the windows at the back of the church with catapults.

For this purpose we collected small pebbles, sat ourselves on a small hill opposite the church and began to smash the windows. This remained undiscovered until the weekend. On the Saturday, the schoolgirls who had the unpaid job of cleaning the church came in, and soon not only the teacher and the priest learned of it, but the whole village.

When we got to school on Monday, the usual curriculum was not followed: there was a general inquisition.

Since no one had seen us and the interrogation yielded nothing, suspicion rested on two school friends who always went about with Tesching guns (these were guns with unrifled barrels). They must have been the culprits. After a mighty beating from the teacher, all was forgotten. One of the boys was the son of a peasant, the other the son of an artisan. Apart from my brother, no one found out who had done it. But from him we got a severe reprimand: what we had done was individual terrorism, and socialism rejected individual terror.

Another lesson I learned was how to treat animals. One day two school friends came by and told me to come with them to steal from sparrows' nests, an occupation which was permitted. Unfortunately, it did not stop at sparrows' nests. Other birds had their nests plundered. A tit had made her nest in a hollow willow tree. Our hands were too big to fit in, so we enlarged the hole with the help of a knife and managed to get the eggs out.

While we were doing this, we were surprised by some children from the neighbouring village, who threatened to tell their teacher. When we went to school the next day, there was an interrogation on who had been stealing from tit nests. Although the teacher knew that it had been us, we denied it. On the following day, the teacher from the neighbouring village turned up with the children who had seen us. Then we had to admit that we had been out for sparrows' nests, but had happened upon the tit's nest.

Since we knew that there would be a beating, we had stuffed exercise books down the back of our trousers. But one of my friends had a hardback book down his trousers. He was the last to be beaten. The teacher did not notice anything with us; but we celebrated too soon — the teacher noticed the hardback book at the first stroke.

My friend had to take his book out in front of the whole class and then take his beating without any protection. Then the two of us had to go out in front again, and although we denied having had any protection, we got our strokes again.

On this occasion, my teacher told me, as he had often done before: 'Hippe, you always get mixed up in every foolish prank, and you could be top of the class.'

With play, household chores and reading, and taking part secretly in the evening discussions when my father did not notice, I reached the summer of 1913. The construction of the surface works for the lignite mines was virtually finished. There was no more well-paid work in bridge-building for my brother and two brothers-in-law. They could have found work in the pit, under far worse conditions, but they did not want to. So my brother returned with one brother-in-law to Leipzig, and the other went back to Berlin; they found work again there, since the economic crisis had eased off considerably. I was the one who regretted their departure the most.

All I had left was the books they had given me on their departure, and the newspapers which they sent me from time to time. But my greatest joy was the many weekends when my brother and sister came by from Leipzig, for then I had an opportunity to talk with them on subjects that interested me.

I went to Leipzig as often as I could. I told my father that I was going to see my elder sister, Alma, but in fact I used to go my sister Ottilie's house, where my brother lived as well. I got the fare from the money I had saved at home.

My sister Frieda lived at my parents' house with her son until he was six. I regarded him as a younger brother, not as a nephew. Frieda was the only one who ever learned a trade, and she was my father's favourite. She had a tailor's workshop; she had obtained qualifications and was able to take on apprentices. Most of her customers were peasants. I was allowed to deliver the completed dresses, and I often received ten or twenty pfennig from customers. And then at weekends Frieda gave me 50 pfennig.

On Saturday evening, a crowd of young people came to my sister's flat in Leipzig, to talk. Sometimes we played cards as well, skat or something similar. But on Sundays we all went to the Lunapark, an amusement park for young and old alike. The thing I liked best there was a trip on the roller coaster. Even though not grown-up, I was allowed to take part in the discussions at my sister's house; at home I was forbidden even to have an opinion.

2.

AN APPRENTICE DURING THE FIRST WORLD WAR

Summer and winter had passed and my school years were drawing to a close: a new period in my life began. Although my father was religious, he did not go to church; my mother, on the other hand, was a liberal woman who had learned her views on life in her parents' house. Her ancestors had been peasants of small means, but her father and grandfather had been railwaymen who had worked on long-distance trains. Her grandfather, as she often told us, had said to her: 'Emilie, rather than go once to church, you should go ten times to the theatre; you will learn more about life there than in church.' In spite of this, I and all my brothers and sisters had to go through the whole process of confirmation. My confirmation was the last time I was ever in a church.

It was understood that I should be apprenticed, but I was never once asked which trade I would prefer to learn. A friend of my father, who was a self-employed craftsman in the village and ran a joinery, persuaded my father that his profession was the path to riches. So I would become a joiner.

By Easter 1914, my father still had not found an apprenticeship for me. Both my parents decided that, until a place had been found for me, I might as well work in the briquetting factory as a 'blacker'. 'Blackers' were boys between fourteen and seventeen who loaded the briquettes into the goods wagons by day; the night shift was done by older people. In ten hours' work, some 700-800 hundredweight of briquettes had to be loaded.

The worst and heaviest work was when the twenty-ton wagons had to be loaded, since the chute which brought the briquettes from the press ran alongside the wagon. For this work, the pay was twenty pfennig an hour, twelve marks for 60 hours. They deducted 32 pfennig for health insurance, and I got 11.68 marks. My mother had the eleven marks, and I was allowed to keep 68 pfennig as pocket money. It was a great help to my mother, who had never had money in her hand before.

I worked at this until the middle of July. Then, one day, I had to load a wagon — a twenty-tonner. The press was pounding away at 120 strokes a minute. Since I had to start by carrying 30 to 35 briquettes some six metres to make sure that all the briquettes were loaded up, I inevitably missed some of the load. When that happened, I quite often cried with rage and despair. But crying did not help at all, for the press continued mercilessly. In the end I was so demoralised that I let the press run without picking up a single briquette.

On top of all this, the foreman turned up. We called him 'Polack Karl' — a Polish worker who had worked at first on the estate farms, and had later gone into industry and then worked his way up to foreman. He was a willing tool of the management. At first he shouted at me and ordered me to get to work immediately. I refused to do so unless the speed of the press was reduced. Then he told me to clear the tracks of loose briquettes after the end of the shift. I refused again. I told him to do it himself if he could find no one else. Incensed, he threatened me with his fists and came at me over the boards of the wagon. I ran off and he followed threatening to beat the living daylights out of me.

Next to the rapid press there was a mound of nut coals. Since he had almost caught up with me, I defended myself by bombarding him with coals. This helped, since he could now only shake his fist at me. The next day, I was sacked.

In the meantime my father had found an apprenticeship for me, in a joinery connected to a furniture business. But I could not start there until 15 August. So I filled in the time with work about the house. Since it was almost harvest time, there was plenty to do. In the last week of July, I was allowed to go to Leipzig to deliver some things which Frieda had sewed for my eldest sister. On 28 July 1914, there was a big anti-war demonstration called by the Leipzig SPD on Augustus Platz. I marched with my brother, my sister Ottilie and many comrades from the Leutzsch branch of the party in a great procession through the town, with red flags and banners and shouting slogans against war.

This demonstration made a great impression on me. I had never seen so many people together. The square and surrounding streets were filled to overflowing. The adults said that 150,000 people had gathered there, all — so it seemed to me — prepared to prevent war. The next day, the newspapers reported that similar demonstrations had taken place in all the larger towns and industrial areas. A few days afterwards, on 2 August, war became a reality — in spite of these mass protests.

The same leaders who had called on the masses to demonstrate against war on 28 July explained on 4 August — after the Kaiser had declared that he recognised no parties any more, he recognised only Germans — 'In this hour of danger we cannot desert the Fatherland'. This was the answer of social democracy.

For myself, it was one of the greatest disappointments I had ever experienced. I had not yet returned home, though I should have gone straight away. The discussions which took place at my sister's flat interested me more than I feared the scolding or perhaps even the beating I could expect from my father. During those days I saw the same people who had demonstrated against the war on 28 July, now in grey uniforms travelling in goods wagons to the west.

Day and night the trains rumbled out, with slogans painted on their sides such as: 'Every jog — get a Frog; every hit — get a Brit; every slap — get a Jap.' Many of the soldiers I saw had thoughtful faces.

In the evening of 3 August a whole bunch of comrades turned up at the flat, all confused, disappointment written clearly on their faces. This evening was depressing for me, since I had not yet clarified my own beliefs. In this mood, I went back home and against all expectation my father did not berate me. He was in a good mood: 'Now we'll show those Frenchies, we'll be in Paris in a few weeks! In three months our soldiers will be back again' — that was the general feeling in my village. It was maintained by suitable slogans and rumours. One rumour suggested that gold was being transported through Germany by the French in order to finance the Russians, who belonged to the Entente.

Thousands of people got out on the roads to ambush the cars — naturally without success, since they only existed in the imagination of the propagandists. Nevertheless a few cars belonging to good citizens got smashed up because it was believed that they belonged to the transport column.

There was another slogan: 'Foreign spies are in our country: they must be hunted down!'

In the meantime 15 August had arrived, and I had to begin my apprenticeship. The worst of it was that the contract specified that I should be given board and lodging there too. My father had to pay fifteen marks a month for this. These were harsh weeks, until I had got used to the new environment. I was not allowed to sleep in the house where the master and his predecessor, known as the old master, lived with their family, although there was enough room. Opposite the house was the workshop, and above that was the loft for storing wood, and off the side of that was a small attic room: that is where I slept. It was literally only for sleeping in as the working day lasted ten or eleven hours. I ate with the family.

The first thing I learned was how to handle a saw and a plane. The first work I did was making children's coffins. These were made out of the wooden crates in which factory-made furniture was normally delivered. There was a young journeyman in the workshop, who had also served his apprenticeship there. He was a great help to me, and a good friend besides. Gradually I found that my position changed: I was not only employed in the workshop, but I also had to run errands and sweep the yard or the pavement. Together with the journeyman, I had to deliver furniture on a cart which we had to pull ourselves. Despite all this, I learned a lot there. Amongst other things I had to saw by hand planks that were three to four inches thick — one of the hardest tasks in this craft. Although there was a band-saw, it was only for use by the master and the journeyman. Apprentices, in the opinion of the master, had to learn everything from the basics.

After a few months, at the start of 1915, the master was called up, and in June the journeyman went too. Meanwhile, a second apprentice had started. The old master was over 70 and could hardly work any more. I had to do most of the work, since the new apprentice still knew very little and had few skills. In the main, we made only coffins and kitchen furniture. The working day was not as long as it had been, but I then had to do other work about the house, and on top of that I had to play nursemaid for two hours most days. I had so far successfully avoided becoming a member of the Young Men's Christian Association (YMCA) when the old master had dragged me there to a meeting. But when I now refused to play nursemaid, there was a beating.

On the second occasion I defended myself, went to the station and travelled home. I told my father that I would never go back, and I would not be beaten again; I would rather return to the pit to load briquettes. My father accompanied me back to the joinery where the old man had to admit that there was little work to do at that time.

My sister Klara was on a visit from Berlin just then. She suggested to my father that she should take me back to Berlin, since I could learn more in the factory where her husband worked than in my present apprenticeship. My father agreed. My sister went back first to make the arrangements. The first days of the war, the chauvinistic atmosphere in my parents' house and at the joinery had all had a negative effect on me. I only saw my brother rarely, as he had been conscripted as well, and so

I could not turn to him for support. Even the *Halle Volkszeitung*, the regional SPD paper, succumbed to chauvinism. The books and pamphlets which I had read up until then were not enough to fortify me against the prevailing atmosphere. And so I too finally lapsed into the jingoism which reigned supreme.

In April 1916, I travelled to Berlin. My sister Frieda had given me a tie as a present, one with a patriotic black-white-red stripe alternating with a black-gold stripe, all the way down. At the Anhalter Station, I was met by Klara and my brother-in-law; the first thing that happened was that my sister took off my tie and threw it onto the rails under the train. Two days later I began work in the German Weapons and Munitions Factory, in the same department as my brother-in-law; he was a fitter there.

This factory was 100 per cent unionised. I became a member of the German Metalworkers' Union (DMV). After only a short time I gained entry to the trade union youth group and became an active member. The political knowledge which I had gathered at the Leipzig school of my brother and brother-in-law, and which had been largely dissipated during my apprenticeship, was reawakened.

In the last days of April there was a certain amount of unrest among my colleagues — at least that is how it seemed to me. I could not understand it. When I asked my brother-in-law, he only said: 'You will see shortly.' The workforce — especially the night shift — seemed to be spending more time in the toilets than at the machines. Only later, when I had gained the trust of my colleagues, did I discover that the toilets fulfilled a dual purpose: they also served as meeting-rooms.

On the eve of 1 May 1916, my brother-in-law told me that we would not go to work the next day, since the workforce would all be joining an anti-war demonstration on the Potsdamer Platz. We went there at the specified time. Ten thousand workers had gathered in the square, and Karl Liebknecht spoke to them from the platform of the Potsdam local station.

I do not know how long Liebknecht had been speaking when the police arrived. They could not do anything at first; the crowd prevented them from getting up to the platform. More and more detachments were sent in, including mounted police who rode into the crowd with enormous brutality. For a time, the demonstrators put up resistance, and many policemen were knocked off their horses. But in the end they succeeded in clearing the Potsdamer Platz. We were pushed into the Köthener Strasse along with a fairly large group. It was rumoured that Karl Liebknecht had been arrested, and this fanned the resistance of the demonstration even more.

We tried once more to get back to the Potsdamer Platz. We had almost succeeded when mounted police again pushed us back to the end of Köthener Strasse. At the wharves, they launched a mounted attack. Many people had to jump over the bridge railings into the docks in order to avoid being ridden down. I too dared to jump. This was a baptism of fire. For the second time I experienced a workers' anti-war demonstration, workers no longer willing to work for the war and become tools of the generals in the service of capitalism. Slogans like this were shouted through the streets of Berlin until late evening.

Again and again the crowds gathered, and the demonstration could not be broken up even when the military were sent in wearing police uniforms. We marched from Flottwell Strasse in the direction of Lützow Platz and from there in the direction of the Charlottenburg district. We were often split up by the police, but always found our way back to the main body of the demonstration. Then came the shout: 'Karl Liebknecht is at the county courthouse on Tegeler Weg!'; and there was an immediate demand that he be freed. Some military wearing police uniform were waiting at Kirchplatz near the Schloss bridge.

We managed to break through this cordon, and the second, guarding the bridge. From here it was only a few hundred metres to the county courthouse. Other demonstrators reached the courthouse through the castle gardens and across the bridges of the urban railway. But we did not succeed in liberating Karl Liebknecht. Regular police, for the most part on horseback, were deployed, and we had to retreat.

On the following day scarcely any work was done at the factory: the toilets were turned into discussion rooms. Foremen and managers did not dare put a stop to the discussions. The shop stewards declared that the demonstration had been a complete success. We would see that the sacrifice made by Liebknecht and some workers would not be in vain. We discovered that some workers from our department had also been arrested. They had not been charged with treason or high treason, but their exemption from military duty was lifted and they had been handed over to the military authorities.

Karl Liebknecht was put on trial. He was accused of inciting a riot and of a serious breach of the peace. But in the trial he became the accuser, not the accused. In a fiery speech he denounced not only the government and the general staff, but also the imperialist powers in the international arena. He denounced the SPD and the trade union leadership as traitors to the interests of the working class, and said they would rot away on the dungheap of history. At the close, he appealed to the workers to fight for the end of the war: 'Down with the government! Down with the war!'

The demonstration on 1 May, the speech of Liebknecht at the

Potsdamer Platz, and even more his speech in court, made a tremendous impact on me.

I took part in all the discussions of the youth group. I was always there when leaflets were being distributed at the factory or in the workers' districts. Soon I became a delegate to secret meetings. At one such conference, I met Richard Müller, the leader of the revolutionary shop stewards. He embodied for me the very image of a militant socialist.

Apart from my practical work in the youth group, I took up my study of Marxist writings again. In the youth group, I met a comrade who gave political talks and explained to us that a struggle limited only to trade union action was not enough to defend the interests of the workers. Only a change from a bourgeois-capitalist society to a socialist society could guarantee an end to exploitation, overcome class anatagonisms and establish a socialist economy. But this could only be achieved by revolutionary means. And for this it was necessary to create a revolutionary party.

On 2 August 1914, Social Democracy had ceased to defend the interests of the workers. The nucleus of the new revolutionary party lay in the Spartacus League. After some discussions, during which my last doubts vanished, I joined the Spartacus League in October 1916. From that point onwards, I concentrated my political work on the Spartacus League, without neglecting my trade union work.

In Berlin, the Spartacus League increased its influence amongst the factory stewards and the workers themselves. Despite this, however, the leadership did not assume that they could win the majority among the trade union officials or in the factories. Social democracy, especially its left wing, still had more influence. For some time there had been arguments within the SPD. The left wing refused to defend the passive policies of the leadership.

In 1917 there was a split. The left wing broke away from the party and in April founded the Independent Social-Democratic Party of Germany (USPD). Däumig and Dittmann were among the leaders. Spartacus worked within the USPD in order to push its left wing forward.

Large groups of social-democratic workers, and a very large number of party officials, went over to the USPD, amongst them workers who had for a long time been unwilling to participate in the passive policies of the national leadership and their cohorts, the SPD leadership around Ebert and Scheidemann.

No one wanted to hear any more of the slogans which large numbers of Germans had adopted and repeated at the beginning of the war — 'Many foes, much glory', or 'Every jog — get a Frog, every shot — a Russki in the pot.'

Nevertheless, new illusions were created by the foundation of the USPD and by its centrism, its political waverings.

The war had now been going on for more than three years; the chauvinists still spoke of 'peace through victory' despite the fact that the fronts were completely bogged down. The losses at the front became greater, and at home the government was no longer in any position to guarantee food supplies. The famous 'turnip winter' arrived; even the cakes which people bought at the bakeries were largely composed of turnips. The turnip replaced the potato. Turnips were brought in on open goods wagons, even in the winter, so that they froze. When they thawed, there was a hellish stench. People had to queue for hours just to get their ration.

Discontent grew in the factories and at the front. The workers no longer allowed themselves to be pacified, and they threatened to strike. Desertion was on the increase at the fronts. In Berlin there were reputed to be more than 30,000 deserters. The anti-war movement, which the Spartacus League took into the factories with leaflets and by word-of-mouth, and in which the USPD also participated, got a positive reaction from the workers. Campaign committees were set up in the factories of the munitions industry. Their first demands to the government were: 'End the war! Better food! Shorter working hours!' (At that time, there was an eleven-hour day.) The government did not react; the union leadership tried to calm things down, but was in no position to pacify the workers. On the contrary, their willingness to fight increased.

And so the first munitions workers' strike took place. It was not restricted to Berlin, but affected many towns including those in the Ruhr valley, and lasted for more than ten days. More than 300,000 workers took part in this strike. The companies responded with sackings and by cancelling military exemption. I was among those sacked, the head foreman having caught me handing out leaflets in other departments. A few days later I found a job at a supply works which made parts for army trucks. But I did not stay there long, because I was sacked for no reason. By the end of May I had still not found a job, and I received a summons to go to the police.

I went to the local police station. The criminal investigators there asked me about the leafleting which took place before the strike. I denied that these leaflets had any political content or called for the overthrow of the government. They had only called for the end of the war, for sufficient food to be provided and for shorter working hours. I also denied being the author of the leaflets. The Spartacus League had been declared illegal as soon as it was founded, and being a member was as good as having an intent to commit high treason. My friends advised me to leave town for a while, but not to go back to my parents. So I went to Leipzig.

I found a welcome at my sister's house and work at the Hupfeld music works, which had also become an armaments factory. In the department where I worked, which made detonators for grenades, I soon found myself back in the opposition movement.

In this factory there were many comrades belonging to the USPD or who were sympathisers; I worked with them politically as well. At first I could not get in touch with Spartacus. The USPD comrades had no contacts with the League. Later on, I received from my brother-in-law in Berlin the address of a comrade in Leipzig who was a member of the League and who had met my brother-in-law during a trip to Berlin. There were only a few members of Spartacus in Leipzig, and our political work was restricted in the main to theoretical discussions, while the comrades worked together with the USPD, as I did.

The USPD work in agitation and propaganda was not limited only to workers in the factories. With the aid of soldiers on leave, anti-military material was taken to the front. In the newspaper *Vorwärts*, which was sent legally to the front, soldiers often found leaflets from the USPD or the Spartacus League which had been smuggled in by the printers. After the founding of the USPD, local groups had sprung up all over Leipzig.

With the aid of the Spartacus comrades, who belonged to the Leutzsch branch, I was accepted into this group. It was up to the younger comrades to take material for agitational work from their own factory into factories where only single comrades worked. With another two friends we had established a foothold in the Poliphon music works — also an armaments factory — and continually took in material.

In Leipzig, the food situation was even worse than in Berlin. It was not uncommon for workers to be absent from their factory with the excuse that they felt too weak to come to work, as they had scarcely eaten anything for days. Many people attempted to improve their diet by trying to get the peasants in the countryside to sell them more food. But even barter met with little success if you had nothing in your wardrobe to offer. It was especially difficult for the young workers who had the same ration cards as the adults, but bigger appetites. And they were disadvantaged financially as well: certainly they earned as much money as the adults, at least in the munitions industry, but they could only spend a part of their wages.

As early as 1915 the government had passed a law that forced them to save. This law specified that people below 21 years of age could only receive 60 per cent of their wages in their pocket, while the remainder was put into a bank account; the young people could only gain access to this account if they had previously proved to the administrative authorities that the money was going to be used for underwear or clothing.

I too had an account at the Berlin Municipal Savings Bank; the administrative authority was the Patriotic Women's Union, whose headquarters was in the Cecilian House in Charlottenburg, on the Berliner Strasse (today the Otto Suhr Allee). On only one occasion did I receive a small sum for buying underwear, accompanied by the admonition that I should make better use of the money in my account if I turned it into a war loan.

When I made a second application, in order to have a suit made, the clerk responsible remarked that I was not too badly dressed and that it would be better to put my money in a war loan. My reply — that I would rather wrap my money in a dirty rag and throw it into the river Spree, then I would at least hear the splash — provoked such a rage that she ordered me out of the office. My remark that we were dealing with hard-earned money and that I had some claim to it only made her threaten to call the police if I did not leave the room immediately.

I never again got any money from my account until the end of the war. It was not until December 1918, when this money was released by decree of the Government of Peoples' Representatives, that I was allowed to withdraw it.

3.

REVOLUTION IN RUSSIA,

UPHEAVAL IN GERMANY

The *Spartacus Letters* appeared irregularly throughout 1917 and 1918. These *Letters* gave us news of national and international developments. They were a great help to us in our anti-war agitation. Karl Liebknecht and Rosa Luxemburg, who had both been in prison for a long time, were able, with the help of warders or of comrades who visited them, to smuggle out political documents, and were, in their turn, supplied with material from outside. The outbreak of the February Revolution in Russia was an event which gave new impetus to our struggle. We were particularly inspired by one of Rosa Luxemburg's articles which she wrote in Wronke prison:

'The outbreak of the Russian Revolution has broken the deadlock in the historical situation which was caused by the continuation of the world war and the simultaneous failure of the proletarian class struggle . . . The anxious expectation with which Germany receives every speech by Chkheidze or by the workers' and soldiers' council regarding questions of war and peace is tangible confirmation of the fact that . . . only the revolutionary actions of the proletariat offer a way out of this impasse of the world war . . . In any event, even with the greatest heroism, no proletariat of any single country can sever this noose. The Russian Revolution will grow unaided into an international problem . . .

'But now to the German bourgeoisie! . . . German imperialism, which is in dire straits, in a tight corner on the western front and in Asia Minor and unable even to start dealing with the food crisis at home, would like to extricate itself from the whole business as quickly and cleanly as possible, so that it can patch itself up and arm itself for another war. Imperialism would like to make use of the Russian Revolution, and its proletarian-socialist pacifism . . . But to have a republic on their flank, more particularly a republic newly built and governed by the revolutionary socialist proletariat, is too much for the police and military east of the Elbe to put up with . . .

'Who can guarantee that tomorrow, after peace has been signed, and German militarism has its claws out of manacles again, it will not strike the Russian proletariat in the flank in order to cushion a dangerous shock to German semi-absolutism? . . . The Russian proletariat would truly be politically naive indeed if it did not ask itself this question: this German cannon fodder, which allows itself to be led to the slaughter by imperialism on all the fronts — how will it avoid being ordered against the Russian Revolution tomorrow?

'There is only one real guarantee against these understandable worries about the future of the Russian Revolution: the awakening of the German proletariat, the coming to power of the German workers and soldiers in their own country, a revolutionary action by the German people to win peace.' ('The Old Mole', *Collected Works*, Volume 4, pp.258-264.)

This article was discussed not only in the ranks of the Spartacus League. The USPD comrades accorded it great importance as well, especially the lines: 'In any event, even with the greatest heroism, no proletariat of any single country can sever this noose. The Russian Revolution will grow unaided into an international problem.'

The wild frenzy of victory which had gripped large parts of the German working class in 1914 and had persisted through to 1917 were countered by the effect of the February Revolution in Russia, the experiences of war and the bad situation at home, and led to a new consciousness in the more advanced sections of the workers. The other sections adopted anti-war stances because of the decline in the standard of living and individual experiences at the front. And then we in Leipzig received the exciting news that the Russian working class in alliance with the peasants had proclaimed a Soviet republic and had consolidated its power. The effects of the October Revolution were visible throughout the whole working class. The workers were impressed by the formation of workers' and soldiers' committees, and even many social-democratic workers welcomed the victory of the Russian proletariat.

The workers of Leipzig had not forgotten their opposition to the war and their great demonstration of July 1914. The October Revolution was the topic of the day and I too was greatly inspired by it. The peace negotiations between the German empire and Soviet Russia at Brest-

Litovsk following on from the October Revolution were conducted by General Hoffmann on behalf of the military staff of the German armed forces and by Secretary of State von Kühlmann, representing the government. For the German military, 'peace through victory' was still at the top of the agenda.

They demanded the evacuation of the Baltic states and of the Ukraine, and an indefinite armistice. Their goal was to be able to transfer to the western front the greater part of the troops then tied up at the eastern front, in order to bring about a change in fortunes there. As People's Commissar for Foreign Affairs, Trotsky led the Soviet delegation. The negotiations dragged on for several weeks, principally because the German delegates could not agree amongst themselves. There were always disagreements between Kühlmann and General Hoffmann. After one attack which Trotsky launched against the German government, Hoffmann explained: 'I do not represent the German government here, but rather the German High Command.'

While the government attempted to prise the Baltic states and the Ukraine from the Soviet Republic by a proclamation of 'the right of self-determination', General Hoffmann strove for a charter allowing him to occupy the Baltic states and Ukraine with his troops. In Germany there were major demonstrations against Hoffmann's demands. Workers sympathising with social democracy put up the opposition slogan: 'We do not want a Hoffmann peace, we want a Scheidemann peace!' The workers behind Spartacus and the USPD demonstrated for the defence and inviolability of the Soviet state.

I did not work in Leipzig much longer. It was becoming increasingly difficult to get the basics to eat; apart from that I had to work very long hours each day. Together, these two factors persuaded me to return home.

No further action had been taken by the police as a result of my leafleting in the Berlin factory. I went home in January 1918. I could find no work as a lathe worker, since there were scarcely any metalworks in the Geisel valley. But there was no difficulty in finding other work: a new plant for producing tar and oil from coal had been set up in our village, the Lützkendorf fuel plant. It was supposed to help overcome the growing lack of fuel in industry and at the front. Forty-eight retorts had been installed for the coal-liquefaction equipment. Two fitters worked there along with four French prisoners of war. I was taken on immediately. Imagine my joy to find that the fitters were socialists and opponents of the war. I had made political contacts again. There was not much happening politically in the coalfield, since only very young or elderly workers were employed there, and most of the work was performed by prisoners of war.

There was a prisoner-of-war camp inside our works. This consisted of primitive huts surrounded by a high barbed-wire fence. The guards were members of the veteran reserve, together with some auxiliary conscripts. Among them was a man of about 25 years of age, small and crippled, whom we considered a sadist. At midday and in the evening the prisoners had to form two lines, and he made sure that the Russian prisoners in particular were formed up with Prussian exactness. Armed with two sticks, he used to go along the line and rain blows upon the prisoners at the slightest fault. The commander, a sergeant, was rarely in the camp. In civilian life he was an agricultural inspector on a nearby manor.

When we left the works at midday to eat, we advised both the commandant and the guard that their treatment of the prisoners contravened the Geneva Convention. It did no good. On one occasion the guard treated the prisoners especially badly. We took his sticks away from him and beat him up, because we considered that people of his sort could only understand that kind of argument. The commander, who was actually in the camp that particular day, threatened to report us to the police. We told him that if he did not ensure that the maltreatment stopped, he could expect a beating as well. Both my colleagues were in a 'reserved occupation' (and therefore exempt from military service because their employers needed them); only a few weeks later they were both conscripted.

For a few days I worked alone with the prisoners, until the firm sent a new fitter. He was quite the opposite of my previous colleagues. You could hardly even discuss social problems with him. I myself had been inspected for service only a few weeks before, and received the medical classification 'fit for garrison duty at the front'. The reason for this limitation was that I had lost the sight of one eye in an accident. I only stayed a short while longer at that factory; I was conscripted seven weeks before the rest of my age group, as a punishment for my intervention on behalf of the POWs.

Along with a troop of other conscripts, I was dispatched by the Näumburg regional command to Bernburg in the Anhalt area. We were quartered in a school there; our unit belonged to Reinforcement Battalion No.66, and the company comprised three squads. Because there was a shortage of drill instructors, each squad had more than 30 men. The first days were taken up with drill and practising parade marches and salutes — great value was set on these. Then off we went to the firing ranges, where a company drill was arranged on a large meadow.

Our squad leader — I reckoned him to be about 35 years old — ordered us to march in groups wheeling left and right, in the pouring rain. Enormous puddles formed on the meadow. He then proceeded to the next exercise, during which we had to 'lie down!' and 'jump up, march, march!' all over the field. The order to lie down always came when we reached the largest puddles. Together with another comrade, I ran in front of the unit. On the next command of 'lie down!' — naturally just at another puddle — we did not budge. The sergeant stormed over the field in a rage: this was disobeying an order. We claimed not to have heard the order. He sent the unit off, and conducted the exercise with us alone. Now it was alternately 'jump up!' and 'lie down!', and crawling every so often, all over the field, always into the biggest puddles, until it was all too much for me and I really disobeyed the command.

At the next 'jump up, march, march!', I stayed lying down and said that I could not go on. Despite all the curses, I did not move a muscle. Four weeks of army life with all its bullying had been enough for me.

Now the company commander appeared on horseback. The rain had eased off. The sergeant told me to get up and then reported, but nothing happened. We had to fall back into the squad, and then the company drill began. Finally, we marched in a parade past the company commander who took the salute mounted on his horse. After we had been drilled hard for more than three hours, it was back to our quarters — naturally with a 'fresh, joyful song'.

Once we had arrived in the schoolyard, my comrade and I had to step in front of the company, where we were informed that, because of our bad conduct at the training area, we were to report to the NCOs' mess after we had eaten. While our friends could go into town — it was Saturday — we were ordered by our sergeant to report back in an hour with polished rifle and bayonet. Naturally, our arms were then found to be in a 'filthy condition' — or at least that is what the NCOs said.

So we were set to work to clean the boots, belt buckles and side-arms of the NCOs, and some even gave us their tunics to clean. I said that I had neither polish nor shoe polish. But every soldier — came the reply — had to have those. I replied that I did indeed have a cleaning kit, but only for myself, not for the NCOs, sir. With a daily allowance of 22 pfennig I could not afford to buy shoe polish for the officers. So they gave us cleaning things. We really took some trouble, for we still hoped to get into town. But when we returned to the mess, they told us that it all looked 'filthy' and had to be done again.

My comrade and I agreed not to lift another finger and to return all the things exactly as they were. When we went back up, they decided it was all satisfactory and took their belongings back: but at the door stood a bucket and a basin, both filled right to the brim. We were told to carry them down two steps: naturally the water slopped over. Their purpose was achieved: they had an excuse to bully us all over again. We had to wash the room, the hall and the steps right down to the yard. By then it was almost nine o'clock. Filled with anger, we went back to our room and to bed.

Fortunately the six weeks' basic training was soon at an end and we were handed over to the watch battalion. A few days later, the class of 1900 turned up at the school, amongst them many acquaintances from my village and district. Service in the watch battalion consisted mainly in guard duty and fatigue duty.

Twice a week we had either drill or target practice at the firing range. When the shooting was finished, we were sometimes met outside town by the company commander on his horse and led back to the barracks. Then he ordered us to sing a song. But the company did not always feel like singing, especially after four hours' drill. One day, we simply did not respond. He turned us round, and made us do a punishment exercise on the road. Then off towards town we went. 'A song!' came the order again. The company struck up with 'I was born in Hamburg'. We knew the commander could not stand that one. He shouted for us to stop, but the song was sung right to the end. At least he did not ask us to sing any more that day.

There were older soldiers in the watch battalion too, people who had been wounded at the front: having been signed off as 'fit for garrison duty', they were completing their service here. In my room there was a comrade, born in 1897, and I struck up a friendship with him. I helped him when he was called for a medical examination, by wrestling with him a few days beforehand. As a result, his wound opened up again and he was not certified as fit for the front. He was extremely interested in politics, and was, as I later discovered, a member of the Spartacus League. It was not at all difficult to discuss the situation at the front and at home with the older soldiers, but it was more difficult with the comrades who belonged to my age group.

There was one occasion when the musketry NCO in charge of the firing range and guard duty must have overheard something of our discussions and put us on fatigues.

Now, after this had been going on for several weeks, my comrade asked: 'Do you want to help us teach Berger a lesson? He goes down to the river Saale every evening with his girlfriend. After curfew we can get over the wall and come back by the river.'

I was in. After curfew, when the corporal on duty had left the mess, we went down and pretended we wanted to use the latrines in the yard. We had put on our belts under our shirts, and our side-arms — a kind

Oskar Hippe in army uniform, 1918

of bayonet — were hidden in our trousers. We waited until the guard who did the rounds inside the barracks had reached the furthest point.

In a flash we were over the wall, and ten minutes later we were down at the river Saale. There we found our victim. Without saying a word, we slapped him with the flat of the bayonets. We calmed his girlfriend, who began to shout, by telling her that she would not be harmed, that we only wanted to teach this tyrant a lesson.

In less than an hour we were back inside the barracks. The next morning, when the company reported for guard duty, our man was absent. He was unpopular even with his fellow NCOs.

The company sergeant who asked for him was told that Berger was still in his room. When the company sergeant ordered someone to fetch him, he eventually appeared. He was somewhat embarrassed, but did not say anything about what had happened, only explained that he had fallen and did not feel well. We never discovered whether he knew who had beaten him. In any case, we were not given so much fatigue duty after that, except in the Solvay works, a chemical factory producing artificial manure. There we had to work ten hours, but were paid five marks a day.

One day, as we reported for guard duty, I could not believe my eyes. In a group of NCOs there stood a man with whom I had worked in Berlin at the German Weapons and Munitions factory, in the lathe section, and who was also a member of the Spartacus League. I introduced him to the comrade who shared my room. One evening, at the start of September 1918, he suggested that we smuggle some weapons out of the barracks to help the organisation. They were to be picked up in a certain cemetery by a civilian who was also a comrade. We managed to achieve this twice without being discovered in the investigations which followed. In all, eight rifles were smuggled out.

At the end of September we were invested. It was said we would be deployed behind the front. We got three days' leave, and then, only a few days later, a long transport train with several garrisons — around 2,000 men — was rolling towards occupied Belgium. On the way we were fed several times, the last time in the town of Düren. Whereas in the garrison we were usually fed with 'barbed wire' — which is what we called the terrible food — at the refreshment points we received good portions, with a lot of meat.

Antwerp was the first intermediate station, and we stayed there a week. We were housed in part of a convent which was crawling with lice. The other wing of the nunnery was still occupied. A lot of coming and going soon developed between the two wings of the building, until the commandant felt obliged to place a guard at every connecting door. But that had little effect. One evening it was my turn for guard duty, and the traffic was very heavy that evening. But I was really plagued by the lice, who were gnawing away at my skin. I put my rifle down, stripped down to my waist and began to hunt down the lice; I squashed lots of them. The comrades who were passing through were of less interest to me.

During the day we were busy on the slopes outside the town. Entire trench systems were laid out there, with barbed-wire entanglements, which we had to work our way through.

There was also practice for gas alerts. For these, a low-lying building had been constructed, and we were led through it in groups to test whether our gas masks were working. Then one morning we were queueing up for our food, and we wondered why there was more than usual — there was even an 'iron ration' with it. Then came the order to march out. After 30 minutes we fell in for roll call. Only about half of the men who belonged to our transport were there. A few days before, doctors had inspected us for our suitability for deployment. A lieutenant-colonel made a short speech and told us that we were going to defend bridges behind the front line. We marched through the town to the station; it was more like a demonstration. From the train came continuous shouts against the war: 'Equal rations, equal pay, then the war can stay away!' Or, if an officer threatened us: 'Out with the light, out with the knife, let him have it within an inch of his life!'

Marching in front of us was a division from the garrison at Aschersleben in the Harz. Most of them were comrades who had already been at the front. The transport train stood ready at the goods station. At the end of the train stood a group of soldiers handing out ammunition to the division in front of us. When these comrades had received their ammunition, they seized the remaining ammunition boxes and refused to climb aboard. The officer, after several unsuccessful demands, ordered them to be disarmed and taken before a court-martial. The comrades — around 100 men — then retreated to a small hill opposite the station. The rest of us were ordered aboard the train without any ammunition. When the train was ready to leave, it was shot at from above, until the steam boiler and the tender looked like sieves. We stayed there until after dark. We did not know what happened to our mutinous comrades. Our train finally left the station with a new locomotive and reached Mons on the Belgian-French border with no further delay.

Telling us that we were to be guarding bridges was only a 'sedative'. Two days later we were sent to the front, although none of our unit was fit for field service. In my case, the medical check, because of my missing eye, had pronounced me only fit for garrison duty.

At the part of the front where we were deployed, we faced British troops. There was only sporadic fighting during the day. At night, we retreated to occupy makeshift positions. We suffered many casualties, and were rarely stood down. We were outside Mons again. That day, the British launched an attack to encircle us. The mood among the troops was anything but a fighting one. Everyone knew that the war was lost. In this situation, we called for a retreat, so that we should not be captured. This was on our own initiative. We called on the two companies lying to the right and left to join us. It was not far to the station, where a train stood with steam up. We climbed aboard and forced the driver to leave immediately. If we had remained in position, we would certainly have been captured. The British had put their cavalry into the field as well, which the older comrades told us had not happened for two years.

We reached Brussels with great difficulty and after many stops. Since our food had run out, we tried to get more there. It was a few days before the armistice. People refused to give us anything since we had no valid papers. When we threatened to go and get the food ourselves, they decided that they would supply it after all. Our train had open goods wagons, with no side walls, and it was already bitterly cold. We warmed ourselves around small field stoves. We were often shunted on to side lines, since closed trains transporting military units were given precedence.

Later we discovered the reason for this: in Berlin, the government of Prince Max of Baden had resigned. The Government of People's Representatives had been formed as the provisional government by leaders of the SPD and USPD. But the general staff remained unchanged. Ludendorff and Hindenburg had announced that they would lead their troops through the Brandenburg Gate as an army unbeaten in war. They did not succeed, but that was not thanks to the effort of the provisional government, and especially not of the Social-Democratic leadership.

Hundreds of thousands of Berlin workers demonstrated their determination not to let the butchers of the German people march through Berlin as unbeaten army commanders. Soldiers' committees were formed in all the units, companies and regiments, in ours too. Our chairman was the comrade with whom I had worked in Berlin and who had left for the front from Bernburg. It was he who had also kept the troop together from the first days of mutiny all the way back to Halle. In the regiments where the Spartacus League and the USPD had little influence, the soldiers' committee was often composed of officers and NCOs. Again and again at the stations — even in Halle — we received the order to report to our regiment in the barracks. But our intention was to travel on to Berlin.

The Halle soldiers' committee and the station authorities informed us that we could travel no further as a single transport, since the wagons were required in the central German industrial area. In reality, they simply wanted to prevent us from staying together as a unit. The soldiers' committee in Cologne had already tried to prevent us from travelling any further until we had surrendered our weapons. On the platforms lay mountains of rifles, carbines and machine-guns. Since we did not wish to come to a confrontation with comrades, we readily surrendered our weapons.

In Halle, we told our comrades not to report to barracks on any account, but rather to try to reach Berlin individually and then to meet up again at a prearranged spot. My parents lived not far from Halle. I decided to travel home first before starting on the journey to Berlin. I took the first-shift train in the morning into the industrial area. Apart from my mother and sister, no one was there. My father was in hospital in Halle as a result of an accident at his work. My mother sent me off to the nearest pit because of my lice, so that I could have a bath and get on some civilian clothes.

My uniform and underwear were stuck in a vat and boiled. But even after a short time, the itching began again. That day my brother came for his midday meal, since he too had not travelled back to his garrison at Stendal. Together with another comrade, he had spent the last six weeks making forced marches from one place to another in order to avoid a 'hero's death' at the last moment.

Thousands had done the same. If they were stopped by the military police, they explained that they were looking for their regiment. In the towns, hundreds and thousands of deserters were hiding; as I have mentioned in Berlin alone there were more than 30,000 of them.

I told my brother that I still had lice even after bathing and boiling my clothes. He asked whether I had changed my braces. Indeed I had not. When we looked, we saw that the new invasion had come from there. After another bath, I finally got rid of the lice.

In the evening my father turned up as well. Nothing remained of his confidence in victory. His loyalty to the Kaiser had given way to a great disappointment. He still rejected our point of view, that a socialist society should replace the bourgeois-capitalist one. When we argued that the bourgeois-democratic republic in place of a monarchy was not enough, that it was now time to clear away social inequality, or else the cost of the war would come down on the backs of workers, my father countered with the bogey of Soviet Russia, where, it was claimed, all freedoms had been abolished. That was the way it had been explained to him by the *Generalanzeiger*.

My brother wanted me to stay at home, for there was enough political work to do there. But I was drawn to Berlin, partly because I felt that other tasks needed to be done there, partly because I had promised my friends and comrades to meet them in Berlin. I stayed in Berlin with my sister. Through my brother-in-law I contacted the Spartacus League again. Immediately, I participated in agitation: leaflets had to be distributed, meetings guarded; I took part in demonstrations and especially in discussions on the streets and squares.

There was little work available. Industry had been crippled by the end of the war, and had to readjust to peacetime production. I had to try to earn my daily crust by casual work. On the days when no work was available or when I did not have much political work to do, I spent my time reading. The *Spartacus Letters* still appeared at intervals. As a soldier I had had little opportunity to examine these. Now I tried to broaden my political horizons. There was an article by Leo Jogiches which interested me, written as early as August 1917. It read:

'After several mighty struggles, the Russian working class has succeeded in making the Provisional Government adopt the following as the official formula for the war policy: no annexations, no reparations, peace on the basis of the self-determination of nations. At first sight, this proletarian policy has won a complete and emphatic victory . . .

'But a general peace cannot be brought about by Russia alone. The Russian proletariat can put down the resistance of its own ruling class, but it cannot exercise any crucial influence on the imperialist governments of Britain, France and Italy, since there, naturally, the decisive pressure can only come, as in Russia itself, from within, only from the British, French and Italian proletariat . . .

'The apparent weak point of true socialist war policy lies in the fact that revolutions cannot be made "on command" . . . But this is certainly not the duty of the socialist party. The only duty is always and unflinchingly "to tell it like it is", that is, to present to the masses clearly and sharply their responsibilities at the given historical moment, to proclaim the political programme of action and the slogans . . .

'Today, like three years ago, there is only one alternative: War or revolution! Imperialism or socialism! To proclaim this loud and clear, so that each in his own land can draw the revolutionary conclusions — this is the only proletarian-socialist peace work which is possible today.' (*Spartacus Letters*, published by the Communist Party of Germany-Spartacus League. No.6, August 1917.)

Leo Jogiches pointed the way for the German working class. It could not continue as a kind of feudal estate, without winning class rights, and acting as a kind of jailer for capitalism. He called on the German workers to follow the Russian example. But he also demonstrated how critically people were following developments in Russia. The slogan of the Spartacus League — socialism or war — was opposed by the majority Social Democrats with: 'Socialism is on the march!' On the advertising pillars of Berlin and throughout the empire appeared posters announcing that we were 'on the road' to socialism:

'Only adventurers chatter about revolution. We Social Democrats know that the power of capitalism is broken. The republic is our passport on the road to socialism.'

The German people did not fight for the republic; it fell victim to it. Scheidemann declared openly — and also wrote in his memoirs — that Ebert had reproached him for proclaiming the republic. 'I hate revolution like sin', is what Ebert was supposed to have said to the last chancellor of the empire, Max von Baden. In the Spartacus League, we knew that a revolution had not really taken place on 9 November, although even we spoke of the 'November Revolution'. For us, the collapse of the monarchy was only the first step in a social movement leading to revolution.

We knew that a revolution was not a single act, but rather a chain of collisions and conflicts with the ruling class, which is never ready to submit itself to the will of a democratic majority, but rather defends its predominant position with all means at its disposal, with the help of the powers which the state has built up — the army, the police, the courts and the church. On 6 December, we saw how strong the counter-revolutionary forces, including the majority Social Democrats, considered themselves, only four weeks after 9 November.

Spartacus, together with the Red Soldiers' League, had organised several meetings and marches in support of its policies; these had been authorised by the police. One demonstration moved from the Wedding district through the Chaussee Strasse to the city centre.

In front of the Maikäfer Barracks (the headquarters of a regiment of guards), the street was blocked by several machine-guns. The soldiers of the counter-revolution shot without warning into the crowd; eighteen people were killed, 30 wounded. A second demonstration, which came from Charlottenburg and was also heading for the city centre, almost collided with a demonstration by the SPD, at the Grosse Stern; the latter included republican army soldiers who were armed. A participant in the Wedding march arrived and reported the events in the Chaussee Strasse.

The leaders of the demonstration managed to divert it in time, so that there was no conflict. Some time later it became known that the future chairman of the SPD, Wels, who was city commander of Berlin at that time, had issued orders to shoot in an emergency. Those killed in this cowardly attack in the Chaussee Strasse were buried, after many arguments, in the cemetery of the martyrs of March 1848, in Friedrichshain.

We saw how strong the counter-revolutionary forces considered themselves to be in the last days of 1918. The right-wing parties openly called for the dissolution of the workers' and soldiers' committees, on the grounds that they constituted a parallel government to the Government of People's Representatives. The majority Social Democrats did nothing to stop this agitation from the right; on the contrary, in conferences of the workers' and soldiers' committees, they tried to weaken the influence of the committees.

In reality, the highest ranks of the army, which still remained unchallenged and whose job it was to demobilise the army, had become the parallel government. Major Schleichmann was allowed to take part in the sessions of the Government of People's Representatives, as link man for the High Command. There he was permitted to demand the death penalty for those who carried weapons without permission. He did not succeed, but even without the death penalty on the statute books, the military still went out and murdered.

Since the overthrow of the monarchy in November, the People's Marine Division had been quartered in Berlin, élite troops of the socialist-democratic forces. The majority were members of the High Seas Fleet, which had been moored in harbour for almost the entire course of the war. When the marine commanders tried in desperation to send the fleet against the British fleet shortly before the end of the war, the crews refused the order. Reichpietsch and Köbis, two sailors, were condemned to death as 'ringleaders' and shot.

From that point onwards, the sailors were always in close contact with representatives of the USPD. After the collapse, they came to Berlin as the People's Marine Division. At Christmas 1918 there was a bloody battle in which the Marine Division also participated. The Spartacus League did not take part. Sixty-seven people lost their lives. The order to shoot at the Marstall, in which the People's Marine Division were quartered, came again from the city commander, Wels. He gave it without the knowledge of the three USPD members of government, who resigned forthwith.

Immediately after the November collapse, the Spartacus League took over the Scherl publishing house, which for years had printed the *Lokal Anzeiger*, the organ of the Conservative Party, and brought out the *Lokal Anzeiger* under the title of *Rote Fahne (Red Flag)*. From that day onwards, it became the organ of the revolutionary workers, and was soon distributed everywhere.

Numerically, the Spartacus League was a small organisation, but hundreds of thousands demonstrated under its slogans.

The plenary committee of the workers' and soldiers' committees had its headquarters in Berlin. Its meetings took place in the Busch Circus, next to the Lustgarten. Rosa Luxemburg and Karl Liebknecht were not members of the plenary committee, and the Spartacus League was only weakly represented among the delegates. Nevertheless, we regarded the committees as the most important instrument for working towards a socialist republic. Liebknecht tried to gain support within the plenary committee. He was quite clear that we had to win the majority in the committees if we were to reach the stage of the socialist revolution.

From the very first days after the collapse of the monarchy, the SPD had supported the bourgeois-democratic republic and the republican army which had attracted many workers to its ranks. But the workers did not allow the republican army to be used against either the revolutionary workers or the People's Marine Division. That task was therefore given to the Lüttwitz Freikorps, which was then just being set up, and to Maercker, the Guards and Cavalry Protection Division and others.

Just as the SPD had supported a pacifist policy from 1914 until the end of the war, so now they hung on to the old state apparatus for dear life. The Freikorps served them as an instrument against the revolutionary working class. Even after the fall of the monarchy, they led the fight against the left wing. They came out with a whole series of slanders, especially against the Spartacus League. They described the leadership and members of Spartacus as agents of the Bolsheviks wishing to destroy freedom.

In the last days of December, the Spartacus League issued a call to a conference in Berlin; this took place on 30-31 December 1918 and 1 January 1919. The conference was supposed to decide on the tactics of the Spartacists, and particularly whether the struggle within the USPD was to be continued or whether the left should unite in a new, revolutionary party. Liebknecht argued before the delegates the necessity of splitting from the centrist USPD in the interests of the revolution.

On the basis of the national conference of the workers' and soldiers' committees, held between 16 and 21 December 1918, which voted to hand over power to a parliament yet to be elected, the leading comrades of the Spartacus League argued for participation in the elections to the National Assembly. But the majority of the conference opposed the leadership. This was the same majority which later, in October 1919 at the Heidelberg party conference, rejected a united front with other workers' parties, and which refused to work inside the General German Trade Union Federation — ADGB — and instead demanded the construction of its own, separate, trade unions. Rosa Luxemburg and Leo Jogiches also suggested to the conference, on the basis of the weakness of the revolutionary workers' movement, that the new organisation be called the 'Socialist Party'; the majority, however, decided on the name 'Communist Party of Germany-Spartacus League' — KPD.

The activities of the members of the new Communist Party increased after the founding conference. The People's Marine Division still occupied the Marstall; the printing district was in the hands of the revolutionary workers. The *Rote Fahne*, now the central organ of the KPD, continued to be printed at the Scherl works. The owners were demanding the return of their presses.

The Government of People's Representatives also wanted to weaken the KPD and drive it out of the printing district. There were provocations almost daily on the part of the armed bodies of government. When the Berlin President of Police, the USPD member Emil Eichhorn, was sacked, the workers spontaneously occupied the newspaper offices. This was the signal for the 'Noske Gangs', as the revolutionary workers called the Freikorps. There was a short but bloody fight, which the workers could not win. They were armed only with rifles and a few machine-guns, while the Freikorps went out with heavy artillery and fired shells into the printing works.

On this occasion again, the republican army refused to go in against the defenders of the printing works. Many of the fighting workers were arrested. The leaders of the action, continuing their work even after the defeat, advised those who managed to escape arrest not to return to their homes, but to seek shelter in illegality. Workers' districts were subject to house-to-house searches; the fighting workers of Berlin had suffered a grievous defeat.

4.

AFTER THE NOVEMBER UPRISING

I was instructed by the party to take a report to Halle and not to return to Berlin for the time being. The KPD was relatively strong in the central German industrial area, especially in the Geisel valley coalfield. The party introduced me to a comrade who worked as an engine driver at the Elise II pit, and who was chair of the KPD branch in Mücheln, a small town in the coalfield. Since no youth group existed here as yet, it was my task to set one up. I made my home in my parents' house.

Each evening I spent at the trade union building: that is where comrade Haubenreisser lived. On 15 January, a courier brought us the news of the murder of Rosa Luxemburg and Karl Liebknecht. On the very same evening, party officials and shop stewards met to discuss how the workers should respond to this.

The local executive of the USPD was also meeting in the trade union building, likewise deciding on their response to the murder of Karl and Rosa. In a joint meeting of the KPD, workers' committees and the USPD, we decided to call a protest demonstration for the next day, which would end up at the market place in Mücheln. Fifteen thousand people had gathered at the square when comrade Scheibner, the USPD chair, opened the meeting. There were similar meetings in Querfurt, Schafstädt and Lauchstädt, towns near Mücheln.

A protest resolution to the government demanded that the murderers of Karl and Rosa should be punished. Then the news reached our meeting that the chair of the District Workers' Committee in Querfurt had been arrested. (The workers' and soldiers' committees at this time were authorised by the provisional government, and thus were official bodies.) This man had tried to round up all the weapons which the peasants in Oberwünsch, a farming village, had received from 'Orgesch', an organisation of right-wing military groups. The peasants had beaten him up, attached him to a chain and locked him in a large kennel.

The masses, who were already stirred up by the news of the murder of Rosa Luxemburg and Karl Liebknecht, demanded of the organisers of the meeting that they march to Oberwünsch to free the chair of the District Workers' Committee. Hundreds, including myself and many other young workers, marched to Oberwünsch. The leadership lay in the hands of an old miners' official by the name of Karl John. We were joined by demonstrators from Querfurt and Schafstädt. Just before the village, we were shot at. In the meantime, demonstrators from Lauchstädt had met us. Although we had no weapons, it was decided that we should enter the village from all directions and try to force the peasants to hand over their weapons and free the District chair. And in most cases, this tactic met with success.

But in one street, a farmer and his three sons — all four army officers — had entrenched themselves. As we later discovered, they had also armed the Russian prisoners of war who were working on their farm, and told them to shoot at us. Sheltered by the houses, we succeeded in reaching the farm and getting through the gate. But before we could cross the farmyard, several of us fell wounded. The peasant and his uniformed sons were disarmed; the Russian POWs were left alone. They were simply told that they had shot at revolutionary workers.

Our leaders decided that the farmer and his three sons should be tried before a people's tribunal — naturally, only a symbolic trial — to be held in the inn across the road. They were brought from their yard into the main room of the inn.

The way there was lined by the demonstrators who — still enraged by the murder of Karl and Rosa — hit the prisoners as they passed. Although the leaders tried, they did not succeed in stopping this entirely. The people's tribunal was held, and condemned all four to a long jail sentence. They were found guilty of acting against bodies of the government and their representatives, which was the equivalent of high treason. But they were told that the monarchy had come to an end, that the republic had taken its place, and that this, if the workers had their way, would eventually be a socialist republic. Although the chair of the District Workers' Committee, now free again, put in an official complaint against the peasants of Oberwünsch before the High County Court in Naumburg, nothing ever came of it.

Instead, a few days later, workers who had participated in the events began to be arrested; I fell victim to this as well. One of the first arrested was the miners' official Karl John. The charge sheet included riot, serious breach of the peace, looting and assault. The charge of looting came about because several demonstrators, having entered the farmer's house, had cleared out a part of the smokehouse. This was understandable in those years of hunger after the war, even if not politically defensible. I was taken in handcuffs from Mücheln to Halle by two policemen. We travelled by rail, in a 'shift train' taking hundreds of workers to Halle and Merseburg. The workers were greatly perturbed, but luckily there was no confrontation with the policemen. At Halle, we took the tram from the main railway station to the central prison — the 'Ox-head' as it was popularly known. For weeks, my parents had no news of me.

Only in April, when we were transferred from the Ox-head to the remand prison, did I at last have a chance to get word to them. In Halle, the political climate since the November uprising had been determined by the Workers' Committee. Later, the SPD and USPD joined in. In the central German industrial area generally there was a strong left-wing movement, in which the USPD played a decisive role. In March 1919, the government transferred the 'Maercker Freikorps' to Halle. The story was that they were there to restore the peace, which in reality no one had actually disturbed. Both the unions and the KPD and USPD protested against the presence of the Freikorps and demanded their withdrawal.

The only reply was the arrest of trade union officials, regardless of whether they were town councillors or Communists or members of the USPD (Independent Social-Democratic Party of Germany). The workers reacted with a strike. Then the central strike leadership was arrested as well. There were clashes with the military. There were battles at the town theatre, in the market place and in the Stein Strasse. After three days, the working class of Halle was beaten. Hundreds were dragged off to the Ox-head.

Although the Maercker Freikorps were supposed to be 'republican' and 'democratic' — at least that is how the government described them, and they were later incorporated into the official army which was 100,000 strong — they were no different from the other Freikorps in their brutality against workers.

Guard duty outside the cell-blocks was also undertaken by the Freikorps. If a prisoner showed himself at a cell window, the cry rang out: 'Get away from that window!' If this order was not immediately complied with, a shot would be fired. The members of the Maercker Freikorps were mostly high-school students, young people of seventeen or eighteen, whose faces were almost completely covered by their steel helmets: but they were completely at home with their antique rifles. In the eyes of the workers, all the Freikorps were the same — reactionary and monarchist. But Noske, as war minister, took part in the meetings between army officers and the officers of the Freikorps which directed their deployment.

At the end of April, around 85 of us were transferred from the Ox-head to the remand prison. The food was bad, just as it had been in the Ox-head, mostly 'barbed wire' and dried vegetables. If you were unlucky and were served last from the pot, you generally got a thick layer of sand at the bottom of your plate. Additionally, in the mornings and evenings, there were two slices of bread. If my mother had not been around at this time, I would have starved. She came to visit me once a week, with a big basket over her shoulder containing underwear and some food, including a large home-baked loaf.

In contrast to the Ox-head, we did not have to worry about any tricks at the Stein Strasse prison. The screws treated us correctly and we were not plagued by bedbugs. In the meantime, we got to see the indictment. As I have mentioned, we were charged with riot, serious breach of the peace, looting and grievous assault. We were defended by Dr Barbasch, a famous lawyer in Halle who had already played a role in the socialist movement before the war. After a period of detention, most of the accused were spared further imprisonment; only comrade John, as supposed ringleader, and those few who had been witnessed in acts of assault and looting (or so our lawyer was told), were kept in prison.

In July, we were allowed to return home. Our solidarity ensured that those who had to remain imprisoned were provided for. During the period of our arrest, our organisation had been further strengthened, and even the youth organisation now showed some promise. None of those arrested kept away from political work. On the basis that 'whatever does not kill us can only make us tougher', we threw ourselves into our work again.

The Mücheln branch of the KPD did not restrict itself to local matters. A series of surrounding villages also came into the Mücheln district organisation. The miners' community at Neubiendorf, attached to the Cecilie pit which belonged to the Werschen-Weissenfels Lignite Company, provided the majority of branch members. Many members and officials of the miners' union had enrolled in the KPD. The lignite works in the Geisel valley was going at full blast. Workers came not only from Merseburg and Halle, but also from Sonneberg in Thuringia, and they had been recruited from the Bavarian Forest district.

Most of them were housed in huts which had sheltered POWs during the war. The barbed wire had been removed, but the people in the huts still lived cheek-by-jowl just like the POWs. The beds were pushed closely together or stacked in bunks. In one corner there were army surplus metal lockers, 30 centimetres wide, and in the middle of the room a stove. Those who slept near the stove sweated all night, while those sleeping around the walls could never get warm.

At first it was very difficult to make contact with the workers in the huts. During their spare time they usually played cards; and 'King Alcohol' also played a major role. It was not unusual for pent-up aggression to burst out into fist fights, which often led to bloodshed.

These men worked either on the spoil heaps or down the pit. It was very heavy work which had to be done in all weathers, even when it rained. When they returned from their shift, they had to dry their wet clothes at the only stove in the hut. These workers were also the worst-paid. The men who lived in the huts never had any money to spare, and they were always in debt at the company store.

It was difficult for me to find employment in the coalfield in my trade as lathe worker. There were a few metalworks in Merseburg. At the Leuna works, where 25,000 workers were employed at that time, there was a lathe shop and capstan lathes. But there was no opening for me there, since those who already had work also hung onto it. The majority of the metalworkers from Halle and Merseburg had found work in the lignite coalfield or in Leuna.

I received no unemployment benefit, since young people living with their parents could not legally qualify for support. My brother, who also stayed with us, worked at the Cecilie pit on the spoil heaps, since he could find no work in Leipzig. So, since I was still without a job four weeks after my release from prison, I started at the same place as my brother. This was 45 minutes from the pit. If you were lucky, you could get there on the pit train, though that was forbidden in the safety regulations. Most of the time you had to walk there, because the train was still being loaded. The workers living in the barracks had even further to go.

The spoil heap lay in the middle of open land; the waste — including clay, sand, stones and even perfectly good soil — had been piled up here for many years. The company did not concern itself that good land was being destroyed.

The work at the tip was very hard. There was a shelter for bad weather, but when the trains arrived immediately one after the other we could not really use it. Sometimes the ground became so wet in the rain that the rails sank in and the wagons tipped over. The trains had sixteen to eighteen wagons. There was a bonus for the drivers of the power shovels and the train drivers, and for the team leaders, if more than eighteen trains were completed in a shift. The workers on the teams never got anything extra.

Sometimes, when the ground under the rails was slippery from rain, the first few wagons were derailed. If the pins that joined the wagons were not pulled out quickly enough, then the whole train could slide down. On one occasion the whole train, complete with locomotive, fell down the embankment. That put paid to the bonus for that day and the following day, since the wagons had to be pulled back up again; there was a special team looking after the locomotive. The team leader fumed, but it did not bother the men much.

Apart from myself and my brother, there were another two men from the village. They belonged to the USPD, it is true, but in discussions they always supported our arguments. These discussions always aimed at explaining to the men from Bavaria or the Thuringian Forest the difference between the social classes and the exploitative nature of capitalism. These men had never heard anything about a progressive workers' movement before. They knew nothing about trade union struggles or of the workers' parties. We often brought them leaflets or the *Class Struggle*, the regional paper of the Communist Party. Between trains, if the rails did not have to be adjusted or tightened, discussions took place. They called my brother 'the propaganda minister'.

Gradually we gained some influence over our colleagues. On top of this, younger men, who had got to know local girls and married them, often moved into the houses of their politicised in-laws: many of them, who had only just joined the union, then became organised politically. The workers' committees brought up with the management the subject of the appalling conditions in the huts. But nothing got done about it, neither at the Cecilie, nor at the other pits. After the men in the huts had been persuaded that only a strike could bring any improvements, the union delivered an ultimatum: if better living quarters were not provided immediately, then there would be strikes at the plants. But even then the management did not react. Only when the strike had been called did they give in.

For us in the the union, this was a great victory. Not only did our colleagues declare their solidarity with us in future struggles, but now they became active on their own account. This was to be shown most clearly in the struggles against Kapp in 1920, when many workers from the barracks marched alongside us against the putschists. In the meantime I began to build up the Communist Youth League (KJV) with other young workers. We found fertile ground for this. The groups in Mücheln and Neumark were especially strong. The Mücheln branch of the KJV had well over a hundred members. Now we had to underpin our organisational success with ideological foundations.

Both the Merseburg regional sub-committee and the regional leadership in Halle gave us support by supplying lecturers who gave talks on the foundations of scientific socialism. A popular subject was the Russian

Revolutions of 1905 and 1917. In the early days especially, we conducted our educational evenings as seminars, so that all the members could take part in the discussion. At the first leadership elections, I was selected to attend a delegate conference of the Merseburg sub-region.

In November 1919, my sister Martha fell ill. Her husband had been killed in the war. In Mücheln there were only two doctors for some 20,000 people. My sister complained of pains in her abdomen, and she had diarrhoea and a high temperature. Since she could not attend the surgery, it was some days before the doctor could see her at our house. His diagnosis was tuberculosis.

When my mother suggested that it might perhaps be typhoid fever, he declared: 'Frau Hippe, your daughter has tuberculosis, that is quite evident.' He gave her treatment accordingly, without taking any precautions to prevent the spread of infection.

My sister Frieda now lived in the village, though she still came to our house regularly. It was not long before she began to show the same symptoms. A short time later, it affected my sister Emma, who was married to a man in the village. In spite of this, the doctor did not change his diagnosis. Only when my mother fell ill — she being registered with the Railwaymen's Health Insurance as an employee's relative — did a doctor from the insurance decide that it was typhoid and order her transfer to the local hospital in Merseburg. I, too, suffered the same symptoms, but continued to go to work. Since I had no faith in the doctor, I went to a homeopath in Leipzig. The medicine which he prepared for me brought some relief, but my complaint remained, and so I was taken to the hospital as well.

There were seven of us lying there in hospital, five adults and two of my sister Frieda's children, while my sister Martha's two children and my father and brother remained alone at home, since they had been spared. My brother looked after the children, washed the clothes, cooked the meals, and was very proud one day when he came to visit and reported that my sister's two daughters, who never usually wanted to eat carrot stew, had eaten more than a plateful for him. Later, when my mother and I had returned home, we found the carrots in the plate drawer of the kitchen table, where the two girls had shovelled them when unwatched.

My sister Frieda and my sister Ottilie from Leipzig, who had come to look after things, both died. The doctor was never called to account, although the true facts were known both to the hospital and the health authorities.

The trial arising from the events in Oberwünsch took place in January 1920. Eighty-five people sat in the dock, except me, who still lay in the hospital. None of the accusations were withdrawn. The defending lawyer pleaded for acquittal, on the basis that neither riot nor breach of the peace could apply. After all, the accused, in danger of their lives, had simply wanted to liberate a representative of the young republic, a man who, as chair of the District Workers' Committee, was simply complying with an edict of the government. The removal of food from the farmer's house could surely not be treated as looting, but rather as theft of food, and even that had only been committed by a few of the accused. Similarly, the accusation of bodily harm was without foundation, since it could only have been committed by a few of the accused and against the will of the main accused, Karl John.

These speeches for the defence scarcely made the slightest impression on the judge. The trial, which lasted several days and during which the accused barely got to speak, ended with the speech of the public prosecutor in which fifteen years penitentiary were demanded for the accused Karl John. For the other accused, he demanded between three and five years penitentiary or prison, and for the Sitte brothers, who were accused of participating in the looting, eight years penitentiary. The judge chose these sentences.

Only my friend and I, who were sentenced in the summer of 1920, received 'just' eighteen months' prison. We came under the amnesty which the government announced after the Kapp putsch. Of the other men sentenced, only comrade John and the brothers Sitte were released under a later amnesty. A great number of workers were angered and embittered by the sentences, and there were protest demonstrations and strikes. The KPD and USPD tried in a major campaign to explain the role played in this matter by the SPD, the German Democratic Party and the centrists, as the Trojan Horses of reaction.

Neither the Government of People's Deputies nor the first government constituted during the National Assembly at Weimar had got rid of the old ministerial bureaucracy or the monarchist judiciary, who were permitted to continue to pass judgement in the name of democracy. On 13 January 1920, the government of the Social Democrat Gustav Bauer supplied ample evidence that it was not simply an oversight that the ministerial bureaucrats and the monarchist judiciary had not been sacked and replaced by democratic forces, but rather that it was the intention of the government to proceed in alliance with these reactionary forces against the rebellious working class.

When the law on works councils was being read, a demonstration of factory workers at the Königsplatz demanded the implementation of Article 165 of the Weimar Constitution. Article 165 proclaimed that waged workers and salaried staff were to be given parity with employers in deciding wages and working conditions and to be given a full say in deciding overall economic development. The government, in its confrontation with the unions and the opposition in the workers' movement — KPD and USPD — had promised to apply Article 165 in full, and further, to complete the 'socialisation' of key industries. But it did not keep a single one of its promises.

The law which now lay before parliament proposed the election of separate workers' and employees' committees, which would then meet to form the works council. Additionally, there was only to be a right of complaint, but not a right of co-determination, and not a single word about cooperation in production. A central committee of shop stewards formed by the KPD and USPD called the demonstration on the day that the bill was being considered. More than 100,000 workers congregated. Many of them had already left their factories at lunchtime.

For no apparent reason, the soldiers and policemen hidden behind the pillars of the Reichstag shot into the crowd. Forty-two workers met with their deaths and over a hundred were injured. The newspapers reported that the police had laid into the retreating crowd with a brutality which had not been seen even in the strike of the munitions workers. In the central German industrial area, there were enormous demonstrations and protest strikes, but there were no other actions.

The bloodbath in front of the Reichstag brought to a close a year in which the revolutionary section of the working class had been obliged to abandon positions which it had won in the first months after the war. The forces of reaction had regained the upper hand with the help of the SPD. Apart from the 'Army of 100,000', new Freikorps had been formed. In the beginning, big advertisements for the Freikorps were to be found, even in the Social-Democratic press, inviting people to join up. Only protests by members forced the party leadership to prohibit such advertisements. The revolutionary section of the working class was beaten in many places in Germany, but not conquered.

5.

PROLETARIAN BATTALIONS

In the early afternoon of 13 March 1920, the news came that the government had been toppled and that Freikorps and army detachments had marched into Berlin, amongst them the infamous Ehrhardt Brigade which had made a name for itself in earlier battles against workers. On the very same evening, shop stewards belonging to the USPD and the KPD met under the chair of comrade Scheibner to discuss what should be done. Many of those present considered that the majority Social Democrats had received fitting payment for their treachery. But most were of the opinion that the question now was one of preventing a putsch by the generals which would be directed against the working class.

Even while we were meeting, news arrived that the General Commission of the Trade Unions had called a general strike. The leaflets reached us the next morning, signed by the chair, Carl Legien, who had previously opposed Rosa Luxemburg with his phrase: 'General strike is general nonsense.'

That evening, we decided to support the strike, and the same night comrades and trade unionists and shop stewards went into the factories to get things moving. The factories were immediately shut down. The trade union representatives and the party officials were instructed to turn up at the trade union centre the next morning to discuss the next moves.

Early the next day, we heard the call which the Ebert-Noske government had sent back to Berlin as it fled towards Dresden. All of a sudden the national government in flight addressed the populace as 'workers and comrades'. They demanded the immobilisation of the entire economy, and a general strike to the bitter end. This call was only signed by the SPD members, since the bourgeois ministers had refused.

The workers in the factories had not waited for the call from the government, but had acted quite independently. The general strike was supported throughout the country. It was, incidentally, the first and last time that civil servants participated almost to a man.

In the meantime, the government was not safe even in Dresden; it moved on to Stuttgart. In the early hours of 14 March came a report that the army battalion at the Merseburg garrison had joined the putschists. In Halle, apart from an artillery regiment, there was also a battalion of infantry. The working class of Halle, having already started the previous day to fight the troops who had declared themselves for Kapp and Lüttwitz, had succeeded in disarming one section of the putschists.

The other section had retreated to the land around the goods station and the artillery barracks which lay opposite it, and had dug themselves in. The workers from the Geisel valley had grouped into Hundreds and elected a military command, and, together with workers from Merseburg and the Leuna works, they surrounded the barracks.

The command was composed mostly of USPD members, together with Communists and Social Democrats. I found myself in a troop with my brother-in-law. Some 15,000 workers had encircled the barracks. We only had a few weapons — a couple of carbines and some hunting-rifles which we had confiscated from the peasants, nothing else. The command called on the soldiers inside to lay down their arms, but this was rejected by the officers.

Only after we had dug up their water supply did they give in, with the assurance from our command that they could retreat without their weapons. They piled up their weapons in the yard. When more than half of them had retreated in the direction of Leipzig, we noticed that the breech mechanisms were missing from the surrendered rifles, machine-guns and a few of the mortars. The departure of the remaining troops was immediately stopped.

When we had found out where the missing breeches had been hidden — they had been thrown into the latrine pits in the yard — we forced the putschists to climb into the pits and get them out again. As it later turned out, it had still been a mistake to let the soldiers retreat to Leipzig: the Leipzig workers had not succeeded in disarming the garrison there and the Merseburg putschists were supplied with new weapons.

With the weapons seized in Merseburg, we managed to equip four Hundreds of workers. These were mostly young workers who had gained some expertise with weapons during the war. Our Hundred comprised mostly miners from the Cecilie, Elisabeth and Leonhard pits, who all knew each other. We were based at the Rosengarten, a large market garden beside the road between Halle and Kassel to the north-west of Ammendorf.

While the putschists defending the land around the goods station were driven closer together, it was impossible for us to get closer to the barracks. From there, we were shot at with 75-millimetre guns, and our losses were considerable. Next to me, a comrade from the Communist Youth League, who worked as a shot-firer in the Cecilie pit, was badly injured: a fragment from a grenade tore away part of his chin. He was later 'cobbled together' to some extent in the Merseburg hospital.

On the third day of fighting, the putschists were forced out of the goods yard back into the artillery barracks, and some of them were captured before that. In spite of considerable losses, we had advanced to the barracks, and then our command dared launch an attack.

In the meantime, we received a report that an agreement had been reached in Bielefeld by which the national government promised to hand the putschists over to the courts, and the workers, through their trade unions, would retain decisive influence on economic and social policy making.

Of course, the prerequisite for this was an end to the general strike. Discussions took place, both in the strike leadership and in the political committee of the KPD and USPD, in which the shop stewards were also represented, as to whether we should submit to the Bielefeld Agreement or continue the fight until victory.

The political committee, in which the USPD held the great majority, decided to accept the Agreement. The strike leadership was divided. Ninety per cent of the workers on the streets had stated that they were not prepared to lay down their arms and retreat weaponless back to their districts. But still the USPD stood by its decision: after all, the government could not possibly break its word.

The KPD representatives left the meeting in protest and explained to the workers on the streets and in the strike meetings in the districts that they had failed to persuade the political committee with their arguments. Since the workers fighting on the streets could not get the support which they needed, they withdrew to their districts with their weapons.

The soldiers of the national government — these were the same ones who had supported the putsch only a few days before — did not dare to march into the miners' districts. Scarcely had it been signed than the Bielefeld Agreement was broken again. General Seekt, commander-in-chief of the German army, who had refused to support the government against Kapp and Lüttwitz with the words 'Soldier does not fire upon soldier', was allowed to remain at his post. Even then, the Ehrhardt Brigade wore the swastika on its steel helmets. It sang these words in its anthem:

'Swastika on our steel helmets,
Our colours black, white and red,
The Ehrhardt Brigade —
Our name is spoken with dread.
Workers, oh you workers,
How badly you will fare
When the Ehrhardt Brigade
Its arms once more will bear.
The Ehrhardt Brigade
Smashes all to kingdom come;
Woe, oh woe to you,
You working class scum.'

This threat by the Ehrhardt Brigade became a reality when it withdrew from Berlin, and shot twelve people dead at the Brandenburg Gate.

The putsch was masterminded by Kapp and Lüttwitz. However, it had mobilised millions of workers who were firmly resolved to put it down. What was not possible for the working class in November 1918 — to set up a socialist republic in place of the monarchy — could now have been achieved after the putschists had been defeated. In the central German industrial area, armed troops of workers abounded. In the Ruhr district the workers had locked the putschist General Watter in the Wesel fortress.

After the Bielefeld Agreement, the Wesel fortress was indeed relieved by the Army, but General Watter, who had conspired with Kapp and Lüttwitz, was commissioned by the government to take steps against the Red Army of the Ruhr. The workers' battalions were not strong enough to storm the fortress and had to retreat before the occupying soldiers. The Red Army of the Ruhr had refused to lay down arms as the Bielefeld Agreement demanded. In central Germany the USPD had succeeded in persuading armed workers to cease any activities involving force. Many, it must be said, hung on to their weapons and some hid them in disused tunnels at the mines. This was done in the understanding that the weapons would be needed again in the fight against reaction.

The reason that the Red Army of the Ruhr was finally beaten lay in the fact that it fought in isolation from the other workers, and that army units and police battalions were concentrated in the Ruhr district. After the defeat of the workers, the troops under the command of General Watter butchered many more than the number who had actually fallen in the fight.

The national government and the forces of the right were mortally afraid that the workers could follow the example of the Russian Revolution, and drive out the monopoly capitalists and their errand boys and so make a breakthrough for the system of soviets.

All those who thought that the conditions for a victorious revolution were nonexistent in March 1920 — because, safe in their offices, they were in no position to evaluate the movement of the masses correctly — were utterly wrong. The millions who had been set in motion by 13 March did not need the bureaucrats to provide the means for the fight against the reactionary putsch. What they lacked was the political experience to advance positively from this fight. The small Communist Party did not have enough influence over the masses to lead them to the socialist republic. The USPD, which had learned nothing from the struggles in 1918-1919, swore by the Bielefeld Agreement and on decisions made in parliament.

There were long discussions in our party, and especially in the youth movement, about the causes of a defeat suffered despite successful intervention in the fight to defend the republic. In the course of these discussions, there was almost unanimous agreement that Rosa Luxemburg and Karl Liebknecht had not split from social-democratic policies early enough, as the left wing of the Russian Social Democratic Workers' Party had done in 1903. In the last years before the war at the latest, when reformism was showing itself more clearly, that was when the left wing in the SPD should have decided to split. Even if it had not been possible to prevent the war, at least the outcome of the November Revolution would have been different.

These discussions never came to a head, but they did affect the membership of the USPD. The Communist Party had been able to increase its influence within the working class tremendously, despite the split at the Heidelberg Congress. Here, a faction of the party was excluded, having refused to work within the Social-Democratic trade unions and demanded instead a walk-out from the unions and the construction of our own Communist ones. From the exclusion of this faction emerged the Communist Workers' Party (KAP).

In both the Ruhr district and central Germany, the KAP won significant support, including the Leonhard mine. In the works council there, the KAP members dominated, apart from only two members of the KPD. Among the workers in the Geisel valley, particularly amongst the miners, there was a tendency to leave the trade unions because of their betrayal of the interests of the working man. Even inside the KPD there was a faction — albeit weak — which was prepared to found its own trade union organisation. Indeed, the Union of Hand and Head Workers was actually formed, but the majority of KPD members remained inside the ADGB. The KAP had already formed its own trade union organisation, the General Workers' Union (AAU).

The discussions between Communist workers and members of the USPD (Independents) resulted in a rapprochement of ideas. On the Russian question especially, in which there had been almost insuperable differences at first, there were now large areas of agreement. In the late summer, official discussions between the central committee of the KPD and the party executive of the USPD were begun, with the aim of unifying the two parties. These discussions bore fruit, and the unification took place in November.

The great majority of the delegates at the unification congress in Halle were members of the USPD. I took part in the unification as a delegate of the KJV. Neither the right wing of the Independents nor comrade Ledebour agreed to the unification. The right wing soon returned to the SPD. Ledebour founded an intermediate organisation which remained without any notable support.

The official membership of the Unified Communist Party (VKPD) was given as 500,000, but not all those whose delegates had voted for the unification even joined the new party. Later, there was talk of 375,000 members. After the unification congress, both organisations took the unification process down to local level.

The first meeting of the membership in Mücheln had to elect new officials. After reports by Comrade Haubenreisser of the KPD and Comrade Scheibner of the USPD, which were followed by a lengthy discussion, the election took place. The first secretary of the Mücheln branch of the party was Haubenreisser; Scheibner was elected as his deputy. While the majority of party members came from the USPD, the ratio was inverted in the Communist Youth League — 90 per cent of its members had already been in the KJV.

The Unified Communist Party had more votes in the industrial belt than all the other parties put together, including the SPD. In the Mansfeld district, as well as in the Harz foothills, the party had won considerable support among the small farmers and peasants. In many communities, the VKPD dominated. Any communal policies made there were always in the interest of the working population. But in the factories as well, working conditions and wages were improved with the aid of strikes.

The great political influence of the party was a thorn in the flesh of the employers and the Prussian government. In the early part of 1921, the Prussian government, with the blessing of the national government, sent several battalions of police into the copper mining district of Mansfeld under the pretence of preventing the theft of crops from the fields.

It was quite clear to the workers and trade unions of that district, and to the regional leadership of the KPD, what the real intention was. At that time of year (March) there was nothing in the fields that could be stolen. The whole undertaking was intended, on the one hand, to provoke the workers, and on the other to intimidate the populace.

When nothing happened after the local and regional organisations had protested and demanded the withdrawal of the police units, the workers at the slate mines stopped work. The police responded with the arrest of party and trade union officials and launched such vicious attacks against the people that there was a general outcry. Then we found out that those arrested had been beaten by the police. The tension among the workers, and indeed in the entire population, increased rapidly.

The KAP called for resistance. The workers, who had already defended themselves against the attacks of the police, went for the weapons which had been concealed in disused tunnels after the Kapp putsch, and gave the police a hard fight. Max Hoelz, who had already fought against the armed forces in 1919 in the Vogtland district, came to the fore again. Together with Klempin, alias Utzelmann, who was also a member of the KAP, he organised the armed uprising.

The workers of the central German industrial area, some of whom had already downed tools and closed their factories, followed a call by the trade unions and declared their solidarity with the men in the Mansfeld district. Many members of the KPD and the youth movement had already gone to the aid of the workers fighting in Mansfeld, in the military sense as well. The workers at the Elisabeth and Elise II pits had taken up position in the south-west of the Geisel valley, on the spoil heaps, in order to prevent the police from entering the valley from that direction.

Only when the Prussian government had sent even more police battalions to central Germany, and students had organised themselves as temporary 'volunteers', did the Communist Party declare itself to be in solidarity with those in struggle.

In the meantime, the uprising had spread out over the entire industrial belt. In Gröbers and other villages in the Bitterfeld coalfield, there were battles with the police. At Ammendorf near Halle, the workers fought a police battalion to prevent them from entering the Geisel valley lignite coalfield. They had blown up the railway bridges. According to our information, only the regional leadership of the KPD in Halle had declared its solidarity with the fighting workers, while the party centre in Berlin was still 'standing to attention'.

Our members were of the opinion that the Halle regional leadership had only declared solidarity in order to avoid isolation. While the pressure from the police increased steadily and more and more units were deployed, the workers remained alone in their fight.

There were no actions to support the uprising in any districts or towns except for the Moers district on the left bank of the Rhine. In Mansfeld the workers were forced to abandon their positions. They had partly removed themselves to Halle in the belief that there was fighting there and that the police had been beaten there — at least, that is what they were told by the central leadership of the struggle. Others, under the leadership of Max Hoelz, wanted to withdraw to Czechoslovakia via Sangershausen and the Harz.

In a village near the Unstrut valley, the police forced them to stand and fight. Some of them were captured, the others tried to avoid arrest. Just outside a neighbouring village, some of the workers being pursued had hidden in a hayloft belonging to a peasant. This hiding place was betrayed by peasants who had been stirred up by stories that the workers had tortured police officers and even killed them. Peasants armed with dung forks searched the barn, stabbing the hay and fetching out the men hidden there; none escaped with his life. Max Hoelz had succeeded in escaping from the area with a small troop, but he too was arrested later by the police.

There were scarcely any fights in the Geisel valley. The police, together with the Freikorps of student volunteers, came in from the west, north and east. Klempin, who had stationed himself with some of his men in the Geisel valley, gave the order to occupy the Leuna works. The leadership thought that the Leuna works could be defended for a long time since the police would not dare attack the defenders of this enormous chemical works with heavy artillery. More than 3,000 fighters had gathered inside the works, not all of them armed, and their weapons fairly poor anyway. Apart from rifles and machine-guns, and two mortars, there was nothing. Ammunition was also scarce.

Reinforcements came once more from the workers of Halle and Ammendorf, but, again, only some of them carried weapons. They told us that the police were following them on foot. That same night, the works was surrounded on all sides. When the police demanded that the weapons be surrendered, the leadership of the insurgents said that they would only agree under two conditions: the withdrawal of the police from the central German industrial area, and safe passage for the workers involved. Otherwise, resistance would continue to the very end.

At first, nothing happened. We did not know that no one apart from ourselves in the Leuna works was putting up any more resistance. The police attack began the following evening, at first without any support from the artillery battery which had been positioned in the mill in the village of Leuna. The attack, which came mainly from the north-west, was successfully repulsed.

On the morning after that, there was another attack, this time with artillery support. There were areas in the Leuna works containing high explosives. Our leaders, who had counted on our opponents not using heavy guns, had to provide a suitable answer to this attack. They had improvised an armoured train. On the very first day, mechanics had started building a train, using the sheets of iron which were in plentiful supply, goods wagons and a locomotive. Three times, this was driven out with a crew to attack the gun battery, and each time we succeeded in driving off our attackers, but not in destroying the battery.

The fight had lasted almost a week. The north-western sector of the works was partially destroyed, although greater damage from explosions had been avoided. The works management, as we later learned, had taken such explosions into their calculations. Gradually our ammunition ran out, although food was still abundant since we had the run of the canteens which were stocked to feed large numbers of employees. Our leadership then spread the word that any fighters not allocated to specific positions should try to escape from the works. The works were about six kilometres long; west of this land ran the railway between Berlin and Frankfurt, while the river Saale flowed on the other side. To the south lay the Merseburg gasworks, to the north the Korbetha Station with an extensive network of railway tracks.

Some of us were able to get ourselves to safety in this direction, since the police were in no position to seal the whole place off hermetically. And at night people could escape to the south and reach home via Kayna and Rossbach.

This freedom, to which I had escaped like many others, did not last long. The remaining fighters surrendered the next morning. They were interned within the works, in one half of which nitrate was stored. The police, who had not been allowed into the district since the Kapp putsch, now went in. Systematically, they searched all the workers' districts. I was denounced to the police by my uncle, a master baker. He accused me of having taken part in the fighting. I was escorted to Leuna together with the miners' official Karl Bairich, who had still belonged to the SPD before the 'March days' but was now in the leadership of the strike, and many others.

At Leuna we were kept in a nitrate silo. The silo was of concrete, some 500 metres long and 36 metres high. At a height of 30 metres there ran a mobile gantry with a bucket, which was used to shovel the nitrate up and out to tank wagons via pipes. Because of the danger of explosion, there was only one entrance to the silo, an iron door measuring 1.80 metres by 70 centimetres. We were herded inside through this narrow opening, where hundreds of comrades were already crowded, many of them lying on straw. Up on the gantry, which was reached by a narrow ladder on either side, were heavily-armed police, with hand-grenades on their belts.

There was still a state of emergency, which had been declared when the fighting first broke out. Each day, civilians came into the silo, accompanied by policemen. They were looking for prisoners who were supposed to have been involved in terrorist actions. If they met anyone who was known to them as a communist, then the individual concerned was led out and, as we later learned from workers who were on emergency cover, was put up against the wall and shot.

All this lasted for three days. Later, when the state of emergency in the area of fighting was lifted and the works started full production again, no more executions took place, but the police harassment continued. Each day, when the food was distributed — this work was performed by policemen — there was some outrage or other. After all the prisoners, some 3,000 in all, had received their food, the overseer asked who wanted more. Naturally, many people went up again, especially in the first few days. But it was very unusual for there to be any more. Usually the police simply flung the remnants among those waiting and then waded in with rubber truncheons.

Amongst the prisoners there was an older comrade, aged 65, the mayor of a village near Leuna. He was mistreated several times. On one occasion, two guardians of the peace grabbed his long beard from both sides and started punching him. Beatings took place for any reason you care to mention. In order to prevent any prisoner from ill-considered reaction to the police provocations — for the police were just waiting for an excuse to be able to throw hand-grenades or use machine-guns from the gantry — each group of a hundred in the silo set up its own security squad. This stopped the prisoners from putting up a fight. The harassment continued until the day we were transferred to Wittenberg.

The responsibility for all these bullyings and beatings lay with the provincial president of Saxony, Otto Hörsing. Hörsing was a leading member of the Social Democratic Party. To the honour of one police battalion stationed in Erfurt, it must be said that it never over-reached itself whilst in service. Most of its members were Social Democrats. We learned from them that the workers who had fought or participated in strikes in Halle and the Bitterfeld district were now locked up in the Moritzburg, an ancient fortress in Halle. They said that, when the prisoners were allowed out for an hour, their hands were tied together above their heads with barbed wire.

Most of the policemen in service were members of the Freikorps —

students among them — and it was these who started most of the trouble. I do not know how long the state of emergency lasted. It could have been eight or even ten days after my arrest. During the fighting and the strike, only emergency working took place in the pits and at the Leuna works.

After the end of the emergency, full-time working began again. Despite this, the harassment of the prisoners did not stop. A great deal of unrest began to spread among the workforce at the Leuna works, who saw what was going on. The chair of the shop stewards, Bernhard Koenen, a brother of Wilhelm Koenen (both of them later occupied leading positions in the Communist Party), informed the management and Hörsing that the workforce would begin an unlimited strike if the prisoners were not accommodated outside the works and if they continued to be treated so inhumanly. This warning obviously made an impression.

Two days later we were loaded into waiting goods wagons early in the morning. Prior to that, we had received food for a full day. No one knew where we were going. A passenger coach was coupled in between every two goods wagons, occupied by policemen, with a machine-gun on the roof. That same morning, the first train left the works amidst the friendly waves of the men. We travelled through Merseburg, Halle and Bitterfeld, to Wittenberg on the river Elbe. Wittenberg had been an important garrison town during the time of Kaiser Wilhelm, but now only a few battalions of police were stationed there.

Our train stopped outside the town. The first prisoners who were disembarked were put up in the fortress outside the town. The rest of us, including myself, flanked by police, were marched through the town to the artillery barracks. There, 300 of us were accommodated in the riding hall, which was furnished with straw around the walls and in the middle. By evening, all the barracks were fully occupied by prisoners, brought from Leuna in three trains. Another hundred men came with the last transport and were herded into our riding hall.

Overnight, peat dust, which lay in the hall along with the straw, was thrown up in the air by the movement of 400 men. Luckily we were able to clean ourselves outside at the pump. The police battalion which had been so reasonable with us at the Leuna works had come with us to Wittenberg. Often, policemen came into the horse stalls to ask why we had gone on strike and taken up arms. We told them that we who were now kept here as prisoners had defended the republic against Kapp and Lüttwitz one year ago in Halle and Merseburg. But this year we had reached for our weapons because those we had defended last year were now arresting our officials and wanted to smash our organisation.

Our arguments clarified things for most of them. Over the weeks, they came to us as often as they could, under any pretext, in order to discuss things. They always warned us against trusting their officers.

The food was much better in comparison to Leuna. Every day there was plenty of hot food. They gave us enough bread and margarine for two days, so that we had to think of ways of 'making it last', since there was no way of storing it.

In the meantime, examining magistrates had been sent from the High County Court at Naumburg, who began to question the prisoners. Nothing could be proved against most of them, except that they had taken part in the strike. If they were not leading officials, they were set free.

Anyone who was said to have taken part in the fighting was imprisoned on remand. For this purpose, once most had been released, the castle barracks were furnished as a prison. One day I was brought before the examining magistrate. He accused me of having participated in the fighting in the Geisel valley. I told him that there had been no fighting at all in the Geisel valley, and so I could not have participated in it. But he was quite happy with the statement made by my uncle, Böhme the master baker, who claimed to have seen me with a rifle in my hand. Thus I changed from 'prisoner in protective custody' to 'prisoner on remand' and ended up in the castle barracks. I lay there on the upper floor with my brother-in-law, Werner Eser, and eight others.

The castle barracks were located quite close to the banks of the Elbe. When we discovered a boat on the bank one day, we decided to risk escape. Three of us secretly set to work. We made a rope out of bedclothes. Of the ten in the room, two others apart from us three were told of the plan. They also helped us make the rope long enough. Earlier, we had noticed how the guards made their rounds. One misty night we dared to let ourselves down. We managed to get clear of the castle without being noticed. Water still lay on the meadows in places, but we managed to reach the boat. To our horror we found that it was chained up. Using a stone we succeeded in breaking the lock, and we rowed to the other side of the Elbe without being spotted. From there we walked to a small station outside Bitterfeld, and caught a workers' train into the town.

We risked telling the workers that we had escaped from the castle barracks in Wittenberg, where we had been held accused of riot and breach of the peace. They gave us money so that we could continue our journey to Halle. In Halle I had relatives who helped us further. They warned us to take care, since the police were still on the lookout for suspicious characters. All the same, we risked the journey home.

Scarcely had we arrived than my sister told us that the police had arrested Karl Bairich, the old comrade who had been active in the SPD and the trade union even before the war. He was released from prison a sick man, and a few years later he died. He had been active both in the Zeitz district and later in Ammendorf, where lignite coal was mined in deep pits. In Ammendorf he was sacked for his trade union activity. He found work in the Geisel valley, because he was one of the few builders of drainage channels who could dig such channels underneath the coal. There he laid the foundations for the mineworkers' union. He did not take part in the uprising, but because he was the chair of the central strike leadership, he was arrested and condemned to several years of imprisonment.

We had only been a few hours at home when the 'Sipo' (that was the Security Police) arrived.

Fortunately, our house stood right next to the Emma pit. The colliers hid me in a gallery. Together with my brother-in-law, who had sought shelter in the pit with me, I went in a circuitous route via Klobikau to Frankleben, to catch the first tram into Halle. In the evening a comrade from the solidarity committee had come to the pit. He told us that we should report to the office of the Hand and Head Workers' Union in the Lerchenfeld Strasse in Halle. In addition he gave us papers that certified us as refugees from the uprising. In Halle we received a ticket to get us to Gelsenkirchen, some money for food and a membership card of the organisation, with a letter for the members there urging them to help us further.

Things almost went wrong at the Halle railway station, for the police were making a raid. But railway workers helped us and hid us in the luggage room underneath the station. The train finally got us to Gelsenkirchen, and we reported there at the office of the Hand and Head Workers' Union. We were given some pocket money and taken to a comrade in the workers' district. He was also a member of the union and an official. We could stay with him for the meantime, until our papers had been put in order. Then they would try to find work for us at a colliery.

We had already been ten days in Gelsenkirchen, but we still had no work. One day a comrade came and informed us that we should go to Krefeld for a short time to work. There too we stayed with friends in the party. We could see everywhere that the spirit of solidarity was highly treasured. Unfortunately, there was no work here either, but we did get employment papers. I received papers in my own name, in which it was claimed that I had worked for eighteen months at a fitter's in Krefeld. Werner, my brother-in-law, who was an unskilled worker, received papers as a building labourer.

We travelled from Krefeld back to Gelsenkirchen. Finally we were able to start in the coking plant at a pit in Castrop-Rauxel. We could stay at the single men's hostel, but it was crawling with lice. I naturally did not want to stay there under those conditions.

Workers were also sought for the Emscher-Lippe pit. We struck lucky and were able to start there as haulers. The pit management allocated us rooms with miners' families. I lived at the house of a hewer who worked at the rockface. My host was 36 years old, but from his appearance you would have thought he was 60. The work of a stone hewer is one of the toughest in the mining industry. The hewers do piece-work and drive the main and secondary sectional cuts — called 'contracts' — through the rock. Holes two metres deep are bored with stone drills above, below and to the side, and these are filled with dynamite. In this way, fifteen cubic metres of stone is blown away each time and the whole section is filled with dust.

In theory, before any clearing up is done, the whole place should be sprayed with water, but since they are doing piece-work, the workers have no time for that if they want their wages. So they work in a cloud of dust which floats around for more than an hour. None of the workers who worked at the rockface ever reached 65; they all became invalids early on.

We worked as haulers. Our task was to collect the coal which the hewers had cut from the seam and shovelled into a pulsating chute, to wheel it through a connecting tunnel to the hoist; down below it was coupled to a train by another hauler and taken to the loading station by a compressed-air locomotive. We did our work at a depth of 800 metres. During the first days we got a strange feeling when we were carried all the way down in 75 seconds, but we got used to it with time. No one bothered about where we came from and what had brought us to the Ruhr district. Germans from every part of the country, Dutchmen, Italians, French and Belgians — they were all there. There was a comprehensive comradeship, every one was there to help his colleagues. The continual danger which surrounded the men also kept thoughts of solidarity awake in them.

Every so often the pit foreman, who went round once a day — sometimes twice — and let us know when we could 'butter' (that is, have breakfast), would sit down with the men, and there would be conversation. On one such occasion he asked me — since I was supposed to be a pipe fitter — whether I might want to take over maintenance work in the pit with another colleague. Here the work papers which I had got in Krefeld came in useful. I agreed immediately, since I really had done some work like that when I had helped set up generators during the war at the fuel plant at Lützkendorf. That same day, he introduced me to my colleague.

That evening I had to go in on the night shift to do some necessary repairs. We had been told to ensure that the spraying equipment worked properly, and we were to connect up the 'Lutten conveyors' — these were large pipes with a diameter of 400 millimetres — and the compressed-air motors which made the chutes pulsate.

On many days there was no work for us at all, so we just had to go around checking equipment; on other days there was hardly enough time to complete all the outstanding work. In those cases we had to come in at night in order to keep up with our repair work. One day — I was about to connect the compressed-air motor to the vibrating chute, which the men at the seam had moved some five feet — when there was a sudden thundering like in a storm. The men grabbed their belongings and fled from the seam. I did not understand what was happening, since I had never heard such a thing, and went on working at the connection of the motor. Then a colleague came back and shouted to me: 'Get away quick! The seam is collapsing!' Scarcely had I left the seam than it and the connecting section collapsed with a terrifying din. If my colleague had not come back, I would have been buried under the piles of rock.

For the moment, no more coal could be got from the seam, and the collapsed area had to be rebuilt by men on a repair team.

Around 3,000 men were employed at the pit, most of them on day shift. Three shifts were worked; the first and second were called 'haulage shifts' during which coal was got out, while the night shift was reserved for repairs so that the day shift could win coal again. The journey down the shaft was tremendously fast. Within 25 minutes, 650 men were brought to the foot of an 800 metre shaft. From the loading point, which was the central point of the mineshaft, we still had to walk for 40 minutes to reach the face where the coal was. At that time, the men could not be driven to the coalface for safety reasons. After they arrived at the face, they first of all 'buttered'. Everyone sat on the tool chests, and ate and discussed: every day there were new problems. In addition, the men were organised into three different trade unions: in the Mineworkers' Federation, in the General Workers' Union, and in the Union of Hand and Head Workers.

In those twenty minutes there was some very lively discussion. Christian trade unionists — as at most other pits — were hardly represented. But I knew of one pit in the neighbouring village of Waltrop where the men were organised almost one hundred per cent in the Christian Trade Union.

There was a crowd of comrades living in Datteln who had fled from central Germany like us and had found work here. Together with comrades from the Mücheln and Neumark branches of the Communist Youth League, we founded a local branch of the KJV there in Datteln. After the events of March, any public intervention was virtually impossible. So we registered our group as a Workers' Cultural and Rambling Organisation. Our daily discussions on the tool chests provided a good advertisement for our League. The young workers especially had an open mind to our positions. In a relatively short space of time, we were able to expand our local branch considerably. On Sunday we were always on the move, either on long or short rambles in the surrounding countryside or agitational marches in a specific direction.

On one occasion we reached Waltrop in the middle of a procession by Catholic youth. There was enormous excitement when, quite unwittingly, we stumbled right into the middle of this procession carrying our red pennants. It almost turned into a punch-up, but one of our comrades managed to convince the Catholics that we were not there for a struggle involving muscles but rather for a spiritual struggle. In the end there was a discussion about social and cultural problems.

On another occasion, when we returned one lunchtime to Datteln after a short excursion into the neighbourhood, we again stumbled on a procession by the Catholic Church. We were just turning out of a side street into the main street when the head of this procession bumped into us from the right. They had to wait until our group was out on the main road. We deliberately slowed down our march so that it appeared as if the procession was marching behind the red pennants. We had the laugh on our side, for Datteln was overwhelmingly protestant.

Our main area of work was among the trade unions, both within the Mineworkers' Federation and in the Union of Hand and Head Workers. Our motto was: trade unions are preparatory schools for socialism; without the political awareness of the masses there can be no successful fight against capitalism.

One of the important political problems for us lay in understanding the causes of the defeat after the Kapp putsch and again in March 1921. The reasons for the defeat in 1920 had been discussed immediately after the end of the fight against the putschists, and we had come to the illuminating conclusion that the defeat stemmed mainly from the treacherous politics of the Social-Democratic 'workers' leaders'.

Despite these bad experiences, it was clear that many workers still had illusions in social-democratic policies. Paul Levi, the chair of the KPD, suggested at that time that the communists should form a 'loyal opposition' in the event that the SPD and USPD came together in government. But the USPD rejected such a coalition. So the Social Democrats had commissioned Hermann Müller with the affairs of government.

The new government was thus constituted partly from those forces which only shortly before had been involved in suppressing and disarming workers' militias — those organs of the working class in which Communists, USPD members and Social Democrats had struggled together against the counter-revolution. The Social-Democratic ministers in the new government were themselves hated by their own membership for their role in the Kapp putsch. Only yesterday, the generals with whom they formed a government today had beaten and murdered workers in their thousands, regardless of their political loyalties. We could never expect such a government to represent the interests of the working people.

The SPD paid the price for this in the parliamentary elections which followed in June 1920, when the number of votes they received fell from 11.5 million to 5.6 million.

Far more difficult than arriving at a correct evaluation of the politics of social democracy was the task of getting a clear perspective of the causes of the defeat of the struggle of March 1921. Both in the Communist Youth League and in the KPD, there were heated arguments about this. The chair of the party, Paul Levi, handed in his resignation after he had described as 'putschism' the decision of the party to call a general strike and to participate in the armed struggle. Levi was later expelled from the party because he made the controversy public.

Each one of us who had experienced the events in central Germany from the very first days and who had stood at the centre of the events had no doubt at all that the party had not wanted the fight and had not organised it. Nothing at all had happened during those days in the Berlin and Lower Rhine regions, where the left wing was strong. (At that time we knew nothing of the events in Hamburg, where there were shipyard occupations.) The KPD was surprised by the events. The fact that it did not pay enough attention to the course of developments must be chalked up as an error. Within the framework of our discussion on the wrong position of the party, it became clear to us that Paul Levi's critique of 'putschism' was not justified and that there were fundamental political differences behind his resignation. The actions carried out by the KAP together with Max Hoelz had been laid at the door of the KPD.

In these discussions, it became clear to us that the party should have faced up to the dangers threatening itself and the working class in good enough time, and not, as happened, let them roll over it. A revolutionary party had the duty to lead the working class in every situation; it should pursue neither vanguard nor rearguard policies — as Lenin once said. Its duty must be to keep its finger on the pulse of the working class and at the same time seek clarity on the the intentions of the government and the counter-revolution.

6.

1923

In the summer of 1922, the national government declared a general amnesty. Only those who had been condemned as 'ringleaders' were excluded from this, such as Max Hoelz and some others, and those who had been found guilty of 'criminal activities'. Most of the comrades who had gone underground for safety after the March days were now able to return to central Germany. This had been agreed in a joint meeting of the party and the Youth League. I returned home as well, although it was debatable whether I would find work.

After my return to the Geisel valley, I found to my joy that the party and Youth League were still very active. The workers still had confidence in them. My political work consisted mostly in building up the Youth League. Inflation was running high, but had still not nearly reached its highest point. In any struggles that took place, the trade unions fought for full settlement of wage claims and a sliding scale of wages.

I found a job as a works mechanic at the Elisabeth pit. I was employed in the workshop with two comrades, one of whom was also an official in the Youth League. Our work was very varied. We went everywhere in the works, sometimes in the compressor house, sometimes in the drying loft or separating area, or again down below in the pit. But our working relationship did not last. Management soon found out who I was. And they found a reason to sack me. We went to the industrial tribunal. At the first hearing, judgement was made in our favour, but at the appeal the management won.

So, after a short period of employment, I was out of work again. Soon, inflation had made worthless the little money I had saved. There was no question of finding another job here. Doors were closed against me throughout the district, at whatever pit I applied, even though workers were sought. After a long search, I finally got work in Frankleben, an hour's journey from our village. After the war, a steelworks had opened up in this village. The chair of the shop stewards there was a member of the KPD and he had considerable influence on recruitment. The work which I received through him was admittedly not in my line, but that was not important to me. The decisive thing for me was, firstly, not being a financial burden on my father, and secondly, being able to continue my political work in a factory. If there had been no inflation, then my wage would not have been bad: we did piecework and the pay was better in the steel industry than in coal.

At that time, my father was negotiating with the management of the Emma mine over the purchase of our property. The house lay right next to the pit, and since the loaded trains went past at short intervals, there was a real danger of structural collapse from the vibrations. The management of the mine offered my father the sum of 25,000 Reichsmarks. Both my brother and I and friends of my father advised him not to sell, but rather to negotiate an exchange for a piece of ground in the village or the next village. Both parties finally agreed to these terms.

There was no exchange made on the first properties which my father was offered, because the architect of those sites had reserved the first right of sale for himself. He belonged to the Stahlhelm (Steel Helmets), an organisation which was supported by the parties of the right. It claimed to be a federation which cultivated the cameraderie formed in the 'community of battle in the trenches', but in reality it was intended as a paramilitary force to support the parties of the right in their fight against the workers. This man did not want my father to get hold of one of these plots — we were regarded as the 'communist Hippes' locally. As I have already said, my father was conservative and had loved his Kaiser. Now that he no longer paid any attention to politics, the fact that I was an official of the Communist Party and its Youth League reflected on the whole family.

After further negotiations, my father was offered a property which had been utterly neglected. Two acres of land and one of meadow came with the property. It lay in the village of Krumpa, at the edge of the industrial area. My father finally agreed to this exchange. The village of Krumpa was almost entirely inhabited by peasants who were influenced by an estate owner and member of parliament for the German National Party by the name of Seibicke. Many of them also belonged to the Stahlhelm organisation.

In the spring of 1923 we moved into our new house, together with my sister Emma, who had got married in the meantime. She gave birth to her

On the way up: with communist comrades near Jonsdorf in the Zittauer mountains (Oskar Hippe seated right)

second child there. The peasants in the village refused to sell her milk for her children. So she had to walk every day into the industrial area. My father also felt the effects of the peasants' boycott. On our previous property we had some ploughed land and another two acres of land. When we wanted to plough our new land, the peasants refused to do any ploughing for my father. Even my uncle, who owned a bakery and a farm, was not prepared to help my father. So we were forced, the five of us in the family, armed with spades and hoes, to turn over more than two acres of earth. Fortunately, the solidarity of the workers made itself felt: comrades from the party often came and helped us till the fields. The behaviour of my comrades made a certain impression on my father, but left no permanent marks.

If the peasants and the squire believed that they could shake me in my political convictions, then they were wrong. On the contrary, I devoted every spare minute to party work. There was not so much conflict with my father as before, because I worked with my brother-in-law on the renovation of the house. In the fifteen months that I continued to live there, we altered the property totally. The peasants with their sabotage and clannishness did not achieve their object. The small number of workers who lived in the village joined the Communist Party.

Finally, the peasants tried direct pressure on me. One evening I had to address a meeting of the Communist Youth League in the trade union building in Mücheln.

Some of the young comrades — most of whom came from Mücheln and district — had to go in the same direction as myself afterwards. So we went together as far as Neubiendorf, a mineworkers' hamlet. When we split up, the master tailor Bergener, who had been visiting in Krumpa, told me not to go home since the peasants were waiting for me in the village, hoping to make an example of me. All the young comrades, and the older ones too, said they were prepared to see me home.

A red flag was quickly found, and off we marched to Krumpa. When we reached the village, we struck up the 'Internationale'. At the fire station on the village square there really was a mob, and even the policeman was there. But they did not expect this escort. I got home unscathed, and my comrades marched out of the village again, singing. The policeman did not intervene.

It was the year 1923 and inflation had reached almost its highest point. Politically, government and capital had not carried through its intention, which was to smash the revolutionary movement with the aid of the Social Democrats. On the contrary, the influence of the Communist Party had grown even further. The trade unions were fighting organisations in the central German area; wage rates now only existed on paper. The factories were shaken by strikes, because the employers were not prepared to offer any wage agreements which matched the continual inflation. The government urged the workers in the trade unions to maintain discipline and to take into account the economic situation. In the factories, unrest had reached gigantic proportions.

We did not have to exert ourselves too much to convince the men that a struggle was the only solution. In the continual confrontations, the management soon found out who were the active trade unionists. They believed that they would have some peace once they had thrown these 'elements' out of their factories. But they did not reckon with the class-consciousness and preparedness for struggle amongst the rank and file. In most cases, those sacked stayed on in the factories since the workers declared that they would not return to work until their colleagues were reinstated. However, reinstatement was not always possible, and many men had to remain sacked. In most cases, these were younger workers, and one day I found myself among them. Now, admittedly, I had plenty of time for political and trade union work, but not a single penny to contribute towards my mother's housekeeping.

Again, I was in conflict with my father, who could summon up no sympathy for the struggle of workers for the security of their existence. I had an ally in my mother, even if she was only able to support me morally, since she was financially dependent on my father. In spite of this, she sometimes managed to slip me twenty or 30 pfennig so that I could buy a couple of cigarettes or a glass of beer. She often asked me in worried tones: 'My boy, how is this all going to end?' She had not forgotten my imprisonment. She feared that something similar could happen to me again, but I never heard a word from her about paying more attention to finding work and leaving politics to someone else.

I did not let myself be influenced by my father's speeches. Like me, a large majority of party officials were unemployed. Despite material distress, we continued our work inside and outside the factories. Inflation was now running at a furious rate; strikes multiplied. On many days, the same works came out three times. The women stood in front of the factories to get some money from their men so that they could buy things straight away. Despite that, they could often only buy a loaf of bread with three days' wages.

Looking back on it, the year 1923 was a decisive one for the German working class. The question of power was posed to the proletariat more sharply than ever before. Capitalism had been shaken to its foundations by war and crisis. The German working class had gathered much experience in numerous struggles. It is true that, in the face of the economic crisis, it still fought for the realisation of economic demands which would secure the basic requirements for existence. But more and more struggles took on a highly political character.

The year 1923 was the year of the occupation of the Ruhr. The French army had occupied the entire Ruhr district to ensure the delivery of coal as war reparation. All the parties, including the Communist Party, took part in passive resistance. The German government continued to pay the wages and salaries in full. In Essen, demonstrating workers and French troops clashed in front of the Krupp works, and there were deaths and injuries as a result. But the KPD had nothing to say in those days except to reproach Cuno's government: 'The nation is collapsing. The German bourgeoisie cannot even protect the frontiers of its fatherland . . . it crawls before Poincaré's bayonets.'

Soon the SPD leadership got to thinking that the politics of passive resistance might lead to military developments, and the parties of the centre joined them. In the course of 1923, an agreement was reached with the French government under Poincaré. But the revolutionary workers continued their fight against inflation and social deterioration. In central Germany, they worked towards the overthrow of the Cuno government with strikes. From Munich came the threat of the counter-revolution with its march on Berlin — even at that time, Hitler played a significant role; in Saxony and Thuringia workers' 'governments' were formed for defence by Social Democrats and Communists; the majority of workers in the central German industrial area, as in all the other flashpoints of the class struggle in Germany, knew what was at stake.

Party and trade union officials were fully deployed; for us there was scarcely any time for a private life; inflation had reached its final phase and the Reichsmark of earlier days now had a value of billions; work had no value any more. In those days, the rank and file were ready for anything, and there were even scenes of machine-smashing. We always had to speak to the men and hold them back from ill-considered actions.

In this situation, there was no end to the provocations against the working class and the KPD. But now they were initiated not so much by the government as by the Stahlhelm. This organisation — as was demonstrated again later — played a decisive role right up until 1933 and made a considerable contribution towards Hitler's victory.

In Eisleben, a town in the Mansfeld copper-mining area, the trade union alliance had called a demonstration and rally for their trade union day, as was the case every year in all regions and districts. The Stahlhelm used this occasion to call a counter demonstration. In the central German industrial area it was only a weak organisation, and its field of recruitment was limited to the agricultural workers on the estates outside the industrial districts. Therefore, it fetched its people from the surrounding areas — Thuringia, Saxony and Lower Saxony — and marched them into the industrial area.

The Joint Trades Union Committee, for its part, called for solidarity from the workers in the Halle region and asked them to participate in the defence of the trade union day. The 'proletarian battalions' already existed.

The trade union alliance had demanded a ban on the Stahlhelm march on the grounds that there could be serious clashes. But the police turned down the application and arranged the Stahlhelm demonstration for the morning and the trade union one for the afternoon. Men from the surrounding area had responded to the appeal by the Eisleben trade unionists in great numbers. In addition, the regional proletarian battalions, especially the Workers' Rambling Association Defence Corps, were strongly represented.

When the procession of the trade unions came through the streets of Eisleben in the afternoon, the Stahlhelm, who were still in full force in the town, tried to rush into the demonstration from the side streets. Apart from a few skirmishes, there were no major confrontations. The police remained entirely neutral. The march reached the Eselswiese, the open space at which the trade unions intended to hold their rally.

During the speeches by the guest speakers, nothing happened; the day's programme continued with sideshows and dancing. Only in the evening, when the men from out of town were leaving and marching to the station, were there clashes which were provoked by the Stahlhelm.

The route from the rally to the station went round the edge of town through a sort of park. At a point where the park was crossed by a stream, there was a fight between the Workers' Rambling Association Defence Corps and a group of 'Young Stahlhelm'. The stream, which was quite full, could only be crossed by a narrow footbridge. It was at this point that the Naturalists were attacked. But the little sons of the petty bourgeoisie had not considered that workers' fists not only work hard but also punch nicely. Their attack here did them no good. The spades with which they were armed were soon taken away from them. We gave them a punching and many of them became well acquainted with the waters of the Böser Sieben, as the stream was called.

But the fight was not finished. The Young Stahlhelm received succour from their elders, and we received the support of our colleagues. The fight lasted several hours. Whenever we had pushed the Stahlhelm back to its 'headquarters', the police shoved themselves between the two sides and forced us back. And so the Stahlhelm found more support and energy. When the fight was at an end, there were several wounded on both sides. But we could say, without exaggeration, that we had taught the Stahlhelm a lesson that day.

It was late at night when we got home. When I stepped into our house, my mother and sisters stared at me flabbergasted, and cried. When I asked what the matter was, they finally told me that Holland, a carpenter and member of the Stahlhelm, had told them that he had seen me lying dead on the streets of Eisleben. Apparently the wish was the father to the thought. When my mother had recovered from her shock, she did not want to let me go again. She asked me never to place myself in such danger again. To calm her, I promised her that I would take care.

Our colleagues had travelled home on the train, while the Stahlhelm were taken there and back on lorries supplied by factory management and estate owners.

Some weeks passed before the Stahlhelm launched a new provocation. In 1921 in Halle, a group of the Communist Workers' Youth — an organisation with strong syndicalist tendencies — had blown up the Kaiser Wilhelm monument. This was an action which could only harm workers in struggle. The monument was rebuilt, and it gave the Stahlhelm the opportunity to march about town at its unveiling. Despite a protest by the municipal authorities in Halle, the provincial authorities gave permission for this demonstration. Halle belonged to the so called 'red belt' of the central German industrial area.

Hörsing, the president of the province, knew the situation in the town. He knew about the events a few weeks earlier, and their outcome. Despite this, he authorised the Stahlhelm demonstration, although they were travelling into Halle not just from the region but from outside as well. Again, the workers of the region did not leave their comrades in the lurch. Communist youth came from the neighbouring regions and from Berlin. When the workers and the proletarian battalions were marching in, the police, strengthened by teams from outside, cut off the town in a great encirclement. As we came in on the shift trains from the Geisel valley into Halle, we were prevented from travelling any further than Ammendorf. All passenger, local and works trains were stopped there; only long distance trains could travel through. Some of the demonstrators from the Geisel valley tried to reach the town via the Saale valley at Passendorf. The rest of us in the group had not even left the station at Ammendorf when an express train from Frankfurt-am-Main rolled into the station and had to stop. We jumped aboard this train.

When we reached Halle, thousands of workers were demonstrating at the Riebeck Platz near the central station. We joined them and marched in a big demonstration through the town. Near the Volkspark, a large community hall belonging to the Halle workers and administered by a cooperative, the police attempted to break up the procession, but they did not succeed. Later, when the police reinforcements arrived, we were forced into the Volkspark and locked in. Some units of the police were taken away to be deployed elsewhere. We used this opportunity to attempt a breakout. This met with success, for the police were too weak to hold us back. More than 3,000 of us marched into the town centre. In Ulrich Strasse, which was a shopping street at that time, the shopkeepers had hoisted black white and red flags. I do not know where the petrol came from, but in any event the flags were doused in petrol and ignited, and the black-white-red splendour went up in smoke.

The police did not succeed in sealing Halle hermetically, and so the workers were in control of most of the streets of the town. We learned that the comrades who had left us in Ammendorf to try to reach the town via Passendorf had been attacked by the police and shot at. One of my friends, Kurt Kittlemann, was killed in this attack. He was married and the father of two children. Later on, we bore him to his burial in a great funeral procession, which was in reality a fighting demonstration.

The Stahlhelm was forced out of town and lay protected by the police in the fields at Passendorf. As we travelled home the next morning, there were a few small groups of Stahlhelm in the waiting rooms at the main station, also making for home. They were cruelly mocked by ourselves and the workers who were travelling to Leuna and the lignite coalfield. There were agricultural workers there, who told us that they had been forced by their employers — estate owners — to take part in the Stahlhelm demonstration.

The Stahlhelm made a third attempt to provoke the working class of central Germany when it marched through what was once the battlefield at Rossbach between Mücheln and Weissenfels. At Rossbach, Frederick the Great had defeated the French and allied troops in 1757. This time they wanted to march into the district and set an example, or so they said. For this task, they had gathered their troops from all over Germany, and this time the party and trade unions had also made preparations. All the trade union buildings were occupied. The youth organisation functioned as a courier service which brought news from the rallying point of the Stahlhelm. At the spoil tip of the Pfannerhall pit, there was a battle with members of Young Stahlhelm, who were also trying to get news from the coalfield. They were properly sent packing.

The workers in the Geisel valley, reinforced by their colleagues from

Merseburg, Weissenfels and Halle, patrolled the coalfield itself. On this occasion, no police came into the Geisel valley. By evening, still nothing had happened, and still not a single Stahlhelm was to be seen. The youth organisation, which had set up its observation post on the spoil tip at the Pfannerhall pit and could easily observe the movements of the Stahlhelm from there, reported that largish groups of Stahlhelmers had driven away in lorries. Despite this, we continued on red alert. Our leadership ordered everyone to remain in the trade union buildings or in houses, while small groups were to continue to observe the country surrounding the Geisel valley.

Still nothing happened until the late evening. All the men who came back from outside reported that more and more Stahlhelmers were driving off. It was almost midnight. I left the trade union building at Mücheln together with comrade Franz Wiesner. Our task was to spy out the land around the railway station at Mücheln and discover whether there were any groups of the Stahlhelm there. We had not got very far from the trade union building when we were addressed by three people in civilian clothing, who asked the way to the station.

Since they did not seem suspicious, we told them to come with us. The station at Mücheln lay outside the town. Beside the road leading there stood the 'Crown Prince' pub, the local used by the Stahlhelm. As we got close to the village of Zorban, our three civilians suddenly vanished, and figures jumped out of the ditches to the right and left of us. Nothing could be seen clearly, it was a dark night; the few lamps that lit the street had gone out. We were attacked. While comrade Wiesner managed to escape and ran back to the trade union building, I was surrounded. I stood with my back to the wall and tried to defend myself with a bottle in my hand. Where I found it, I do not know. All of a sudden, there was a shot, and I felt as if someone had hit my left shoulder with a hammer. The bottle fell to the ground, and I could not move my left arm any more. Then I was seized by several men in Stahlhelm uniform and dragged into their pub.

There I noticed among the others a man — also in Stahlhelm uniform — with a pistol in his hand. We knew him as 'pale Emil'. He was a foreman at the Elise II pit, which provided coal for the Leuna works. The administration building at this pit was a bastion of the Stahlhelm.

The Stahlhelmers discussed what to do with me. There were also two cops in the pub, who seemed entirely unmoved by the whole affair. While 'pale Emil' argued for taking me off to the Elise II administration block, a second group said they should take me to a doctor because I was bleeding heavily. Suddenly the door flew open and around a hundred workers, roused by comrade Wiesner, entered the pub.

Now, all of a sudden, the policemen woke up and tried to intervene. The Stahlhelmers, who had no idea how many workers there were, tried for their part to force my comrades out of the pub. There was a punch-up, during which the men in uniform had to leave in a panic by the back doors. I was bleeding heavily from the left shoulder. I was taken to a doctor by three comrades. The bullet had lodged, as an x-ray the next day proved. The doctor, who was a sympathiser of the Communist Party, was of the opinion that it should not be operated on, since the bullet was too close to the heart. It was better to await the healing process, and the bullet would assuredly be encysted. To this day, the bullet still sits in my left side.

The Communist Party filed a suit against the Mücheln branch of the Stahlhelm for malicious assault, and against 'pale Emil' for attempted murder. I stood as co-plaintiff. But scarcely a week had passed before the High County Court at Naumburg charged myself and comrade Wiesner with breach of the peace, riot and destruction of a hostelry, in which I was supposed to be implicated with a group of workers. In this way, the accusers became the defendants. All our protests — there were large mass demonstrations throughout the Geisel valley, in Merseburg, Ammendorf, Halle and Weissenfels — were in vain: the accusations stood. After a few months we heard that the charges against us had been dropped. However, the case against the Stahlhelm was never proceeded with either. Similar things happened in the Bitterfeld and Zeitz coalfields.

Despite all the provocations, in which the right-wing organisations and the organs of the state were involved, they did not succeed in breaking the resistance of the workers. On the contrary, the influence of the Communist Party and the trade unions grew steadily. In the central German industrial area it was now the KPD who called the tune in politics. We had succeeded in integrating fully into the party and trade union those workers who had arrived in the coalfield in 1919 and 1920. The KAP had lost its influence, and many of its members had returned to the KPD; the General Workers' Union, which was close to the KAP, had split and now led only a shadowy existence. Only the Union of Hand and Head Workers had maintained its strength, although the party was working to bring these colleagues back to the ADGB union as well.

In July 1923, the KPD centre issued a call to its members, urging them to be on the highest alert:

'The Cuno cabinet is bankrupt. The crisis at home and abroad threatens a catastrophe in the next few days. The Fascists in south Germany have decided at their meetings . . . to seize the opportunity offered by the declaration of the Rhineland Westphalian buffer state . . . to strike out for themselves.

'Ludendorff and Hitler have everything ready for a march into Saxony and Thuringia. The North German Fascist organisations . . . have made all their preparations for the military overthrow of Berlin and Hamburg . . . The officers of the German army are equipping the Fascists . . . '

Another declaration in the *Rote Fahne* stated:

'We communists can only be victorious in the fight against counter revolution if we succeed in leading the social-democratic and non-aligned working masses with us in the fight, without and against the treacherous party and trade union bureaucracy . . . United proletarian defence organisations must be organised from the factories outwards, despite any resistance . . . The plans of the Fascists have been laid in the minutest detail, in military fashion.

'They have issued the call: "Conduct the civil war in the most brutal and forceful manner". All workers who offer resistance to the Fascists would be shot by them if caught. To defeat strikes they intend to shoot every tenth man among the strikers. The Fascist uprising can only be defeated if we oppose white terror with red terror.

'If the Fascists, who are armed to the teeth, kill proletarian fighters, then the latter must destroy all Fascists without mercy. If the Fascists put every tenth striker against the wall, then the workers must put every fifth member of a Fascist organisation against the wall . . .

'The KPD must lead the entire proletariat into battle under its banner . . . The Party must also state clearly that, if required, it will issue the call to battle alone and alone take over the leadership of the fight . . .

'Only when we have the will for victory and for the taking of power, only when every communist is ready to sacrifice everything for the salvation and liberation of the working class, only then will our party be the party of victory. Only then will it create the revolutionary workers' and peasants' government which will seize the material assets and control of production from finance capital, and so save from slavery the working class, the office workers, the civil servants, the heavily-burdened middle class, and oppose French imperialism with a united nation which is ready to fight.'

In central Germany and in the Ruhr district, the proletarian batallions had been built up on a cross-party basis and in great numbers, while there was scarcely anything else in the country apart from that. Now the construction of these groups was supposed to proceed with increased energy. In places where it was possible, these were to be built as organs of a united front; where it was not possible, then as party organs attracting non-party people. Where the party now began to construct workers' self-defence organs in other parts of the country, it was done quite hectically.

In Saxony and Thuringia, the Social-Democratic organisations found themselves under strong pressure from their rank and file. The chair of the KPD, Heinrich Brandler, who had travelled to Moscow in the decisive August days of 1923, returned at the beginning of September. None of the middle-ranking officials in our district knew what had been decided there, but everyone was clear that things were now on a razor's edge. Everywhere in Germany, as in the central area, strikes took place. Workers demanded actions which went far beyond wage strikes. So the weeks passed. In the meantime, Heinrich Brandler travelled to Moscow again.

When he returned on 8 October, not only the members of the party but also the other workers were prepared to defend themselves against possible attacks by the Fascists, the army and the 'Black National Army'. In Saxony and Thuringia, in quick succession, workers' governments were formed by the SPD and KPD.

On 12 October, Brandler, together with Paul Böttcher and Fritz Heckert, entered the Saxony government of the left Social Democrat, Zeigner. At that time, a workers' conference was convened in Chemnitz, to discuss the critical food supply situation. The KPD used one intervention at this conference to call for a general strike.

Everyone knew that an action like that at that time would mean a general uprising. The conference rejected the call. So the KPD sent couriers from Chemnitz into the districts, advising them to stand down from their preparations for uprising. All the couriers reached their destinations, except the one for Hamburg. And so the Hamburg uprising took place. For three days, several hundred workers fought against a superior number of police.

For the members of the KPD, and even more for the workers who were sympathisers, the defeat was a great disappointment. Generally, people were of the opinion that we should investigate the reasons why the preparations for the general strike had been called off. Later, in the internal arguments in the party, through so-called 'Discussion Documents' which had been made available to the membership, we learned of a letter written by Stalin in the late summer of 1923 to the members of the Politbureau of the Russian Party, in which he warned against calling a general strike in Germany, because it might lead to an uprising. He claimed that the revolutionary situation had finished in central Europe, and said that the German comrades had to be restrained. Amongst the party membership there was a general feeling that Heinrich Brandler, when he was in Moscow at the beginning of October, had agreed with Stalin's evaluation.

The governments which had been formed in Saxony and Thuringia were completely legal. The Social Democrats and Communists had a parliamentary majority in those states. They demanded from the new Stresemann government some action against the reactionary forces in the south. In Saxony, Heinrich Brandler had managed to get the proletarian battalions legalised as a sort of auxiliary police force. The national government took this and the inclusion of some Communists in the state governments as an excuse to act with force against the governments of Saxony and Thuringia.

The Social-Democratic President, Ebert, gave the commander-in-chief of the German army full powers for this 'imperial execution'. The army occupation claimed many victims again. The hunt for Communist Party officials now began in the whole of central Germany. The party talked of 8,000 to 9,000 arrests. While the large towns and industrial areas throughout Saxony and Thuringia were occupied, there was no occupation of the Geisel valley or of the Bitterfeld coalfield. The feeling in our group and the neighbouring party groups was that the October events could have led to a victorious revolution if only Heinrich Brandler had abandoned his opportunist policies. He had lost all credit in the party at that time.

On 23 November, the KPD was banned. The Communist Youth League had planned a regional conference for the beginning of December. It took place despite the ban. The public house in which the conference was held lay at the edge of town, on the Dolau Heath. It went ahead as planned at the weekend, without interruption. The main points on the agenda were: 'The October defeat' and 'Our future tasks'. In the industrial area, despite the ban, our work continued almost legally.

After the October defeat, the factories were closed to me. And there was no prospect of receiving any unemployment benefit in the foreseeable future. My father informed me that he was no longer prepared to feed me. All the attempts of the party to find work for me were unsuccessful. For political reasons, I should have remained in the Geisel valley: I had important functions in the party and the Youth League, and was also a delegate at regional level. However, after a discussion with the regional leadership in Halle and Merseburg, we agreed that I should leave the district and find work elsewhere. I then got in touch with my sister in Berlin. At the beginning of January, I left the Geisel valley to set up home in Berlin.

7.

ON THE BLACKLIST

Even in Berlin, it was difficult to find work; the economy was only slowly recovering again after inflation had ended. My girlfriend, who had been working in Magdeburg, had also come to Berlin and had got a job in Königswusterhausen. One day, when she was visiting me in Berlin, she introduced me to an uncle of hers. He was employed as head of security at the Bergmann-Rosenthal works, and said he would try to get work for me with his firm. After a few days he wrote to me to tell me that I could start in the warm press department. My girlfriend's brother also lived with him, and I knew him from central Germany; he was also a member of the Youth League. He wanted me to move in with them. His uncle, Herr Marold, gave his permission. My sister, who lived in a single-bedroom apartment in the Charlottenburg district, was only too happy for me to move out.

So I now moved to the Lichtenberg district, in the Frankfurter Allee. It was really a big apartment — three bedrooms — but at that time the building had no sewerage. The toilets were in the back yard. All the tenants, regardless of whether they lived on the ground floor or four floors up, had to go down to the yard whenever they needed the toilet. The conditions throughout the Lichtenberg district — only workers lived there — were such that the sewage simply ran into cesspits.

I shared a room with my friend Ferdinand. To get to work each day we took the suburban train, which was then a steam train, to the Rosenthal station in the north of Berlin. When I reported for work, the manager told me that there was no vacancy on the warm press, and I would have to spend some time first on the hydraulic press. Three shifts operated at this press. I did not like these changes of shift; on the other hand, I could not abandon my job just like that, since there were no other prospects. I talked the matter over with my landlord, Herr Marold. He promised he would talk to the foreman; perhaps he could even get me into the lathe shop — I only needed to be patient. Many weeks passed and I still manned the hydraulic press. In the meantime I had become shop steward. Since I had got involved in the current wage negotiations right from the start, and had won some advantages for my colleagues, I soon earned their trust.

Along with the two shop stewards from the other shifts, I negotiated with the works committee chair and the management. Herr Marold soon found out that I had political leanings. One day he came to ask me to ease off a bit in the wage struggle. My activity would eventually rebound on him, since he was after all the one who had found me work. I replied that I was grateful for what he had done, but that it was not my fight now but that of the works collective to which I belonged; therefore I had to maintain solidarity, and could not even consider easing off. Thereupon he told me that, if that was how things stood, I could not remain in his house any longer. My sister suggested to me that I move to her mother-in-law's, in the Wedding district. That is what I did.

A short time afterwards, since neither the management nor the works committee chair could come to any satisfactory settlement in the wage dispute, we decided to down tools at the end of the morning shift. Everyone agreed that a strike was the only way of winning our rights.

We packed the furnace full of mouldings so that the next shift would be able to do their work. We informed the department head that we were no longer prepared to work after the months of negotiations with management had reached no solution. The manager appreciated the situation immediately. He knew that, once the mouldings had reached a certain temperature, they would melt if left in the furnace, so he called the works manager. A few minutes later, he appeared on the scene. He told us to start work again immediately, otherwise we would be sacked on the spot.

We were sure of our strength, and he knew it, for the first mouldings were beginning to melt. Then the works committee chair turned up and told us that we were out of order and that he was no longer prepared to represent us and that he would inform the trade union leadership. He told the men that they would do well to return to work immediately, and that he would then ensure that the negotiations reached a swift conclusion. This was grist to the mill for the works manager. Intimidated by the behaviour of the works manager, the first few started work; indeed even two of the morning shift declared themselves ready to work.

The manager told my colleague and myself — both of us shop stewards in the organised trade union — that we were sacked. We scarcely had time to collect our things before being escorted to the gates by the works security. The official of the metalworkers' union told us that we would get nothing from a tribunal: our biggest mistake had been to pack the furnaces full of mouldings. He unequivocally denounced the behaviour of the chair of the works committee. We learned from our colleagues who remained in the factory that, immediately after our action, the management had stated their readiness to raise the piece-rates far above those for the warm press. Our strike was successful.

In the first months that I was in Berlin, I kept in contact with the party, but without being active in the district branch to which I belonged. My main area of activity in those first weeks was trade union work in the factory. I noticed from reading the *Rote Fahne*, but even more from the people in the district branch, that there was still unrest in the party. Berlin was one of the three regions which almost unanimously backed the opposition. Along with comrades Schwarz and Korsch, who led a strong workers' opposition, the group around Ruth Fischer and Arkadi ('Max') Maslow demanded an extraordinary party conference. Besides Berlin, the Hamburg and Lower Rhine regions stood firm behind the opposition, but in other regions too there was a strong movement against the Brandler-Thalheimer Central Committee.

In March 1924, the party conference, which had to be conducted in secret, took place in Frankfurt. There the politics of the Brandler leadership were condemned. Not a single delegate voted for Heinrich Brandler. In place of him and August Thalheimer, we elected Ruth Fischer, Arkadi Maslow and Ernst Thälmann. Among the masses, confidence in the party remained the same after the October defeat as before; the workers accepted the revolutionary words of the party at face value.

One proof of this came in the parliamentary elections in May 1924, when the KPD candidates polled 3,700,000 votes, and had 62 members elected to parliament. The KPD defended revolutionary slogans — 'For proletarian dictatorship', 'For soviet power' — which were closely linked to preparations for armed uprising. Arming the workers, went the argument, was the most important task of the party. It was absolutely necessary to familiarise German workers with the idea that the proletarian battalions would be necessary in the daily struggles.

In February 1924 in Magdeburg, the organisation called 'Black-Red-Gold — The Standard of the Nation' (Reichsbanner) was founded. The chair of this paramilitary group was Otto Hörsing, the president of the province of Saxony, who had let the police battalions into the

Mansfeld area in 1921. This organisation was supported by the SPD, the Catholic Centre Party and the German Democratic Party (DDP), later renamed the 'State Party'. In popular parlance, the group was renamed 'The Scandal of the Nation' (Reichsjammer), because it soon became obvious that, although formed to combat the right wing, the group's politics were anti-left; it was destined to remain an organisation with no power at all.

After my dismissal from the Bergmann-Rosenthal works, I did not remain without work for long. Pipe benders were needed for the pneumatic mail department of Zwietusch at Salzufer in the Charlottenburg. I applied, and after an interview with the department manager, I got the job.

At Zwietusch, more than 70 per cent of the employees were women. Only in the pneumatic mail department were there only men; all the other departments were mixed. I quickly built up a good relationship with my colleagues. Without exception they were organised in the trade union, and a small number of them were politically organised, including some members of the KPD. At that time the reorganisation of the party, which had been decided on earlier, was under way. From now on, the comrades working in the factories would meet in 'factory cells'.

For our factory this change had a very positive effect, as it did in many other factories. In our cell we had 32 members of both sexes. Once a week after the end of the shift we met to discuss problems relating to the factory and trade union. Above all, we now had the opportunity, as never before, of preparing our factory meetings properly. These factory meetings took place after work. Unlike now, the works management had no right to attend these meetings; they were only allowed in at the invitation of the works council. This body, which — in accordance with the laws governing works councils at that time — comprised one committee from the shop floor and one of office workers, was led by a Social Democrat.

As Communists, we had a relatively large majority in the shop floor committee, while the committee of office workers was dominated by Social Democrats with a couple of bourgeois representatives. After I had already become shop steward, I also became a member of the works committee in the elections of 1925. In my department and elsewhere I intervened on behalf of my colleagues, insofar as the agreements on wages and conditions allowed me. In this connection, I had very few difficulties with my departmental manager, but rather more with the works management. I had won the trust of the men by my uncompromising stance in the works meetings. And so I was often buttonholed by them on any number of questions, even outside the officially allotted time, which was something the works committee did not view favourably. I was continually being told by the chair of the works committee that I should remind the men of his office hours.

At Zwietusch the trade union, unlike most of the other factories in the Berlin metal industry, had never yet succeeded in downing tools on 1 May. We had discussed both in the factory cell and in the works committee the possibilities for getting the workforce to demonstrate alongside the workers of Berlin in the Lustgarten. In the works committee we agreed to put up a notice on the main noticeboard urging the workforce to take a day off on 1 May and to get themselves along to the place mentioned.

According to the law governing works committees, all notices should be countersigned by the works management. But as we knew that the works management would not sign a notice like that, we put it up without their signature. On the very next day — 30 April — the works management demanded that the notice be taken down again.

In the meeting of the works committee which followed, the majority maintained that the notice should be taken down again since the workforce had had 24 hours to see it. No one paid any attention to our objections that the management would then have 24 hours to put up their own notice saying that 1 May was to be worked. The end result was that the chair took the notice down on a majority vote. Within the very next hour, the predictable notice from management appeared not only on the main noticeboard, but in all the departments as well.

A few of us in the factory cell met to discuss what to do about this. At my suggestion we decided that I should leave work at the same time as the seriously disabled, who were allowed to leave the factory ten minutes before everyone else. I got myself a pass-out from my department manager which authorised me to leave work half an hour early. In the meantime, the other comrades were to arrange for both the bridges to be watched — the factory lay between the March Bridge and the Charlottenburger Bridge — to give advance warning of the arrival of police. In the afternoon, I left the factory at the same time as the disabled. A little later, when the rest of the workforce came out, I climbed up a gate-post to give a short speech on the significance of May Day.

The management on the third floor were furious. The works security tried to clear the area in front of the gates. That did them no good, since the workers gave push for shove. All of a sudden you could hear the sirens of the police, as expected. With a few short sentences, I finished off my call to join the demonstration on the next day. The police could find no reason to intervene. I made myself scarce down a small alley which led to the River Spree. The workers cleared the street. When we arrived at the rallying points the next morning, most of our workers were there. We marched to the Lustgarten carrying banners which we had prepared. For the first time, we had succeeded in closing down the Zwietusch factory on 1 May and in enrolling its workforce among the fighting workers.

When I turned up at work on the morning of 2 May, the works security manager stood in front of the gates with two men who prevented me from going in. When I remonstrated that I was a member of the works committee, they paid no attention: I stayed outside. Even a telephone call to the chair of the works committee and the subsequent protest by the works committee achieved nothing. In the course of the day, I went to the headquarters of the German Metalworkers' Union in the Linien Strasse in the central district to speak with an official.

He told me that they would speak to the works management again. If he had no luck, then they would lodge a complaint with the employment tribunal. They advised me to report to the gatekeeper for work each morning and to advise the works committee of my readiness to work.

Ten days later I was still outside the factory when I received news from the union that it had reached the following agreement with the works management: pipeworker Hippe will be reinstated; the days on which he was prevented from working will be paid in full; his rights and responsibilities as shop steward will be respected in full. At the factory I received a warm welcome from my political friends and colleagues, and was urged not to retreat from the struggle. From then on, I always felt the shadow of the management behind me.

Our work in the factory cell proceeded; in all the other factories in Berlin, the party reported good results. In the large plants like Siemens, the cells were even subdivided. The cell only met as a unit for political discussions, in order to ensure that the discussions did not become too narrow but rather covered a wide range. The vast majority of the factory cells published their own factory newspapers.

There had to be an article on political fundamentals in every issue, while all the other articles dealt with problems in the factory and trade union. In our factory, three comrades were responsible for the paper. In addition, there was a group of sympathisers who collaborated on it. The costs of the newspaper were met out of collections amongst the workers. Sometimes we could even give part of the proceeds to 'Red Aid' (Rote Hilfe) or to the International Workers' Aid.

After my dismissal had been withdrawn, there was one foreman in particular who tried to provoke me. It was August, and I had some business in the quality control department. There I was speaking to a colleague who wanted some information from me as shop steward in a matter concerning wages. While we were still talking, the foreman came up and told me to get out of the department immediately. I replied that I would, as soon as I had finished giving the man the information he needed. That very same day, I received notice of instant dismissal as I had infringed work discipline and had behaved unacceptably in front of a superior.

We went to the employment tribunal again; again the DMV presented my case. Two witnesses from the quality control department confirmed that I had only stayed a short time in the department and had told the foreman that I would go as soon as I had finished my discussion with the colleague. Two other men, on the other hand, claimed to have heard me say to the foreman: 'You can't tell me what to do.'

On cross-examination, they could no longer remember precisely what they had heard. Later we learned that they had been threatened with losing their jobs. Despite these attempts at intimidation the employment tribunal gave the following verdict: reinstatement, or, for every six months of employment to date at the firm, payment of one month's wages as compensation. The works management decided to pay the compensation.

I received regular financial support from the German Metalworkers' Union for the seventeen weeks that it all lasted. From then on, the gates of the Berlin metal industry were closed to me. Wherever I asked for work, I was always turned down, although workers with my skills were in demand. We knew that blacklists existed. These were of course forbidden by law, but the metal industry cared little about that, since the governments of Prussia and elsewhere never did anything about this violation of the law.

Although I was no longer employed at Zwietusch, I still belonged to the factory cell and did agitational and propaganda work with the comrades to spread the party's influence in the factory politically and in the trade union. Comrades who were sacked were allowed to belong to their erstwhile factory cell until they had found work elsewhere or the party had another use for them. It was especially important for me to continue to function in the factory cell, for a large number of the comrades there belonged to the Left Opposition.

The unemployment benefit which we received — I had got married in the meantime — was not a lot. So I had to see how else I could earn some money, since we had bought some furniture on hire purchase. A political friend, who worked for Kosmos Publications, offered me a job selling the *Evening World* newspaper (*Welt am Abend*) for three hours each afternoon, at a fixed wage of fifteen marks per week. For every paper that I sold, I would get another three pfennig. With this income and the benefit, we somehow got through the days.

In addition, I had set up a stand to sell the *Rote Fahne* at the Jungfernheide Station. I started with three newspapers, and after a few months I had built up sales of over a hundred papers, and some 30 *Workers Illustrated (Arbeiter-Illustrierte)* and a few copies of the *Evening World*.

When I was later employed by the Charlottenburg Council, I could not find anybody who was prepared to take over my stand, until my wife declared that she would not let what I had built up go to waste: she herself went there until someone was found to replace me.

My wife, whom I had met at Zwietusch when she was an active trade union official there, sympathised with the KPD. Although she was not yet a member at that time, she attended the branch meetings at the invitation of the political secretary. One day when she was there, we had an important problem to discuss. Although we were already close friends at this time, I proposed that 'the colleague Gertrud Mankowski' should be excluded from the meeting, since there was a rule which said that non-members should not be permitted to attend closed meetings. At first the comrades argued against it. But when I gave them the ultimatum that either colleague Mankowski should go or I myself would go, it was decided that Gertrud should no longer take part in this meeting.

This did our friendship no harm; on the contrary, she joined the Communist Party a few months later. On 12 October 1926 we were married. When she informed the personnel department a few days later, it only took a few more days for her to be dismissed 'due to lack of work'. In reality it was a belated revenge, for the employer took on someone else a few days afterwards. Unfortunately we learned of this too late to be able to take action against the firm at a tribunal.

My wife, the third child of a working-class family, grew up with six brothers. Her family lived in a two-room basement apartment which was sometimes also occupied by a lodger if her father was out of work and could not meet the monthly rent. As early as eleven years old, she was employed as a child's maid, and was later employed at the house of an engineer at Siemens, where she had to do household chores as well as look after the children. Of course this affected her attention at school. She often came to class without having done her homework because on the previous evening she had come home from her job too tired to do any schoolwork.

Her parents, both father and mother, were illiterate. Her father came from the Rawitsch district in the province of Poznan. Although attendance at school was obligatory there, the children were 'given away' by the teachers to peasants who employed them to watch over the geese, or, if they were bigger, as shepherd boys. Gertrud's mother, who came from Galicia, which then belonged to Austria, had barely attended school. Thus she had no support from her parents and no stimulation to advance herself academically. Only later, when she had already left school and had gone

Gertrud Hippe selling the papers of the KPD

to work, did she realise what she had missed. With help from colleagues at work and by systematically reading socialist literature and by writing, she was able to catch up on quite a lot.

When Trude left school at Easter 1915, she left her job as maid to start work as an unskilled worker at Siemens — at a weekly wage of eight marks for ten hours a day. She often said to me that the foundations for her rebellion against bourgeois society were laid at Siemens.

In 1919 she became a member of the Metalworkers' Union, and when she started at the Zwietusch company she became a shop steward in her department. Between 1919 and her dismissal in 1926 she was a active official of the DMV. When she joined the KPD, her work in the trade unions took on a greater political significance. She played a lively role in the arguments inside the party.

Amongst our friends, who consisted entirely of party comrades of both sexes, there were often political discussions when we got together. At the weekends, our hikes in the countryside around Berlin or further afield turned into political seminars, since there was a strong feeling of cooperation and solidarity in our circle which was maintained even during the inner-party arguments.

After it had become clear in 1924 that the Reichsbanner organisation, which had been set up to defend the republic against the machinations of the paramilitary bands of the right, also followed a right-wing, pro-capitalist political line, the central committee of the KPD decided that it was necessary to build up a paramilitary organisation of its own. This decision about the founding of the 'Red Front League of Fighters' (Roten Frontkämpferbundes — RFB) was made while the Brandler-Thalheimer leadership was still in charge. Like the groups of the right-wing organisations and the Reichsbanner, the RFB was to wear a uniform.

In honour of the People's Marine Division, the service blouse of the navy was to be worn, with a military cap and a belt. Like all the other groups, and incidentally most of the proletarian battalions earlier, members of the RFB also carried a stick made of oakwood. The first meeting leading up to the founding of the RFB took place in Jena. At that time I was still in the Geisel valley and was a delegate of the proletarian battalions.

It was my opinion that we should stick to the decision of the Frankfurt congress which was to spread the battalions throughout the country and build them up everywhere. They had lasted through the putsch by Kapp and the period after that. They should also be good enough for the future when the fight against reaction and the capitalist state needed leadership. In Germany, without a doubt, it was time to stop playing soldiers and to start educating the masses towards self-awareness. But a majority voted for the founding of the RFB.

For some time, the battalions and the RFB marched side-by-side. But the RFB, since it had the support of the central committee, was able to develop very quickly. Only in central Germany, where the proletarian battalions had a long tradition, did they last a little while longer. It was especially those groups which had grown out of the Workers' Rambling Association which had the most stamina. Apart from the RFB, the Red Youth Front and the Red Women's and Girls' League were founded as well.

The leadership of the RFB had actually succeeded in attracting a large number of workers who were not politicised. Ernst Thälmann and Willy Leow, in the leadership of our organisation, soon both began to defend the Stalinist line in the Party, along with Walter Ulbricht. They were also the ones who were later to remove the Fischer-Maslow Central Committee.

In the inner-party arguments in 1924-1925, the RFB was also intended to play a certain role — at least, that is how the Stalinist group in the party saw it. In the Charlottenburg party district, to which I belonged, it was decided to send members of the left majority into every local district and into the Red Youth Front, to prevent the RFB from being drawn into party discussions. That is how I became a member of the Red Front League of Fighters, although I had no liking at all for military games. When I was working in the No. 2 Party Branch in the district, the inner-party discussions there at least were in full swing.

Hermann Buschmann, the leader of the No.7 Branch, was determined, along with his deputy Willy Wisse, to bring the members of the branch into the Stalinist faction. The discussions began to cover a wider ground, and they were no longer simply concerned with the causes for the defeat of 1923. On the contrary, the Stalinist faction was now using the RFB without any reservations in their struggle against the Internationalist Group. These discussions, when they were carried out on the highest political level, had positive results.

In our area, we managed to win many of the RFB comrades to the party. I became political secretary after only a short time in the No. 2 Branch. Our 'Friends' Evenings' were mostly devoted to political education. Marx, Engels and Lenin were the three theoreticians whom we studied. In particular, Lenin's *State and Revolution* and his book *'Left-Wing' Communism: an Infantile Disorder* contained themes which interested the comrades.

In Berlin, the RFB grew into a strong organisation in a relatively short time. In workers' districts like Wedding and Neukölln, the divisions contained thousands of people. In Charlottenburg, where we were, the division was 500 strong, and there was the Red Youth Front with 200. At joint demonstrations, which nearly always took place in the Lustgarten, the RFB was fully represented; in addition, it formed a security cordon at all party meetings.

Besides the RFB, in our district there was a Workers' Sport and Culture Group, named 'Libertas', in which judo was practised alongside other sports. Its members were also politically active, and they participated in rallies and demonstrations alongside the KPD. When Libertas was marching with us, the police were much less aggressive than usual.

National meetings of the RFB all took place in Berlin. The members, some of whom were unemployed or on poor wages, were not always in a position to buy their League uniform immediately. Only when the RFB leadership gave the members the chance of buying the clothing on credit did the outward appearance of the RFB become uniform. The first national rally took place in the Lichtenberg Stadium, with around 30,000 people and the support of the people of Berlin.

Year by year, the number of participants grew. The last rally, which was attended by several hundred thousand people, took place on the Weber Field in the Friedrichshain District. The place could not hold everybody, and the divisions, grouped by district, marched in an unbroken stream past the national leadership. Public buildings like schools were rarely required for accommodation, for almost all the comrades from out of town were lodged in private houses. When the march started, the workers of Berlin had gathered at the sides of the streets to supply the marching columns with drink and bread. When they marched back to the railway stations, the people lined the streets again to bid them farewell.

On days like that, it seemed as if the KPD exercised complete power over the working masses and had become the leader of the working class. In reality, however, things were different: the party was greatly weakened by its inner conflicts, and was in no position to make much long term political use of such rallies.

8.

CONFLICT WITHIN THE GERMAN COMMUNIST PARTY

At the Tenth Congress of the KPD in July 1925, the Stalinist faction led by the Brandler-Thalheimer group succeeded in taking over the central committee. Although the Fischer-Maslow central committee had been elected at the Ninth Congress with an overwhelming majority, this majority was made up of several factions and could not withstand the machinations of the Stalinists, who received massive support from Moscow. The Tenth Congress of the KPD was the turning point.

At the congress both Ruth Fischer and Ernst Thälmann spoke about the Bolshevisation of the Communist Party. In reality, however, this congress marked the turn towards Stalinisation.

In the time between the two congresses, a new group had been formed alongside the Fischer-Maslow faction and the Stalinist faction — the Scholem-Rosenberg group. Connected with this group was the Weber group, which had its support in the Rhine Palatinate. From these two there later emerged the group of International Communists, the Trotsky faction.

In addition to these, there was the Korsch-Schwarz Group, which could be described as ultra-left. They were not prepared to submit to the majority decisions of the delegates on the tactic of the united front or the trade union question. The group included comrades Schumacher, Kayser and Weyer, the organisers of the Red Building Workers' League and other groupings. At the time of the Tenth Congress there was already a small Trotsky faction in Berlin, which was especially strong in Charlottenburg and led by a worker in the flooring trade, comrade K. Lorenz.

In the party, this group was regarded as a right-wing deviation. It did not put in an appearance at the congress, since it had been unable to get delegates either in the city leadership or in the districts. Later, when the German left in the Lenin League gave support to the Russian internationalists around Trotsky — Preobrazhensky, Rakovsky and Joffe — in their fight against Stalinism, these comrades had largely disappeared from active party work.

With regard to the German question, the representative of the Executive Committee of the Communist International (ECCI) at the congress adopted the following position: the military defeat in world war, together with the decline of the economy, had created an objective revolutionary situation. This, however, failed to come to anything in October 1923. But his explanation did not go into the reasons for the defeat. Equally, the representative said nothing about Heinrich Brandler, who had cancelled the signal for uprising after the Chemnitz shop stewards' conference. Nor did he say anything about Stalin's letter of the summer of 1923.

The most diverse groupings which turned up at the party congress were depicted as petty-bourgeois manifestations by the Fischer-Thälmann central committee and by the ECCI representative, even though such different conceptions were defended in the half-dozen groups that neither the central committee nor the ECCI man could ignore them. Comrade Ernst Meyer, who had come from the Spartacus League and played the role of mediator at the congress (he had been party chair before Brandler), was also thrown into the pot of petty-bourgeois soup.

An American socialist, the writer Max Eastman, had published a book shortly before the congress, entitled *After Lenin*, and had discussed critically the different ideas of Lenin and Stalin. This critical investigation of Stalin's policies dealt mostly with the delays in industrialisation and the collectivisation of the agrarian economy demanded by the Left Opposition in the Communist Party of the Soviet Union. Investigations like Eastman's were characterised at the congress as part of a concerted action by world reaction and petty-bourgeois ultra-lefts: Mr Chamberlain was said to be organising a new holy alliance against the land of Soviets, Kautsky was mobilising the Second International in support of Chamberlain by calling openly for armed intervention against Russia, while Mr Eastman, as a paid agent of the bourgeoisie, was busy disorganising from within any resistance by the international proletariat to the united campaign by all the capitalist nations to defeat the workers' revolution.

As Marxist internationalists, we were told, we already knew — and history had already proved — where these disorganisers stood, obstructing the powerful resistance of the German and international working class.

One of the most important themes at the party congress was the question of the trade unions. Although the Frankfurt party congress had succeeded in taking some united decisions about the trade unions, and the Union of Hand and Head Workers had been disbanded, the comrades who had run this organisation were not completely convinced that they should start their work in the ADGB. In the course of lengthy discussions, both the ECCI representative and the central committee, especially Thälmann, as well as most of the representatives of almost all the factions, argued for a Leninist answer to the trade union problem.

Thus, the ECCI representative explained that the main task of the moment was to purge the party, with an iron fist, of all the ultra-left deviations; this struggle was not simply some minor episode which could be ended in a few days after the congress by a complete amnesty for the youthful excesses of the old left comrades — they had done untold theoretical and practical damage to the party.

Almost all the speakers from the central committee argued the same line, even Ruth Fischer and Ernst Schneller, Wilhelm Pieck, Ottomar Geschke and others. Ernst Thälmann said that since the trade unions were politically neutral, we were obliged to bring politics into the unions. We should not be frightened by the trade union bureaucracy. The level of political conviction had to be raised in our own ranks, members had to be convinced of the necessity of trade union work. Comrades had to approach trade union work with the same zest that they had when shouldering their rifles.

It did not take long for the very same comrades who had pleaded so persuasively for work in the trade unions to submit to the Stalinist line. Only a few years later they fought just as fiercely for separate trade unions, and then expelled as enemies of the party all those who resisted.

Under the slogan: 'Down with the spirit of factionalism', the central committee representatives and those who shared their position began their arguments with the most varied critical groupings. Their goal was to crush any other opinion. They argued that the party was so strong and united since Frankfurt that factions were now out of place. In so doing, they quoted Lenin from 1921, when he defended his policy of not allowing factions in the Communist Party of the Soviet Union. At that time, Lenin justified his behaviour by saying that factional debate was just not possible at a time when there was a fight against counter-revolution. The ban on factions was only intended to be temporary. But now they were trying to suppress any other opinions.

I do not wish to go too deeply into the problems of the Tenth Congress of the KPD, but I would recommend reading the report of the proceedings, since it brings to light the fundamental differences between the Internationalist Group and the Stalinist faction. The resolutions which were voted on at the end, and were accepted almost unanimously, do not show the real differences which characterised this congress.

This congress marked the turning point in the party, away from Leninist policies towards the Stalinist line.

In Paragraph 6 of the new statutes, sub-section (c), we have:

'A binding recognition of the decisions of higher Party organs by the lower ones, a strong Party discipline and a swift and exact execution of the decisions of the ECCI and leading Party organs. Whichever organisation extends its activity throughout a certain area will be regarded as higher than those Party organisations which limit their activity merely to individual parts of this area.'

In sub-section (d) we have:

'The discussions of Party questions will be conducted by the membership only until such time as they are decided by the relevant Party organs. After a decision has been taken by the Congress of the Comintern, the Party Congress or the leading Party organs, it must be executed without question, even if some of the members or the local organisations do not agree with the decision.' (*Bulletin of the Tenth Congress of the KPD*, Number 12, Berlin, 24 July 1925.)

These were the formal tricks which the Stalinist faction used to push its policies within the party.

The discussions following on from the Tenth Congress which took place in the factory cells, local branches, town leaderships, districts and regions, showed that the rank and file did not agree with the outcome of the congress. Both in Berlin and in the rest of the country, some of the membership formed factions. They demanded of the central leadership an open discussion on all questions which were not clarified at the congress, in particular on the Russian question.

The central committee at first attempted to discipline the comrades in the local branches and factory cells, and responded with expulsions. But the membership refused to be intimidated, and demanded freedom of discussion. In Berlin in particular, the most important districts had a majority supporting the opposition forces. One of the strongest groups in the German organisation, led by Werner Scholem, Hugo Urbahns, Ivan Katz and Anton Grylewicz, took their lead from the comrades of the Leningrad Opposition around Zinoviev. On 1 September 1926, they addressed the central commitee with a statement which had been signed by 700 party officials. Part of this read:

'Statement on the Russian question.

'Party Comrades! With this statement, the undersigned have seized the initiative for solidarity action with the Russian Opposition. We are utterly convinced that the majority of communist workers would declare themselves for the Leningrad Opposition if they had the chance to find out about the real contradictions in our sister party in Russia, on the basis of unprejudiced information and a multilateral discussion . . .

'The new organisational steps against the various leaders of the opposition which have brought the most important section of the Comintern — the Communist Party of the Soviet Union — to the brink of a split should make clear to the least active comrade the enormous responsibility which weighs on him if he is obliged to make a decision on the Russian question. In Russia there are two opposed opinions. The Leningrad Opposition, which was already represented at the Fourteenth Congress of the Communist Party of the Soviet Union by the most prominent of the old Bolsheviks like Zinoviev, Krupskaya, Kamenev etc., has now come out with a programme which has until now been withheld from the Party and the Comintern.

'Even at the Fourteenth Congress, the German left declared itself in solidarity with the Leningrad workers and demanded the lifting of the ban on discussion. Today we are in no doubt that we share the political standpoint of the Opposition in the Communist Party of the Soviet Union . . .

'In this struggle, the Leningrad Opposition makes a stand against any acquiescence to the possibility of socialism in one country, and stands for an undiminished struggle to advance the revolutionary movement in the other countries, without losing momentum in the construction of socialism in Russia, until socialism triumphs with the victory of world revolution: against the idealisation of present conditions in the Russian state industries as consistent socialist industry . . . against the over-acceleration of the new economic policy, when it is broadcast especially crassly in the familiar slogan "Enrich yourselves!" and finds expression in practice, for example, in the new land laws, in barter and free trade etc. . . . against any loosening of the dictatorship of the proletariat in favour of the town or village bourgeoisie by an extension of Soviet democracy etc. . . . against the advancement of non-proletarian elements in the Communist Party of the Soviet Union; for the swiftest possible creation of a Russian cadre with industrial workers and the village poor, as the most natural enemies of the capitalist counter-offensive in town and country; against the wrong course inside the Party which adopts mechanistic measures of oppression (limitation of freedom of discussion, disciplinary actions etc.), for the extension of Party democracy and the encouragement of all comrades in responsible work without reference to their position in the Party . . .

'If there is an opposition in the Communist Party of the Soviet Union, represented by comrades like Zinoviev, Krupskaya, Kamenev, Lashevich etc., which stands up against the official party line, and whose platform is supported by a comrade like Trotsky who only a short time ago was being fought by comrade Zinoviev, and whom the group led by Stalin took the greatest possible trouble to woo; and if, in addition, old and experienced comrades, who have proved their loyalty in the Revolution, and have been tested in the battles of the Revolution — if these comrades turn to conspiratorial methods, then it is unworthy and fatal for anyone to try to resolve the political questions behind this stance with a mechanical use of the accusation of breach of discipline . . .

'We consider it quite intolerable that a serious and relevant discussion of the Russian questions, that is, the fundamental questions of revolution, is forbidden and that everyone is branded as anti-Bolshevik, as a traitor, social fascist etc., as soon as he expresses opinions which more or less coincide with the views of the Russian Opposition . . .

'Such methods as these can only ruin the Comintern! The significance of these events for the Comintern is obvious. The witch-hunt now developing against Zinoviev etc. will be understood by every politicised worker as an attempt to liquidate the Comintern as the revolutionary organisation of the world proletariat . . .

'We cannot keep silent when these facts are before us. We demand that the discussion is brought back to a political level. We demand the immediate publication of the stenographic report of the last meeting of the central committee and Central Control Commission (CCC) of the Communist Party of the Soviet Union, and of the Fourteenth Congress . . . We demand an end to the monopoly on the taking of minutes which the central committee has claimed for itself. We demand that the discussion be carried out within the broadest framework . . .

'We further demand the lifting of all disciplinary measures and the reinstatement to the Communist Party of Germany of the honest revolutionary comrades who have been expelled for political reasons . . .

'We demand real party democracy in the Comintern and in the Communist Party of the Soviet Union and KPD.

'We reject most emphatically any revision of Leninism. Back to Lenin, to the real, pure, unfalsified Leninism! That must be the watchword in this discussion.'

To this were appended the signatures of 700 party officials from Berlin and the rest of the country. I signed as well, but my name appeared as 'Hoppe, O.' due to a printing error. The list of signatures was not complete, since the leading comrades did not want too much time to be wasted, and so the statement was not passed to the members of factory cells for signature.

The statement on the Russian question was followed by extensive discussions. In the regions where the leadership was in the hands of the Stalinists, any criticism of the policies of the Communist Party of the Soviet Union and its Stalinist leadership was answered by attempts at mass expulsions. In the district of Charlottenburg, the left were in the leadership and they decided which comrades were to represent the standpoint of the central committee. In most cases it was comrade Ernst Meyer, who adopted a conciliatory attitude. The discussion, which was conducted at a high level, made it possible for the local leadership to avoid expulsions at least in the early stages.

In actual fact, the united opposition succeeded in forcing the central committee to organise conferences in the regions and districts and even to discuss both the Russian and German questions. In Berlin, the discussions were conducted at first at the district level, then at the party workers' conferences of the Greater Berlin region. Conferences of Berlin officials met in the Sophie Rooms at the Hackesche Markt. Up to 2,000 comrades took part in these discussions.

The inner-party conflict lasted over three years, and only in 1929 did the Stalinist faction succeed in gaining general control of the party. Unfortunately, I am not in a position to reproduce the resolutions which we passed during this period. In 1933, my library and all the material I had collected was confiscated by the Fascists during a search of my home.

But it was not only the Russian question that was discussed in the party; the politics of the central committee under the leadership of Thälmann and Neumann also stood at the centre of the arguments. Thus the election of Hindenburg as President in 1925 and the tactics of the central commitee played a role in the discussion for a long time, because these very things showed how the principles of the united front had been grossly neglected.

In the first election the whole party had supported the candidacy of Thälmann, since it was clear that no single candidate would win the first round. But it was different in the second round, when the parties of the right supported Hindenburg, the butcher of the First World War and a died-in-the-wool monarchist. The SPD withdrew their candidate, Otto Braun, and, together with the Centre and the State Party, supported the bourgeois politician Marx.

Instead of calling on the SPD to nominate a common candidate against Hindenburg, the central committee again put up Thälmann as its own candidate for the second round. The candidacy of comrade Thälmann was debated at a party workers' conference for Greater Berlin: for the Left

Opposition, the presidential election was a question of fundamental importance hingeing on the correct application of the united front policy, and was not simply a question of the lesser evil.

So at this meeting they fought for the tactic of the KPD renouncing its own candidate in order to force Social Democracy to unite with the Communists and the left wing of the liberal parties for a candidate who could prevent the election of Hindenburg the monarchist; unfortunately, this met with no success. The Brandler group voted with the Wedding opposition in this argument, while the Committed Left (the Korsch Group) supported the candidacy of Thälmann.

In the large popular meetings, the presidential election was not so much debated as swayed by the deployment of paramilitary groups. Even the Communist Party largely renounced agitation amongst the masses, and sent in the Red Front League of Fighters along with the Red Youth Front to help its election campaign. The members of the Stahlhelm and the 'Young German Order' drove through the streets of Berlin in long columns of lorries.

Their journeys were not simply aimed at drumming up support for Hindenburg. From their vehicles they bombarded the local offices of the communists. Even the local offices of the SPD and the republican parties were smashed up. As a result of this terrorist deployment of the Stahlhelm, the Red Front and the Reichsbanner came out to defend the other parties. In Wilmersdorf and in other districts there were regular street battles. The police only intervened if the Stahlhelm was threatened with defeat.

Once, in the Bundes Allee, where the Brandenburgische Strasse comes in, two lorry loads of the RFB were attacked by several lorry columns of Stahlhelm. A street battle developed in which workers from Wilmersdorf were attacked as well as other lorry crews. Despite its superiority in numbers, the Stahlhelm had to retreat.

Another time, we received a report that the people from the Charlottenburg Reichsbanner had been attacked in the Berliner Strasse near the town hall and were besieged in their local offices. Two lorries full of RFB immediately drove off there to liberate the Reichsbanner. From that day on, there was a very good relationship between the RFB and the Charlottenburg Reichsbanner, which was often put to the test later in the fight against the terrorism of the Fascists.

However serious the inner-party discussions became, the opposition groups always maintained the unity of the party towards the outside world. The KPD was in everyone's eyes the basis for the struggle against the class enemy and against the reformist ideas of social democracy. Regardless of whether it was a question of distributing leaflets, organising meetings, providing security for them or — as was common between 1925 and 1929 — conducting house-to-house propaganda, the opposition comrades and those expelled from the party were always there.

House-to-house and 'courtyard' propaganda was primarily conducted in workers' districts; it began on Sundays at about nine o'clock and did not normally last longer than three hours. We began with a song of struggle, and then a comrade made a short speech highlighting the social distress of the working population. Then the comrades split up and called at the apartments to discuss current problems with the tenants. It was rare that we were denied entry. On the contrary, we were often invited in for a cup of coffee because 'it was easier to talk like that'.

As I said, the activity did not last longer than three hours. But it often turned out that we were 'detained' longer in an apartment, especially if we were talking to a sympathiser. Or the discussions were continued out on the street. If the meal at home got cold, then we were given a talking-to. Once when I came home later than agreed, there was a note on the table: 'Am at Klara's, dinner is in the oven'. By evening my wife had calmed down again, after I had explained to her that I was not late because of a lunchtime drink or a card game, but because I was engaged in necessary political work.

On 1 April 1926, the party called a central demonstration in the Lustgarten. As always, the place was jam-packed. The 1 April is my birthday. After we had marched home again, I met up with a few of my comrades and some friends in the RFB in a small cafe in the Rückert Strasse in Charlottenburg, to celebrate my birthday with a glass of wine.

When we left the cafe at about nine o'clock, there was an argument between two comrades and an officer of the vice squad in the Wilmesdorfer Strasse. This policeman had previously belonged to the political police and had shot dead a worker for no apparent reason at a demonstration at the start of the 1920s.

Several prostitutes stood at the corner of Goethe Strasse and Wilmesdorfer Strasse. The policeman now claimed that they had spoken to us and threatened to take them down to the station. The two comrades told him that he had accused the women unjustly, and confronted him with his own past. Then there were recriminations on both sides, which threatened to turn to violence. While the officer from 'vice' summoned support on the police telephone, my friends and I went down Goethe Strasse, in the hope that the other two would follow us. But they did not budge.

In the meantime, a police van rolled up, and the two of them were arrested. I went back to see if I could help them, only to be arrested in my turn on the word of the policeman from the vice squad. A comrade who presented himself as witness was also arrested, with the explanation that witnesses get arrested too, and was taken to the police station in Herder Strasse.

After almost 24 hours, we were released and told that proceedings would be started against us. And sure enough, after a short time we received a summons to a hearing by the state prosecutor. There we were informed that we were accused of riot and serious breach of the peace.

We received legal aid and a lawyer through Red Aid, which was a party organisation. The trial took place in August before the magistrate at Moabit. Although our attorney did not turn up, the trial proceeded regardless. Our application to have the trial postponed was turned down.

Although I was completely innocent in the whole affair, the state prosecutor pleaded for an exemplary punishment and demanded that I be given nine months prison for riot, serious breach of the peace and being a ringleader. For the other accused he demanded seven months' imprisonment. The court sentenced me to seven months and my fellow-accused to five months. No warrant was issued for our immediate arrest.

The next day I went to the office of our lawyer to ask him why we had had no representation. He apologised and said that he had been called away from Berlin that day. After a consultation with the comrades who stood trial with me, we asked for an appeal to be made; this was granted. I learned from my friends in the Charlottenburg district, including comrade Max Hesse, that there had been no legal representation by order of the party, since we were known as oppositionists.

At the appeal hearing a few weeks later — the charges of riot and serious breach of the peace had been dropped, only simple breach of the peace now remained — once again the lawyer did not turn up. The hearing had already got quite far when a young lawyer who was not fully qualified turned up in place of him. His defence speech was very shaky. I believe that even without him the penalty would not have been any different. The state prosecutor, with duelling scars on his face — he looked as if he had once been a student member of the Freikorps — again demanded a severe punishment, since that was the only way to clear the 'terror from the streets'.

Our case was that the KPD rejected individual terror, that we had been on our way home on the evening of 1 April and that the incident only occurred because of the provocative behaviour of the officer from the vice squad. My sentence was cut to five months — the charge of ringleadership stood; the other comrades came away with three months each. I sat out my sentence in Tegel prison in the winter of 1926-1927. The first four weeks were spent sticking paper bags together and assembling toys. Then

I was employed on work outside in the Tegel forest, together with other detainees. We had to fell trees there, which were later cut up for firewood for the prison staff. Twice a week my wife came out to bring me tobacco and food which friends had collected for me.

The wives of other married prisoners also came to bring extra food for their men. There were sixteen of us out there in the wood with a single guard. I was the only political prisoner in the group. The guard was a patient man, who paid no attention either to our conversation or our methods of work. In the evening, when we returned to prison, he made sure that nothing was taken off us during frisking, although it was forbidden to take any tobacco or food with us into the prison.

Since I received newspapers every time my wife came, I had the opportunity of catching up on the news when we were locked in each evening. Because I was occupied outside, the time passed very quickly; the day of my release arrived. My political friends were waiting for me outside the gate, more than twenty people. We marched down the Scharnweber Strasse with red flags and singing the 'Internationale', and celebrated in a party meeting room. My wife was still at the Jungfernheide Station, at the newspaper stand where the *Rote Fahne*, the *Evening World* and the *Workers' Illustrated* were sold to Siemens workers in the morning.

In the evening, comrade Hesse told me that he had spoken to a Social-Democratic town councillor who could intercede for me. At the Charlottenburg cleansing depot, a comrade who was chair of the works committee there had been fired. He had accepted a present from the firm involved when he was buying horse blankets. The party laid great store by maintaining some influence at the depot. So, with the aid of a Social-Democratic councillor, I began as a worker in the cleansing department.

The work was very hard. At that time there were only 200-litre bins. Since most of the homes in Berlin were still heated by stoves, the full bins weighed up to four hundredweight, and if they also contained the ash from the central heating, then they were even heavier. At first I had to do a 'reserve' trip, which meant two trips a day, shovelling the cinders into bins and carrying them out of the cellar to the lorry. The bins were carried by two men with belts. My shoulders were torn to shreds and festering: I asked myself every day whether I should not just chuck in the job.

My wife encouraged me to do just that and to find another job: 'You are killing yourself with this back-breaking work.' But I kept on. My shoulders healed again and I was put on a normal trip. But now there was a new difficulty: although some of my colleagues were members of the party or sympathisers, they did not want to ride with me. The reason? I did not drink spirits. On these trips, which were near the Wittenberg Platz, there were two wholesalers in the alcohol trade; there we took the rubbish directly from the cellars and were then allowed to drink as much schnapps as we wanted. Since I turned down the schnapps, the cellar master did not offer the others as much. I did not want to abandon my principle of being anti-alcohol. Finally the problem was resolved when a colleague named Schulz said he would ride with me.

However, my job in rubbish collection did not last long. In March there were elections to the works committee; the previous chair, who had let himself be bribed in the matter of horse blankets, had been sacked on the spot. Now the Social Democrats wanted to use this as an excuse to limit the influence of the Communists and take the chair for themselves. I was put forward by the party and the comrades at the depot to speak on behalf of our party's candidates. I myself could not stand for election since I had not been there for six months.

The workforce at the cleansing depot was organised 100 per cent in the State and Council Workers' Union, the majority of whose officials were in the Communist Party. In two works meetings I succeeded in convincing the men that their interests were best served by Communist shop stewards: even the colleague who had been sacked had always fought unconditionally for the interests of his members, and besides, the party had distanced itself from his behaviour. The new works committee which was then elected was of the same composition as the old one, and its chair was once more a Communist.

In the middle of April, the winter season ended; although my contract had no time limit, I was dismissed along with other men. 'Due to the ending of the season' was what was written on my dismissal notice. But everyone knew that I was dismissed because I had actively campaigned for the Communist candidates. After a few weeks the council personnel office offered me a job as street sweeper in the cleansing department, and the offer was even made within the terms of the union agreement on conditions of employment, which stated that new vacancies were to be filled first by previous employees.

Since there was no chance of getting a job in the metal industry, I accepted. I was to report to the depot at the Hebbel Park. The foremen there were long-serving soldiers — so-called 'twelve-year men' — some of whom were organised in the Stahlhelm. I made sure that I gave no cause for complaint in my work, but I also continued my political and trade union agitation there. We had only a half-hour break, which I used to encourage trade union activity; the foreman tried to forbid this. But I told him that my trade union activity was protected by law and that he had no right to stop me; and besides I would complain to the works committee. From then on he did everything he could to get me removed from his patch; finally he told the personnel office that he could not accept the responsibility if anything happened to me, since I only had one eye, which was dangerous when working on the streets.

A little later, a new hostel for the homeless was opened in the Sophie Charlotte Strasse. I received a transfer there from the personnel office. Sometimes it happens that even the right wing can do something good: in this new job everything was better for me; in any case, I was grateful to my foreman. For one thing, he had released me from that mindless work on the streets, and secondly because I was paid more. But even more important was the fact that honest and liberal people were employed there and the colleagues with whom I had daily contact were quite in order in terms of the trade union and politics.

Three hundred homeless people were taken in there, only a few of whom were social dropouts. At that time there were already far more than a million unemployed. Benefit was then linked to income, and for most people it did not cover all expenditure. At least half of the inmates were on welfare benefit, which at that time was just a little over six marks a week. They had absolutely no chance of finding a room elsewhere, since any landlady would immediately turn away unemployed people coming from a hostel.

Among the inmates were representatives of all trades; a few had found work again but nowhere to stay. They had to be woken up between four and six o'clock. One of them spoke seven languages and, as he told us, had been employed at Siemens in the international department. Since we could not believe this, we asked friends who worked at Siemens, and they confirmed his story: he had been sacked and replaced by a younger man at a lower wage,

On 'Black Friday' in 1929, the great economic crisis in America began. At that time, it was said in economic circles: 'When America coughs, Europe gets TB.' In Germany, more and more factories closed down; the number of unemployed rose, finally to more than six million. Many small tradesmen had no work; small businesses with not much turnover had to give up because they could not afford the rent for their premises. Despite this, modern hostels for the homeless, even those which had barely been opened, were closed down, including the one in which I was employed.

All the employees of the hostel in Sophie Charlotte Street were transferred to other jobs. I ended up in the surveyor's office, where I was supposed to conduct surveys along with a trained surveyor and another colleague. Here again I was in luck. The surveyor, Herr Friedrich, was a liberal man, and he and my colleague Karl Henzel ensured a very pleasant working environment. I could express my opinions freely there, even on politics.

The technicians and surveyors were mostly social democrats or liberals; even the leading director, Herr Teschner, had nothing against discussions on current affairs, even on the most controversial topics. We had to take our breaks in restaurants or schools, for our work area stretched right across Charlottenburg. Here the three of us often held discussions. Herr Friedrich belonged to the German People's Party, and his idol was Stresemann.

My colleague sympathised with the KPD. Whenever Friedrich reached a sticky point in these discussions, he would always say: 'Ah well, let's get back to work again.' We always countered with: 'But the break isn't finished yet,' whereupon he would reply: 'Well, I'll go out and fill in the reports.' He discussed with us the work which had to be done, although he bore the responsibility alone. I must say that my years of employment between 1929 and 1933 were my most pleasant. Herr Friedrich was arrested in 1945 by the Russians and taken to Sachsenhausen, and never returned. He joined the Nazi party, the NSDAP, after 1933, like many others in the surveyor's department. But I cannot believe that this man did anything which could possibly have justified his fate.

In the meantime, the factional struggles in the KPD continued. The Stalinist leadership in the central committee had allied itself with the Brandler-Thalheimer group in the fight against the left, and succeeded in weakening it. Whereas the left had at first formed a united grouping after the October defeat of 1923, now these conflicts brought out various differing standpoints.

In the first phase of the struggle, the leading figures of the left, from Korsch to Ruth Fischer, Hugo Urbahns and Anton Grylewicz, had fought for the implementation of Marxist-Leninist policies against the nationally-blinkered conceptions of the Stalinists. One of the leading figures of the left was Karl Korsch. In 1920 he parted company with the left wing of the USPD to join the KPD, although he had some reservations about the '21 conditions' for membership of the Comintern adopted at that year's congress. In 1923 he was a member of the short-lived Social-Democratic and Communist government in Thuringia. Korsch, who later joined the ultra-left wing, became the theoretician of this group.

The original united faction of Scholem-Katz-Rosenberg-Korsch-Schwarz fell apart, and Korsch and Schwarz stood with their group in fixed opposition to the Comintern. Together with Schwarz, Korsch published the bulletin *Communist Politics*.

Unlike Korsch, Ernst Schwarz only came into the socialist movement after the end of the First World War. In 1918 he was a member of the SPD. In 1920 he joined the USPD and, along with its left wing, moved to the KPD. In 1926, together with Korsch, he was expelled. In parliament, where he was still an elected representative, he publicly denounced the 'counter-revolutionary policies' of the Soviet Union. In the autumn of 1926 he split from the *Communist Politics* group and brought out his own paper, *Committed Left (Entschiedene Linke)*, and drew nearer to the KAP, at least in his views. A short time later he left the 'Committed Left' group and eventually left the workers' movement.

Ruth Fischer was elected leader of the Berlin party organisation in 1921. The Berlin region, the most important and largest next to Hamburg and the Lower Rhine, was left-wing; Ruth Fischer became the leader of the left in the Party, alongside Arkadi Maslow, who was less of a public figure.

The relationship between the Communist International and the German Party was becoming more and more tense, especially after 1925 when there was a split with the left. The ultra-lefts — Scholem, Katz and Rosenberg — attacked the politics of Ruth Fischer. The left-wing leadership was thereby weakened, and the Comintern attempted to foist its preconceptions on German politics. When, in August 1925, the 'Open Letter' of the ECCI against Ruth Fischer was accepted, her influence had passed its peak.

She attempted to mobilise her supporters to salvage the leadership for the left. But she did not succeed; some of her supporters returned to the line of the ECCI, especially those who were dependent on the party. Another section gravitated towards the ideas of Hugo Urbahns and Anton Grylewicz.

Things were made more difficult when the Comintern called Ruth Fischer to Moscow and kept her there for a time. In June 1926 she returned to Germany without permission, for which she was charged with a serious breach of discipline. In August 1926, together with Maslow, she was expelled from the party, and tried again to bring the left together, along with Urbahns, Grylewicz and others. At that time she was hoping for the support of Zinoviev, who meanwhile was in opposition to the policies of Stalin.

Anton Grylewicz joined the USPD in 1917 and was among the leading revolutionary shop stewards who were most involved in the outbreak of the November revolution. In 1920 he went over to the KPD with the left wing of the USPD and became organisational secretary for the Brandenburg district of Berlin. After he had been removed from the central committee as a result of the 'Open Letter', he continued as an influential leader of the Fischer-Maslow group.

In 1927 he spoke for the Left Opposition at the Eleventh Congress of the KPD and was expelled. Until 1930, comrade Grylewicz was national organiser of the Lenin League. In February 1930, with a group to which I also belonged, he left the Lenin League; in the period that followed he was a leading Trotskyist and published Trotsky's writings in German.

Hugo Urbahns joined the north coast regional leadership of the USPD at the start of 1920 and was delegated to the unification congress in Halle. Along with Ernst Thälmann he now became leader of the Communist Party on the north coast. During the Hamburg uprising in October 1923, it was he who ensured an orderly retreat. As supposed leader of the uprising, he was arrested, and, despite being a member of parliament, remained in prison on remand for a year. At the start of 1925 he stood before the court as the principal accused. He declared to the court — 'I accept full political responsibility. I would rather die in the fire of revolution than rot away on the dungheap of democracy!'

From the very beginning he represented the views of the Left Opposition and in November 1926 he signed the Statement of the 700, whereupon he was expelled. In 1928 he became leader of the Lenin League, and remained in that position until 1933.

When the Nazis started an extensive propaganda campaign in 1932, with rallies, demonstrations and public meetings, representatives of the KPD were also invited to speak at them. One such occasion was in the Pharus Rooms in Wedding, where Goebbels was billed to speak. In an article in the *Rote Fahne*, the KPD rejected the idea of sending a speaker. However, comrade Urbahns presented himself before the Nazis.

He appeared with his own self-defence organisation, to which we in the Trotskyist opposition of Bolshevik-Leninists also belonged. Goebbels guaranteed Urbahns absolute safe conduct. Urbahns replied that he needed no such guarantee, for his guarantee lay in his comrades who stood 140-strong in a U-shape before the platform or stood in the aisles. In a devastating speech against the demagogy of the Nazis, comrade Urbahns declared that the final discussion with them would take place on the barricades.

The German leadership marched behind the Stalinist leadership without any reservations. They accepted the fact that active branches throughout the country, which had had 100 to 200 members in the period of the Ruth Fischer central committee, and which had won ever greater influence in the political arena in their struggles with other parties, shrank to half strength as a result of the policy of expulsions.

For example, there was a worker's letter in the *Bulletin* (*Mitteilungsblatt*) published by the Left Opposition, which said:

'You would hardly think it possible that the number of members in the Aachen district has declined so much. The party here is ruined. Districts which had 100 to 200 comrades in 1923 and during the Ruth Fischer central committee, now consist of five to ten comrades. The only district which has managed to maintain itself is the Western district, with 70 comrades. Western once had over 300 comrades, and it keeps going only because left-wing comrades are active there.

'Who should shoulder the blame for the destruction of the Aachen district and its branches and where are the comrades now? The main guilt lies in the wrong line adopted by the party, and a large share of the blame must fall on Michael Sommer, who is a big boss on the central committee. Once he used to be an exemplary member of the Christian Workers' League and the Youth Congregation; now he is looking for alliances with the Christian Socialists. There is no description for the dirty tricks, cheap lies, despicable libel and treacherous means employed by this central committee boss. We will write about the doings of this central committee youth some other time.

'It is sad that many comrades who have been expelled have become politically indifferent. One section has joined Pfemfert [member of the KAP and of the syndicalist General Workers' Union], another is suspended in mid-air and has no opinion. The Urbahns group, which makes steady advances here every week, has given itself the task of catching those comrades from Aachen and district who have resigned or been expelled. It wants to get the Aachen district back to the level it was at in 1923 and during the Ruth Fischer central committee, that is, a left-wing region in the western black earth.'

Contributions like this came flooding in to the offices of the *Bulletin of the Left Opposition* and later to the *Flag of Communism*.

Neither the Committed Left nor the Fischer-Maslow faction were permitted by the Thälmann-Neumann leadership to defend their ideas in the central organ, *Rote Fahne*, nor in the regional papers, nor in the theoretical journal the *International*. So the Opposition had no choice but to publish bulletins to make themselves understood by party members.

In the sub-regions it was becoming increasingly difficult to get the same speaking time as the Stalinist speakers, in factory cells or branches or at party workers' conferences. For those comrades in particular who were employed in party-owned businesses — the *Rote Fahne* publishing house, Kosmos Publications, Russian Trade Delegation etc. — it was now almost impossible to speak unless they wanted to place their jobs at risk. Some of these comrades capitulated and no longer took part in the fight. On the other hand, however, these comrades supported the left financially.

In the first edition of the *Bulletin of the German Left Opposition*, in January 1927, the editors published a statement which had been submitted by Trotsky and Kamenev to a session of the extended ECCI. Thälmann, who at that point was a member of the ECCI presidium, had refused to accept this submission, and had also refused to allow the two comrades to speak. Part of this statement read:

'In voting against the resolution of comrade Stalin, we consider it necessary to explain the reason for our vote as follows:

'We categorically reject once again the accusation of a factional character in our stance. Our whole criticism is made against mistakes and deviations from the proletarian line and dictated by the revolutionary proletarian policy of our party, in order to preserve, secure and buttress the domination and growth of the socialist elements in our economy and the inseparable connection with the international revolution — as Lenin taught . . . We reject decisively and categorically the baseless accusations of pessimism and scepticism. In reality we maintain an unshakable belief that the proletariat, under the leadership of the Communist Party of the Soviet Union, can and will conquer the elements of capitalism in the economy of the USSR, will overcome all difficulties and, with the aid of the international proletariat, will construct socialism in the USSR.

'If we take pains in concentrating the attention of the party on the kulak danger, then it is not so that we should capitulate before them but rather to encourage the party to base itself more securely on the village poor and the agricultural workers and, with the firm hand of the proletarian state to guide them, help them gain the support of the peasants against the kulaks.

'It is not correct to say that we want to exert pressure on the peasantry in order to promote a policy of industrialisation. We say that the alliance of proletariat and peasantry must be preserved at all costs. Without that, the dictatorship of the proletariat is doomed to failure in the USSR.'

The leadership of the Russian party under Stalin had based their struggle against the left on a conflict between 'Trotskyism' and Leninism. It must have been obvious to every clear-thinking party member that a fight conducted like that was only an attempt to divert attention away from the real differences of opinion which had been aroused by the blatant Stalinist deviation from the class line, and to draw attention to old differences which had already been resolved or clarified during the Leninist period.

In reality, the left in the Communist Party of the Soviet Union represented the Marxist-Leninist position, while the Stalinist faction in the International was trying to push through a policy which was directed primarily towards 'the construction of socialism in one country' and only secondarily corresponded to the interests of the international working class.

Stalin's position signified an abandonment of the world revolution. The communist parties now served him only as the means to prevent a military invasion of the Soviet Union by the imperialist powers. In Stalin's eyes, the Social-Democratic leaders and the members as well were lackeys of imperialism. The treachery of the Social-Democratic leaders was one thing, but the struggle of Social-Democratic workers with their illusions of reaching socialism by the parliamentary road and reforms — that was quite another. But they were not therefore social fascists; as before, there was still a need for a united front policy.

The task of the KPD was to split the Social-Democratic workers from their leaders, by united actions, instead of tying them even closer to their leaders by erroneous policies — like the theory of social fascism, or the construction of separate unions (Revolutionary Trade Union Opposition — RGO). The trust which the Social-Democratic workers placed in their leaders was greater than their trust in the leaders of the KPD.

The political mistakes of the KPD pushed the members of the SPD back into the arms of their leaders, isolated itself more and more from the factory workers and put an end to its independent power in the trade unions. What follows will show that in 1931 even the left wing of the SPD refused to merge with the Communist Party and instead proceeded to found its own party.

The Fifteenth Congress of the Communist Party of the Soviet Union at the end of 1927 signalled a change not only for the Russian left, but also for the left in the European communist parties. In the course of the so-called 'Bolshevisation' of the Comintern — in reality, it was the Stalinisation — a halt was called to the previous developments, which effectively brought about the end of Marxist-Leninist policies.

The end result of the congress was the capitulation of the group around Zinoviev and Kamenev which was temporarily in alliance with the group around Trotsky, and the expulsion of the Marxist-Leninists supporting Trotsky, Rakovsky, Preobrazhensky and Radek.

But if Stalin believed that he had silenced the Left Opposition with these expulsions, then he was wrong again. Trotsky was exiled to Alma-Ata; from there, together with the comrades who still remained, he continued the struggle for the internationalist position.

Kalinin, who represented Stalin, answered the capitulation of Zinoviev and Kamenev with a mocking speech. So not only had this wing of the Opposition humbled itself before Stalin and his supporters, but it had lost all credibility with its German counterpart, the Fischer-Maslow group. If it had not been for the statement by comrades Smilga, Muralov, Rakovsky,

Radek and others, who appealed to the delegates on 18 December at the Fifteenth Congress and thus voiced the position of the Internationalists, then the struggle for the Marxist-Leninist position would scarcely have continued so decisively. This statement said:

'Expelled from the party we remain loyal to the programme of our party, to its traditions and its banner. We shall continue to work for the strengthening of the Communist Party and its influence in the working class.'

They stated that they would comply with the decisions of the Fifteenth Congress and dissolve their faction, and also rejected the idea of founding a second party; equally, they wanted to defend their ideas where they disagreed with those of the Stalin faction, but within the framework of the party constitution. However, in contrast with the Zinoviev-Kamenev group, they stood firm on their own positions:

'The expulsion of the Oppositionists, like the other repressive measures against them, is aimed only at uprooting and destroying all trace of opposition ideas in the party. But since these ideas reflect the historic interests of the proletariat, they will live on in the party, despite the repression, and find new supporters.

'Bolshevik workers are the quintessence of the party: at a time of approaching danger, their voice shall be decisive for the fate of the party and of the Revolution. This voice is our voice.'

The struggle by the best elements in the Russian party, as expressed in the statement of principles at the Fifteenth Congress, not only gave new impetus to the Russian comrades, but also provided encouragement in the International for those fighting the Stalinist faction. Although a large proportion of the leading comrades had already been expelled in Germany, those of the left who remained in the party still regarded themselves as a faction of the KPD, unlike the ultra-lefts around Schwarz, Katz and, to a certain extent, Korsch.

Exactly as in the Russian party, the German Stalinists worked with slander: they had nothing else to oppose the arguments of the left.

The juggernaut of expulsion rolled on unstoppably; everyone who made any criticisms in the party was given their notice. Amongst them were comrades who were in the branch leaderships in trade unions, or were active as shop stewards or chairing works committees. On 19 January 1929, I too was expelled. We continued to be regarded as communist comrades by the membership at grassroots level. And it was also possible to discuss problems with them; this applied both to the party and the RFB.

Entire local branches were thrown out of the party, for example in Bruchsal, Rathenow, Suhl and elsewhere. To the outside world, although expelled, they still represented the KPD, with the only difference that these groups now put forward the positions of the Marxist-Leninists in actions and in propaganda. In Suhl in Thuringia, it was not just a single branch: there, the whole district was expelled.

The chair, Guido Heym, came from an old socialist family. By trade he was a toymaker. As early as 1913 he had worked as editor of the Erfurt *Tribune* newspaper. He came to the KPD in 1920 along with the left wing of the USPD. From the very beginning he was on the left wing of the party, and became editor-in-chief of the Suhl *People's Will (Volkswillen)*, the organ of the KPD.

At first the Stalinist leadership tolerated comrade Heym, since the Suhl branch and the majority in the district stood behind him. But when he declared at the start of 1928 that the *People's Will* would appear as the organ of the Left Opposition, he and the entire district were expelled. Most of the members went with him into the Lenin League. However, soon after the foundation of the League, he went over to the SPD with some of the comrades from Suhl.

The Opposition, which in 1927 operated as a loose organisational collection of those on the left who had been expelled from the party, decided at a national conference on 4 March 1928 to take on a tighter organisational form. The resolution adopted there showed a strong inclination towards the founding of an independent party. A powerful minority spoke out against such a formulation at the conference, but could not get the vote.

It was decided that the founding conference of the Lenin League should be called in Berlin for 8 and 9 April 1928, which was Easter. The reason the majority gave for this was that we would miss a golden opportunity if we did not strengthen and rally the Leninist forces.

Despite its objections, the minority took part in the preparations for the founding conference, in order to maintain the unity and solidarity of the organisation. The Charlottenburg comrade Max Hesse had voted for the resolution. In 1918 he had been a member of the soldiers' committee in Spandau, and had simultaneously joined the Spartacus League. He had always been on the left wing of the KPD. After unification with the USPD, he had become chair of the Charlottenburg district.

I had worked closely with him ever since I first met him in 1924. Through Max Hesse, who was a close confidant of Ruth Fischer, I got into the more exclusive factional meetings which usually took place in the Halensee apartment belonging to Ruth Fischer. Ruth had a habit of chairing these meetings from her bed, although she was neither ill nor disabled.

Together with Ruth Fischer, Max Maslow, Paul Schlecht and others, Hesse soon left the Lenin League again. In Spring 1929, like Guido Heym, he went over to the SPD and became the Charlottenburg chair. Any credibility he had left after his support of the national conference resolution of 4 March 1928 vanished utterly when he attempted to take part of the left with him to the Social Democrats. At the founding conference, the minority succeeded in maintaining its position; they were able to ensure that the Lenin League described itself as a faction of the KPD which continued to fight for the reform of the party.

If the struggle had taken place mostly inside the party before the foundation of the Lenin League gave a firmer footing to the organisation, now it found added impetus outside the party. The *People's Will* was made available to us as the central organ. Soon we also had the *Flag of Communism* (*Fahne des Kommunismus*), which was supposed to act as a theoretical journal, though it was not entirely up to this task.

Additionally, there were still many ways of holding discussions with party comrades. On discussion evenings which we held in the districts, many KPD members turned up. There were also members of other organisations who were interested in our point of view and took part in the discussion. There were always tremendous arguments whenever we stood up to speak at public meetings of the KPD, as for example at one meeting where Hermann Remmele, one of the most loyal Stalinist partisans, was speaking. The theme was 'The Soviet Union, land of socialist construction'. We were well-represented with our group, having more than 50 members in Charlottenburg alone.

Two days beforehand, the infamous SA Storm Troop 33 had attacked people attending a KPD meeting in Ahlert's Rooms in Berliner Strasse. The SA Storm Troopers had shot at those leaving the hall from their position in Lohmeyer Strasse. There were two dead and several injured. The police did nothing. Our attempts to catch the Storm Troopers failed when we were shot at ourselves, even though we had no weapons.

The meeting at which Hermann Remmele was speaking also took place in Berliner Strasse, at the 'Turkish Tent' public house. The platform declared that the meeting should be treated as a memorial meeting for those killed and injured by the SA attack. But Remmele disregarded this. After he had spoken about the victims for a few minutes, he went on with his speech about the Soviet Union.

I quickly asked for speaking rights, and soon got them, after a vote had been taken. When Remmele had finished, I did not find it difficult to tear his speech to shreds. At the end of my contribution, I explained that the October Revolution led by Lenin and Trotsky had indeed given the signal for the permanent revolution, and that, as before, the international working class and the extension of the revolution to other countries was the best guarantee for socialism in the Soviet Union.

I was greeted with applause even from the ranks of the RFB and the rest of the audience.

In his closing remarks, Remmele did not attempt to prove that Stalin's policies were Leninist. Rather, he launched a furious bombardment of slander against the Opposition and myself. My attempt to argue with him by heckling was answered by his call on those present to throw this 'agent of imperialism, this counter-revolutionary' out of the hall. No one stirred. Remmele then shouted: 'If no one will bother to throw this counter-revolutionary out, then I'll do it myself'; interrupted his speech, climbed down from the platform and told me to leave the hall. At the same time, he grabbed me in order to drag me out. When I told him to let go of me, otherwise he would be in trouble, he paid no attention. On the contrary, he kept on pulling. So there was nothing left to do but defend myself.

Since my fists were harder, he went down. But that was the signal for a row of RFB heavies to come to Remmele's aid. The RFB men piled into me. Hermann Krüger and Willi Fieber, members of the district leadership of the KPD, tried to intervene — by the way, they were sympathisers of the Lenin League.

The whole thing ended with me and some other comrades leaving the hall, along with others, badly bruised and bloody. On the street outside, the discussion went on far into the night, until the police broke up the street meeting at half past two.

Such occurrences were frequent, and always provoked by the KPD; the result was that many supporters of the party renounced their loyalty or became sympathisers with us. It was mostly members of the Communist Youth League who let themselves be drawn into such provocations. They drove through the streets in closed vans belonging to the *Evening World* and hurled stones at Opposition comrades who were putting up posters. They did not shrink from attacking Opposition groups with clubs.

A new turn was taking place in the German Communist Party. This change was again to be traced back to a turn in the Russian party. Whereas it had followed a right-wing course in the years 1925-1926, completely neglecting industrialisation and instead devoting itself to the villages, that is, the kulaks, now, from the winter of 1928-1929 onwards, it followed an ultra-left course, which was called the 'Third Period'. By supplying a new set of figures for the industrialisation plans laid by the the Left Opposition, they tried to make up for the ruinous years when industry was not built up.

The German party took its cue from this new line, and attacked the Social Democrats and the ADGB trade union organisation with ultra-left slogans. It was aided in this by the tools of Stalinism such as the theory of social fascism, of the construction of 'red' unions and the abandonment of any real united front policies.

In that period, the forces of Social Democracy grew almost as great as those of the Communists, with the only difference that the KPD drew its voters from the growing number of unemployed or petty bourgeois who had fallen on hard times, while Social Democracy mostly influenced factory workers and the majority of trade unionists. Without making any changes in its policies, without a return to Marxism-Leninism, the KPD found it impossible to win the mass of factory workers away from the treacherous leadership of the SPD.

At first the KPD found credibility amongst its own members who thought that it was now prepared to pursue policies which would enable them to bring Social Democrats and their sympathisers to the ranks of communism. But the party neither abandoned its ruinous theory of social fascism nor did it give up its policy of a 'Revolutionary Trade Union Opposition' (RGO). In the matter of the united front, it wavered between attempts at a united front from below and then from above. It turned to the Social-Democratic workers with dozens of appeals, but without success. On the contrary, it achieved the opposite: the Social-Democratic workers clung even tighter to their leaders.

In the meantime, a real opposition under the leadership of Seydewitz and Rosenfeld had emerged in the SPD, which at first made an attempt to strengthen the left wing of the party in the hope that they could exert pressure on the party leadership from within and so push the SPD towards socialist policies. Seydewitz and Rosenfeld did not yet see at that point that the leadership of the Social-Democratic party was fully integrated into the bourgeois system, playing its role in the swamp of bourgeois and petty bourgeois 'liberal parties', and was no longer capable of taking up the fight for socialism. At the side of Brüning, the emergency Chancellor, they believed they could save the democratic republic.

Consider here a short extract from a speech by Hans Vogel, a delegate to the SPD Congress in 1929:

'There are only two possibilities: either a purely bourgeois government or a government with whose leadership our party is as closely involved as possible. Here again, it is a question of the lesser of two evils, and I would consider the second alternative as the lesser evil.' (SPD Congress, 1929, Document 81.)

Later, when Brüning had dictatorial powers, then his purely bourgeois government was regarded as the lesser evil compared to a government which included the NSDAP or under its leadership.

A sixteen-point programme of struggle was proposed at the SPD congress which, amongst others, contained demands which could only be supported, such as the reopening of factories which had been closed down, the confiscation of the property of unpatriotic large industrialists, confiscation of the operating capital and the entire property of employers who sabotaged production, establishment of industrial contracts with Soviet Russia, confiscation of country estates with the land being handed over to agricultural workers and peasants for their use.

These demands had scarcely been proposed than they were forgotten about in their enthusiasm for the Brüning government.

In 1929, the 'grand coalition' still 'governed' under the leadership of the Social-Democratic Chancellor Hermann Müller and Finance Minister Rudolf Hilferding. But policies were no longer dictated by the national government. Industry and the banking world, together with the National Bank, put their ultimatums to the government. When the government once more fell into financial difficulties and tried to arrange new credits with the banks, the president of the National Bank, Hjalmar Schacht, laid down humiliating conditions.

In a dictatorial fashion, he demanded liquidation of debts, increases in taxation and a lowering of real wages, otherwise the government would not receive a penny. At the same time, the German People's Party (DVP) demanded the resignation of Rudolf Hilferding. The SPD leaders swallowed these demands, and into the shoes of Hilferding stepped a representative of the DVP.

However, the Social-Democratic leadership gained no advantage from its retreat before the reactionary demands inside and outside the government. In March 1930, the coalition collapsed in the argument about unemployment benefits. The DVP demanded a lowering of the social security contributions, which would inevitably have led to a decrease in unemployment benefit.

The number of unemployed had already risen to over two million in the winter of 1928-1929, and had hastened the processes of radicalisation. In the parliamentary elections of 1928, the KPD had already gained a further 1.3 million votes over the presidential elections of 1925, and now had 3.3 million voters. The unemployed demanded that the government put an end to unemployment and raise the benefits. They expressed their determination in large mass demonstrations and there was rally after rally throughout the winter of 1928-1929. In Berlin, some of the demonstrations were led by the RFB in full uniform. Even after the ban on the RFB, which resulted from the bloody events of May 1929, we saw several demonstrations like that.

I remember one demonstration which marched along the Kurfürstendamm and through the Zoo district on Christmas Eve. Thousands of RFB members in uniform, and tens of thousands of unemployed, marched through this bourgeois shopping area. There were hardly any police to be seen that day. Although the demonstration was entirely peaceful, the honest bourgeois fled down the Underground entrances clutching their packages.

Perhaps they were frightened because the cry of 'Hunger!' rang out time and again from the rows of demonstrators; that day the well-fed bourgeois felt that he had been left in the lurch by his police force.

In Berlin, the situation was very tense. The Prussian government and the Berlin police president had nothing with which to reply to the demands of the demonstrating workers other than to break up the protests by force;. That only added to the fury of the unemployed and the working people. So the Berlin police president banned all open-air processions. But the KPD called on workers to take to the streets on 1 May, the day of struggle of the international working class, and to demonstrate for its just demands. The Social-Democratic police president did not lift his ban.

The KPD printed a statement in the *Rote Fahne* of 13 April 1929, which read:

'The 1 May 1929 is a day of struggle! The 1 May 1929 is a symbol of the proletarian offensive against the crimes of capital, of the bourgeoisie and of Social Democracy. The Communist International and the Communist Party are the only force that can call on the workers to demonstrate on 1 May under the time-honoured slogans of proletarian solidarity and proletarian class struggle. Take up the fight in all the factories, in all the trade unions and mass organisations! Vote unanimously for work stoppages and the revolutionary mass demonstration!

'No demonstration for "battleship socialism" [Müller's SPD government had voted funds for the construction of a pocket-battleship], for economic peace or economic democracy!

'Demonstrate on 1 May in town and country under the slogans of the revolutionary class struggle, under the slogans of the Communist Party! Ignore the bans!

'For the defence and strengthening of the Communist Party and the Red Front League of Fighters against the threatened bans of the bourgeoisie and Social Democracy! Against the social fascist policies of coalition, against the dictatorship plans of the bourgeoisie and their Social-Democratic henchmen! For the dictatorship of the proletariat and for socialism!'

On 27 April, the Berlin May Day Committee warned Zörgiebel, the president of police, against using force against the demonstrating workers. Any police provocations initiated by Zörgiebel on 1 May would be answered by a mass strike by the workers on 2 May. Both appeals, on 13 and on 27 April, were made as if the ruling class was no longer strong enough to hold on to its power, as if the working class already had enough strength to take power.

What was the reality in the factories? The influence of the Communists had virtually sunk to zero as a result of the policies of the KPD. More than 75 per cent of factory workers heeded the advice of the Social Democrats and trade unions not to participate in the demonstrations of the Communists. On the other hand, the Prussian government was determined to prevent any demonstration. At any place where workers had met up or gathered to demonstrate, the police, led by reactionary officers, intervened and split the workers up. In many places, workers defended themselves against the brutal behaviour of the police, and built barricades to limit the mobility of the police. Twenty-eight workers were left dead on the street.

The KPD tried to portray the fighting as an organised battle on the barricades, involving the whole Berlin working class. In reality, there were fights only in Neukölln and Wedding. The call made by the KPD met with little response in Berlin or in the rest of the country.

These days showed how much the influence of the party had declined in the factories. The *Rote Fahne* was banned for three weeks; the RFB was made illegal in Prussia. The political responsibility for this fell on the Social Democrats and their government officials in Prussia. For left-wing workers, old memories were reawakened from the Noske period, when the Government of People's Deputies suppressed the demands of the workers with machine-guns.

9.

THE END OF THE WEIMAR REPUBLIC

Towards the end of 1929, Berlin was shaken by a great scandal. The textile firm of Sklarek had made enormous profits out of supplying the public utilities of Berlin. Some of the senior municipal officials of Berlin had allowed themselves to be bribed by Sklarek, including the Lord Mayor, Böss, who belonged to the Democratic Party. All efforts by the town hall to cover up this scandal ended in failure. The newspapers were full of the 'Sklarek affair' for weeks on end. The scandal burst like a bomb, because it had been known for a long time that the gentlemen of the Berlin council, with their enormous salaries, had been engaged in shady business. And now came the proof — Messrs Councillors had been conducting business with capitalist profiteers! The so-called 'Sklarek fur', worn by the mayor's wife, played an important role in the story. Berlin was in a furore. This excitement even spread out to the province; the scandal contributed considerably to the radicalisation of the population, both working and unemployed, from which the NSDAP in particular made gains.

The first Brüning cabinet, which was a dictatorial government and ruled on the basis of a state of emergency, was only kept alive by the toleration of the Social Democrats. In July 1930, when a motion was put forward to lift the Brüning state of emergency, not only the Communists and the Hugenberg-Hitler block voted in favour, but also the Social Democrats. Brüning remained in the minority by a vote of 225 to 236. He then dissolved parliament in the hope of getting a decisive majority in the elections. But the elections which took place on 14 September 1930 did not give him the decision he wanted.

The Social Democrats lost half a million votes and were reduced to 8.5 million voters, while the Communists gained 1.25 million and rose to 4.5 million. The workers' parties together polled 13 million votes, which was an increase over the 12.5 of the previous elections. But when you consider that there were four million new voters in this election, which the NSDAP could largely claim for themselves, then the landslide of the September election is clearly seen: the NSDAP grew from 800,000 voters in 1928 to 6.5 million voters and 107 seats. In the period after 1923, Fascism had been a latent danger in Germany. But these elections showed that it had become an acute threat.

The elections were a turning point, not inside parliament, but outside. The slogan of the Social Democrats was one they repeated often: 'Berlin is not Rome — Germany is not Italy'. This was how they tried to explain that Fascism could be victorious in Italy but not in Germany. The KPD thought that the process of radicalisation among the German working class would be sufficient to isolate the SPD and the trade unions, and hoped to gain large sections of the petty bourgeoisie with slogans against the Versailles Treaty which spoke of 'national and social liberation', and thus to succeed in stopping the Fascist danger.

Our organisation, which still regarded itself as a faction of the KPD, concentrated all its efforts on making clear that a policy of national and social liberation was not enough to defend the interests of the working class, the peasantry and the petty-bourgeois layers. Rather there had to be a policy which could win over the millions of workers who still followed the Social-Democratic leadership. The nationalism of the NSDAP could not somehow be outdone by a revolutionary party.

The leadership of the KPD simply brushed aside our reminders that the Bolsheviks had not only succeeded in isolating the Mensheviks in the period between the February and October revolutions, but had also managed to win broad layers of the petty bourgeoisie and the small peasants. As the NSDAP grew in strength, so the terror of its Storm Troops (Stürmerabteilungen, the SA) against the organised working class also grew. One of the biggest provocations by the SA was an attack on a band of musicians belonging to the Charlottenburg RFB in Lichterfeld.

This band, under the baton of the acting branch leader, Wisse, had travelled to Luckenwalde by train to play at the invitation of the Luckenwalde branch of the RFB. On the trip home in the evening, two extra carriages were attached at the town of Jüterbog, which were occupied by two SA detachments also travelling to Berlin. They had been on an exercise in Jüterbog.

The train stopped at Trebbin, and the Storm Troops made their first attempt to attack the band. Only the presence of mind of the guard, who made the train leave early, prevented the attack. At Lichterfelde-East, where the train had a longer stop, the SA terrorists succeeded: all 26 of our comrades were beaten up so badly that they had to be taken to hospital, many of them seriously injured.

The attack took place on a Sunday. On the Monday morning, the Berlin-Brandenburg district leadership of the KPD and the regional leadership of the RFB distributed a leaflet in the factories of Berlin which called for a powerful demonstration in the square in front of the Charlottenburg castle. Masses of Berlin workers responded — some estimates put the number at almost 300,000. The square in front of the castle and all the streets leading off it were packed with demonstrators. Twenty-five thousand RFB supporters assembled with the Red Youth Front and the Red Women and Girls' League at the 'Knee', the place that is now Ernst Reuter Platz.

Ernst Thälmann, the chair of the party and national chair of the RFB, arrived by Underground to speak to the crowd. Even as he spoke, a mounted police battalion approached and demanded that the demonstrators leave. Without waiting to see if this order would be obeyed, the battalion rode straight into the crowd. The commanding officer hit Thälmann in the face with the flat of his sword so that blood spurted out and smeared his RFB shirt.

Now there was no holding anyone back: in less than two minutes, not a single policeman remained on horseback. There were comrades in the RFB who knew how to handle horses; the front legs were splayed out so that the animals stumbled. It was impossible to say what happened to the policemen. The demonstrators then spread out across the width of Bismarck Strasse and marched down it. A small troop of police came out of the Berliner Strasse. It was disarmed by the women and beaten up. Three large armoured cars stood outside the German Opera House.

Since the demonstration had grown larger, with more and more people joining it, the police were powerless. The three armoured cars were overturned, the policemen disarmed, and their rifles smashed on the kerbs.

That day, Marx's statement that 'When the idea takes hold of the masses, it becomes a material power' achieved its full meaning. There were no more policemen to be seen on the streets. In Wilmesdorfer Strasse, into which the demonstration turned, a single Storm Trooper tried to provoke us, but he very quickly fled into a tram car. A policeman on the tram tried to protect the provocateur, and both received a good beating. The demonstration marched onwards up Pestalozzi Strasse, Lietzensee Strasse and Danckelmann Strasse to the castle. At the start of Danckelmann Strasse there was a traffic policeman on duty. Since his political allegiance was not branded on his forehead, he was beaten up as well; it turned out later that he was a member of the Communist Party.

When I arrived at the castle, there were already many speakers addressing the crowds. There were no police there either, for they had retreated to the police barracks in Schloss Strasse. The RFB sections from Charlottenburg and Zoo district had been instructed to maintain order. We were the last to leave the square after the close of the rally. We had got as far as Lohmeyer Strasse when a battalion of police armed with rifles drove up, and in Kaiser Friedrich Strasse formed two rows — one kneeling, the other standing — and shot over our heads. We did not allow ourselves to be provoked, but turned into Brauhof Strasse and marched to the 'Werner' pub in Wall Strasse.

Later the party and the RFB leadership found it impossible ever to call upon the masses in such a way again, although there were occasions enough. The erroneous policies of the KPD, in not seeing the SPD as an opponent of Fascism, but its twin brother, the absence of a united front policy and the attempt to set up its own separate trade unions — all these things isolated it more and more from the factory workers.

The NSDAP recruited its SA detachments from the unemployed, the lumpen-proletariat and de-classed elements, and held them together with soup kitchens and schnapps. The Nazis used these SA terrorists to attack party meeting places, public meetings, even public houses which were hosting festivities by left-wing workers' organisations. The terror campaign was intended to intimidate. The Storm Troops did not even shy away from murder.

In 1929, as I have already described, they shot at people leaving a peaceful public meeting of the KPD in the Ahlert Rooms. The victims included two dead and several injured. The authorities did nothing.

On another occasion, at around the same time, the Charlottenburg Workers' League organised a social in the Kaiser Friedrich Rooms, which were at the top of Spielhagen Strasse; the Communist Youth were also involved. Suddenly, late in the evening, several taxis drove up. SA terrorists jumped out, tore open the doors and shot into the festive crowd. Again there were dead and injured.

Most of these attacks involved the infamous 'Sturm 33' group, which was led by the 'Red Cockerel' (as Storm Leader Hahn was known because of his red hair) and by Maikovski, and was based in Hebbel Strasse. One comrade who lived in this street could only return to his house if accompanied. He received no police protection, such as was offered to 'upstanding citizens' in similar circumstances.

Once the Nazis tried to storm the 'Werner' in Wall Strasse — the Sturm 33 group was involved again — and to smash it up, as they had done repeatedly in other districts. The place was quite full that evening, since the RFB was holding a meeting. Although I had already been expelled from the party at this time, I was there too. I was there quite often to have discussions with people; quite a few sympathisers went there. The Nazis attacked from two sides, from Berliner Strasse and Weimar Strasse. A real battle developed. Wall Strasse was purely a workers' street. More and more workers appeared from their apartments to come to our assistance. A scrapyard near the pub served the workers as an arsenal. Together we beat the Fascists into retreat. Soon, members of the Workers' Samaritan League appeared, to treat our injured.

The Fascists often carried out attacks like this, but they never came back to Wall Strasse. Only when they took power, on 30 January 1933, did they come back out of the city centre and try to attack us again. They had no luck that night either: they had to retreat carrying the body of their leader Maikovski.

At the turn of the year 1929-1930, there was a fundamental discussion within the Lenin League about the Russian question, a question which had already played a significant role in the preceding months. After the departure of Ruth Fischer and Max Maslow shortly after the capitulation of the Zinoviev-Kamenev group in 1928, two groups had formed around this question, with quite different perceptions of the Soviet Union.

The group around comrades Grylewicz, Seipold, Joko and Schoeler, to which I belonged, based itself on the conception of Trotsky and the Internationalist Group, who defended the idea that the Soviet Union was still a workers' state, but a degenerated one ruled by a parasitic bureaucracy. The group around Hugo Urbahns, which included amongst others Deutschmann, Spieker and Spielberg, were of the opinion that the Soviet Union had ceased to be a proletarian state and that the Thermidor had been victorious.

Between 1923 and February 1930, our group was in close alliance with Hugo Urbahns' group in the struggle against the Stalinist bureaucracy. But when he then began to accuse the Communist Party of the Soviet Union and the Comintern leadership — which had ceased to be the class party of the international working class — of being agents of the counter-revolution, it became impossible for us to fight to correct the mistakes of the Communist Party from within the Lenin League.

Approximately half the members of the Lenin League left the organisation and continued working as an independent group under the name of 'United Left Opposition (Bolshevik-Leninists)'. Thus a long alliance of struggle ended in a split, but one that was necessary to prevent us from going down with the two workers' parties — although that is exactly what happened anyway.

The Lenin League had stopped being a faction of the Communist Party; it considered itself to be an independent organisation which had taken up the fight against Fascism and reaction quite separately from the two workers' parties. Apart from the *Flag of Communism*, the Lenin League was able to use the *People's Will* as its central organ and weekly paper — indeed, it appeared three times a week before the split.

For the Lenin League, the revolutionary party was no longer at the top of the agenda; Hugo Urbahns laid most stress on the formation of workers' councils. He thought that the party could be replaced by soviets. Workers' councils became a fetish for him. In January 1932, he spoke at a meeting against the Communist Party's claim for the leadership of the working class:

'The leadership will lie in the hands of the councils, which will be elected by the masses themselves, and not created at the command of a single party!'

Hugo Urbahns earned tremendous applause for this statement, but that was no proof that he was correct. On the contrary, according to the basic doctrine of Marxism and Leninism, the proletariat can only be victorious if it has created a revolutionary party beforehand. As oppositionist communists, we continued our fight for the Communist Party.

At first it was very difficult for us to continue our political work, since we had to start by finding a replacement for the *People's Will* and the *Flag of Communism*. In the beginning we had to be content with a bulletin sheet which appeared at irregular intervals. Only in July 1931 could we publish the first edition of the *Permanent Revolution*.

'The title of this newspaper is the slogan of a movement which has been opposed to the official leaders of the communist movement for a number of years: "permanent revolution" is the strategy on which the fight for freedom of the working class will proceed. The theory of "socialism in one country" which has been nurtured by Stalinism is the kernel of the incorrect policy now infecting the revolutionary workers' movement throughout the world. To claim that we can realise "socialism in one country" is no more and no less than to negate the international character of the social revolution.

'In Germany, the falsification of Marxism and Leninism has the effect of an increasingly obvious abandonment of international perspectives and an increasingly blatant stress upon the national standpoint. The slogan of "national and social liberation", the replacement of the Marxist concept of the social revolution by the un-Marxist concept of the "people's revolution" — these are sure signs of the ideological confusion in the leadership of our party.

'This confusion must be countered by a clear Marxist programme, whose kernel is the theory of "permanent revolution". "The socialist revolution begins on the national arena, develops internationally and ends in the world arena. As a result, the socialist revolution becomes a permanent revolution in a new and broader sense of the word: it does not end until the new society has won a final victory on our planet." (Trotsky)

'Permanent revolution therefore means for us a socialist revolution with definite international perspectives and the unconditional rejection of all those slogans about socialism within national boundaries or national liberation which have been borrowed from the arsenal of reformism and nationalism.'

With these Marxist conceptions we continued our fight against Stalinism. We also had to guard against the ideas of the Brandler opposition. They had actually taken up the fight against the Thälmann-Neumann-Ulbricht leadership on many German questions — united front, trade union policies — but they had no standards with which to gauge the Russian question.

In a situation where capitalism in Europe was rotting away, the German Social-Democratic bureaucracy represented the most rotten part of the Second International. It was neither willing to break out of the embrace of the bourgeois parties nor to take up the fight against the Fascist threat. And in this situation it also rejected its own left-wing workers. While reactionary forces were in league with the Storm Troops of the NSDAP in an attempt to deal the death blow to the Weimar republic, the leadership of Social Democracy refused to form a united front with the communists and the left-wing forces which had once been in the SPD.

The theory of social fascism made it very easy for them to reject any thought of a common struggle with the KPD. The SPD continued to rely on the parliamentary system and hoped to get a president — Hindenburg — in the presidential elections who would protect the national constitution, since, as they thought, the army obeyed the president. Hindenburg, so they claimed, would never permit the constitution to be undermined by the Fascists. And even if the Fascists dared to come out against the army and police, they were not strong enough, and would be defeated — so ran the thoughts of Social Democracy. Thus, the republic would win seven years' grace — since presidents were elected for a seven-year term — in which to stabilise the economy and crush the parties of dictatorship, and so stabilise the democratic system.

In the autumn, a left wing of the SPD, led by Seydewitz and Rosenfeld, split away. The differences between the left and the party leadership went back to 1929 (around the defence programme and the construction of battleships), when the left first made a concerted stand against the leadership at the Magdeburg congress of the SPD. When the party supported the state of emergency called by Brüning, the conflict reached its peak — or at least that is how it appeared in the liberal Berlin press. In reality, the Seydewitz-Rosenfeld group constituted a leadership that was continually being forced by the workers in the SPD to do something against the party's support for the bourgeois parties and the Brüning government.

The conflict between the party leadership and the 'left' leadership blew up over a secondary question, to wit, the right to publish the newspaper the *Torch* (*Der Fackel*). It is easy to believe Seydewitz and Rosenfeld when they stated that it was not their intention or desire to split, let alone to found a new party. They were not the lead players in this situation, but rather the unwilling participants; the socialist workers in the SPD were the ones who demanded a clear fighting programme. Even before the first national conference of the SAPD (Socialist Workers' Party of Germany) at the end of 1931, we told their leading comrades that, in a situation where everything was balanced on a knife edge, there was no room for a third party. Rather, they should see the necessity to enter the Communist Party with their 20,000 or 30,000 members, and so force Thälmann, Neumann and Ulbricht to perform a 180-degree turn in their policies and return to the Leninist path, since that was the only way to defeat Fascism. Instead, the SAPD leaders set out an eclectic mishmash of demands whose goal remained utterly obscure — a typical document of centrism.

We wrote in the *Permanent Revolution* of October-November 1931:

'The fact that it is possible in this situation to use such vapid policies and half-cocked ideas to rally perhaps 20,000-30,000 workers to a new version of the USPD is the strongest objection and the most damning indictment of the policies of the KPD leadership. If the central committee had not made serious mistakes, there would have been no power on earth to stop the SPD workers coming to communism in a new situation. However, they have made another mistake on top of the wrong tactics already adopted: we read in *Pravda* the description "left social fascists" in an article about the founding of the SAPD. Such a mistaken and foolish description, on top of all the other errors in the past, obstructs any application of a Leninist policy for a united front. The consequence of this phrase is that, at the first public meeting of the SAPD in Berlin, the discussion was conducted with fists and led to the break-up of the meeting.'

After Hitler had come to power I spoke to an official of the SAPD — in the prison at Luckau, where we were both doing time for 'conspiracy to commit high treason'. He answered my question as to the motives which had driven them to found the SAPD with the following argument. The betrayal by the SPD of the interests of the working class, and its unwillingness to defend democracy and the legal state, and the paralysis of the KPD by dogmas and its loss of influence among the factory workers, these were the factors which had forced them to found a third party. When I objected that both the SPD and the KPD had had millions of voters, and that the SPD was still strongly represented in factories and trade unions, he explained:

'We too had workers and were a workers' party. In Berlin, Breslau and in parts of Saxony we were also strongly represented in the factories, although we only had a few workers in our ranks in the rest of the country.'

'But how did you think that, in the short time left before the crisis, you could hope to rally the millions of workers and isolate at least the SPD? It must surely have been obvious to you that a revolutionary Marxist party can only lead the workers to victory if it has previously destroyed the mass basis of the SPD?'

This question remained unanswered; neither did the comrade have any idea at all of how Fascism could be defeated. We also discussed the appeal which our organisation had sent to the founding conference of the SAPD at the end of March 1932. He could remember it and said we were correct in many things. Here are some extracts from this appeal:

'Valued comrades! Your party congress is taking place a few months after the emergence of your organisation. We would like to take this opportunity to direct your attention in a comradely fashion to the questions which the present situation has placed at the top of the agenda.

'The emergence of the SAPD reflects on the one hand the deep crisis in the capitalist economy, and on the other hand both the class betrayal of Social Democracy and the serious mistakes made by the leadership of the KPD. These three factors determine the basis for your party's existence. The deep crisis in the economy and the tremendous sharpening of the class struggle with which it is connected will not permit a long life for a party wavering between reformism and communism. The complete bankruptcy of reformism and the unconcealed betrayal of the SPD have increased the dissatisfaction in the ranks of the social-democratic workers to the point where they have broken with reformism.

'But as a result of your incorrect evaluation of the Communist Party, you have no clear idea of the revolutionary solution, but rather only succeeded in creating tremendous ideological confusion within your own party concerning the basis of the revolutionary movement.

'That is why it is not enough to be correct about certain questions where the KPD is wrong; rather, the SAPD should make a fundamental declaration about what separates them from the Communist International.

If these differences are mainly only of a tactical and organisational nature, then why the need for a new party? Why not concentrate all your strength on a reform of the Communist Party and the Comintern? Why not support the left wing of the KPD in its fight for the reform of the Communist International? These questions must be answered clearly and unequivocally! It is no coincidence that the most important part of your declaration of principles is also the weakest and couched in the most general terms. You must prove clearly here what it is you want!'

Just how utterly undialectically the SAPD leadership approached the political problems posed to them by the political situation in 1931-1932 is shown by the parliamentary elections of 1932. In July, the KPD won a further 780,000 votes over and above the elections of 1930; the SPD lost more than 600,000 votes. In the November elections, the SPD lost another 710,000 votes, while the KPD won another 610,000. In Berlin, the Social Democrats lost over 75,000 votes, while the Communists could report an increase of 138,000. Against the 7.25 million votes of the SPD and the six million of the KPD, the SAPD only polled 45,000 in the parliamentary elections of 1932.

We knew that the elections did not resolve political problems, but the 1932 elections showed that trust in the Communist Party was not yet abandoned, that only the Stalinist line prevented the KPD from becoming the leader of the masses. The centrist stance of the SAPD, however, blinded it and befuddled its brain. It justified its step in forming a third force by pointing to the party-egotism of the Social-Democratic and Communist parties. The SAPD claimed that class interests rose above the party-egotism of the other two workers' parties. That is how the SAPD tried to establish its claim to lead the German working class.

In his pamphlet, *What Next? — Vital questions for the German proletariat*, Trotsky wrote in 1932:

'The SAPD is without a programme. We are not discussing the matter of a formal document; the programme holds water only in the event that its text is tied up with the revolutionary experience of the party and with the lessons gained from battles which have entered into the flesh and blood ot its cadres. The SAPD has none of these. The Russian Revolution, its separate stages, the struggle of its factions; the German crisis of 1923; the civil war in Bulgaria; the events of the Chinese revolutions; the battles of the British proletariat (1926); the revolutionary crisis in Spain — all these events, which must live in the consciousness of a revolutionist as luminous guideposts for the political road, are for the cadres of the SAPD only murky recollections culled from newspapers and not revolutionary experiences lived through and assimilated.' (Trotsky, *Germany 1931-1932*, 1970, pp129-130).

The SAPD was not armed with any of these fundamental principles. It rightly condemned the incorrect trade union policy of the KPD. But its criticism fell on arid ground and was thus equally false. Any weakening of the trade unions and social-democratic organisations must be rejected if one cannot use this to rally the members for actions directed against capitalism. Also incorrect was their alliance with the Brandler group and the Lenin League, and it was no use claiming that this alliance was only to help the propaganda for a united front. A united front is not built by forming propaganda alliances with small groups; a united front is built out of united action between social-democratic and communist organisations, that is between communist and social-democratic workers.

Wherever the SAPD intervened in struggles, it showed its contradictory position. They attempted to delay the fight against Fascism almost until the very point when it took power. Only under the influence the the KPD dissidents Paul Frölich, Jakob Walcher and August Enderle, who split from Brandler and Thalheimer in March 1932 and joined the SAPD, did the position of the SAPD alter, and they finally called for an immediate fight against Fascism. Misled by their impressions of the bureaucratic regime in the KPD, which had nothing in common with Lenin's democratic centralism, the SAPD had unfortunately 'thrown the baby out with the bathwater' and replaced Lenin's communism with Paul Levi's opportunism. He justified his transition to the reformist camp as follows:

'The organisational form in western Europe can only be that of open mass parties, which can therefore never be directed at the command of a central committee or the command of some central body.'

In August 1931 we issued a call in *Permanent Revolution* addressed 'To all communists! To the revolutionary proletariat of Germany!':

'Even today the position of the German bourgeoisie is not certain . . . It makes every attempt to hang on to its social order that has long since been outdated . . . How is it possible for the German bourgeoisie, whose weaknesses are so manifest, to stand up so strongly to the working class? The responsibility for this must lie firstly with the SPD and the trade union leaders who have held the workers back in their fight against the bourgeoisie, because they had to support "the lesser evil" of Br üning. The bourgeoisie not only achieved its goals without meeting resistance, but Fascism has also managed to continue growing . . . The role played by the SPD was made much easier by the incorrect policies of the present leadership of the KPD and Comintern.'

In the edition of October-November 1931, we addressed a call to the central committee of the KPD:

'We are writing this letter in full knowledge of the seriousness of the present situation. The events of the last few months have brought the crisis to such a point that we most likely face a decision now: either the seizure of power by the revolutionary proletariat, or, for the bourgeoisie, the possibility of crushing the workers' movement in blood with the terror of a Fascist regime . . .

'In the KPD's assessment of the danger, there are two main lines of thought:

'a) The victory of Fascism is the necessary prerequisite for the victory of the proletariat under the present conditions; we cannot "leap over" this stage. We are not throwing ourselves into the fire, but are rather playing a waiting game, by observing the unavoidable victory of Fascism and its equally inevitable collapse; then and only then will it be our turn. The rule of Fascism does not frighten us; it will destroy the economy faster than any other government!

'b) The victory of Fascism signifies the suffocation of the German revolution for years to come and also the certain death of the USSR; to prevent Fascism from coming to power is the revolutionary duty of the German proletariat; the fate of the proletariat is totally bound up with this task.

'We consider that the idea of retreating and so letting the Fascists seize power "provisionally", so that we can strengthen ourselves at its expense, is a *betrayal of the proletariat*. The experience of Italy speaks volumes. The Italian experience is as nothing compared to what European Fascism can achieve when supported by the bourgeois classes and the lumpen proletariat. Even if we accept that the proletariat will suffer a defeat in the decisive battle against Fascism, then this fight is still unavoidable and absolutely necessary. A defeat in battle is still preparation for the future. But to be defeated after a powerless capitulation simply means burying the future for decades to come.

'In addition to all that, we have no reason to believe that the decisive battle against Fascism *before* its seizure of power must necessarily end in defeat. The Fascists undoubtedly have the support of the professional fighting cadre of the officers; but the great mass of its hangers-on is largely composed of human dross, and their fighting qualities are significantly less than those of the proletariat.

'*Victory is possible, victory is probable, we must do everything to secure it.* That is the only possible way for revolutionaries to pose the question in the present situation.

'The question of the victory of Fascism in Germany is also a question of the fate of the USSR, regardless of whether you look at it from an economic, a political or a purely military point of view. But that means that the Soviet Union must throw all its forces into the fight, so that it is in a position to secure the future of the socialist economy in the USSR in inseparable connection with the future of the European revolution over Fascism. That is the only possible strategy for the Communist Party. The Communist Party must therefore adopt initial positions which are based on the irreconcilable and unconditional struggle against Fascism in order to destroy Fascism in the inevitable and open battles for the seizure of power.

'*The united revolutionary class action of the proletariat must be organised against the victory of Fascism.* This can only be realised if all revolutionary forces, regardless of which camp they currently find themselves in, unite for this common and immediate action. We are quite aware of the fact that the conditions for this are extremely unfavourable. Despite this and because of the seriousness of the situation, history calls upon the KPD to attempt to create a true unity of struggle within our class.

'We therefore propose the following:

'That the KPD approaches all political groups, trade unions and workers' organisations who declare themselves ready to fight Fascism, with the aim of issuing a common appeal for *a joint campaign of action against Fascism.* This appeal must include:

'1. The creation of action committees with representatives from factories, trade unions, political groups and other workers' organisations. It is of the greatest importance that the action committees truly reflect the various tendencies of the revolutionary workers in the localities.

'2. The joint action campaign should call a constitutional congress with delegates from these action committees throughout the whole country, and this should be called in the shortest possible time. This congress must represent the concentration of the proletariat against the concentration of reaction.

'3. The congress must be organised from the start as a proletarian parliament in opposition to a possible Fascist parliament or a Fascist government comprising extra-parliamentary or parliamentary forces.

'4. The congress must address three tasks concretely: a) the preparation for a general strike to prevent Hugenberg and Hitler taking power; b) the formation of a joint, cross-party workers' militia; c) the elaboration of a common minimum programme which will decide the next steps to be undertaken by the action committees.

'Although defensive in character, this action would, under the correct leadership and given the objective possibilities mentioned above, contain all the elements necessary not only for the proletariat to pass to the offensive against Fascism but also for the overthrow of the bourgeoisie itself.'

Wherever we had our strongest support — in Oranienburg in Berlin and in Bruchsal in south-west Germany — we did not content ourselves with appeals to the KPD, the SAPD and the Lenin League; here we also proceeded to turn directly to the workers in the factories. In Oranienburg we had a strong group; comrade Schneeweiss, an active party worker, had won the majority of the local KPD branch to his ideas, with the help of a few comrades from Oranienburg and the district organisation of the Left Opposition (Bolshevik-Leninists). The Stalinists got no joy from starting to expel people: on the contrary, the expulsion of Helmut Schneeweiss and his friends in the party simply meant that even more comrades supported him.

In Oranienburg it was possible to conduct public meetings without the Stalinists being able to interrupt them. In effect, the group around comrade Schneeweiss, working closely with the Left Opposition, constituted the local Communist Party to the outside world. Their meetings, which were attended by up to 600 people and at which I spoke along with other comrades from the national leadership of the Left Opposition, resulted in Committees for a United Front being set up in Oranienburg and the surrounding district, in which the KPD also participated. Comrade Ruf, a KPD town councillor, repeatedly stated at these committees that it was high time that a united front was formed, since that was the only way to prise the SPD workers away from their leaders.

In Schmachtenhagen, Sachsenhausen and Birkenweder, other Committees for a United Front were formed. The SPD participated officially, while the KPD always tried to break up the committees.

In Birkenweder, the KPD under the leadership of their comrade Schnellbacher finally 'succeeded', by resigning from the committee with their representatives. His reason: the formation of a united front depended on the level of maturity of the workers and could only be realised if a high enough level had been reached.

After the ban on the RFB in 1929, Helmut Schneeweiss seized the initiative and set up his own self-defence organisation which was recruited mostly from erstwhile RFB comrades. Helmut Schneeweiss came early on to the workers' movement; in 1920 he had joined the communist youth organisation. He won the trust of the Oranienburg workers in the unemployment movement, and he was always an active official of the KPD until his expulsion. In 1927-1928 he made up his mind to leave the KPD because he thought that its policies would lead it into isolation. However, he stayed on and soon found his way to the Opposition. His expulsion from the party followed a well-attended meeting addressed by Hugo Urbahns, at which the audience got really carried away.

The small town of Oranienburg always had a high percentage of unemployment; after 'Black Friday' it rose to sixteen per cent. Comrade Schneeweiss also chaired the Unemployed Committee at that time. In his negotiations with the mayor, he always managed to get subsidies for the unemployed which were over the average. He marched on the town hall with 2,000 unemployed and went into the mayor's office with a delegation. At one of these meetings, the mayor said to him: 'Schneeweiss, you act as if you owned half the world.'

To which Schneeweiss replied: 'I represent 2,000 hungry unemployed people against a single well-fed mayor who has no conception of the hardship suffered by the hungry millions.'

As early as 1923, this same mayor, again during discussions about a particular problem of the unemployed, asked whether Schneeweiss was a member of the Communist Party. Schneeweiss replied:

'It is not my party membership which is under discussion here, but the problems of the unemployed; you would do well to make a note of that.'

After the meeting at which Hugo Urbahns spoke, Helmut Schneeweiss turned to us and asked for a discussion. I was appointed by the national leadership to speak to him. I explained our position to him in lengthy discussions. I told him that, unlike Hugo Urbahns and the Lenin League, we still regarded the Soviet Union as a degenerate workers' state ruled by a parasitic bureaucracy, and that only by a reform of the party could we return to a class policy of the Leninist type; this, and not the formation of a third party, was the only way to gain a victory over Fascism. Helmut Schneeweiss accepted these points of view and joined the Left Opposition (Bolshevik-Leninists).

On 1 May 1932, comrade Schneeweiss managed to get all the proletarian organisations — with the sole exception of the KPD — to participate in a joint demonstration, and afterwards they all worked together in the fight against Fascism and reaction. The KPD tried to organise its own demonstration, but it only managed a meeting with 60 people.

Leon Sedov, Trotsky's son, who was studying in Berlin, came to Oranienburg on several occasions to meet comrade Schneeweiss and his friends. At the end of 1932, after discussions in Copenhagen with Trotsky which I also attended, Roman Well, a leading member of the Left Opposition (Bolshevik-Leninists) — but also, as it later turned out, an agent of the Soviet secret police — tried to get comrade Schneeweiss to return to the Communist Party, because, according to Well, the present situation made it possible for work inside the KPD to meet with more success than work from outside. Schneeweiss refused. Even earlier, the Berlin-Brandenburg district leadership tried to win comrade Schneeweiss and his group back to the party, but these attempts, like Well's later one, failed. The KPD, with no arguments left, tried to spread slanders and accused him of criminal activities, a method which they had tried earlier on other comrades — but again they had no success.

In Oranienburg, the Left Opposition (Bolshevik-Leninists) held the initiative, for even the SPD workers participated in the formation of a Committee for a United Front. Our comrades in Bruchsal in Baden worked from the same perspectives. We held the initiative in Erkenschwick in the Ruhr as well.

At a meeting called by the unemployed and welfare workers, attended by more than a thousand workers, our comrades called the political tune. After a speech by a comrade from the Left Opposition, the meeting voted to form a fighting committee in which all organisations would be represented, which would fight for the interests of the unemployed and for a political struggle on the basis of a united front. At the next meeting, which was supported by similar numbers, the Left Opposition proposed a resolution which called for a common struggle against Fascism, and an alliance which would include both works committees and unemployed committees to answer any attempts to reduce wages or unemployment benefit with strikes and demonstrations. The district committee of the ADGB, the German trade union federation, was called upon to organise the fight for the rights of the working population outside the district.

At another meeting which followed, also attended by factory workers, it was decided to pursue a political line on the basis of the united front, as follows: against the dictatorship of the generals and against Fascism; against any reduction in wages or benefits; for a 40-hour week, with no cut in wages; for workers' control of production; for a national alliance of works and unemployed committees; for the defence of the Soviet Union.

These proposals were circulated to the leaders of the KPD, the SPD, the ADGB, the Anti-Fascist League and the Reichsbanner, in order to unite all these organisations on this basis. The resolution was accepted unanimously and published as an open letter in various newspapers, and at the same time distributed in large numbers as a leaflet. At an enormous meeting, the like of which Erkenschwick had not seen for years, attended by all the workers' organisations, an action committee was formed. Represented on this were the Unemployed Committee and the KPD with three seats each and the SPD and ADGB with two each, all other organisations having one seat each.

In Berlin the leadership of the KPD tried to stop our activities every way they could. For example, we printed leaflets with the appeal originally published in our October-November issue, and handed them out in all the workers' districts and outside the factories, and pasted them to walls late at night.

The party mobilised the Communist Youth League to prevent us from pasting up these leaflets. The young member named Schönwald, a nephew of Hermann Remmele, organised so-called 'ambush commandos' who drove through the streets in vans belonging to the *Evening World* newspaper and hurled stones at our bill stickers. Once they also tried to chase us away with clubs, but that did not turn out very well for them.

Since our finances were very limited indeed, our newspapers could only appear in a very limited print run (4,000 copies). Larger runs could only be done for special editions. On the other hand, our pamphlets, which were mostly written by Trotsky, reached a far larger circle of politically-interested workers; the pamphlet *What Next? Vital questions for the German proletariat* was published in an edition of 10,000 copies and then went into several reprints. The same went for the pamphlets *Against National Socialism*, *Will Fascism really be victorious?* and *How can National Socialism be defeated?*

So that large numbers of Berlin workers could find out what was necessary in these historic times, we painted in capital letters two feet high outside the large factories the slogan: 'Trotsky demands: a workers' united front between SPD and KPD!'

This was especially effective in places where the river Spree and the canals ran past the factories, for we could paint the slogan on the embankments, at Zwietusch in Charlottenburg, for example, and opposite the Siemens works in Siemensstadt. We carried out this work with four comrades, two painting and two on the lookout. Once we even painted outside the Russian Embassy in Unter den Linden. There, comrade Müller was arrested, while the others managed to escape, but she was not even charged. In 1948, after my arrest by the Russian military authorities, they also charged me with that one, although they had no proof at all.

Although my apartment only consisted of a single room, from the spring of 1931 until autumn 1932 it became the 'committee room' of the national leadership. My wife protested many times. Although she was convinced of the necessity of the political work, as I was, she considered that we should conduct these meetings in a pub instead of smoking up a small apartment. But, for reasons of security, we did not want to move to a pub.

At that time there were already arguments between, on the one side, Roman Well and his brother Adolf Senin, and the majority of the national leadership on the other side, although no one knew at that time what role the two brothers played as paid agents of the Stalinists. Leon Sedov, Trotsky's son, regularly took part in the political life of the organisation.

His main work, however, consisted in the publication of the Russian Bulletin, the organ of the Russian Opposition, which was printed on the same presses as the *Permanent Revolution*. Although comrade Sedov, in common with every member of the national leadership, was fully conversant with all details of our political work, he too knew nothing of the intentions of the two brothers. And that is not to mention the fact that Senin was the link man between the German organisation and Trotsky until November 1932. With his wife, Leon Sedov was one of the last to leave Berlin after the victory of Fascism in the spring of 1933, when he moved to France. Until that time I was in continuous contact with him.

At the turn of the year 1931-1932, the factories owned by the Berlin town council cut the working week by three hours. This meant that, in the administrative offices and the technical departments, every second Saturday was not worked. I used this Saturday to discuss with workers and unemployed in and around the labour exchange and to offer them our material, newspapers and pamphlets. Almost every time, I came into conflict with officials of the KPD. By contrast, a rational discussion was possible with comrades of the SAPD and SPD. At least where we were involved, the KPD people could still not tolerate opposition communists criticising their doctrinaire policies.

They called us agents of imperialism and counter-revolutionaries, and threatened that, when they were in power, they would have us all shot. My reply to this was: 'If you surprise us all and come to power, we shall be quite happy to stand before your rifles, but we fear that we shall meet each other again in prison.'

On 20 July 1932, Franz von Papen ended the activities of the Social-Democratic government of Prussia with the aid of one lieutenant and ten men, and the SPD appealed neither to the Prussian police nor the millions of workers in factories and unemployment offices for them to defend a constitutionally elected government, but rather declared that it was only yielding to force. On that day, it became clear to us that the victory of Fascism was inevitable. A party which had the support of the Prussian police — at least, that is what they always said — as well as millions of factory workers, but was still unwilling to fight in such a situation, is condemned to defeat. The only tragic thing was that, with the SPD, millions of workers were also disenfranchised.

It was clear to us that we would have to prepare for underground activity. Directly after 20 July, we discussed in the national leadership what steps were necessary in order not to be taken by surprise by illegality. Then, in the first days of August 1932, we reconstructed our organisation into cells of five; each cell in the districts had to be quite sure which comrades they could take underground. In the event of illegality, our newspaper would no longer be issued as *Permanent Revolution*, but would be published as *Our Word (Unser Wort)*.

Despite all this we did not neglect our agitational work. Both our meetings and our discussion evenings continued, and we still attended meetings called by our opponents where our comrades spoke up in the discussions. In Nürnberger Strasse in Charlottenburg there was a fairly large meeting hall which was maintained by all the opposition groups, including ourselves. What we called 'Contradictory Evenings' were held there; it was the only place where a proper discussion could be conducted and where even comrades from the KPD took part. We had left the Lenin League because we did not wish to disappear into isolation with it on account of its sectarian behaviour. The formation of the Left Opposition (Bolshevik-Leninists) was then the necessary and only way to fight for the Leninist line with communist workers, and still continue as a faction of the KPD.

After leaving the Lenin League, we kept in contact with it, just as we had kept in contact with the comrades of the Committed Left in the years 1925 to 1929, although comrades like those grouped around Ernst Schwarz had formed an extra-parliamentary group on the model of the one formed by Otto Rühle in 1919. This group refused to form a united front with the social-democratic organisations, and refused to work in the reformist trade unions.

We were convinced that these ultra-left groups had no substance and so would simply fold up when faced with our arguments. In the Charlottenburg district we were able to recruit 95 per cent of the membership of this group, and in Berlin as a whole and throughout the rest of the country we were able to win the majority of the Committed Left. There were only loose contacts with the SAPD and the Communist Party Opposition (Brandler group). During the period of illegality, it was possible to recruit members from the Lenin League. With the recruitment from the Committed Left — some eighteen comrades of both sexes were involved — our Charlottenburg group rose to over 40 members. Immediately afterwards, a number of younger comrades from the Communist Youth League and the Anti-Fascist League joined our group. We had organisational successes in all the other districts of Berlin and the rest of the country. Ninety per cent of our members were workers and some of them were still in the factories.

Despite this, the Charlottenburg group was too weak to undertake any independent actions along the lines of those in Oranienburg, Bruchsal and Erkenschwick. The large majority of committed revolutionary workers still placed their trust in the Communist Party. In conversation they were happy to give us credit in many matters and they supported us in discussions with KPD members.

We summarised our policies in a leaflet for the workers in factories and unemployment offices. We pointed to the dangers then threatening the German working class. We defended ourselves politically against the theory of the inevitable collapse of capitalism, which was propounded both by the KPD and by sections of the SPD. Our position was that capitalism would always find a way out if it was not overthrown by the working class. We pointed to the steadily increasing danger posed by Fascism if the working class, through its parties, was not ready to bring capitalism down. Capitalism would make use of the National Socialists to smash the workers' organisations and give total power to the monopolies. Because of the tremendous danger, we kept repeating our calls and appeals, which were directed primarily at the KPD, in order to try to pull it back from its ruinous policies at the last minute.

Thus, for example, when Papen dissolved parliament in September 1932, we wrote:

'No to a referendum — yes to extra-parliamentary action! Demand an immediate conference of all works committees and unemployed committees!

'A government which has not been elected by parliament has dissolved parliament. On 12 September all the democratic rights gained by the workers in the struggles of 1918 were taken away. With the help of Brüning and the path smoothed by the Social-Democratic leaders, the Papen government has set up a dictatorship. The illusions that the majority of the people determine the politics of a state are completely shattered. Never before has there been such a clear justification of the communist theory that parliament is merely an instrument of the trust-kings, bank-barons and the lords of agriculture. The bourgeoisie is acting outside parliament and spits on the decisions of the majority of the people.

'In this situation, with the bourgeoisie only acting outside parliament, it becomes obvious to everyone that the working class can only defend itself by using the same methods . . .

'Defend democratic rights; organise mass strikes against the Papen programme; call a congress of works committees and unemployed committees to take concrete measures for this defensive action.' (*Permanent Revolution*, third week of September 1932.)

Particularly during the presidential election of 13 March 1932, when we tried to throw our political weight into the scalesith a special edition of *Permanent Revolution*, we found that not only sympathising workers in the KPD, but also many SAPD comrades and Social-Democratic workers were in agreement with our ideas:

'For a workers' united front! Against the dictatorship of the generals! Against any reduction in wages or benefits! For the 40-hour week! For workers' control of production!'

They fought for these slogans alongside us. The desire for unity existed among large parts of the working class: only the leaders of the two workers' parties worked against it. The KPD did not want to back down from its theory of social fascism, while the leaders of the SPD played down the dangers and based themselves on parliamentary activity.

We went into 1933 in the knowledge that the victory of Fascism could no longer be prevented. In the final four weeks, our activities increased in spite of everything, because it was clear that the fight would continue, indeed that it had to continue. We had predicted often enough that, if Hitler's march to power was not prevented by a united front of the workers, then it would be a long time before Fascism was smashed. The Nazi terror became even greater. Now it was not only the SA involved in attacks, but also the SS.

Whereas previously the Party had simply defended itself against National Socialist attacks, with the aid of the Communist Youth and the 'Antifa' (Anti-Fascist Action League), now the illegal RFB attacked the meeting places of the SA along with people from Antifa. I was able to convince comrades at the places where the Antifa met that actions like that could lead nowhere except to fatalities and injuries:

'The NSDAP needs actions like these because they mistakenly believe that they can intimidate the militant workers. But we must mobilise the entire working class; with individual actions like these we will only alienate a section of the workers. It should be your duty to convince more and more workers of the necessity for the political struggle, and to prepare your organisation for the last battle against Fascism.'

Many young workers, who already belonged to the Antifa, understood this. In the first days of January 1933 there was a confrontation between the Nazis and people from Antifa, who were on their way home from a meeting at a pub in Schiller Strasse (the 'Schillerglocke'). At the corner of Schiller and Wilmesdorfer Strasse, the Antifa people were attacked by the SS; eye witnesses reported that the SS man named von der Ahe was killed by shots from his own friends. There were arrests, not of SS people, but of a few Antifa members, including the leader of the Antifa in Charlottenburg, a young worker who was also a member of the Communist Youth League. Richard Hüttig was his name, and it could be proved that he was at a central meeting in the city centre on that evening; in spite of this he was accused of murder and incitement. His trial took place at the end of 1933; he was condemned to death and executed. Today, his picture hangs in the Charlottenburg town hall in honourable memory of a resistance fighter.

My wife was almost dragged into this trial as well. She had been a member and active official of the Workers' Samaritan League for several years. Someone had accused her of being present at the scene of the crime. In reality, on that evening she had been at the meeting place of the Samaritan League in Wall Strasse, listening to a talk by a doctor. In spite of this, our apartment was searched immediately after 30 January 1933. Fortunately she had not used her first-aid box recently and it was dusty, and so could not have been used in the previous few weeks.

In the judgement of the crime investigator, 'This woman cannot possibly have been at the scene of the crime.' Luckily there were more than 50 witnesses, including the doctor, who had seen my wife at the meeting.

On 5 January 1933, the Nazis demonstrated at Bülow Platz: directly opposite stood Karl Liebknecht House, headquarters of the KPD. This was a great provocation by the NSDAP, but the demonstration was permitted to go ahead by the Berlin police president — unlike the time on 1 May 1929 when every demonstration was banned and 28 workers were killed. The Central district, like the surrounding districts, was a working-class one. The Communist Party called for a counter-demonstration to protect Karl Liebknecht House. Tens of thousands of workers answered the call, and we took part as well. A strong cordon of workers protected the party headquarters. The police tried to break up our demonstration but did not succeed. The SA columns remained outside Bülow Platz. Finally, the police deployed two armoured cars, but again without success. The workers controlled the streets of the Central district until late at night. It was the last big demonstration in which the Berlin working class showed its willingness to fight.

10.

IMPRISONED BY THE NAZIS

In the decisive days leading up to 30 January 1933, our members were active at all the meeting places in the districts of Berlin, holding discussions with comrades; I worked from party headquarters, the 'Werner' in Wall Strasse. I was there on 30 January as well. In the last days, even the comrades of the KPD and the RFB became certain that Hitler would win. Only the extent of the victory remained unclear to most of them.

In the evening, the report came over the radio: Hitler had been handed the office of Chancellor by President Hindenburg. There was pandemonium; workers came into the building from Wall Strasse and the streets around — Wall Strasse being a workers' street — and everyone wanted to know: what happens now? We put forward the proposal that party officials and known members of the party should keep away from their homes, for we had to expect massive arrests.

The place was full to bursting, hundreds more comrades and sympathisers stood out on the street. Then the word raced through the crowd: some columns of the SA and SS, who had been screaming their adulation of Hitler at the Chancellery, were now marching back to their districts. And indeed, after a short time, we heard the marching columns, singing the 'Horst Wessel' and shouting 'Death to the communists', and getting closer. One column, including Storm Troop 33, now came up Berliner Strasse from the 'Knee' (today's Ernst Reuter Platz). They turned into Wall Strasse and, as they had tried several times before, they launched an attack on the 'Werner'. But on this evening of 30 January, once more the Nazis were sent home with bloody heads.

Barely another twenty minutes had passed before a comrade came into the pub and told us that there had been another confrontation with the SA in Richard Wagner Strasse, during which the SA had fired shots. Their 'storm leader' Maikovksi was reported to have been shot dead by his own people during this shoot-up.

We stayed together that night until the grey dawn, and naturally we discussed the events of the past few hours and the attack by the SA. Even the party officials present were in a pacifist mood that night. I had already arranged with my wife a few weeks earlier that she should put a prearranged signal at the window if there was any danger. I could see our apartment from Krummer Strasse, and since there was nothing at the window, I quickly went upstairs to tell her that I would stay at my sister's for safety's sake. I met my wife there every day, for we had heard of extensive arrests. It was primarily the SA, who had been appointed as the auxiliary police nationwide, who carried out the house searches and arrests. Since there had been nothing at my apartment yet, I went back home. I later learned that they wanted to come and get me as well, but that the owner of the shop in our building, who supported the SA, had prevented them.

This man was an enthusiastic agitator for his party. When I came home from the surveyor's office in the late afternoon, there were always many people, including a lot of workers, standing in front of his shop, talking. The SA man had a habit of reading aloud from Hitler's *Mein Kampf*, and always argued on the basis of the latest edition. Since I also possessed a copy of *Mein Kampf* — a first edition — I made a note of all passages which were different and, when I took part in the discussion, told him that what he was saying was not quite right.

Then I would go upstairs and fetch my copy of the book and had the last laugh when I proved to him that the passages were different in the two editions. Later he spoke to me and asked me whether he might discuss things with me. I agreed and invited him to my apartment where we talked about various topics related to Marxism-Leninism and 'National Socialism'. Naturally we could not change each others' minds. I do not know whether these discussions accounted for his intervention on my behalf.

In February 1933 we held yet another discussion evening in Wieland Strasse in Charlottenburg. More than a hundred people came to the premises, and I had agreed to give a talk. The theme was: 'Hitler has won — what now?' I had been speaking for about half an hour when suddenly the windows shattered, the doors were thrown open and police and SA auxiliary police stormed in and announced that everyone was under arrest. We were led out with our hands above our heads, and the police lorries were already waiting to take us to the Berlin police headquarters on Alexander Platz.

Since the police cells were already overflowing we were accommodated in the corridors on the upper floors of the building. After the initial interviews, most of those arrested were released. At that time, only the key positions of the state apparatus were occupied by the Nazis. For myself and a number of other comrades, our stay at the police headquarters lasted a while longer. My 'interrogator' had previously been a Social Democrat, and told me that he had not long to go before picking up his pension and would be happy to get out of this building. Luckily for me, no one knew who my examiner had been and I was released along with the other comrades, and was able to continue working in the surveyor's office, after I had explained to Director Teschner why I had not been at work.

A great feeling of despair spread among the members of the KPD, but more especially amongst the RFB people, because of the capitulation to Fascism; many RFB people joined the SA. This transfer of allegiance, however, did not limit itself to the RFB — many members of the Reichsbanner applied to the SA for membership. Even in the political parties — especially in the SPD and the State Party — there were people who carried three membership cards in their pockets: that of their own party, and then one for the KPD and one for the NSDAP. For a long time after 30 January, they only ever pulled the NSDAP card out.

The greater part of the comrades in the national leadership of the Left Opposition initially went underground, and eventually emigrated. Apart from comrade Eugen Bauer (Erwin Ackerknecht) and Leon Sedov, Alfred Schoeler and myself, there were hardly any members of the national leadership left in Berlin. Fritz Belleville, responsible for Frankfurt and the southern German region, was still in Frankfurt. Anton Grylewicz must have left Berlin immediately after 30 January and emigrated to Prague, where he was soon arrested by the authorities, acting on information from the local Stalinists, and was only set free again after an intervention by the left-wing Social Democrats.

Oskar Seipold had left Berlin for East Prussia. This district was one he had represented as a member of the Prussian parliament, where he had joined the Left Opposition and where he organised our work.

Comrade Bauer was in Berlin until the middle of May, and we organised our work with him. Agitation by discussion had become dangerous, since no one knew any more who supported what. So we pasted leaflets and small posters at the most important spots, particularly near large factories. Only the leader of each group of five knew which streets were going to be postered. We were out on the streets again on 28 February; comrade Klemz and his group were late and did not go with us. At Lietzov Platz — a square near the Charlottenburg town hall — he met us, quite out of breath: 'The Reichstag building is on fire!'

We immediately stopped our work and went to my apartment to clean ourselves up. Brushes and paste pot had already been hidden by the roadside. When I led the comrades back downstairs again, we were stopped by the police, who searched us, but found nothing incriminating.

We managed to publish another two editions of our paper *Our Path* (*Unser Weg*) in Berlin, but after that we had no further opportunity since our printer refused to do the work. In the meantime we could only manage to keep our comrades and sympathisers informed by means of short bulletins. From April onwards we began to receive *Our Word*, which was smuggled over the German border from Basel. We received 300 papers this way, but that was not nearly enough to deliver to all our comrades and friends.

We managed to find a solution. In the town of Lüneburg, where I was having a holiday, I got to know a comrade who had once been a member of the Communist Workers' Party (KAP). He was prepared to work with us, and we developed a close friendship with him and his family which lasted until his death in 1968. With his help and that of a photographer, we photographed the paper on to one frame 13 centimetres by 18 centimetres; a magnifying glass which was bought at Woolworths for three marks was delivered along with the photo to our friends and comrades, who could then read the paper quite normally.

There was another important problem to be overcome: on the premises of the Energia Press, at 91 Gitschiner Strasse, Berlin SW61, where the *Permanent Revolution* and our pamphlets had been printed, there were stored some 2,000 pamphlets, including Trotsky's *What Next?* A decision was taken by the national leadership to save this material whatever the risks. We agreed with a Charlottenburg comrade, Gustav Schröder, who had a job as janitor at 44 Leibniz Strasse, and with Franz Wegner, a comrade from the Berlin district leadership who was later part of the national leadership, that Wegner and I would transport the material, while Schröder would ensure that it was sealed in behind a brick wall in the boiler-room at number 44 Leibniz Strasse.

We borrowed from a friend of my wife's a handcart about six feet long. We walked from Charlottenburg to Gitschiner Strasse with this cart. Prior to this we had observed the printworks for a few days, since the Gestapo had searched the works several times in February, but, as the printers (members of the KPD) told us, they failed to discover the pamphlets. We had got a supply of rags from a comrade who owned a wholesale business. Within half an hour we had managed to get the pamphlets tied up in packets, down the stairs, thrown the rags over them and were off with our cargo back to Charlottenburg.

The very same day we built a second wall in front of the piles of pamphlets, and no one but us three knew of their existence. Only in 1945, after the occupation by the Allied Forces, did they again see the light of day. It almost ended badly: comrade Schröder, who had separated from his wife during the war, had married a KPD sympathiser who wanted to hand the pamphlets over to her own party. We learned of this just in time and were able to prevent it.

There was another crisis: when all production stopped in Berlin, the water-table rose by more than a metre and most basements were flooded, including the one in Leibniz Strasse. Some of the pamphlets were floating on the water, but after we had dried them out they were still usable. I stored the rest of them at my home and that of my daughter.

In this situation, where the best forces of the German working class had taken up the fight against Fascist barbarity, a letter circulated amongst the comrades of the SAPD. It was written by the chair of the ADGB, Leipart, to his friend Wilhelm Keil. He wrote:

'I could not answer you earlier and can only do so today with a few words, since, as you will understand, I cannot get much peace in these disturbed times. Unfortunately, this also affects my health, which has never been very robust. In my lecture at the School of Politics, which I repeated shortly afterwards at the Academic and Political Club in Munich, I included a great deal of national warmth.

'For example, when I mentioned the various official speeches made on radio etc., I said that they had deeply injured my national feeling and that my German heart had been filled with sorrow. For it is a real disgrace to see what is now being done to the prestige and reputation of the German people. Naturally many mistakes have been made — we have already spoken about them face to face. But I still do not understand the party leadership. Where has Breitscheid got to? — I recently asked Otto Wels, who seems to be quite lost and has no idea what to do. I have no intention of making any more political statements, for I do not consider that to be wise, given my responsibilities.

'My primary concern must be for the trade unions, for it is possible that some good may now come of the fact that I have always been somewhat retiring in the political sense.'

And here is an extract from a report of a meeting of the national committee of the ADGB, on 5 April 1933:

'Leipart began with a report on the developments of the last few weeks and the measures taken by the national committee. The discussion regarding the role of the trade unions in the new state is now in full swing. Up until now there has been no clarity about the future organisational form of the trade unions and the limits to their authority. In its declaration of 20 March and in repeated statements to government authorities, the national committee had made clear that it recognised only one guiding principle for its activity, and that was to advance the economic and social interests of the working population.

'Although the trade unions have dedicated themselves to this task in the past few weeks just as they have done for decades, there have been many cases where their property and institutions had been subject to attack and the activity of their officials blocked. The trade unions have a right to the protection of the state. All the more when their political behaviour and activities have given no cause at all for violence . . .

'The trade unions believe that any German government should be proud of the national effectiveness of the trade unions, which has lasted through war and peace. Their history is one of the mobilisation of the determined forces of the German people for the construction of a social order which has created the spiritual and legal basis for the inner unity of the nation.

'The value of this work of national education was particularly significant during the fateful times of world war. But in every crisis of the postwar period, the trade unions were still the bearers and vanguard of the will to unity among the German people and of the fight for its independence. The trade unions proclaim their allegiance to the nation; this means that workers direct their efforts of their own free will for the good of the whole people. No German government can close its eyes to this fact . . .

'The reconstruction of the economy after the war, and the securing of its existence in the face of the unforeseeable catastrophes in the recent crises — these would be unthinkable without the education of the German workers in spiritual and social responsibility. The trade unions therefore believe they have a right to expect that their historic contribution should be recognised by a government which has set itself the great goal — also recognised by the workers — of founding the inner and outer liberty of the nation of the creative forces of the entire people.'

So, while tens of thousands of trade unionists, SPD and KPD members, and even workers belonging to no party, lay in the torture chambers of the Gestapo or were suffering in prisons and concentration camps, in these very same days the politically rotten leadership of the trade unions had the gall to throw themselves dishonourably at the feet of the Fascists.

But it did not stop there. They also thought they should do something more to gain recognition as the paid torturers of the nation. Thus, the ADGB leaders gave out a statement in which they broke off all ties with the SPD and called on all their members and officials to take part in the rallies organised by the Hitler government on 1 May at Tempelhof Field.

The organised workers and most unorganised workers refused to follow the trade union leadership, and stayed at home. All attempts to cajole them came to nothing. Then, on 2 May, the trade union offices were occupied and transformed into offices of the 'German Workers' Front'.

While the Communist Party had been banned directly after the seizure of power, the SPD continued at first to be legal, and its elected representatives still sat in parliament. They too tried to save themselves. While the executive of the Second International protested against the terrorism of the national government, demanded the release of those imprisoned and called for the reintroduction of democracy, the party chair, Otto Wels, resigned from the Bureau of the International, in order to distance himself from this criticism of the Hitler government.

But this did not help them, nor did their parliamentary vote in favour of Hitler's 'Peace Resolution' on 17 May 1933, nor their denunciation of their own executive members then in exile. The party was banned, their seats annulled.

Just as the SPD had conducted their policy of civil peace during the First World War, in the closest possible collaboration with the 'all German' nationalists and the Hohenzollerns, so in 1933 they now tried to preserve legal status — at the price of collaboration with the NSDAP.

Nor did the bourgeois parties act any differently; they had supported the Weimar state together with Social Democracy, and now they voted for Hitler's Enabling Act. One of the best-known MPs belonging to the State Party, Theodor Heuss, campaigned in his party for a vote in favour of the Enabling Act. Despite this, Heuss managed to be elected the first President of the German Federal Republic after 1945.

After my first arrest in February 1933, my wife and I were both certain that my regained 'freedom' would only be of short duration. The national leadership had decided — with my vote being cast against it — that I should go to Switzerland with Fritz Belleville to organise underground work from there; I refused, giving as my reason the fact that political work must suffer if all the leading comrades were out of the country.

Since I possessed an extensive library, including important documents dealing with the work in the KPD and the International, I talked over with my wife how best to safeguard the books. At first we thought about my sister, but since my brother-in-law was an unreliable fellow when it came to politics, we rejected that idea. My wife's brother was not even considered. So that only left my niece, who, with her husband, had a summerhouse in Röntgen Strasse.

Both were happy to agree. Since it was not possible, for safety reasons, to transport them all at once, we moved the books packet by packet. We had already removed some of them when, one day, my wife was taking some more over; she stopped on the way to ask my sister if her daughter was already at the summerhouse. Suddenly she was stopped down in the courtyard by SA auxiliary police and told to hand over the package. Since she refused, she was taken away to the police station in Kaiser Friedrich Strasse.

My wife was neither prepared to say what she was doing with the books, nor to tell them where I was or where I worked. But the police must have found out my place of work some other way, for a few hours later they turned up in Ruhleben where we were surveying near the Underground station.

Then I was taken to the Kaiser Friedrich Strasse police station as well. In a short interview, I explained to the officers that the books were very valuable to me and that I had asked my wife to get them out of our apartment. But my sister had refused to keep them for me. Fortunately, my wife was quite close during this interview, and could hear what I was saying. She was released again, while I was taken away with other prisoners at midnight in a big police assault vehicle to the police headquarters on 'Alex' Platz.

A heavy machine-gun was fixed to the top of the driver's cab, and to the side and the back stood policemen armed with carbines. We went firstly to the police cells, where nothing at all happened for two days. Then on the third day the first interrogation took place; I was accused of instructing my wife to move the books in order that we could make new leaflets against the 'national government' with this material. I denied this accusation and told them that if I had intended to use the books in question as the basis for subversive material, then I would hardly have taken them to my sister, who was completely apolitical.

Further interrogation sessions took place, and the officers involved were almost always the same as those when I was first arrested. As I later learned, the previous officials were replaced only in early summer with members of the NSDAP. After I had refused to sign a report, even at the risk of being moved to Oranienburg, which is what they threatened me with, I was released again.

Once again I was accepted back into the surveyor's office; Director Teschner and my surveyor were outraged when they heard why I had been arrested. In the meantime, a house-search had been carried out at my apartment shortly after my arrest, which resulted in the confiscation of my library. Since, as I have already mentioned, we only had a one-room apartment, I had had to keep most of my books in the loft. Apart from my books I had built up an extensive collection of newspapers, including copies of *Angriff* (*Attack*) and *Völkische Beobachter* (*People's Observer* — both Fascist papers).

I do not know how the Gestapo knew that my newspapers were stored in the loft. I can only assume that other residents in the building had informed the Gestapo. So everything without exception was confiscated, including the copies of *Angriff* and the *Völkische Beobachter* — all except a single copy of *Problems of the Chinese Revolution* which a comrade had borrowed to read in 1932. She had dirtied the binding and returned it to me in a plain cover.

My wife told me that the official who came kept picking it up when he saw it, but then put it down amongst the books which were not objected to. Luckily I and my wife had managed to get the most important books from my collection over to my niece's summerhouse before this. There we buried them at the side of the path. Then I made a sketch map so that they could easily be found again.

Unfortunately things did not go according to plan. Up the hill from the summerhouses there lay a coalyard belonging to the firm of Krebs. During my stay in custody between 1934 and 1936, this coalyard moved several metres in the direction of the summerhouses, and the spot where I had buried the container was buried under nine metres of building rubble. The books, which had been wrapped in oil-paper, and the chest which was lined inside with imitation leather, still lie there today.

At the same time as I was losing my books, there were book burnings of Marxist and so-called 'decadent' literature in squares all over Berlin and in the rest of the country as well. One of these book burnings, in Unter den Linden outside the Humboldt University, lasted for several days. But not all books were burned; most of them were put into storage. Large numbers of Marxist and socialist books were taken to the Jewish synagogue in Eisenacher Strasse, and few remained in private hands. Most people, including our comrades, had got rid of their precious books out of fear.

In 1937, when I was at home again for a few months, I visited some friends — the wife of the former regional MP, Kasper, who lived with her partner in Grün Strasse in Charlottenburg. I got involved in a private argument while I was there. The pair of them had managed over the years to acquire a piece of land with a house. They could not agree who should get the piece of land when they separated. Their extensive library lay on the floor. They wanted to burn it. I protested, and said it was irresponsible to start burning Marxist literature themselves, and suggested to them that, if they were neither willing nor able to look after their books, I should take them to safety.

My sister had separated from her husband in 1936 and now lived alone with her daughter in the apartment. She agreed to find as much space in her attic as she could for the books. Transporting them was largely left to my wife and my sister — I did not take part in it at all. They were stored at my sister's along with leaflets and newspapers which we published between 1933 and 1944 — but unfortunately only until February 1944.

During a bombing raid, several phosphorus canisters fell on the front building and the side wings of the building at 26 Krumme Strasse, where my sister lived, and an explosive bomb fell on the main building. Along with the house and the furniture, the books and illegal material went up in flames.

After the defeat of the German working class in 1933, we succeeded in winning a number of comrades from the Communist Party. We agreed with them that they should continue as members of the party, as it seemed to be easier to convince comrades of the incorrectness of Stalinist policies from within. We managed to win a number of young comrades who took part in our activities. Only at the end of 1933 did we cut our ties with the KPD, because their bad organisation was resulting in arrests of more and more people. In the meantime we had also stopped putting up posters and leaflets. It had become too dangerous, since SA men in plain clothes were always out and about looking for bill-stickers.

Our Word still appeared every fortnight and 300 copies were sent to us, which, when distributed to many places in Brandenburg and central Germany, meant that each group only got a few copies. I suggested, especially to the comrades in Oranienburg, Halle, Luckenwalde and Weissenfels, that they copy the paper photographically. I knew from comrade Frieda Lehmann in Halle, with whom I was always in contact, that this procedure was carried out in Halle and Weissenfels.

Despite this we were still only a small organisation, only reaching limited groups of workers. Most of our comrades were unemployed, but it was even difficult to discuss with the unemployed, since the Fascists were beginning — albeit only in a limited fashion — to find sympathisers among them.

During the last phase of the Brüning government, which was followed by the governments of Papen and Schleicher, the KPD had attempted with its policy of a 'united front from below' to reach the Social-Democratic and Christian workers. Despite a flood of agitational material, most of which contained correct slogans, they did not succeed in gaining the trust of the trade unionists and factory workers. Only at the unemployment offices did support grow: the KPD had become the party of the unemployed and the petty bourgeoisie. Their public activities continued right through to May of 1933, with the result that thousands of comrades disappeared into the prisons of the Nazis, without achieving anything.

Fascism had succeeded in confusing sections of the working class. But they did not convince broad layers, as was shown by the elections of 5 May 1933, the last 'free elections'. The KPD could only conduct illegal campaigns. Karl-Liebknecht House was occupied at the end of February; machinery, matrices and manuscripts were confiscated. No one campaigning for the KPD was allowed to stand outside the polling stations; despite this, 10.5 million people still voted for the Communists and Social Democrats on 5 May 1933.

I continued to be employed at the Charlottenburg District Office as surveying assistant. At the start of May, I was supposed to be dismissed along with many others according to the provisions of the 'Law concerning the Reconstruction of the Public Service Offices' of 7 April 1933. The director of the surveyor's office, Teschner, tried to keep me on and to this end he negotiated without my knowledge or permission with the works group of the NSBO — the so-called trade union organisation of the NSDAP. He explained to me that my employment would continue if I was prepared to sign a statement in which I abjured all my previous political opinions.

I told Herr Teschner that I would be prepared to sign a statement of loyalty, even ten statements of loyalty, if the NSBO so desired, but not a declaration of principle like that. Teschner went back to the NSBO with this. The leadership of the NSBO, however, wanted a statement of principle, which would have made my position with my colleagues quite impossible. Herr Teschner advised me to sign regardless, since the power of the Fascists was certain to last for a long time. I replied that I knew that it was going to be at least a decade before they had to resign following a lost war. He said that, in my position, he would take up the offer. He wanted to send me to evening class and train me to be a surveyor's technician. Despite this attractive offer, I was not prepared to abandon my principles.

When Director Teschner went on holiday in August, Herr Friedrich, with whom I was always doing surveying work, stood in for him. In the meantime, most of the political 'unreliables' had long ago been dismissed. Then, one Saturday morning, I was handed a blue envelope by a messenger from the surveyor's office, which instructed me to report immediately to the office. It was obvious that I was about to be dismissed. When I reported to Friedrich, he was extremely uncomfortable at having to give me my notice. I was banned from the building and had to leave without delay. In the afternoon, Friedrich turned up at my apartment to apologise and give me some advice for the future. He could not understand when my wife told him not to worry about us. If it was necessary she would take to the road with me, for communists were quite used to discomfort.

A few months later I was in a cafe in Schlüter Strasse speaking with a comrade from out of town about some work which had to be done. Quite unexpectedly, Friedrich in full official uniform walked in with a collection box. When he reached our table, I could not resist telling him that I was still 'the same'. He went on, red to the tips of his ears, without replying. Teschner had also joined the NSDAP, along with some other former members of the SPD.

The Left Opposition had largely switched over to underground work. In our work against Fascism, we had already given ourselves the task of building up communist cadres who would be in a position to gain the trust of the workers in the coming crisis of Fascism, so that they could work together to overthrow the Nazis. Our comrades were also supposed to build up a relationship not only with members of the KPD, with whom there were already good contacts, but also with comrades in the SPD, the SAPD and the Lenin League, and convince them by means of intensive education that Fascism could only be defeated by the unity of the working class. *Our Word* was a great help to us in this connection.

We discussed again and again in our meetings the problem of the seizure of power by the working class and its revolutionary party — which would have to be created anew since neither the KPD nor the SPD had proved capable of leading the working masses to socialism. After Hitler's victory we no longer considered that the KPD could be reformed, and we changed our course. Against this background, I had also got in contact with comrades Weber and Weidland, who had brought almost the entire Rathenow branch of the KPD to the Lenin League in 1928.

These comrades were admittedly still in solidarity with Hugo Urbahns, but were prepared to argue with us about the role of the Soviet Union — 'either state capitalism or degenerated workers' state'. Unfortunately, after my arrest in January 1934, the comrades in the national leadership did not keep up this contact.

Our cells of five worked at their tasks conscientiously; the leaders of each group regularly reported on their work to the meetings of cell leaders. Until then we had no losses to report, for the Gestapo had not succeeded in stopping our work. One of our youth groups worked in Wilmersdorf, led by two active young comrades, Walter Haas and Oskar Grossmann. In December 1933 it was reported that the entire group had been arrested. The Berlin leadership told everyone who had worked with the youth comrades to suspend their operations until new instructions were issued.

As in the spring of 1933, I had arranged with my wife that she would put a sign at the window if there was any danger. (Since the arrest of the young comrades, I no longer stayed at home.) On 5 January 1934, I had just collected my unemployment benefit from the dole office, and was taking it to my wife. I went beforehand into the building in Krumme Strasse opposite ours, to see whether I could go home. Everything was OK, and I did not want to stay long. Scarcely had I entered the apartment than the bell rang. The criminal police stood outside and told me I was under arrest. They barely gave me enough time to say goodbye to my wife.

Down in the street a van stood waiting to take me to 'Alex' Platz. This time I would not get back home quite so soon.

Some ten days before my arrest, comrade Kurt Müller had been arrested. With his wife, who also belonged to our organisation, he ran a small lending library from a stall. But he was released again only a few days later. On the day of his release, comrade Klemz — who also had a lending library — turned up at his house: both were skilled metalworkers by trade, but had gone into this other business as a result of mass unemployment. As greeting, Kurt Müller said to him: 'Do not shake hands with me, I am scum,' but without explaining what he meant. He disappeared the next day. At first no one knew where he had gone, until his wife told us that he had made lengthy statements to the police and was now trying to go abroad.

In fact he succeeded in fleeing to Denmark (he now lives in Stockholm), as his wife informed us after receiving a short telegram from him. Comrade Herta Müller told us that he had been picked up by the infamous Storm Troop 33 and taken to Brauhof Strasse. There he had made some lengthy statements. Since he had been in the Left Opposition for quite a long time, he knew a few things. In particular, he had told them everything he knew about my activity in the group. We told comrade Herta Müller that she should keep out of any political work for a while, for we had to assume that she was being followed. For the third time I landed up in the 'Alex'.

The Gestapo man took me to the cells. When he handed me over there, the 'screw' on duty told him that there were no empty cells. The Gestapo man replied: 'It is vital that the man be kept in a cell by himself!' The screw replied: 'You get me a cell, or arrange that another one be emptied. Then I'll take this man off your hands.' They could not agree, so the Gestapo man dragged me off again.

There were two apartments down in the basement which had been turned into temporary jails by the Gestapo; he took me down there. When I went in, I saw the youth group. Comrade Grossmann put his finger to his lips to tell me — 'Be careful of third parties!' The place was full to overflowing. On the floor was some straw, upon which the inmates sat or lay. Thus warned by Grossmann, I did not let myself be drawn into conversation, but just told them what was absolutely necessary.

In the evening I sat down close to Grossmann: he told me that there were several stool-pigeons in the room, including one man who had been involved in the trial resulting from the burning of the Reichstag building — I forget his name now. I thought that my arrest had been caused by one of the young comrades, but Grossmann explained that none of them had made any statements, nor had they been beaten. All had stated unanimously during their interviews that their contact had been someone named Lind, alias Messer, who had instructed them to start their political work again. Now I knew that there was no danger from that quarter; the reason for my arrest had to be Kurt Müller. I was extremely lucky to have spoken to the youth comrades before my first interrogation.

In the morning I was taken out of the temporary jail before the official opening-time, and taken upstairs to a single cell. It was not long before I was taken to interrogation. The inspector whom I met there was the same man who had arrested me and taken me to the 'Alex'. He demanded that I should make a statement about my underground work, since they already knew more than I could guess. Since I already had some experience of the criminal police, I did not fall for that one and replied that he should first tell me why I had been arrested. When I stressed that I had engaged in no political activity after 1933, he burst out laughing.

I still only spoke in monosyllables, because I was working on the basis that the Gestapo should tell me why I was arrested. This lasted for days, and still they had not got me. In one of the next interviews — in the meantime, a second official had joined him, but I was still not shaken by that — the inspector said: 'Let us have a confrontation.'

I was led into a neighbouring room. After a short while I stood in front of a comrade whom I did not expect to see: Erich Albrecht, the leader of the Charlottenburg group. He welcomed me with the words: 'Oskar, you can tell them everything; the police know more than you think.'

I tried to build a bridge to him, to get him to retract his statement, and explained that I did not understand what he meant. The inspector ordered me to be quiet and asked Albrecht whether he stood by his statement: he said yes. He was immediately taken back to prison, and my interrogation continued.

'Well, Hippe, you certainly didn't think' — he used the familiar 'thou' form of address — 'that your best friend would drop you in it, did you?' Any further denial would achieve nothing now. The only question was, which tactics should I adopt.

On that day I only admitted that we had been rebuilding our

organisation in Charlottenburg for some time, and had taken up our work against Fascism again. For that reason, we had published a few leaflets and distributed *Our Word*. Now he wanted to know names. I maintained that we always did this work in a group of three — Albrecht, Müller and myself. Naturally, they did not believe me and wanted more names and the names of the men behind it all.

Albrecht had confessed that he had given me the money for the papers he had sold. I explained that I still had that money. Now I remembered what the young comrades had confessed — they had said that their contact was a man named Lind, alias Messer. In fact, the name really did exist, but it was a cover. The comrade concerned was a member of the national leadership and lived in western Germany. I gave this name as my contact. Immediately, he wanted to know where he lived and when he visited me or when I met him. I had to react quickly and said that he used to come to my apartment, but now the 'meets' took place in the open air. 'Where and when is the next meeting?' On 28 January, at two in the afternoon, at Olivaer Platz, I said. I gave these details in case I could escape if a suitable opportunity arose when we were there.

After my arrest, my apartment was occupied and it remained so for almost four weeks. In the end my wife was also arrested. Since I had made no statements, they hoped to squeeze something out of her. Immediately after my arrest, my wife had drawn up a list of comrades who had to be warned. She wrote this 'stiff', or secret message, on very thin paper. She told the officer in the apartment that she had to visit her sister-in-law in Krumme Strasse, since she had to run some errands for her. One of the officers said he would accompany her to her sister's. Once there, she slipped the message into her sister-in-law's mouth with a kiss, and told her why she had come. Even when she went shopping, there was always an officer with her. She told all the shopkeepers that nothing could harm her now, since she always had a bodyguard. In this way, everyone in the street found out that I had been arrested.

During the occupation of my apartment, two comrades came to visit. Comrade 'Sascha' (Alexander Müller) brought material with him, even though I had told him personally that the youth group had been arrested and that all work had to cease until further instructions were issued. And a second comrade came, who did not belong to our group, but only came from time to time for information. We called him 'the Chatterbox'. Both of them, as I learned later, were also arrested. Alexander Müller, like myself, was accused of conspiracy to high treason, while 'Chatterbox' was released again after a spell in detention.

Before my wife was arrested, she spent three weeks, night and day, with two Gestapo men in the apartment. Our home only consisted of one room and a kitchen. Forty per cent of all apartments in Berlin were one-room apartments. During the day, the two Gestapo men were in the room, and my wife had to stay in the kitchen. At night, it was the other way round — so my wife was able to sleep in the room, while the other two spent the night in the kitchen.

For these three weeks, my wife was constantly accompanied by one of the two, regardless of where she went. There was also a rabbit in the apartment, which my wife had brought with her from central Germany — she always had to have animals about her. His place was under the kitchen window in a box. One night the animal managed to get out of its box and peed all over one of the Gestapo boots. The SA wore laced boots which enclosed the calf as well. The whole upper part of the boot was completely soaked. On the following morning there was great excitement. My wife was angrily accused, and she answered that even the rabbit could not stand Nazis.

This incident had no further consequences. None of the comrades who had been arrested made any statement about my wife. Since I had as yet made no confession apart from things which they could already prove against me, her arrest was made in the hope that they could force a confession from her. She was taken first of all to the police barracks in Klein Alexander Strasse, which was occupied by the SA auxiliary police.

My wife knew a lot about the organisation, and knew a series of names. Despite being tortured, she said nothing. On one occasion she had to stand out in the corridor along with other women who had been arrested. They were taken in turns to interrogation. Outside, they were hit by SA people, kicked and beaten with rifle-butts. When they fell down unconscious — which happened repeatedly with my wife — they had cold water thrown over them until they came to. During these tortures of my wife, three of her vertebrae on the spine were broken. To this day she walks bent over and rarely without pain. But she has kept her sense of humour.

On 28 January 1934, at two o'clock in the afternoon, the inspector was with me at Olivaer Platz in order to 'nick' the supposed Lind. I had not reckoned that the officer would take as many men with him as there were streets leading into the square. I had told the inspector that I was supposed to meet my man on the Konstanz Strasse side. I walked up and down for quite a time with the officer dogging my footsteps but no one appeared. Once, I saw my sister coming out of Lietzenburg Strasse.

She had failed to find comrade Klemz, who usually stood with his bookstall at the corner of Kurfürstendamm and Knesebeck Strasse, and was returning up Lietzenburg Strasse. I had to ensure that she did not see me. I reacted as quick as a flash, and ran across the square to the other side, to Paris Strasse. The inspector came pounding after me, wanting to know why I was running. I lied, and said that I had seen my contact there. I had to give a description — height, age and clothes — and tell them where he had run to. The inspector immediately sent his men searching in Paris Strasse and the neighbouring streets, naturally with no result.

In the meantime, my sister had disappeared. The inspector, together with another officer, went to my apartment with me because he assumed that the 'comrade' would go there. We waited in the flat for almost an hour. During this time I had a couple of chances to speak to my wife briefly. She told me that Müller and 'Chatterbox' had been arrested. The inspector ranted and raged before he took me back to the 'Alex'.

On the next day, when I was taken to interrogation again, we went to a different floor of the building. Another officer sat at the desk. For the past three weeks I had not been hit once. My martyrdom began on that day. Scarcely had I entered the room, before any questions were posed, than I was beaten up. 'I won't put up with you for long, you'll be sentenced to death anyway if you do not give us a full confession.'

Now it was not simply a case of the comrades in my district, now they wanted me to name the comrades in the national leadership. In spite of the blows I was now dealt with increasing frequency, I told them that I did not know any names. This lasted for days. At the beginning of February, I do not know which day, when I was taken to interrogation, there were four SA men in the room. The inspector threatened: 'If you refuse to make a statement here, then you will certainly confess where we're going to take you now.' He handed me over to the SA men. I did not have to walk down the four steps that led out. I simply rolled down them, kicked without respite.

A van stood ready to take us to Charlottenburg. We drove through the zoo. The trees were showing tender green already, unusually early. These signs of life being renewed in nature gave me the courage to put up resistance against whatever was coming to me. I will never forget that day or the six which followed. I knew what to expect: Storm Troop 33 — to which the men escorting me belonged — had set up a torture chamber in what had been the Cooperative store in Brauhof Strasse, and had installed all their equipment there. In the six days that I was there, six people were carried out dead. The people in neighbouring buildings could hear the continual cries of pain from those tortured.

On the first day, I was kicked and beaten in a basement room without a bed. There was nothing to eat. On the following day I was taken upstairs for interrogation. It was already late in the evening. I did not leave that room for three days. As I had not eaten anything for more than 24 hours, I asked for something to eat. I received blows in reply. The Storm Troop leader led the interrogation. He was the son of a well-known dentist in Charlottenburg; he lay on a chaise-longue with an alsatian at his side, a cavalry whip in his hand which he used to underline every unsatisfactory word that I uttered. From time to time he ordered ten or fifteen lashes on the buttocks.

They had made a special chair, over which I had to lie. While one of the SA men sat on my neck, another took a square piece of wood which had a screw through one end — this also functioned as a hinge. This piece of wood was placed over the back of the knees. It was like being placed in stocks. A third man put a wet floor-cloth over my buttocks, and then they began to beat me with a steel bar encased in leather. The wet floor-cloth was supposed to prevent the skin from breaking, or so we learned later from other prisoners. As had already been the case at the 'Alex', they wanted to know the names of comrades in the national and Berlin regional leadership. I told them that our organisation, after the leading comrades had emigrated, had been crippled and that we had only recently been able to start rebuilding it again.

And that is what I maintained despite all the beatings. They confronted me with Müller's statements, and read some of them to me. I denied ever having belonged to the national leadership or the Berlin regional leadership. Müller must have confessed in order to be released, I said: just bring him up here and I would show that there was not a single true word in all his statements. The only thing that was true was that we had recently built our Charlottenburg group, and even then it only consisted of Albrecht and Müller. Naturally, they did not believe this, and repeated the beatings, with the additional threat that I could only expect to leave this building in a coffin. Despite all this, I stuck with what I had said at the start, when comrade Albrecht had confirmed his confession at the confrontation.

It was the third day of my stay in this SA cellar, the second day of my interrogation. There was scarcely a white patch left on my body, apart from my chest, which I protected with my hands. My whole body was swollen and covered with patches of every hue. In between times, I had also received something to eat, but only dry bread and water. On the third day, late in the afternoon, I had reached the point where I did not care what happened to me; the only thing that kept me going was the thought that I must not, under any circumstances, weaken and give names, even if they beat me to death, for then it would all be over.

They had given me half an hour's rest, and then an SA man brought a tray with three salt herrings, straight from the barrel, a glass of water and a packet of cigarettes. The Storm Troop leader then told me that I could choose between the cigarettes and the glass of water or the salt herring. If I confirmed Müller's confession, then the interrogation would stop, and I could help myself to the cigarettes and the glass of water. But if I kept silent then I would have to eat the three herrings.

I reached for the three herrings. Despite the scales which were still on them, despite the salt and the entrails, I ate the fish all up — although not without disgust. They left me alone for a while, and the salt took its effect in my stomach. I felt like bursting. The Storm Troop leader then said: 'Well, Hippe, there is still time! The glass of water and the cigarettes can still be yours.' I said that even if he gave me double the number of herring, I could tell him no more than I already had. And in fact I did not have to eat any more herring. To compensate, I was beaten again; but they could not make me change my mind about saying anything else.

Late in the night I was taken down to the basement again. Despite the pain, I fell asleep. When I woke up again, I noticed that it was morning. Some light came through the windows, which had been boarded up with wood. The pains, which I had not really felt badly during the interrogation, were almost unbearable now. Above all, I was dying of thirst. But nothing stirred outside. Nor was I taken to interrogation again as expected.

At around midday, an SA man came and brought me some stew in a cooking-pan. It was the first warm meal which I had received. Nothing else happened that day. I tried to sleep, but the cold kept waking me up again. On the following morning I was taken upstairs again. I braced myself for an interrogation. But there was nothing like that. The Storm Troop leader informed me that I was to be taken back to the 'Alex'. But if I said anything at all about what had happened, then they would come and fetch me again. And this time I would not live a day.

Thus, just as I had come, so I was taken back. The inspector sent me down to the police cells immediately. I was only taken for interrogation on the following day. When I was brought back to the cells, the warder asked what had happened to me. I told him only that he should not pretend that this was the first time he had seen such a thing — I had not been on a picnic. The inspector mocked me at the first interrogation after that: 'Hippe, you could have spared yourself all that.' I answered that he should not have expected me to make different statements in the cellars of the SA from those I made to him. If he wanted, I said, he could happily continue with their methods, but the result would be the same for him as for the SA. I was taken up for a few more interrogations, but there was no serious attempt to get anything out of me.

Towards the middle or end of March 1934, I was transferred to a remand prison. During these weeks since January, I had lost all sense of time. I still wore the underwear that I had on at the time of my arrest. They were completely smeared and crusted with blood as a result of my maltreatment. I applied to the investigating magistrate for my sister to be allowed to visit and to bring clean underwear, and this was granted. I had learned of my wife's arrest through the inspector. I was able to give the dirty and stained underwear to my sister; she told me later that she had shown my clothes to friends and acquaintances.

In the remand cells there were 'completely normal conditions', unlike in the police cells. Three times a day there was something to eat and every day you were allowed to move about the courtyard for half an hour. I was later able to buy a newspaper from my own funds. All the cells were overcrowded, sometimes with two, sometimes three people in them. Only so-called 'spies' were kept strictly in isolation; they also went for exercise separately.

At first I was sharing with a prisoner who belonged to the Stahlhelm. He had been arrested, so he told me, because he and his friends had resisted the order that they enrol in the SA, and because they criticised the policies of the NSDAP. He was the same age as me and came from a middle-class family who supported Kaiser and empire, and regarded private property as something given by God. Despite this, it was possible to have a discussion with him. He had become a soldier as late as 1918, but, unlike me, he did not get sent to the front, which he regretted a great deal.

I shared a cell with him for around six weeks, until he went to trial. He was also accused of 'conspiracy to commit high treason'. When he returned on the afternoon of his trial, he was swearing fearfully. He had been sentenced to two years' prison. A few hours later he was taken away to the transit cells. I remained alone for ten days, until a new 'billet' arrived. My new cell-mate was a member of the KPD, a printer by trade. Until his arrest, he had lived in Friedrichshagen near Berlin, where he belonged to the branch leadership.

He was arrested along with a group of people accused of participating in the preparation of subversive material. Like all the others whom I spoke to in prison, he had gone through the 'loving care' of the Gestapo. He could give me details of the events in Köpenick, where people in the Reichsbanner had been sewed into sacks and thrown into the river Dahme. I was with this comrade for six months, and I still have a fond memory of him; we had discussions every day, especially about the period between 1928 and 1933, and on the question of how Fascism could be defeated, and how long it would remain in power. It continued to interest me: if you spoke with individual members of the KPD — and this had also been the case before 30 January 1933 — you could usually have a factual discussion with them; and in many cases, the members agreed with us, as did this man.

Our cell looked out on a courtyard where Thälmann walked once a day. We often heard encouraging shouts for Thälmann from the other cells; indeed, it is true to say that scarcely a day went by without these shouts being heard; my cell-mate sometimes joined in. Although he agreed with many of the criticisms which we made of the party and the Comintern, he was not prepared to commit himself to our position which stated that the KPD had stopped being the party of the revolutionary working class. We exchanged addresses, but never heard from each other later, though I sent him a postal greeting after my release so that he would remember me.

In general, the warders were bearable; indeed there were some among them who confided in us that they had once been members of the Social-Democratic Party. When they told me this, I was reminded of Trotsky's words when he expressed criticism of Social Democracy: 'Your members in the police force — and this applies to the prison warders too — will be first and foremost servants of the Prussian state, and only then members of your party.'

One day we got a new warder who demanded that our wash-basins — in every cell there were tin basins — should shine like a mirror both inside and out. For this purpose we were given a red tile which we had to crumble into powder, and then we used the powder to rub the bowl clean. I told him — and my mate stood by me — that I was not prepared to make my bowl shine like a mirror; it was quite sufficient that it was clean. In any case, when we had been given the bowls, they were dull and not gleaming. If he thought that we needed a mirror to observe the changes which we underwent while in prison, then there was nothing to stop him from asking the administration to provide us with a mirror. He threatened me with disciplinary punishment, but it went no further.

At the end of May I had my first hearing. I was taken down to the basement of the prison, and there I saw my wife again for the first time. She was still very weak, but in good spirits. She told me that she had no great interest in this first hearing, for we now had no apartment any more. The furniture had been stored in a cellar by friends, since there was no more money left to have them put into storage. Our landlord had told my sister that he was prepared to keep the apartment for us. But my wife had refused since she did not know when or if I would return home.

At this first hearing, only 'Chatterbox' was released, while my wife remained in custody, although there was no evidence against her. My wife had told the investigating magistrate: 'After you have kept me prisoner here for months although I am innocent, and you have beaten me until I am half-crippled, you could at least see to it that I am decently looked after.' At a second hearing which took place in October, she was set free. When the magistrate asked her where she would go, she said that she would go to the refuge for the homeless.

On 10 June, I received notice of the charges against me. Together with me, another eleven people stood accused: the first six mentioned in the charges were members of the Communist Party, and amongst the last six were three youth comrades who had been in prison since December, and comrade Müller who had been arrested at my apartment. We were accused and tried alongside the KPD group because comrade Cholleck was a sympathiser of our organisation and had had contacts with both the youth group and myself.

The trial took place in November 1934 in Court No. 4 at the Berlin Supreme Court. Many of our friends and comrades knew of the date, since I had told my sister when she was visiting. The trial took place in a room which could contain around 200 spectators. Before we were taken to the courtroom, we had the opportunity of meeting in a cell and talking briefly with each other. We agreed that comrade Grossmann and I would answer the accusations of the state prosecutor, and would defend our organisation's position. Our comrades, in contrast to the members of the KPD, openly admitted their actions.

Grossmann spoke first. He accused the capitalist system of breeding Fascism; it was not us and our organisation that belonged in the dock, but capitalism, which was incapable of solving any of the problems facing it. I too, when I was called, answered the accusations by admitting everything in the charges. I explained that, on the basis of Marxist theory and the many years of experience since my earliest youth, both during the war and in the whole period of the Weimar Republic, I had come to the conclusion that 'National Socialism' was not capable of solving the political, economic and social problems either.

I mentioned Hitler's *Mein Kampf* in which he had written, amongst other things, that either there should be an agreement with Britain for the return of our colonies and Alsace-Lorraine which had been taken from us in the shameful peace of Versailles, or the sword would decide the issue. But, I said, since capitalism was neither willing nor ready to reach an agreement, but would rather defend its booty to the very last, there would be war between the rich capitalist countries and the so-called 'have-nots'.

We communists, however, maintained that all the conditions had long been present to raise society to a higher, socialist, stage. If, in the conflict between capital and labour, it had not been possible in 1933 to attain this new society in the interests of all mankind, then the blame lay with both the workers' parties, the SPD and the KPD.

'My lords,' I concluded, 'you can condemn us, but that will not change the fact that this system will collapse, collapse as a result of a lost war. Whether we survive or not, is not the most important thing; the most important thing is that, sooner or later, socialism will be victorious and will usher in a society which serves all mankind.'

I was the only one to receive a spell of hard labour; all the other comrades in our group were sent to prison. Comrade Grossmann, as I learned after my release — he had Russian citizenship — was deported from the country; unfortunately, we could not find out where. After the judgements were passed, I returned to my cell for a short while, to pick up my few belongings. Then I spent two days in the transit cell until I was taken to Plötzensee.

Plötzensee was a prison which housed many of those condemned to death and where some of them met their deaths. My cell, which I shared with other prisoners, lay right next to 'death row', where those condemned to death waited, including a good friend of mine, Richard Hüttig, who, as I have already mentioned, was arrested for murder after the fight between people from the Antifa and the SA at the start of January 1933. Every day I saw him as he went in chains for exercise. When he was beheaded, so friends who later came to Luckau told me, he died as an upstanding fighter. Richard Hüttig was a member of the Communist Youth League, a leading official in the Red Youth Front, and leader of the Anti-Fascist Action League.

When we saw comrades who had been condemned to death, walking their circles with their hands chained behind their backs and not knowing whether they walked for the last time, we swore that we would continue the fight against Fascism unswervingly.

I only stayed a short time in Plötzensee; then, with others, I was taken by rail in a prison transport to Luckau. The journey lasted two days, since our route took in several prisons.

As soon as we passed through the gates of Luckau, we stopped being human beings. From that day onwards we only existed as a number. Everything was taken from us at reception, we were given a brown uniform with yellow stripes down the trousers and arms. Nine hundred prisoners were housed at Luckau Prison, including 700 politicals; 'criminal' and 'political' prisoners sat apart.

The 'criminals' were in sections thirteen and fourteen, the 'politicals' in all the other sections. I was put in section six, where there were already

86 politicals, including Brandt, the Magdeburg MP, and the Secretary of the RGO, Braun. Several members of the Lenin League and comrades of the Communist Party Opposition (Brandler group) were also there, but the majority were KPD people.

While we spent the days in the so-called 'workroom', in the evening after work was finished we went to the dormitories. The upper floors of the cell-block lying opposite the main building had been redesigned for that purpose. Previously, this space had been used for store-rooms; now, with overcrowding, areas had been sectioned off with wire-netting, and these now functioned as sleeping quarters. We slept right at the top, on the floor, with comrades from two other sections.

We were watched by two guards the whole night through. Although there was supposed to be absolute quiet after lock-up, quite loud conversations took place. The two guards at first tried to restore quiet, but without success. Despite a ban, we smoked up there in the sleeping quarters too. Comrades who were employed outside the prison, in the kitchens or in other outlying places, brought tobacco back with them and shared it out in the evening.

It was not uncommon — so the comrades who worked outside told us — for cigarettes and tobacco to be handed as presents to the prisoners. Reveille was at six o'clock in the morning, and then it was off to the workroom where, after breakfast — which consisted of a ration of dry bread and a bowl of coffee substitute — the work commenced. The men from section six had to fix wire-netting made of brass wire across a framework of wood. Since the wire was very inflexible, our hands suffered and often bled. A quota was set, which meant that a predetermined amount had to be completed each day. The working hours lasted until six o'clock in the evening.

After we had washed, we returned to the sleeping quarters. This pattern of events was repeated every day in the same sequence. During the day only one guard watched over our section; he sat like a teacher in school on a high chair, in order to observe the prisoners better. There were guards who were very strict and threatened every offence with disciplinary action.

But there were also guards who sometimes allowed us to converse. One of these guards had previously been in the SPD, and when he was on duty in our section, it was like a Sunday. He was a keen chess player, and with him around we could converse in low tones while the trusty — that was the man who had to look after all the cleaning — kept a lookout at the window to make sure that none of the warders came across the yard. This warder was an opponent of the 'National Socialists' and expressed this quite unequivocally.

We would gladly have had him on our section all the time, for then our imprisonment would have been far easier to bear. However, the guards were changed around regularly. Our free time, which was supposed to last half an hour every day, was only allowed on Sundays and consisted of the so-called 'bear dance', in which everyone ran one behind the other in a circle round the yard; during the week, exercises took place instead. The 'commanders' here were criminals, three lifers, all three sentenced for murder. One of them was an unpleasant bloke, a 'slave-driver' as they used to call them in the army.

The whole group marched in columns the whole time, 'left and right wheel, quick march'. The chief warder — we called him the 'Lion of Luckau' because of his powerful voice which rang out over the yard whenever something displeased him — was a one-time sergeant in the Imperial German Army, and sometimes he took over the command himself. Comrades who were released later than me told me that, from 1937 onwards, the prisoners had to exercise with wooden rifles. At the beginning of February 1935, the 'workforce' decided to reject the quota, since it could only be met if the comrades disregarded the injuries to their hands.

A discussion preceded this decision, since the former MP Brandt and Braun, the RGO Secretary, proposed that every comrade should deliver ten items fewer than the quota. I and some other comrades spoke out against this, and suggested that, while we should indeed deliver about ten too few, this shortfall should differ according to each comrade. We were accused of 'opportunism' and 'retreat before the class enemy', and a vote was demanded. The overwhelming majority — more than three-quarters — voted that every comrade should make the same number of items. We, in the minority, submitted to the majority decision, and the next day ten items per man was missing from the quota. On the third day a guard came from the administration block, gave us a warning and ordered us to deliver the full amount the next day.

After he had gone away again, there was another short meeting — the decision was upheld. On the following day we had our 'own' guard again; he knew about the threat from administration and told us that things could get bad for us. The trusty stood at the window as was usual when this guard was on duty with us. All of a sudden he shouted: 'The "Lion" and a group of guards with carbines are coming across the yard!'

They came up to our building, and after a few moments they came into our room. Everyone jumped up from their seats — that was the rule — and the guard reported: 'Section six reporting with 87 prisoners at work.' The 'Lion' told us to step into the aisle, and the group of guards stood opposite us with rifles aimed. Before the head warder spoke to us, he had the rifles loaded with the safety-catches off. He told us that what we were doing was mutiny, and that he could have us shot on the spot; he demanded that we name the ringleaders who had organised this action.

Nothing happened, everyone remained silent, no one had any fear that someone would step out of line and 'squeal' — amongst 700 political prisoners there were only two men to watch out for, and there was no one in our section who would 'sing'. The head warder worked himself into hysteria. The whole thing seemed quite ridiculous to me, and this must have shown on my face, for I was suddenly dragged out of the line with two other prisoners — including RGO Secretary Braun — and taken to the cell-block by the head warder.

Since I was the last of the three, I received the blows from the rubber truncheons. Down in the corridor in the cellars, we had to strip off our clothes and were then thrown into one-man cells where we remained for ten days; for three days we remained naked. On the fourth day we were taken to the administration block and interviewed separately by the director in the presence of the head warder.

These interviews were repeated daily. Despite all the threats that they would leave us to stew in the cellars — it was still winter, and the cells down there were unheated — no one said a word. On the eleventh day we were split up on to different floors in the cell-block. I was put on the fourth floor, in a cell which also contained Comrade Bibach, with whom I had stood trial.

There were three of us in a cell of eight square metres. Our work was to make doormats from sisal grass; there was a quota here as well. During the day the cell was full of dust from the task of splitting the sisal. I did the work for a few days, then I went to the doctor and told him that I could not continue with it, since my left hand would not move properly and I kept having headaches — the Storm Troop leader had injured my left hand with his 'SA dagger' in the cellars of the SA and had hit me on the head. At first I had no success.

Since I kept going back to the dispensary, I was eventually released from the work, and was permitted to grow my hair longer — all the prisoners in Luckau were shorn to the scalp. I had to stay on in the cell; I was obliged to twine the sisal for hours, if I could. I did not need to exercise in the yard with the rest of them, but could run in a loose formation. Our 'commander' for this exercise was a lifer, who told us that he had killed his bride out of jealousy.

Relatively speaking, this group had it easy. It was here that I got to know a former MP for the KPD, Roman Chwalek, who was now in the same isolation cell as Karl Liebknecht had occupied during the First World War.

This cell had two rows of bars and a close mesh wire-netting across the window. He was very open to our political ideas in the Left Opposition of the KPD. We used the time while 'marching' for discussions.

During these discussions it often happened that we did precisely the opposite on the command 'right turn, quick march'. But thanks to our 'commander' there was no trouble. Only if one of the warders was near did this cause a rumpus.

It was extremely difficult to communicate anything political in the cell-block; we tried to establish contact by using 'stiffs' for secret messages. Since the trusties were also 'politicals', this worked; they acted as 'postmen' between the cells. It was a dangerous task for the trusties, and they had to watch out for the guards, except the one who had played chess with us in section six. This one knew about the postal system and kept an eye on the stairs so that nothing went wrong.

Sometimes we had one warder who was still a sergeant in the auxiliary police and came on duty wearing an SA uniform; he was a nasty sort, well-known as a slave-driver and not very popular even with the guards.

At one midday break, while we were waiting for food, I was standing second in line holding my bowl, and he screamed that I was a 'communist pig' because I was not standing straight. I replied that I had certainly been condemned as a communist, but for that reason I was nothing like a pig. 'If you don't shut up,' he shouted, 'I'll throw you over the railings!' I then stepped out of the line and said that he should get on with it if he was brave enough.

Boiling with rage, he let all the bowls be filled, but not before sending me back to my cell and locking the door. The next day, I had to report to the chief warder, who welcomed me with a 'thunderstorm' because I had contradicted an officer. I told my side of the story. I had expected some kind of punishment. Surprisingly, nothing happened; the chief warder told me that the man had had no right to call me a pig.

In the meantime, a functioning news network had been established in the area, and all sections were now in contact with each other. The committee had decided that on 1 May, at a predetermined signal, the 'Internationale' should be sung early in the morning. Since 1 May was a national holiday in the Third Reich (the 'day of German labour'), only a Sunday shift of guards was present. All the sections took part in this demonstration — except the two containing the criminals. Down in the yard, the 'Lion of Luckau' ran around like a wild animal, not knowing what to do.

In the meantime, the governor had turned up. All the verses of the 'Internationale' were sung right through to the end. On the following day our warders told us that the song had been heard over almost the whole town. There were interrogations again, but, as with the incident on quota-refusal, there was no one to give the administration any clues. The directorate tried to get something out of us in day-long interviews, but every comrade remained silent and told them that they did not know whether it had been an organised demonstration.

Despite the presence of the auxiliary guard, who, although he passed as a 'tough man' inside the prison, gave the prisoners quite a lot of freedom outside, the comrades working outside did not tell tales out of school. So the investigation into the First of May Singing Incident petered out. For the whole time that I stayed at the Luckau prison, contacts and communications amongst the comrades were maintained, with the help of two guards.

I remained in a cell with three other comrades until I left Luckau. The only one who sat alone in his cell was comrade Chwalek. All the comrades who knew him knew of his militant behaviour — in his factory, as an MP in Parliament, but especially standing accused before the court, where he quickly became the accuser. In Luckau he made a major contribution to directing the political work. He was also one of the few leading officials in the prison who did not hesitate to support the ideas of comrades in other political groupings if he considered them to be correct, and even openly defended them in discussions — in contrast to the erstwhile MP Brandt and the RGO Secretary Braun, who continued to defend Stalinism and the 'line of the party' unconditionally.

The days and weeks dragged on interminably, the working day was long and monotonous, especially in the cell-block where I was always cooped up with the same comrades. When the 'free time' was finished, I was always looking forward to the next one on the following day, since then I had the opportunity of discussing many political problems with comrade Chwalek.

Even if we were not often of the same opinion, we were at least in agreement in our evaluation that the rule of the Nazis would last many years and that they would not be overthrown by the working class but by Hitler's opponents in war, and we also agreed that the construction of a revolutionary movement would depend on those comrades who had led the resistance against Fascism. I only saw comrade Chwalek again after the end of the war, when he was giving a talk in his capacity as national chair of the FDGB (Free German Trades Union Confederation of East Germany).

Not one of us imprisoned in Luckau knew what would happen after our sentences had been served. Until now there had been no releases. From comrades who had been recently sentenced and had only just arrived at Luckau, we learned that comrades released from other prisons had been sent to the concentration camps. The decision between release or concentration camp did not lie with the penal authorities — only the SS took that decision. And then the first releases began at Luckau. At the start, we could not find out whether the comrades went off to 'freedom' or were sent to the camps. But the two guards who had given us news earlier came to our assistance.

In the spring of 1936, my release date came up. Together with comrade Walter Cholleck, a sympathiser of our group who had received the same sentence as me, I sat for two days in the basement — already dressed in civilian clothes — and waited to be taken to the release cell which was situated in the administration block. Suddenly the door opened and Cholleck was told to accompany the guard upstairs. The official who fetched him did not even give us time to say goodbye to each other properly. A short 'Auf Wiedersehen', and Walter disappeared.

In more than two years' imprisonment, I had experienced all kinds of things: in the spring of 1934 I had been subjected to the maltreatment of the Fascists in the cellars of the SA. Despite their threat that 'You won't get out of here alive', I did not despair and survived the torture. How often I had spoken with comrades before this about what would happen to us if we had to continue the struggle in illegality. We were quite clear that everyone had to expect the worst. Nevertheless, the way that Comrade Cholleck was dragged off still gave me a shock. I was certain that he was being taken to the concentration camps — he was partly Jewish. I passed a sleepless night.

The next morning, I was taken to the release cell; there, during the course of the day, I received my release papers, a ticket to Berlin and was instructed to report to the police when I got there. But I still thought I might be taken to the concentration camp. In my mind I went through the days and weeks which I had spent with the Gestapo and in the cellars of the SA.

After I had spent a night in the cell, the door did indeed open on the morning of the following day. The secretary who accompanied me to the gate warned me to take the direct route to Berlin, and to report to the police on the following day. And yet I was still not convinced that I would get home unscathed. At every moment I expected the Gestapo to take me to Berlin and then off to the camps. It was only when I was sitting in the train and nothing had happened that I believed in my release.

11.

A 'FREE MAN' IN THE THIRD REICH

My wife, who had visited me several times in prison, had told me that we no longer had an apartment. After her own release, she had been put up by my sister. Since there were now four people living in a one-room apartment, she could not stay there long and had moved in with the mother of one of our comrades, who had a one-room apartment with a boxroom in Pestalozzi Strasse. But there was no room for me there, the boxroom being only 7.5 square metres, and I had to stay with my sister at first. For the first few weeks we lived apart, my wife in her boxroom, me at my sister's.

On the day after my release, as I had been instructed at Luckau, I went to the local police station to report with my release papers. There I was told to report each day at a certain time. Every day for the first three months, I did just that, and the police officers did not force me to say 'Heil Hitler'. I said 'Good day', as I always did when I was dealing with officials. Later, I only had to report to the police station every other day, then twice a week, and after six months I did not have to report at all. Apparently they thought that imprisonment and the registration duty had succeeded in demoralising me.

During these six months I only made contact with one comrade from the national leadership of our group. They advised me not to carry out any political work while I still had to report to the police, because it was likely that I was being tailed by the Gestapo. Nevertheless, I was in contact with our Charlottenburg leadership through Georg Klemz, the bookseller. Although the group of five had continued its political work after our arrest, there had been no more arrests. Both *Our Word*, which still reached Berlin from Switzerland, and the photographed pages, were still distributed, and sometimes even leaflets could be handed out — these were not produced by the Charlottenburg group, but by the Berlin regional leadership.

In the first six months after I returned home, I often received a visit from the acting branch secretary of the Charlottenburg RFB, who urged me to to take up underground work with his group. I refused. Firstly, because our group of five had made a decision that there should be no more cooperation with the KPD, since arrests were now including ever widening circles of people, not only in Berlin, but throughout the country as well, and secondly, because there were rumours that this this particular comrade was to be treated with caution. (We never established whether these rumours were true.) In any case, it was a fact that with the aid of their agents, the Gestapo had succeeded in penetrating groups of the KPD.

In its approach to underground work, the KPD still worked from the premise that the victory of Fascism would only be short-lived, as Hermann Remmele had suggested in the illegal *Rote Fahne* of February 1933. On every visit which I received from comrade Wisse, he tried to involve me in the illegal work of his group. Only when I told him that it was irresponsible to speak like that to a comrade who had only just got out of prison and who had to report daily to the police, and who was probably under observation — only then did he stop coming.

During my imprisonment, my wife had drawn supplementary benefit, which amounted to 8.35 Reichsmarks; after my return, this payment was stopped, since I was still eligible for unemployment benefit. For the two of us this amounted to 12.30 Reichsmarks. Out of that, 3.90 Reichsmarks went on rent, so that we had 8.40 Reichsmarks left for food. No one could live on 8.40 Reichsmarks in those days, so I was obliged to moonlight. A friend of mine, who had a coal business in Weimar Strasse, managed to get me an hourly-paid job with a baker who had a stall at the weekly markets. Five times a week I carried his goods to market on a handcart, and fetched them back at the end of the market. For this I did not receive much money, but I always got a bag full of cakes to take home. Sometimes, if trade was slack, the bag was quite large, and we could have friends round for tea and cakes. In this way we were able to secure the means of existence.

It was intolerable that I and my wife had to live apart. Yet we could not even think of getting our own apartment. My efforts to get an apartment, or at least a room, out of the housing office were in vain; they told me that I was registered on the waiting list and would have to wait until something turned up.

Quite out of the blue I received an offer from a one-time member of the KPD, who had stopped his political work in 1932, shortly before the defeat. In 1931 this man, along with many others, had been sacked by Kraft AG, the largest taxi firm in Berlin. He had rebuilt an old taxi which this company had sold off, and turned it into a pick-up truck which he used to make deliveries to customers for a furniture shop. It had become a profitable business for this comrade. But he had no time to look after his plot of land in Spandau, and he asked me to live in his house there for the summer. Naturally we jumped at the chance; our only responsibility was to look after the land.

We lived there until November 1936, although we were still registered in Charlottenburg. No one in this new place knew that we were political refugees. In the meantime, we had also taken up our political work again, and the meetings of both the national leadership and of the executive of the Charlottenburg groups took place in this period on this plot of land in Spandau.

In 1933, the Western allies did nothing to curb the excesses which were directed principally against the organised sections of the German working class. Apart from a few protests from the democratic organisations of the West, nothing happened. On the contrary, neither the French nor British governments objected to Hitler suppressing the German workers' movement. The most powerful evidence was this: in 1935, when Hitler reintroduced military sovereignty and shortly afterwards reoccupied the west bank of the Rhine, with the advice to his general staff that, if the Western allies offered any resistance, they were to retreat to the east of the Rhine again, then the Western powers did nothing at all, although it was obvious that this was the first step towards the Second World War.

At that time it would have been possible for the Western powers to declare war against Hitler for breaching the Versailles Treaty, and for them to have won without great losses, as the Berlin-Rome-Tokyo axis did not yet exist. There were strong disagreements between Hitler and Mussolini concerning the South Tyrol. Hitler had nothing but his Storm Troops — the SA and SS — and an enthusiastic petty bourgeoisie which saw the glory of empire shining as of old in the resurrected military sovereignty. On the other hand, there was a defeated working class and the ban on workers' parties and trade unions. The workers in the factories still opposed 'National Socialism' as they had done before. Only after the military victories in Poland in 1939 and against France in 1940 was there a growth in confidence in the strength of the regime.

The bourgeois governments in Paris and London recognised the mood of the German workers better than the leaders of the Communist and Social Democratic parties. They knew that, if Hitler were to be defeated militarily at this point, then the workers' movement would draw the lessons from its defeat of January 1933 and take up the fight against capitalism under a new revolutionary leadership. That was why the governments in Paris and London let Hitler alone — in order to complete the defeat of the German workers' movement. Hitler and German imperialism were well aware that, on their own, they could never manage to wrest supremacy in Europe and play a decisive role in the world economy. They needed allies, and they finally found them in Italy and Japan. It was not difficult for Hitler to give up his claim to South Tyrol, although he had made promises during the Weimar Republic and in the period immediately after he came to power that he would annexe this area.

The aim of the Western powers was to add fuel to the existing differences between Hitler's Germany and the Soviet Union, so that, at the end of a military confrontation, they could step in and dictate peace terms. Even when Hitler 'brought Austria back into the Reich' and occupied Czechoslovakia, the Western powers were not prepared to fulfil their commitments as allies. France, it is true, had signed a defensive pact with Czechoslovakia, but France did nothing after Hitler's troops had invaded the Czechoslovak republic. Although the Soviet Union had declared in Paris and London that it was prepared to defend Czechoslovakia, France and Britain signed the Munich Agreement with Hitler in 1938.

We were quite sure that this agreement could not last long. Hitler's goal was to drive a wedge between London and Paris. Hitler wanted Britain as an ally, in order to prevent France from being a European power for all time and finally to be able to lead the fight against the Soviet Union. Anyone who had studied Hitler's *Mein Kampf* and the aim of German imperialism knew that Britain had been ascribed a secondary role in the struggle for supremacy in Europe. If Hitler really had succeeded in gaining Britain as an ally, then it would only have been a short-lived alliance which would have collapsed before the outbreak of war.

Under these conditions, it was clear that war was inevitable. The bourgeois-democratic parties had voted for the Nazis' Enabling Act in the Reichstag after Hitler had taken power, and had then dissolved themselves. The workers' parties, both Social Democrats and Communists, could no longer consider themselves as leaders of the German working class. Therefore, at the outbreak of war, a new wave of nationalism and chauvinism would surely break out, one which would also sweep through the German working class — if only temporarily.

We were also certain that it would be impossible to conduct any mass propaganda against the war — at least while workers were gripped by this chauvinism. So we decided to concentrate on educating a powerful cadre, which would be in a position to take up the fight for democracy and socialism in the period after the German army and the Nazis were defeated.

We had already won a series of young comrades in the last phase of the Weimar Republic, some as sympathisers, some as members. Even in illegality, it was possible for our comrades in the factories to convince young workers about out programme. In the existing groups of five and with the help of our paper *Our Word*, we were in a position to deepen their knowledge and train them for the tasks to come. In the meantime, the Nazis had succeeded in ending unemployment. Hitler had taken millions off the streets with the renewal of military sovereignty, with the construction of the autobahns and of the 'West Wall'. The money for all this came partly from the funds belonging to workers' and office workers' insurance schemes and from health insurance schemes.

When the Nazis took power, the health insurance schemes and the pension funds had considerable finances, but by 1938 they were deeply in debt. This involved hundreds of millions of marks, which at that time were considerably larger amounts than today. Further finances were released for Hitler by inflationary measures (such as the 'Mefo' exchange system etc.) and the printing presses of the Reichs Bank threw more and more millions on to the market to pay for increased armaments. Wages and salaries of all branches of the building industry were cut in favour of armaments workers. For workers who laid heating — and water pipes — this meant a cut of more than a third. Here, the hourly wages which had been guaranteed by contract were cut from 1.78 Reichsmarks by 62 pfennig, while the wages of armaments workers were raised. This affected mostly unskilled or semi-skilled workers, who often earned twice the wages of a skilled worker in the building trade. The result was that the skilled workers in the building industry went over to the armaments industry.

The year 1937 was drawing to a close. I still had not found any work, although skilled workers were in short supply, especially in the building industry. Now and again I found a job for a few weeks as a labourer with some small builder. An American of German origins had come to Germany with his millions, because he was enthusiastic about Hitler and his system. He had a villa built for himself in the Schmargendorf area of Berlin. I got work for a short time while this villa was being built, but was laid off again after the foundations were laid, and returned to 'Old Man Crutches', as the unemployed of Berlin called the labour exchange.

One day I went to see the director of the labour exchange in Charlottenburg, to ask him why I had not been given a job in spite of the fact that skilled workers in all areas, especially the building industry, had been sought for months.

The director's answer was: 'For you, we have no more work.' So I had to go and sign on again. My unemployment insurance had run out in the meantime, and I received unemployment benefit. The amount was not a great deal in both cases, and we had to go moonlighting if we were not to starve. My wife went two or three times a week cleaning houses for 30 pfennig an hour and a meal, although this was sometimes only soup. But the fight against Fascism and Stalinism went on, in the knowledge that the international working class under the leadership of a revolutionary party would take its own fate in its hands, clear away capitalism and replace an economy driven by profit with a humane socialism.

The winter of 1936-1937 had driven us out of the summerhouse. We found an empty room in the home of the mother of a comrade — she was called 'Mother Weber' in the Communist Party during the Weimar period. But the rooms were past their best and had bugs — or 'carpet flounders', as Berliners called them. We suggested to Mother Weber that she had the apartment fumigated, and she agreed. She had already put some of her furniture up into the loft, although we had told her to leave the furniture in the room which we were to occupy. There was still panelling over a blocked-in doorway to the adjacent room in the neighbouring apartment.

We asked Mother Weber to speak to the landlord so that he could give us permission to tear down the panelling, for we feared that bugs had nests behind the wood. She got permission, and what we had feared turned out to be true — bugs' nests as big as your hand. Mother Weber had told us when we rented the room that 'now and again' a bug would appear. But it was simply not the case that Mother Weber had bugs — the bugs had her. We wondered whether, in this situation, we should not terminate our lease. But since we had already bought everything for redecorating and for removing the bugs, we decided to stay put. And in fact we succeeded: the bugs vanished — until one day Mother Weber fetched some of her furniture down from the loft, and there! the bugs reappeared in our room after a little while.

In the meantime, through friends, we kept trying to get an apartment. One day my sister came to us with the news that there was an apartment going at number 12 Spielhagen Strasse. She had spoken with the janitor's wife, who was a friend of hers. The agent was a young man and, as Frau Hummel, the janitor's wife, had told her, was no Nazi. That same day I went to the agent to apply for the apartment. Once again it was a one-room apartment, with a small windowless boxroom. I told the agent honestly why I did not have an apartment but now lived in one room with my wife, who was also a victim of the arbitrariness of the regime.

We got the apartment and were delighted to be alone again. But now there was the question of furniture, which we needed to live in any way decently. After our arrest in 1934, our furniture had been stored by friends in a cellar, since there was no money to put it into proper storage. On some of the pieces the glue had come loose and they were on the point of collapsing. The metal beds had rusted and could not be used. While we were in the summerhouse, we had everything needed for a simple life. We had only put into Mother Weber's room the most basic items, since we could not forget the bugs. I spent weeks piecing together and polishing those pieces of our furniture which were still usable. I was helped by my two years' training as carpenter after leaving school. Gradually we settled down again.

Immediately after the announcement of military sovereignty, Hitler passed the so-called Military Service (Unworthiness) Law, which excluded from military service all those who had conspired against the 'Third Reich' and had been punished for that crime. In 1937 I received a summons from the Regional Military Command, instructing me to report at the 'Hotel zum Tiergarten'. This was not to report for duty, but rather a discharge ceremony. Most of the people who had been summoned there were young.

I received a discharge certificate from an army officer, together with a certificate declaring me to be unworthy of performing military service. The Führer had decreed that I was not worthy of wearing the 'honourable uniform of the soldier', and I was thrown out of the army. I was dismissed with the instruction to return home. I did not even want to laugh at this ceremony — although the whole thing was laughable — for I knew then that war would surely come.

In this period we had discussions in our organisation concerning the events in the Spanish Civil War, and about the defence of the bourgeois Republican government and democracy against the attacks launched by right-wing military leaders. These leaders were being supplied with weapons and ammunition by Hitler and Mussolini. Both the French and British governments had an interest in a stalemate between the Republicans and Fascists. They permitted workers' organisations and trade unions in their own countries to send fighters to the International Brigades, while the Soviet government supplied material aid to the Spanish Republican government. But with the weapons and advisers there also arrived the members of the Soviet secret police, the NKVD, who took over the political leadership and suppressed all other political tendencies — in many cases, physically.

In our organisation, after this discussion there was an almost unanimous agreement that it was not possible at this stage to send any comrades to Spain to fight with the International Brigades for the victory of the socialist forces. It was evident from quite early on that — despite heroic fighting by the Republican army and the International Brigades — Fascism would be victorious in Spain as well. Not only had the bourgeois government in Spain and the workers there suffered a defeat, but the victory of the Fascists would have a negative influence on the whole European working class. The bourgeois governments of France and Britain had cut into their own flesh with their 'non-intervention policy'. While they stood by without lifting a finger, watching the Spanish Republic being cut down, they sowed the seed of the Second World War in European soil.

The defeat in the Spanish Civil War had even more serious repercussions on the Soviet Union. The Soviet Union had hoped that, after the victory of the Republican army, they could consolidate their influence over the Spanish government with the aid of the Spanish workers' movement, in the same way as they had been able to extend their influence in France — and to some extent in Britain. But the victory of the Fascists in Spain now presented the danger to the Soviet Union that the bourgeois governments of the West would give a free rein to the Fascists in the fight against the Soviet Union, in order to realise the old goal of the European imperialist power of wiping out for ever not only the Soviet Union, but also the very basis of the October Revolution.

The Stalinists in the Soviet Union and, like them, the sections of the Third International, had to find a way out of this danger in order to survive. Whereas after the October Revolution in 1917-1918 the international working class had prevented the imperialist powers from wiping out the young workers' state led by Lenin and Trotsky, now the German, Hungarian, Polish and Czechoslovakian workers were defeated, and those in other countries seriously weakened. From this point of view, the way was clear for Hitler.

Stalin found another solution — he signed the non-aggression pact with Hitler. Hitler thus managed to open the door to France, and after a short offensive war against France he had the mainland of central and western Europe under his control. It very soon became obvious that the Stalinists' tactic of allying with Hitler was miscalculated. For both sides in this pact, it was a question of who was to be the rider and who the horse.

While large sections of the supporters of the Communist Party had agreed with the theory of social fascism in the years from 1928 to 1932, now they were no longer prepared to tolerate this strategy of allying with the Fascists. On this basis, we were able to convince several members of the KPD — especially younger comrades — of the ruinous policies of Stalinism. But many resigned and followed the road into political oblivion. We continued to lay stress on educating our cadre. As before, it was not difficult to talk to men in the factories about many political problems.

Although the workers were organised almost without exception in the 'German Labour Front' (Deutsche Arbeitsfront) — that is, were forced into it — most of them rejected Fascism; but most of them could not be persuaded to take part in active conspiratorial work.

In 1938 we received a visit from a comrade who had been a friend of mine for years, and who worked as a heating engineer at the firm of Haag AG in Mittenwalder Strasse. He told me that the firm had vacancies for assistants and fitters and that he had spoken to the supervising fitter who was prepared to employ me. Souvang, the supervisor, was in fact a member of the NSDAP, but had previously been a Social Democrat, and had been sent into the NSDAP by his party. I would be able to talk to him about anything.

On the following day I went to Mittenwalder Strasse, and was duly taken on after a short interview. At seven the next morning, I reported to the fitters' foreman, a man named Fels, at the building site. As it turned out, he was also a Social Democrat. He already knew that I had been imprisoned for 'conspiracy and high treason', as did his colleague, who was also left-wing and — as he later told me — had been a member of the KPD.

It was a large building site in the middle of the woods near Heckeshorn. We were building the Air Defence College of the Reich. Our firm alone employed sixteen gangs; 32 men were working there and, as I discovered in the course of time, all had remained trade unionists and anti-Fascists — excepting only one who had joined the SS.

In our hut, which we used for changing clothes and eating breakfast, open discussions took place, even in the presence of the man who had gone over to the SS. There was no holding back the criticism of the German Labour Front, although all the men except me were members of that organisation. I always claimed back the deduction they made from my pay at the end of the month.

The head clerk of the firm, who also functioned as the chair of the 'workers' council', told me that 100 per cent of the workers in the firm had to be organised in the Labour Front. I replied that I would only join an organisation if I was convinced that it represented my interests.

Two other men were employed there who had also been in prison for political reasons — one was once the mayor of Sachsenhausen, a Social Democrat. After six weeks, I and the other two were told to come down to the offices of the firm. Supervisor Souvang informed us that the Ministry of Labour was demanding that we be dismissed. He explained to the director of the firm, who was also present, that, if we three were dismissed, he would not take any responsibility for work being continued by the others. Finally he and the director went back to the Ministry and agreed with them that we could stay. On the following day, Supervisor Souvang turned up at the building site and, in the presence of Karl Fels, the foreman, he advised me to be more circumspect in future during discussions, since he thought that the head clerk was behind this attempt to have us dismissed. But I would not have to worry about my colleagues, as the one who had joined the SS had been transferred to a repair gang.

I remained with Karl Fels at the building site until the autumn of 1939. When we began to test the heating system, we had more time to have a look round the buildings, where we quite often had conversations with men from other firms. We discovered that many of them had also kept their political convictions — if not quite to the same degree as us.

Immediately after the work was completed, I and another colleague went to another building site. In Charlottenburg, a new administrative building for a large coal firm, Bubiag, was being erected at the corner of Kant Strasse and Uhland Strasse, and our firm was putting in the heating. While I was at the Air Defence College site, I had never had to go to the firm's offices, since all the deliveries of materials had been done by van; here it was different. Only four of us were employed there, and we had to take turns to return to headquarters to pick up materials and wage packets.

Two employees regularly came round there with collecting tins in aid of a 'winter aid' charity. I refused to donate anything here either, and always got into arguments with the collectors, until, at the end of 1940, Supervisor Souvang banned me from the building. I had to send one of my colleagues whenever I needed something.

During this time, war with Poland broke out; the troops from Berlin marched through Kant Strasse on their way to board the trains at Charlottenburg Station. In contrast to the First World War, when the soldiers were enthusiastically cheered on their way by the crowds, people stood detachedly on the pavements.

Only after the campaign against France in 1940, when the German army succeeded in less than five weeks in defeating the combined armies of the Western powers, was there a change in the mood of the populace. A tidal wave of chauvinism swept through Germany, sweeping with it large sections of the working population. Whereas the annexation of Austria in 1938 and the occupation of Czechoslovakia had scarcely raised an echo, now the victory in the west brought about something that the Nazis had always hoped for. In those days, weeks and months of 1940, it was scarcely possible to discuss the consequences of war, even in the factories.

The construction of the 'West Wall' and the introduction of military rule had already given our organisation some problems, since young comrades had been conscripted and many of them were sent off to the West Wall. Despite this we were able to continue our discussions in the groups.

In this period a discussion took place in Mexico, where Trotsky lived in exile. It concerned the differences between on the one hand Trotsky and the other Shachtman and Burnham, members of the Socialist Workers Party, the American section of the Fourth International. In the SWP, the Russian problem had been discussed anew after the signing of the pact between Hitler and Stalin. The Thermidor question was once more on the agenda. The SWP, an organisation with a strong section of workers, threatened to split over this question. Shachtman and Burnham defended the thesis that the Soviet Union was no longer a workers' state, but rather that the Thermidor had finally been victorious.

We learned about this debate through a comrade from out of town, who visited us in Berlin. According to his report, it appeared that, after the argument with Shachtman and Burnham, Trotsky finally decided that it had been a mistake to have defended the thesis of a degenerated workers' state for so long and not to have identified the victory of the political counter-revolution sooner. The Berlin organisation continued to defend the thesis of the degenerated workers' state ruled by a parasitic bureaucracy.

In the middle of this discussion, in August 1940, we suddenly had the news in the bourgeois press that Trotsky had been murdered in his Mexican exile. None of our comrades wanted to believe the news; we thought that it was a story cooked up by the class enemy to upset the work of the Fourth International. All contacts with the International Secretariat had already been broken by that time. In September, a comrade from western Germany visited us. He confirmed Trotsky's murder and told us that it had been Stalin's work, carried out by an agent who had managed to win Trotsky's trust. And in January 1941 we received confirmation in the December 1940 edition of *Our Word*; Leon Trotsky was dead.

The death suffered by Trotsky was one which he had had to live a thousand times. Firstly, in watching the murder of thousands of revolutionaries who had stood at Lenin's side and carried the October Revolution to success, but who were not prepared to submit to Stalin's dictates, since the principles of Marxism and Leninism were more important to them. Then in watching the deaths of members of his family, who had been persecuted by Stalin and, through a kind of guilt by association, had been driven to their deaths.

Trotsky knew that Stalin wanted him dead to strike a blow at the entire Opposition in the International. The attempt on his life which had failed made it clear to him and his friends that he had been condemned to death.

When we finally had in our hands confirmation of Trotsky's death, in the pages of *Our Word*, we came out of our strict illegality for the first time, or at least relaxed it. All the older Berlin comrades met at the house of comrade Trigojess in Charlottenburg, at number 1 Knobelsdorff Strasse, together with the leaders of the groups of five, including some from the areas just outside Berlin, in order to honour Trotsky's powerful figure and to reaffirm our commitment to defend the principles of Marxism and Leninism in the fight against Fascism.

At the end of December 1940, Supervisor Souvang asked me to come to the office, where he told me that I would have to disappear from the immediate view of the works council, since the difficulties he was having with the chair were increasing. Karl Fels, who had been supervising a site on the Baltic island of Riems for more than a year now, had asked for some more men; he would be delighted if I could go.

I replied that I would gladly transfer, partly because the thought of working with Karl Fels again appealed to me, partly because I liked the sea. But first I would have to speak to my wife, since the job was quite a long one; Souvang mentioned six to eight months. My wife had no objections, so I travelled to Riems in early January. I was met at the station at Greifswald by an architect named Siechert who had an office there, and was taken by car to Gristow, a small fishing village, from where a cable ferry took us to the island.

It was late in the afternoon when we arrived. After our welcome, I moved into quarters, sharing a room with a colleague. There were two of us to a room in a barrack hall; the workers for the firm had to sleep eight to a room. In the evening, we would sit together and talk about Berlin and about the political situation.

According to our contract, we were allowed three days of paid leave every six weeks. On the very first occasion, neither the people in charge on the island, nor the site foreman, Siechert the architect, thought about how we were to get to the station at Greifswald. Before the outbreak of war, there had been a bus service between Greifswald and Stralsund, but this had stopped now. The next railway station was at Mesekenhagen. To get there, you had to walk for an hour; then there was the problem that none of the fast trains stopped there. Our complaints were ignored, although both the firm and the people in charge on the island had promised to get us to the train at Greifswald in good time.

In the meantime, most of the equipment was completed, the heating system had been handed over and most of the workers had been recalled to Berlin. In the end, only Fels and myself were left at the site. The time when I was supposed to have left Riems had long since passed; I had been

On the island of Riems in 1942: Oskar Hippe (left) with prisoner of war

there for more than a year now. I could only meet up with the comrades in Berlin when I was visiting the city. On those occasions we discussed the political situation and the tactics of our future political work with the leaders of the groups of five.

With the passing to time, my colleagues and I had managed to find a way of getting safely to the station at Greifswald. The driver for the building firm was a 'maid of all work' and always discontented, without noticing how badly he was being exploited. In the evening he often sat with the cook in the POWs canteen. (On this island, more than a hundred Belgian and French prisoners of war were employed, replacing all the workers who had gone off to fight.) He listened to all the conversations amongst the fitters, including those from other firms. In secret conversations with myself and Karl Fels, he became convinced that our way to a just social order was the better one. With his help we succeeded in making the connection with our train on the days we travelled to Berlin.

The inhabitants of the island regarded the fitters from elsewhere as communists. In fact, most of them had once been Social Democrats or simply just trade unionists who made no boast of their rejection of 'National Socialism', but otherwise were in no way activists. Despite that, they tried to collect incriminating material from the evening conversations in the POW canteen. We had learned from the manager of the canteen —who was in fact a member of the NSDAP but remained a social democrat in his beliefs, and with whom we could discuss anything — that one of the workers from the slaughterhouse had been instructed to act as stool-pigeon. This spy often came in the evening in order to surprise us. But since he went around in wooden clogs, we could hear him from miles away and could change our topic of conversation in good time.

One evening he really did manage to catch us, because he had crept up in his stockinged feet. As luck would have it, we were just discussing some economic problems. Despite this, he cried triumphantly: 'Now I've caught you!', and ran off to fetch the NSDAP leader at the base. The canteen manager was able to confirm that we had simply been discussing economic problems, and so the report burst like a bubble.

On Riems, they made a serum from the blood of cattle which was intended to combat foot and mouth disease. In January 1942, the research department on the island was supposed to conduct experiments on the reaction of sick animals to heated stalls. My colleague Fels gave me the task of installing a heating system in three stalls; he himself laid the supply pipes in a conduit. The stalls were too small to work in, so I had to stay out in the open air. I stood on a sand dune with trestle and portable forge, in 30 degrees below zero.

I told Fels that I was quite prepared to complete the stall, but if someone forced me to install heating in the other two, then I would pack my bags and leave for Berlin. So the research department contented itself with a single heated stall, and the other two to be completed in the spring. In the boiler-room, the condenser installation had to be changed, so I moved into the boiler-room with my tools. I was given as assistant one of the French POWs, and got on very well with him.

He often disappeared; when he returned he would tell me that he had been speaking to comrade Thorez and so had been delayed. This comrade Thorez was the brother of the chair of the French Communist Party; I often talked to him as well, and had political discussions. He knew that I belonged to the IKD, the International Communists of Germany, but in many questions he shared our opinions. After the end of the war I never heard anything more of him, although he had promised he would write.

Through Thorez I got to know many of the prisoners of war. Whenever I returned to Berlin, they asked me to get them something, and I could usually oblige. I came back with pocket knives, combs and other utensils; they were always delighted when I had managed to get them everything. My colleagues all knew that it was forbidden to befriend the POWs, and behaved accordingly.

In November 1941, fifteen Russian prisoners came from the POW camp at Greifswald, to work for a Hamburg firm at the request of the president of the island. This firm was supposed to be constructing a 'Düker', a pipeline to be laid on the sea floor between the island and the mainland; until now they had been unable to employ anyone except one fitter. The president decreed that the Russian prisoners should be accommodated on the mainland opposite Riems in a corrugated iron hut which had once served as a garage for a lorry. In addition, they were not allowed to eat the meals served at the canteen, but were given a special meal which consisted mostly of potato peelings.

The question of the conditions in which the Russian prisoners lived brought about the first serious disagreement I had with my colleague Fels. He had been told by the management to install iron bars across the window of the corrugated iron garage. Fels was prepared to this; I refused to help him and told him that it was inhuman to keep the prisoners in a garage.

If he thought that that was a refusal to do reasonable work, then he could send me back to Berlin if he wanted; apart from anything else, this was the sole responsibility of the management of the island and did not lie within our brief. We were here to install heating and air-conditioning equipment, not to build prisons for prisoners of war.

He did not speak to me for three weeks after that, except in matters concerning work. When I told him that this business of ignoring each other was ridiculous, and that it might be better if I returned home, he finally came to his senses and slowly our old relationship of trust returned. With the help of the French POWs we managed to get a pail of food out of the canteen each day, along with two loaves of bread, and take them to the Russian prisoners. After three months, with the winter almost gone, the Russian prisoners were moved on to the island itself. We had often talked about it with the chief chemist, Piel, who was a friend of the camp commandant at Greifswald, and through him and his contact at Greifswald, we finally got the Russians accommodated on the island in permanent huts.

My work at the rebuilding of the water condenser was going well. Despite this, management did not think it was going fast enough, and they demanded that we make the prisoners work harder. I asked the manager to come with me to the boiler-room and read the thermometer: the temperature there often went up to 48 degrees, since the boilers had to remain running. I also pointed out to him that it was not my job to make the prisoners work harder; I was quite happy to use them in my work. If he wanted, then he could give me a second prisoner. He did just that.

Every morning at seven o'clock, when our work began, the few workers who were still at the disposal of the island management gathered for a 'news report' in the boiler house. And how they revelled in the successes of the German troops in the battles against the Red Army! One day, when there was great delight in new successes, I could not prevent myself from saying: if whole sections of any army are wiped out, then that does not happen without a battle, and there must be German losses as well in these battles.

Even that was too much for them. I was called a 'communist swine' by the stoker who worked at the high-pressure boiler plant. I replied that, just like him, I was a German worker and demanded that he take back the word 'swine' — he could think what he wanted about the first word. In the exchange which followed, he reached for a poker to hit me with, but I got to him first, and after one blow, he lay on the floor in front of the boilers.

It did not take long for the manager to turn up: how did I come to hit the stoker? According to the conditions of employment, I could be punished with a prison sentence. Although I had reckoned that the affair would be handed over to the director of the base, I was surprised that nothing else happened. This was because some of those present had to admit that the stoker had threatened me first.

After three months we had finished our work on the condenser. The manager had told Fels that he was very pleased with our work. He knew that he could find nothing wrong with it. Our firm was quite often unable to send two replacements to Riems at the weekends, because of the shortage of workers. So Fels and I often agreed to work through the weekend to carry out work which could only be done when everyone else had gone. We were greatly overworked; despite this, the manager took the French POWs away and gave me a Russian assistant. At first I regretted this, but later found out that I had a real helper in this man. He was a mechanic by trade, and so we got on well. The Russians had learned German at school, even in the primary schools, where it had been a compulsory subject.

The German colleague who had laid the 'Düker' pipeline with the Russian POWs had his wife with him. Since the regulations regarding diseases banned dependants from living on the island, he had built himself a home on the mainland right next to the corrugated iron hut, and had taken a lot of trouble to teach the Russians to converse in German. Almost all the Russians spoke German relatively well. I had a very good relationship with the one who worked with me, as I had had with my French assistants. I could also have political discussions with the Russians. Only two of the prisoners were members of the Komsomol (the Communist Youth League of the Soviet Union), but all of them approved of the social system in which they had lived. But they kept telling me: 'Lenin good, Stalin not good'. We worked together for months. In the morning, before we began our work, we sat on the trestle — our workbench — to smoke a cigarette and drink a beer.

One morning there was great excitement on the island: two of the Russians had run away. They had taken a fishing boat from the mainland and, with a sail they had made themselves, tried to cross the Baltic to their homeland. They had been sighted by the navy to the north of Rügen and brought back. In the evening there was a shout: 'The Russians are coming!' A building worker who had treated prisoners badly on other sites is said to have fainted when he heard that, or so his colleagues told us. But it was only the two prisoners coming back. A few days later all the Russian POWs were taken back to the camp at Greifswald, and we never heard what happened to them after that. When they left, my Josef had tears in his eyes, and fell on my neck crying; I could only tell him to have courage.

In this connection I would like to relate an episode which shook me to the core. One weekend, when I was travelling back to Berlin and was waiting for my train, a goods train stopped opposite me and Russian prisoners were disembarked. Many of them were already dead or so weak that they needed to be carried off the train. As we later learned from the railway workers, this train had been travelling for a very long time and had no provisions.

The 'president' of the island, Professor Waldmann, a strict Catholic and all-powerful ruler of Riems, never spoke to anyone. The seating in the canteen was arranged according to his rules: he ate with the chief chemist; the next rank down was composed of the vets; in the third were the assistants and laboratory workers, in the fourth lowly employees. Each of of these groups had its own dining room. All the remaining personnel had their own canteen far away from the officers' mess, and even we, as fitters and workers for the building firms, were looked after outside. In May 1945, after Germany's capitulation, Waldmann managed to continue in his capacity as president of the island and was given the same full powers in the Soviet Occupied Zone — to which Riems then belonged — as the Prussian government had once given him. However, later there must have been arguments, for he then emigrated to the Western Zone with all his research material.

Even in the workers' canteen, there were regulations handed down by the president, according to which the employees were subdivided into different categories — most of which were ignored. Waldmann arranged that the midday news on the radio should be broadcast in the canteen. There were endless reports of victories on the eastern and western fronts. To the east they talked of 'the destruction of the Soviet army', to the west, it was the 'the destruction of the Anglo-American merchant navy'. One day there was a report that an encircling movement had destroyed an army in the east, with 250,000 men taken prisoner, and the sinking of 400,000 tonnes of shipping on the high seas. Naturally, when reports like that came over the radio, they were greeted by the singing of the German National Anthem and the 'Horst Wessel', standing with arm outstretched.

For a moment we were so surprised that we stood up as well; but at the same moment I said to my colleagues 'Sit down again,' (which we did), 'eating is far more important than this circus.' Of course, someone reported this to the commander of the base, and this time there was going to be an investigation. Schultz was accused; he was a fitter for AEG, who was putting together the machines for a new refrigeration block. (In the refrigeration block they kept seagulls' eggs which were then sent to all the various ministries as delicacies.) But on the day concerned, Schultz had not even been in the canteen. So then they looked for 'ringleaders'. Karl Fels was friendly with the commander of the base and persuaded him to pursue the matter no further. From then on, we only went for our meal after the news on the radio had finished.

There were two attempts at escape by the French prisoners of war. One was successful, the other failed.

A French prisoner who had worked with a German as an electrician came to us and told us that he wanted to try to get back to his home town, Paris. He would need a map of Germany, civilian clothing and enough to eat for a few days; we got him all this. In the evening I was to determine whether the boat which he had anchored at a certain spot was still there. After darkness had fallen, I gave him a signal that all was well. On the following morning he had the guard let him out two hours earlier, which was not remarked upon, since it often happened. Only on the evening of that day did anyone notice that the prisoner was missing. No one had noticed earlier since his German colleague had some business in Greifswald that day. A few days later, we learned from comrade Thorez that the escapee had reached Paris. He had journeyed for some of the time hanging between railway wagons, and sometimes in goods wagons.

Oskar Hippe (centre) with colleagues from Hamburg on the island of Riems in 1942

The second attempt at escape was supposed to be made with the aid of a motor boat which before the war had towed large barges from Sweden across the Baltic with animal feed. The boat was seaworthy; all that was missing was the diesel oil. The would-be escapees asked Fels and myself whether we could get the diesel for them; we would not have to get anything else. We got in touch with the president's driver who was prepared to supply us in instalments. According to his calculations, we would need almost 200 litres. For months we collected the necessary amount of diesel fuel and stored it in the pipes of the heating system.

The attempt was scheduled for a Sunday afternoon, since at that time the guards would be over on the south side of the island. The entrance to the harbour was very narrow and somewhat silted as well, since it had not been used for more than two years. As I remember, twelve or fourteen prisoners were involved in the escape. After they had launched the boat into the water, everything went well at first. But as soon as they got out to the middle of the channel, the boat grounded in the shallow water. They manoeuvred to try to get the boat clear, but did not succeed. To cap it all, a group of women then appeared on the north side of the island. They raised the alarm. The prisoners could do nothing except abandon the boat and return to their quarters. Luckily, in the investigation which followed, none of those involved could be identified.

For my colleagues and I, and for the chauffeur who had supplied the fuel, there now began days of tension and unrest, although Thorez and another man had promised that under no circumstances would they implicate us if anything went wrong. The commandant of the POW camp at Greifswald appeared in person in order to conduct the investigation with the island management. However, it was not Professor Waldmann who led the investigation with him, but the chief chemist, Dr Piel, the camp commandant's friend. After day-long interrogations of the prisoners, who unanimously denied having been involved in the escape or knowing anything about its preparation, the whole thing petered out.

In the meantime the war had also reached the island of Riems. In Peenemünde, the Nazis had built a research centre for so-called V-weapons — rockets which were to be launched against Britain. More and more frequently, air raids were launched by the Allies against Peenemünde. One evening there was a massive raid by British planes. All around us the anti-aircraft guns thundered, and we saw several planes hit and crashing in flames into the Baltic. One bomber, burning like a torch, kept trying to gain height. It flew directly towards our island; it flew right over the roofs of the cattle stalls and, on the other side of the island, on the mainland near the village of Gristow, the machine crashed and exploded. A few days later the corpses of the air crew were washed up — they were Canadians.

The local population, still under the influence of the chauvinistic atmosphere, rejoiced over the shooting down of the machines. The deaths simply did not affect them. Every attempt to speak to them about the senselessness of war was immediately met with protests. We had to bite our tongues at the risk of being denounced. Only two people in Gristow were capable of political discussion, the innkeeper, and the fisherman who had his little house outside the village on the hill called Bückowberg. In the summer, my wife and I stayed with him, and, in the course of time, we developed a friendship. All the other inhabitants were fanatical supporters of the Nazi system.

In the autumn of 1942, workers for the building firm who lived in Greifswald and the surrounding area told us that, a few days previously, two Poles who did forced labour on a farm had been lynched in one of the villages. Two hundred Poles from near and far had had to witness the execution. The victims were accused of having had a relationship with two German girls. At first I could not believe that such a severe punishment could be meted out for this, and I asked an acquaintance of mine in Greifswald for the details. She confirmed that the whole thing had taken place as reported. The two girls had had their hair shorn off, which the inhabitants of the island and the village of Gristow found quite reasonable.

In February 1943 I travelled once more to Berlin to spend my three days' leave there. As always, I had discussions with the comrades about the political situation and our organisation. Very few of our younger comrades remained in Berlin — all of them had been called up to the military, and the 35-45 year-olds had been sent to fight the partisans in the Balkans. Not one of them returned. We learned that one of them had been court-martialled and shot for collaborating with the partisans. For the comrades who remained, it was becoming increasingly difficult to do any propaganda work, but all of us were convinced of the necessity of keeping up all possible contacts and of establishing new ones.

Events took a new course with the defeat of the Sixth Army under Paulus in February 1943 at Stalingrad. It was clear to us that this military defeat also demanded a change in our own tactics. It was no longer a question of training a cadre and steeling them politically, but now also of preparing them for the political fight. But for that it was not enough to have a high political awareness; they also needed military preparedness.

In contrast to the Stalinist party, which placed its trust entirely in the Red Army and awaited liberation by it, I put forward the view in our organisation that it was now our responsibility to work both in the factories and the ranks of the KPD to build up resistance groups of a military nature which, when the Allied troops had reached German soil, would be able to intervene in the fight against the German army. In discussions, it was difficult to convince the comrades of the necessity of this work.

In this period I also received a summons to report to the Third Army Regional Command in Grolmann Strasse in Charlottenburg. When I arrived there, a major sat at a desk and informed me that the time had now come for every German to be put to the test, including those 'unworthy of service' like myself. Now every man could prove how he would stand by the Fatherland in its hour of need.

I told him that I had to consider myself, being 'unworthy of service', as a second-class citizen, and could not even think of signing the voluntary enlistment form which he offered me. I replied that I made a distinction between the rule of 'National Socialism' and Germany. I had always put Germany first, ever since I had begun my political activity. I had fought against 'National Socialism' and had been punished for it. Since that time I had been treated as a second-class citizen. But if the Führer believed that he could not win the war without me, then there was nothing stop him from annulling the Military Service (Unworthiness) Law and making me a soldier. He could think of nothing to answer that, except that we all had to 'serve'. I got so carried away as to say to him that only serfs serve, but free men act according to their inner conviction. After that, I think, the walls came down and he ranted and raged. In the end he threw me out.

After being thrown out I was convinced that the Gestapo would turn up. My wife supported me. She said that there had to be people who had the courage to say what they thought. On the next day I travelled back to my work on Riems. I had arranged with my wife that, if the Gestapo appeared, she was to send me a telegram with some meaningless phrase, signed by another name.

My friends and comrades did not agree with my actions, and accused me of acting against the interests of the organisation. Within myself I knew they were correct. They demanded that I should emigrate, but I refused. First of all I wanted to see what would happen. On Riems I still had time to disappear if they wanted to arrest me. Several weeks went by and the Gestapo did not turn up. We assumed that the major had not reported this argument to the Gestapo, for nothing happened about it even later.

During my absence, the Berlin comrades and the groups in the districts around Berlin had continued to discuss the problem of building military resistance groups. They had agreed on the conception put forward by the earlier minority, which I had represented; with the aid of comrades from the KPD and SAPD in the factories, they had organised groups of that sort amongst sympathisers, since we were not strong enough to do that work on our own. Unfortunately we found that there was no support for our ideas, especially amongst the comrades in the KPD. There it stood: there were comrades who told us that they had fought for long enough and were no longer prepared to help us. But they were among the first to run to the 'self-government agencies' after the occupation by the Allies to offer themselves for administrative work. So we had to abandon our plans.

The battles in Berlin later, when two groups of the German army fought against the SS around Sophie Charlotte Platz and Kaiserdamm, were vindication enough for the construction of military resistance groups like ours. The leader of one of these German army groups belonged to the Communist Party after 1945 and was the first head of personnel in the District Authority of Charlottenburg.

In Berlin, as in the rest of the country, there had been extensive raids by the British air force. They came with hundreds of planes, and the destruction grew greater.

Until then I had only experienced the war from afar, and not just in the military sense. The management of the island was always concerned with preventing any shortfall in food. In November 1943, all the workers from outside were ordered back to Berlin by the firm, to do 'catastrophe work'. When I returned from Riems, I came to a city on the front line. Buildings that had been destroyed were only repaired if necessary. That was the instruction from the Ministry of Labour to our firm. Only once an exception was made, and that was when the houses of some bigwigs were involved.

One day Supervisor Souvang gave me the job of repairing a heating system which had been destroyed in the house of an SS Obergruppenführer, Jüttner. Souvang instructed me to do not more there than I would elsewhere. One entire side of the house was missing, as if shaved away, but luckily the rising main to the expansion tank in the loft was still intact. The instruction to do only what was necessary was grist to the mill for me. I told the SS Gruppenführer that he was still in luck; if the rising main or the expansion tank had been damaged then it would have needed weeks of work. So I reconnected the radiator in one living room and one in a small boxroom, and shut off all the other radiators.

The Gruppenführer glued himself to the telephone to voice his complaints, but the Supervisor of Installations, Souvang, replied that he had sent a very experienced fitter and if he thought that there was nothing else to be done then that met with his approval. As I later learned, they gave the SS leader another apartment.

The firm had still not forgotten my politics. The winter aid collections and other collections still went round as before. As before I refused to donate anything or to sign any list. Souvang told me me that there was only one way to avoid attracting the attention of the chair of the workers' council. He had spoken with his brother, Fritz Souvang, who was head fitter at the Ministry of Transport on Wilhelm Platz; I should start work with him. On the very next day, I started there.

The ministries and the government Chancellery had suffered serious damage. Building workers from all trades were continually engaged in repairing the destruction. All these buildings had good air-raid shelters, but workers from contracted firms had no right to use them. Even at the Ministry of Transport, when there were air raids, we had to seek shelter in the inspection shafts for the telephone wires. It was hardly possible to breathe in there— the dust came down the conduits so thickly. But our firms did not bother about that.

One lunchtime there was another bombing raid, and seven of the Ministry's eight entrances were blocked by rubble. We sat in the boiler-room in the basement, where there were strong pillars with niches coming up from the foundations. One of the bombs exploded very close to us. Fortunately, we escaped the fragments which hurtled past because we were well-protected in the niche. But the principal rising main was hit, and hot water at 70 degrees flooded into the cellar. To avoid being boiled alive, we had to get out of there while the raid was still on.

On the same day my colleague Souvang went to the Transport Minister to protest at the unacceptable conditions for contract workers. If they were not allowed to use the air-raid shelters in the next raid, then the management of the firms concerned would stop all work in the building. A few hours later Ganzemüller, the Secretary of State, came to tell us that, with immediate effect, we were now permitted to use the air-raid shelter. We even managed to receive permission for my assistant, a young Pole, to use it as well.

This Pole was filled with a tremendous hatred for the Nazi regime. It took us a long time to convince him that there were also decent Germans who opposed the Nazis. His hatred was entirely understandable. He came from Warsaw. As a fifteen-year old he had been on his way to visit his sister when he was arrested by an SS troop for transportation to Germany to do forced labour. The same thing happened to countless Poles and Ukrainians.

Since he knew why he was being transported, he had tried to escape. At a favourable moment, he had jumped out of the lorry, but did not get far since the guard had shot at him as he fled. Hit in the leg, he was recaptured, operated on and taken to Germany on the next transport. He came to our firm at the age of seventeen, and slowly came to trust us.

Sometimes I took him with me to Werder, in the fruit-growing district. For this, we had got him a set of civilian clothes. In Werder we bartered for fruit with roofing felt and other items in great demand which my colleague Fritz had acquired. Everything which we came back with was split into three portions; he received the same as us. Sometimes I took him home with me and my wife looked after him. Unfortunately we heard nothing more of him after the war.

While the population starved and had to live on rations, the officials in the ministries were kept supplied with additional foodstuffs twice a week. Stored in a large room in a wing of the basement were gigantic amounts of food and luxuries. We were able to see for ourselves, since we had to do a repair down there. In the autumn of 1944, my colleague sent me to Schwanenwerder. Secretary of State Ganzemüller lived there in a large villa, together with his girlfriend and her mother. I was to replace the existing radiators with larger ones and install a new one in the turret room. The job lasted six days. When we began there was a five-litre jar of olive oil in the kitchen, almost full; when we had finished the job, it was almost empty.

In the cellars were apples and pears, a whole roomful. We could not resist taking something home with us; these people had so much that they would hardly notice if a few kilos went missing.

I was employed at the Ministry of Transport until the end of the war. As soon as one set of repairs was complete, there came another air raid. Unlike earlier bombing raids, they now attacked during the day. One day, a bomb — it must have been a ten-tonner — landed right on top of the air-raid bunker. There was only a slight vibration in the bunker itself and, apart from a few hair-line cracks on the ceiling, there was nothing to be seen. The bunker was said to have a three-metre-thick roof of reinforced concrete.

A few weeks before 20 July 1944 an official of the illegal trade union organisation informed us that there was a plan afoot to overthrow Hitler. We did not know any details, neither the day nor the hour of the attempt. We suspected that the military were playing a leading role.

By that time, contact with our leadership in exile had been lost, and we were on our own. Our contacts in the factories could tell us nothing either; they knew even less than us. So we took a decision in our executive meeting to issue a small number of leaflets and distribute them to our contacts. This leaflet warned these workers against taking part in any unauthorised activity. They should rather wait until the rumours were confirmed. That was our last leaflet.

Unfortunately I no longer have any of the material which was published in the twelve years of illegality, since as I said, a bomb from an aircraft destroyed the building at 26 Krumme Strasse where the illegal material was stored at my sister's apartment.

On 20 July, with defeat staring them in the face, the military attempted to save their own skins. The political and military leaders complemented each other in their desire to wipe out the disgrace of 1918 and to wrest the hegemony of Europe for themselves.

Since the defeat at Stalingrad and with the demise of Fascism in Europe certain, they now tried to replace the rule of 'National Socialism' with a state which they governed. To this end they had had talks in Switzerland. Certain circles in the illegal trade union movement were supposed to supply the democratic veneer. If the coup had succeeded, the working class could have expected nothing from these people.

If the masses had already been demoralised before 20 July, then their disillusionment only deepened afterwards. Even in the ARP organisations discipline had become lax. And in our building the air-raid warden found it impossible to get people to stand watch, although most of the residents belonged to the NSDAP.

The air-raid warden, Herr Hancke, told me that his bosses had called a general meeting of the residents in order to fill the post. In the late afternoon, the head of the ARP organisation in Charlottenburg turned up in a splendid uniform. All the residents of the building who were not at work assembled, including myself and my wife. My wife, by the way, having had training as an auxiliary nurse, had been drafted into the Red Cross two years previously and was called out during emergencies.

When our air-raid warden told his boss that it had been impossible for him to allocate responsibilities, the 'Herr General' demanded the list of names. My wife was first on the list, so he called out: 'Frau Hippe — fire watch for the building!' I spoke out against this and told him that my wife was in no position to take on this responsibility. He threatened to report me; he alone would decide what was done; my refusal bordered on sabotage.

Despite this I could not keep quiet: if he alone made the decisions, I said, then he should first ascertain whether the people he assigned to each task were actually able to do them. He only needed to look at my wife to see that her physical condition, as well as her responsibilities to the Red Cross, prevented her from climbing around on the roof with a fire blanket putting out the flames. And besides, I continued, it was certainly not the way the Führer would take a decision on such a complex matter, from some lofty standpoint, without checking first.

Although there were five men living in the building, including three in the NSDAP, he could not find a single firewatcher. He did not ask me again. At the end of the meeting it fell to a woman with three children to take on the job, because she did not know how to defend herself.

As it happened, I often went up to the lofts with the ARP during raids, sometimes while the alarm was still on, to put out incendiary bombs. Our building would have been burned down if the tenants had not put the fires out in good time. I should stress that the women had more courage than the men in situations like those.

Shortly before the end of the war I almost became a victim of the Nazis. In our building there was a bar — I think it was called 'Zum Ostpreussen'. The barkeeper, at one time a Social Democrat, and on whose premises we often held our meetings during the Weimar period, had kept up his convictions, while his wife had become a 'Nazi-ess'.

One of their sons had become an enthusiastic soldier and was hoping for a commission. During the war he had lost an arm. He was engaged to the daughter of the janitor, with whom we were friendly. On one occasion there was a small party going on in Herr Hummel's apartment — that was the name of the janitor — and my wife and I were also invited.

That evening there was a discussion about the course of the war. I put forward the view that the war was lost. Thereupon young master Rumprecht shouted: 'If we weren't in the house of my parents-in-law I would report you to the local office of the NSDAP!'

I encountered him another time; after my release from Bautzen prison in 1956, I found him in the SPD; he had meanwhile climbed on to the first rung of the administrative section of the Berlin Senate, heading a section in the Constitutional Department.

We could now conduct our political work only with the greatest difficulty. All the young comrades were in the army and stationed on various fronts. There were only people older than 50 in the groups — I was the youngest at 44. A large number of our sympathisers had also gone off to the military.

'General Heldenkau' ('Hero's Claw') was going through the factories looking for 'human material' for the front; the jobs thus vacated were filled by POWs and forced labour. The daily rations, which had until then been better than during the First World War, were now cut back appreciably.

During the years of the war until then, the occupied territories, particularly to the east, had had to pay for the relatively good nourishment of the Germans. But now the expanses of Poland and the Soviet Union were lost, and the Red Army was already fighting in East Prussia.

In the west, the Allies had pushed far forward from their bridge-head at Cherbourg, although the German offensive in the Ardennes was still holding them up. In the east, however, the Soviet troops continued their relentless march forwards. By January 1945 they had reached the river Oder. But it would still be months before the defeat of the army was complete. At Küstrin the Red Army had succeeded in establishing a bridge-head west of the Oder. In the last days of March, the offensive against Berlin began.

At the end of April, Russian troops had reached the eastern edge of the city. On the morning of 24 April we suddenly heard the thunder of guns and exploding shells. We were just sitting down to breakfast at our work in the Ministry. I went out into the courtyard to convince myself that it really was enemy fire, for a few days earlier members of the German army had started to build barricades and to set up gun emplacements.

I was just getting to the door when two shells exploded in the upper floors. We agreed to stop work under these conditions. We were going to meet up again on the following morning to get our tools to safety.

When the firing had stopped, we left the Ministry. On the afternoon of the same day placards appeared at all the suburban railway stations to say that the railway was closed to all civilian traffic and was now at the disposal of the leading ranks of the army for purposes of transporting troops and materials.

The next morning I went by bicycle towards the city centre. Near the Zoo Station, a squadron of Russian aircraft was attacking the bunker at the zoo, which had anti-aircraft guns on its roof. Then it was 'all clear' until the Potsdam Bridge, but I saw the first bodies right after that.

I waited at the Ministry of Transport for my colleagues, but in vain. I could not carry the tool-boxes all on my own, for together they weighed more than two hundredweight. There were only a couple of labourers left in the building, all the officials having fled. I asked one of the labourers to help me take the tool-boxes to safety. His reply was: 'That's all shit — everything is lost.'

People like him, who only yesterday spoke about the 'final victory', were not prepared to safeguard the tools for tomorrow's rebuilding. So I did the work on my own. With the aid of lenghts of piping which I placed under the boxes, I rolled them into niches which were protected by strong pillars. Then I went back home.

I had ridden some hundred metres when a Russian artillery attack began. I hid myself under a fire engine and waited for the firing to stop. Luckily the shells landed on the other side of the canal.

In the meantime, 'People's Storm Battalions' (Volkssturm) had been set up in Berlin, and all males up to the age of 65 were drafted into them.

AND RED IS THE COLOUR OF OUR FLAG

They left me alone, or forgot about me, but I was not offended. The encirclement of Berlin was tightening. On 29 April came a report that Russian troops had reached the Jungfernheide. At that time I lived in Spielhagen Strasse, which ran parallel to Bismarck Strasse.

On that day, a troop of German soldiers marched through Kaiser Friedrich Strasse. They were intending to crack a Russian tank. I tried to make it clear to them that any resistance was pointless. 'The war is lost; come home with us and we'll give you civilian clothes to help you avoid being captured.'

They refused, telling me that the Russians had already been halted in their tracks. The army under Wenck was already supposed to be at Dessau, waiting to relieve Berlin. I only realised afterwards how dangerous it was to argue with soldiers like that. The SS had hanged soldiers from lamp-posts everywhere because they did not want to fight any more, and civilians were hanged because they had spoken out against the continuation of the war.

On the morning of the same day, along one side of Kaiser Friedrich Strasse from Schloss Platz almost as far as Bismarck Strasse, there were double rows of Russian tanks — the light tanks in front, the heavy ones behind; the other side of the road was filled with heavy artillery, also in a double row.

The first Russian soldiers who entered our building in search of German soldiers left the apartments again immediately without harming the civilians. The only thing they asked for was something to drink. But anyone who gave them a drink had to taste it first.

The unpleasant side of things began in the evening when the soldiers who had not been in the front line harassed the women, searched apartments and took sheets and clothing from one apartment into the next. On the second evening, a front line soldier in leather clothing came into our basement and got interested in Edith Hancke, later an actress, who was then fifteen years old.

The combined efforts of myself, my wife and a tenant who knew Russian succeeded in persuading him to leave again. On the following morning, as every day, I went with my wife to fetch water, since the mains supply had failed. We had to walk to a pump in Schul Strasse. We had just filled our bucket when the soldier of the previous evening appeared. He was completely drunk and insulted my wife in the most unpleasant manner. I tried to get through to him. So he turned towards me. He wore a suit that was far too tight for him, and that was perhaps my salvation. When he tried to get a pistol out of his pocket, he failed.

A 'starshina' (sergeant) of the tank division who had observed this drama, climbed down from his tank, disarmed him, and restrained him.

During the days of the battle of Berlin, Russian soldiers tried to get hold of watches. The Geneva Convention permitted every Russian soldier to confiscate one watch in the course of the war. But they did not stop at a single watch — many of them had them strapped right up their forearms.

One day a Russian soldier — who was no longer young — came up with his rifle pointing and shouted 'Watch!' His cry did not go unheeded. All of a sudden he roared with laughter, gave everyone their watches back and declared: 'German stupid. Hide watch! Why give away all?'

A section of the Polish division which was deployed in my part of the town behaved in a very restrained manner towards the German civilian population. There were no attacks of any sort, although on 30 April a 'Werewolf Group' tried to blow up the commander of the Polish unit at his headquarters in a basement apartment at 87 Kaiser Friedrich Strasse. But the Werewolves were discovered in time and shot.

An acquaintance of ours, Frau Andreczewski, had made contact with some Polish officers. She had a perfect command of the Polish language. She had come to Berlin with her husband after the First World War. I was often at their apartment and was able to converse with the Polish officers. When asked about the correct behaviour of their troops towards the inhabitants, they explained that they had not come to Germany to take revenge on the civilian population. Their task was to smash Fascism and to ensure that the treaties of Yalta and Tehran were respected.

My wife had never lost her nerve during the years of the war. But now, with Russian soldiers roaming through the cellars, although nothing had happened to her or any of the women in our building, she angrily demanded that I find a way to get out of Berlin.

All my attempts to convince her that it was impossible came to nothing. I had to go and look, but got no further than Schloss Strasse, in the company of comrade Trigojess, who lived at the corner of Schloss Strasse and Knobelsdorff Strasse. (The meetings of our executive had taken place at his home during the years of illegality.) He came back with me, and with his help we managed to calm my wife down and bring her to her senses.

I survived one more precarious situation: the fighting had finished, but there were still individual soldiers going through the apartments, including ours. I had been able to preserve pictures of Lenin, Trotsky, Marx, Engels, Luxemburg and Liebknecht throughout the Nazi era. With the exception of the picture of Trotsky, I had stood them on top of a cupboard in the hallway. Two soldiers came into our apartment. My wife was alone. Whilst one of them sniffed about the apartment, the other talked to my wife —

who could speak Polish — in the hope of getting close to her. She led him out of the kitchen into the hallway and showed him the pictures. When he saw Lenin, he fetched his friend and said: 'Lenin lives here. Come on, let's go.'

Still during the fighting, on 1 May, I had gone out to fetch some water. A man came towards me on the same side of the street, putting into mailboxes leaflets issued by the North Charlottenburg branch of the Communist Party. I got talking to him. He told me that members of the KPD in North Charlottenburg had refounded the party on 28 April, with the permission of the Russian section commander, and since then they had been out campaigning.

Although he had been a member of the Communist Workers' Party (KAP) for many years, this man had joined them since he believed that a resistance fighter had to take an active role in any situation which arose. I told him that I was also a resistance fighter and until now had been fighting Fascism with an opposition group. I said I would come and visit him as soon as I could. When the fighting had stopped, on 2 May, I went to see him.

I met him again in the party offices of the reconstituted KPD in Tegler Weg. This was comrade Emil Bohn, with whom, as secretary of the district committee of the Free German Trade Union Federation (FDGB), I was later to rebuild the trade unions in the factories. In 1947 he and his family moved to Halle.

12.

POLITICAL RENEWAL

The war had finished but the destruction was unimaginable. Eighty per cent of Berlin was either destroyed or seriously damaged. There was not a single building which had not suffered some damage. All means of transport had stopped, and part of the Underground railway was under water — in the battle for Berlin, the SS had flooded the Underground shafts.

The streets were partly blocked by the rubble and houses which had collapsed. The resistance fighters, with the help of the population in each district, took it upon themselves to clear the rubble and make the streets passable again. The Nazis, who were responsible for the chaos, had to be dragged out of their apartments before they would help with the clearance work.

The Russian occupying power, who exercised all control over Berlin for the first three months, called for the building of organs of self administration. The first news sheets appeared, but only one person in ten could get hold of them, since there was a shortage of paper and presses.

A public order troop was also formed, who did service as unarmed auxiliary policemen. I reported for duty with them. Our main responsibility was to transport and distribute meat and food. A comrade of the KPD, a man from Charlottenburg who had spent twelve years in Brandenburg prison for conspiracy to commit high treason and who had been released by the Russian army, took over the police station on the Kaiserdamm.

He offered to let me take over the police station in Richard Wagner Strasse. I refused because I did not wish to become subject to the orders of the occupation powers, and I saw my task lying in the construction of a militant socialist party which, independently of the occupation powers, would act in the interests of the working class.

My activity as a policeman was short-lived. I always had to remind myself what the role of the police was in the apparatus of the state, serving the interests of capitalist society. And this state too, which would arise under the control of the victorious powers, would either be a capitalist one or, in the Soviet Zone, a bureaucratically-governed state which had nothing to do with the principles of Marxism or Leninism.

So, after twelve days, I left the police and reported back to the surveyor's office from which I had been sacked in 1933 according to the provisions of the Law on Public Servants. Neither Teschner, the head surveyor, nor Herr Friedrich were employed there any more.

The office was managed by a man who had worked there as a volunteer in 1933. Our work consisted in determining the extent of war damage within the administrative district of the local authority.

In the meantime, the cells of five in our Charlottenburg organisation had dissolved and been incorporated into the newly-built regional organisation. Our ranks had been considerable thinned. Of the twelve comrades who had been sent to Yugoslavia to fight the partisans, only a single one had returned.

Three comrades had vanished in the east. Our organisation had lost more to the military campaigns than to the Gestapo and their arrests. We decided to concentrate our main activities in the trade union area and, wherever possible, to penetrate the ranks of the KPD, in order to agitate for Marxism and Leninism.

Only later, when transport was once more provided by the Berlin Transport Authority, did we manage to get in touch with other groups in Berlin.

Alongside the Communist Party, which was the first to be reconstituted — the refounding of the SPD followed on from it — the trade unions took up their work again. In contrast to the trade and professional federations which had existed during the Weimar Republic and earlier, the organisational principles for the industrial federations was this: one factory, one trade union. The umbrella organisation was the Free German Trade Union Confederation (FDGB), made up of seventeen industrial trade unions.

In the district committee of the FDGB in Charlottenburg, the representatives were not elected by the workers, but appointed proportionally by the KPD and SPD; the CDU, which was founded later, got two votes. I was the only representative on the district committee who had been elected by a meeting of building workers.

The headquarters of the FDGB was in Wall Strasse in the Soviet Sector. The FDGB and the political parties were supervised by the control officers of the occupying powers. Officially, they were called trade union officers.

Their task was to set up trade unions according to the rules laid down by the occupying powers.

In spring 1946, a third secretary was to be appointed to the district committee. The working committee offered me the post. I turned it down and told them that I would not stay long in the job, since the secretary of the organisation, Walter, had no time for any opinions but his own, or rather, those of the Soviet occupying power.

The SPD representatives in the district committee announced that they and some of the KPD would support me and that they would guarantee my work. Despite this, I turned the offer down a second time, since I knew the Stalinists' methods better than they did.

When they offered the job a third time and said that I could take over responsibility for youth work, I finally agreed. Firstly, because I was of the opinion that it was worthwhile working amongst and for the youth, and secondly, because I could then influence the youth groups in the rest of the city, since there were no youth sections in the political parties.

However, I laid down one condition: I would only accept if I could be given leave of absence from my job at the surveyor's office in order to build the trade unions. 'But you will always have a job here', came back the echo. I repeated: 'If you want me to work as the paid secretary of the district committee, then get me leave of absence.' I was quite certain that my new job would not last very long.

Comrade Bohn, together with a representative of the CDU, Kozal, who worked in the district committee, went to the personnel manager and asked that I be given leave; this was duly given and confirmed in writing. Together with Bohn, I then began liaison work, while Kozal looked after commercial matters. Each day we attended two, sometimes three meetings — in that period, trade union meetings took place during work hours.

One day our colleague Kozal told us that the trade union officer seemed to know exact details of our political position; he had apparently told Kozal that Emil Bohn was a long-standing member of the Communist Workers' Party and that until recently I had worked as a Trotskyist.

I later spoke to the officer about this and told him that, if he wanted to know anything about me or my political work, it would be better if he came to me and I would give him more reliable information. He was somewhat embarrassed and said that he was a member of the British Labour Party, and that his enquiries had only been for himself.

I replied that, if he knew that I was a member of the Trotskyist Opposition, then he also knew that I had fought with the resistance to the end and that I was not prepared to do anything contrary to my political principles.

At all the meetings where I spoke, I had to defend myself against the standpoint put forward by the occupying powers that the German nation was collectively guilty in the war; this conception was tolerated by all the German parties, without exception.

During the first months after the war, I was not only active in the trade union movement. Immediately after the founding of the workers' parties and our decision to operate initially inside the KPD, I took up work with Emil Bohn in the local branch of the KPD.

Shortly after the KPD was founded, some comrades got together to found the 'Richard Hüttig Group' in Schiller Strasse. I had already worked with some of them during the war. With this group we intended to put down roots for the basics of Marxism and Leninism and to develop our own policies against the Stalinists.

As early as the summer of 1945 I was elected the political leader of the 'Richard Hüttig Group'. I was also elected as instructor for a second group in Windscheld Strasse. The two groups had more than 300 members. There were always arguments with the sub-district of Charlottenburg, whose executive was led by an old Stalinist, comrade Schönwald-Masslovski. Their attempts to prevent me from carrying out my political functions resulted in the members of both groups banning the representatives of the sub-district from speaking to them.

One day I received a summons to the Berlin regional leadership, signed by Bruno Baum, who was then the regional leader of the KPD. Baum wanted to know why I had arranged that members of the district leadership were banned from speaking to the groups which I led. I told him that it was not I, but comrade Schönwald who had been responsible for this decision. Secondly, Baum wanted to know where I stood on the Soviet Union.

I told him that, all the time that the Communist Party of the Soviet Union did not return to Marxist-Leninist principles, then I would not give up my stance on these problems. Besides, I said, the Communist International had been dissolved by the Russian party in 1943, and there were no other ties beyond those of friendship. And the De-Nazification Commissions had accepted dozens of people into the party in the past few months without asking them about the Soviet Union.

'Yes,' said Baum, 'but it's different with you; you could be selected to give talks on Russian questions, and then we would have to know how you stood on the Soviet Union.'

I replied that I still adopted a positive attitude to the October Revolution and would defend it. But Stalinism was another question altogether. It was not I who would have to revise my opinion, but those who had caused the defeats of the German and international working class. And with that we parted.

Only a short time later, I received a letter from the district leadership, telling me that comrades who had been expelled from the KPD in the past could no longer remain members. I went with this letter to the groups which I led in order to explain things to them. Almost without exception, the members of the group backed me up.

So I was able to continue to defend and strengthen my political position for weeks. It was not a question of being a member or leader of these groups — rather, I wanted to be accepted as a full member of the KPD by the Berlin regional and district executives. But my attempts to mobilise the comrades of the two groups did not succeed.

I had told them that I would not take part in any of the political work unless they acted on my behalf — but they remained inactive. So the question of my membership was settled. Perhaps it was a mistake to try to enforce my membership in this way. But in the meantime we had begun to build up our own Berlin groups again; apart from that I was very busy with trade union work; so I did not think it sensible for me to continue my work inside the Communist Party under these conditions.

Our Trotskyist group in Berlin was at full strength again; 52 comrades had taken up their work again, although that was less than in 1933 when we had fought Fascism in illegality. In 1932-1933 and later, we had expected — as did Trotsky — that, in the event of the failure of the two workers' parties when faced with the threatening Fascist danger, we would inherit the communist movement after the collapse. But this hope was not realised.

Despite that, we were sure that neither the KPD in the Soviet-occupied Zone nor the SPD in the Western Zone were capable of clarifying the ideas of the working class or of taking up the fight for a socialist society.

We did not even imagine then that the wave of anti-communist feeling unleashed by the bourgeois parties, supported by the Western occupation powers and made possible by the Social Democratic Party, would swallow us up too. It was a difficult struggle that we had taken up.

In the meantime, comrade Haas, who had been condemned along with me by the Nazi courts for 'conspiracy to commit high treason' in 1934, rejoined us. At the same time, a group of Young Socialists from Wilmersdorf also joined us. The leader of this group, Klaus Schütz, who later became the leader of Berlin city council, had several discussions with me before he joined our organisation, partly in my apartment, partly at his mother's in Konstanzer Strasse.

For a year after my arrest in East Germany in 1948, he remained a member of our group. He came and went in my apartment, and you could say that we became friends. My relationship with Walter Haas was even closer, both personally and politically. In one political discussion, which concerned the Soviet Union — this was at a meeting in comrade Klemz's bookshop in Ansbacher Strasse — Klaus Schütz and Walter Haas defended Stalinism on various points. In 1949 Schütz went off to the USA as an exchange student, and returned a dedicated supporter of Willy Brandt.

In the summer of 1945, comrade Bohn came to see me at my apartment and handed me an invitation to a meeting which was to take place at the home of comrade Weiland in Eisenacher Strasse. Members of a whole series of different groups turned up for this meeting, including people from the Communist Workers' Party (KAP), the Socialist Workers' Party (SAPD), the one-time Brandler group (Communist Party Opposition), the Red Fighters; even some opposition members of the SED (Socialist Unity Party of East Germany) were represented.

The discussion centred around the reasons for the defeat of the German working class by Fascism. On this point, Weiland — and many others with him — suggested that, because the workers' parties had failed both before and after 1933, they would never again be capable of leading the German working class.

So, before anyone proceeded to build a new revolutionary party, we had to investigate not only the causes for the defeat but also the errors inherent in Marxism and Leninism. We had to explore its theoretical foundations in Feuerbach and Hegel in order to avoid any mistakes in future.

Two other comrades and myself opposed this idea. We said that Marx and Engels and Lenin and Trotsky had laid the foundations on which the working class — led by a revolutionary party — could fulfil its historical destiny. The meeting then decided to found a Socialist Working Group called 'New Beginning' (Neues Beginnen).

After I had reported back to our organisation, we decided not to participate with all our forces in this group, but to delegate only three comrades, and to concentrate on our work in the trade unions. Almost 300 comrades had joined the 'Socialist Working Group' (SAG).

Two foreign comrades also worked in it; both belonged to the Fourth International — comrade Kurt Lang belonged to its American section. He had emigrated with his parents and had returned as an American soldier. When the Allied Commission passed the De-Nazification Law, he wrote an alternative draft on which I also worked; this document was then published as a leaflet under the name of his German girlfriend, Rohovski.

His unit somehow got on to him and he was sent back to America immediately.

The second comrade, a French journalist called Benno Sternberg, co-wrote a pamphlet with me which dealt with the collectivisation of agriculture in the Soviet Occupied Zone. Benno Sternberg later joined the French group 'Socialisme ou Barbarie' (Socialism or Barbarism).

As long as I worked with the SAG, I heard no talk of Feuerbach or Hegel; but every weekend there were scientific lectures, for example on Marx's *Capital*, given by comrade Klingenberg, who was once a member of the KAP.

Other comrades, including myself, gave talks on the various problems facing the workers' movement. I was often asked to speak in the branches. In Pankow there was a strong group consisting mostly of ex-KAP comrades. Since the Socialist Working Group was not licensed by the authorities, we still had to operate underground.

I was met at the Vineta Strasse Station by a comrade and taken to an apartment where some 30 people had assembled, including Paula Wünsche. She was the wife of a comrade who had been arrested in the Nazi period and subsequently condemned to death for 'conspiracy to commit high treason'.

I met her again in Hohenneuendorf, where, as 'victims of Fascism', we were permitted a three-week rest in a home belonging to the city of Berlin. In the political discussions which we had there every day, she always supported me on any question, and later she attended the Berlin executive meetings of the Trotskyist groups.

As I later discovered in prison, she did not do this out of conviction, but because she was working for the NKVD. The Pankow group was arrested the day after me, although they were all released again — all except comrade Silberstein, who was later sentenced along with us.

Until now, only theoretical discussions had taken place in the Working Group, without any attempt being made to carry out the conclusions into the masses. Our attitude was that if people thought that the KPD and SPD were the willing servants of the occupying powers, then it was high time that we set up some publication to inform the masses of their tasks.

There was a stormy discussion about whether we should go public with our own newspaper. The ex-SAPD representatives argued that we should have our own paper, and this was accepted by the majority. We then declared that it was nonsense to content ourselves with a discussion circle, and that we would put out our own newspaper and resign from the group.

After only a short time, our newspaper, the *Marxist*, appeared as the Berlin organ of the IKD (International Communists of Germany). The first edition was dedicated to the memory of the dead who had fallen in the resistance fight against Fascism. After the second edition of our paper had appeared, the 'New Beginning' group also put out a newspaper in its own name.

It was not easy to get hold of the paper or ink, since both could virtually only be obtained on the black market. Money was short too — the occupying powers had decreed a prices and wages freeze. In fact, only salaries and wages stayed still. We managed to bring out the *Marxist* every fortnight. Comrades who had emigrated to Britain and were publishing a German-language paper there — *Solidarität* — gave us a great deal of assistance here. Our newspaper was very much in demand amongst the workers and we could not print enough. From the summer of 1948 we received several copies of the *Internationale* from Holland. On the other hand, *Our Word* never arrived.

Solidarität and *Internationale* were brought to us by the two foreign comrades, Kurt Lang and Benno Sternberg. We sold most copies in the Spandau district. During the Weimar Republic and in illegality as well, the Charlottenburg group had always been the strongest, but comrade Heumos had been able to build a group in Spandau that did good work.

In addition to my work as secretary of the district committee of the Charlottenburg FDGB, which I carried out mostly in the factories, I was also delegated to the district Food Committee and the Charlottenburg Control Committee.

It was our responsibility to supervise food shops and butchers' shops and to ensure that the goods were correctly weighed. The shopkeepers tried to save their stocks, especially meat and butter. We found out that an average of 25 grammes were missing on 250 grammes of butter.

On one occasion a woman from the Food Committee came to me and reported that Schwertfeger the butcher in Kaiser Friedrich Strasse had been selling two smoked hams to a leading public servant who did not have the correct food coupons. When I checked on this shop, I found another 26 smoked hams, and Herr Schwertfeger could not tell me when they had come into his shop or how they were then sold.

Most of the short measures reported also concerned this butcher. For these reasons I demanded that the head of the Food Office, Herr Mai, should confiscate the unauthorised goods in this shop and start proceedings against Schwertfeger. But nothing happened. And Schwertfeger was not the only one. One day, when I came home from work, my wife happily told me that a man had brought her a sack of potatoes and a basket of vegetables.

The headquarters of the Food Office was in the Finance Office in Spielhagen Strasse, very close to my apartment. I found Herr Mai still there and asked him why he was sending me potatoes and vegetables. At first he pretended that he did not know what I was talking about. But he eventually remembered and said that they were confiscated goods which were being redistributed.

I told him that he had no right to do such a thing; in view of the suffering of the rest of the population, goods like that should return to general distribution; and I demanded that the potatoes and vegetables be taken away again.

My work in the Food Committee was like the task of Sisyphus; there were complaints from everyone, but scarcely a single contravention was put right.

It was better in the Control Committee for the Victims of Fascism (OdF). There were people there who had actually spent time in penal institutes, prisons or concentration camps; they were members of the SPD or KPD. People would come along wanting us to give them 'whiter than white' documents recognising them as victims of Fascism. Everyone had to provide incontrovertible evidence.

The SS in the concentration camps had used the criminal elements who were then given the 'Red Triangle' and placed in the barracks alongside the political prisoners to act as spies for the SS. These people now had the effrontery to come to us to be given recognition as victims of Fascism.

There were also those who really had been arrested by the Gestapo but were released again after a short time and had done nothing more for the resistance — one example was the brother-in-law of the later Mayor of Charlottenburg, Horlitz.

I knew that he had only been detained for a short time (fourteen days) and had done no resistance work. Some people wanted to give him recognition. They thought — well, Horlitz sits on the district committee of the FDGB, and if he sends his brother-in-law, then it must be O.K. With another two comrades — as the resistance fighters called each other in those days — we fought this idea.

For one thing the Allies had decreed that someone had to have been in the resistance movement for at least six months in order to qualify, but more importantly, the comrade had to be still politically active. But in the last twelve years, this man had not lifted a finger. The majority of the committee voted to refuse him the certificate. From that moment onwards, it was not easy to work with Horlitz on the district committee.

As time went by, Bohn and I found it increasingly difficult to do our work in the FDGB. For example, we had managed to get a meeting of officials to agree that officials employed by the FDGB should get no more pay than a qualified skilled worker, plus expenses. This was taken very badly by all kinds of people, and the resolution was annulled after our dismissal. In the meantime, Walter, the organisational secretary of the National Executive of the FDGB, had succeeded in uniting most of the KPD representatives and some of the Social Democrats into a 'front' against us.

In the spring of 1946, Bohn and I were summoned to headquarters in Wall Strasse. There, with no preamble, Walter told us that we were dismissed without notice. We protested strongly: any decision about the continued employment or dismissal of an official could not lie in his hands alone, but, as we saw it, could only be made by the officials or the works councils.

But Walter permitted no argument and told us: 'Do what you like. You are dismissed because you have broken the rules which apply in the Soviet Zone. If you wish, you can always go to the Labour Courts.'

We replied: 'We have no wish to act out this farce in front of the bourgeoisie. What would they make of trade union employees pressing charges against the FDGB so soon after the collapse of Fascism?' But, we assured him, we would publicise this case amongst the workers.

This development did not surprise me; I had foreseen it and had even told my colleagues in the district committee that anyone who did not subject himself to the ideas of the Stalinists would soon have to leave. We were sacked as secretaries, but the long arm of Walter could not reach us as members of the Charlottenburg district committee.

We used the time until the first delegate elections to tell all the meetings about the methods which the organisational secretary had used. The national chairperson, Chwalek, with whom we had discussed Walter's methods, told us that he disapproved of the whole affair, but that he was powerless, since the final decision was made elsewhere.

After my dismissal, I went back to my earlier job. When I reported back for work to the personnel office at the Charlottenburg District Council, the personnel manager told me that they had no work for me, since all vacancies were filled. I replied that I had been given special leave to build the trade unions, and demanded to return to my work in the surveyor's office. He refused. He claimed to know nothing about my special leave. I replied that I had a letter to prove it, and that this time I would go to the Labour Court.

When he was convinced that such a document really existed, he yielded a little, and suggested — since all the jobs in the surveyor's office were in fact filled — that I work as a heating fitter in the central workshops. I took up the offer.

The head of the central workshops was a member of the KPD, and I got on well with him. In conversation he condemned the practices of his party. At the next shop-steward elections I was voted on to the stewards committee by the Central Workshop (Transport Pool and Schools) department, and when the district works council was constituted, I became deputy chair. It was chaired by Buchwald, a member of the SPD.

During the war he had worked as a railwayman in the occupied lands of the east. His father, an old Social Democrat, had joined that section of the SPD which had united with the KPD in the Soviet Zone.

Representing our members' interests at that time consisted mostly of supplying clothing and shoes to the people in the factories. As deputy chair, this task fell to me. I spent most of my time dealing with the Office of Trade and the Ration Offices. Twice a week I had to negotiate with the heads of these offices. At that time, shoes and textiles were delivered straight to the factories, and only food went directly to the shops.

During all this, my colleagues in the works council, both SPD people and Communists, worked to consolidate their position in the FDGB. At the turn of the year 1945-1946, the Independent Trade Union Opposition (Unabhängige Gewerkschaftsopposition, UGO) was formed. The majority of Social Democrats and all the members of the CDU belonged to the UGO.

This organisation first arose at the instigation of the Western occupation powers. Their so-called trade union officers played the decisive role here: together with two members of the British army, they organised meetings of the UGO and gave talks and directions on how to conduct the fight against the majority in the FDGB. I myself, introduced by my colleague Buchwald, was able to attend some of the meetings. From the very beginning I rejected the unreasonable request that I should become an organiser of the UGO. My primary concern was to see what opposition this faction would adopt in the fight against Stalinism

I told Buchwald that a common factional stance with them was not possible inside the FDGB. After I had already managed to get out from under the thumb of Stalinism when I was in the Communist Party during the Weimar period, I was not now going to submit to the directions of the Western occupiers. From that day on, I no longer let myself be dragged off to meetings of the UGO.

The first delegate elections in the FDGB took place in the spring of 1946, and in the period up to then there were stormy arguments between the KPD and the SPD on one side and myself on the other (my comrades — insofar as they were organised in the FDGB — supported me), which counted against me in the elections. Perhaps it was a mistake to oppose both the Stalinists and the Social Democrats at the same time. At the delegate conference of the Charlottenburg FDGB, I had both parties against me. In order to be elected, 77 votes were required. At the pre-election committee meeting, which was opened by speeches from both the SPD and KPD, they agreed that only fifteen candidates could appear on the voting list — those with odd numbers would be the candidates of the KPD, those with even numbers from the SPD.

My objection that such an agreement contravened the rules of elections was ignored. The men from the building workers' section voted solidly for me, and a few people from SPD and KPD joined them, so that I managed to get 37 votes. But that still meant that I no longer remained on the district committee.

One of the first things I had tackled as secretary for youth work was a call to the city youth; this was distributed as a leaflet and published in *Tribune*, the trade union newspaper of the FDGB. The leaflet appeared with a few amendments, since the stress on the struggle for socialism was not to the liking of the majority on the youth committee.

Although I no longer belonged to the district committee, I received a delegate's card for the next Berlin delegate elections. Two members of the CDU, Lemmer and Kaiser, were also represented at this delegate conference, sent by the Berlin organisation of the FDGB. A rumour went round at this meeting that they had both been members of the NSDAP.

In my speech, I opposed having people who had been members of the NSDAP only yesterday, or who had worked with the Nazis, working in responsible positions in the construction of the trade unions. For making this criticism, I was censured, especially by the KPD representatives. As I later heard from colleagues who belonged to the SPD, both Lemmer and Kaiser were already working closely with the UGO.

Unfortunately, it was almost impossible for our group to get in touch with our friends in West Germany. As individuals, our comrades were refused entry, even if they were unknown to the Soviet occupying power; in many cases they had to do service in the lodgings or kitchens of the Red Army. This happened to one comrade who was detained by the Soviet military for almost a week; for four days he had to chop wood from dawn to dusk in a military camp, and also had to do work in the kitchens.

There was absolutely no free traffic between the zones at that time. There were a whole series of smuggler groups operating out of the Western Zones, who tried to smuggle into the Soviet Zone goods which were unavailable there. Our only contacts with the outside were the two foreign comrades who supplied us with news and material.

During the first eighteen months, the workers' parties — especially in West Germany — were obliged to rely on the forces which had carried on with illegal work during the Nazi period; now, gradually, comrades returned who had emigrated to flee the Nazis. In the SPD especially, new forces came in who had completely abandoned the old principles of prewar Social Democracy and now defended positions which approached those of the leaders of the British or even the American workers and trade unions.

There was nothing left of the guidelines of the Prague Manifesto of Social Democracy and its 'revolutionary' programme (1934); the party developed ever more strongly into the servants of the Western occupying powers. The SAPD no longer existed as an independent organisation, since most of its members had returned to the mother party, the SPD.

In the case of the KPD, on the contrary, many older comrades turned their backs on the party, because they were not prepared to tolerate the policies of Walter Ulbricht, who was now under the control of the Soviet occupying power. At demonstrations, they watched from the sides of the streets as bystanders.

During the war, neither I nor my wife could get hold of any priority coupons. Even here we felt the pressure of the Nazis, and our clothes had become quite worn out. In 1945-1946 there was hardly anything to be had, and only at the end of 1946 did I receive a pair of work shoes and overalls.

There was no point in thinking about underwear or socks. My wife was even worse off. In May 1948, when she tried to ask for some cloth, she was directed to the end of the queue which stood waiting at the office. My wife was a victim of Fascism, her back was injured and she was 60 per cent disabled with a certificate to prove it.

The woman behind the desk was not to be drawn into any argument and told her that there were still lots of disabled people outside the door. My wife complained, without result, to the head of the rations office, Herr Ehrenberg (politically, he was with the SPD).

When I delivered a protest about all this to Herr Carlbergh, the head of the department for Trade and Crafts (Distribution Office), I received the following explanation:

'The number of textile priority coupons which has been made available to us is so small that only a fraction of even the most pressing cases can be dealt with. The difficulties which you have reported are more or less typical of the ones faced by all the consumers in your situation. Therefore, in order to make possible a just distribution of scarce resources and to avoid continual reprioritising of the claimants at their ration offices, we have introduced a reservation system for specially urgent cases.

'We would ask you to tell us your requirements for cloth on the enclosed form. However, we would point out that we have discovered from Ration Office No.6 that, despite the difficulties you report and taking into account the fact that you are a certified victim of Fascism, you have already received overalls and a pair of work shoes, and, as we have also discovered, you were dealt with on a priority basis.'

Carlbergh did not even mention my wife's complaint nor the discrimination in the handling of her case by both the manageress of the ration office and Herr Ehrenberg. By the way, Carlbergh was a member of the SPD.

The same thing happened when we applied at the housing office. I had already submitted a request in the summer of 1945, without ever receiving an answer. Apartments were being allocated unfairly. Only when I was no longer prepared to wait and told the head of the housing office that I would take appropriate action was I given the keys to an apartment which was partially destroyed by bombs and which we had to patch up ourselves.

A special section had been set up at the housing office for victims of Fascism who had lost both their apartments and their furniture as a result of years in prison; this section was supposed to redistribute the confiscated apartments and furniture of members of the NSDAP to victims of Fascism.

After applying, I eventually received an authorisation from the magistrate to fetch furniture from an apartment in Kaiser Friedrich Strasse. Since it was not apparent from the document who had authorised it, we finally decided against fetching the furniture, and stayed in our almost empty home. Later on, those who had got their furniture in this way were forced by the Allies to return the things to their previous owners.

Our comrades in the IKD were all active and, insofar as they could make speeches, they intervened at meetings of both the Communist Party, if they were open to the public, and the trade unions. Very often, our comrades were threatened with reprisals, especially at KPD meetings.

This happened to me once at a public meeting organised by the KPD, addressed by comrade Hans Seigewasser. (Seigewasser was a comrade who, after being a Young Socialist, left the SAPD for the KPD in 1932. He was imprisoned at Luckau during the same years as me — 1934 to 1936.) At this meeting he now told me that, if I did not stop arguing 'subversively', they would render me 'harmless' — they had the means to do so!

But there were other attempts to take us and our criticisms out of circulation. On one occasion the regional chair of the KPD, Schönwald, who was then the mayor of Charlottenburg, offered me a job as head of department. I turned it down and told him that I could not possibly work alongside him and that, in any case, I preferred political work to administration.

In order to avoid crippling my activity, I had to try like the other comrades to improve our rations. Our coupons did not cover what we needed for a healthy diet. The Allies fed miners with special parcels in order to get hold of the coal, the most important raw material for restarting production. But they had no interest at all in those who did general work. I used my leave to go down to Halle with my wife, to the peasants I had known as a schoolboy, and collect ears of corn and beets from their fields.

I was repeatedly urged by my political friends in Mücheln in central Germany to return to my old haunts and take on the job as mayor. They refused to accept my objection that I was critically opposed to the policies of the occupying powers.

When I then demanded that I would return to Mücheln only if I had their unconditional support, even if it meant opposing the directives of the occupying power, they could not agree. So I remained in Berlin.

At that time we also had discussions on reparations to the victims of Fascism. The Allies had decreed, and later passed as a law, that the victims of Fascism had to be compensated. Our argument was that, in contrast to those who had been persecuted for racial reasons, we were not victims but rather resistance fighters. When 20,000 Jewish victims had come together from all over Berlin, we tried to show that compensation should be political first of all and material only in the second place. But they did not want to know.

At a meeting in the refectory of the Technical University in Stein Platz, when I spoke about the necessity for political activity on the part of the Jewish victims as well, there were protests. I was defended only by those who had fought against Fascism with the workers' parties during the Nazi era.

13.

A COMMUNIST IN AN EAST GERMAN PRISON

In 1947, in addition to our political work in Berlin, we finally succeeded in creating some groups in central Germany. Thanks to my connections from earlier years, I was able to organise people in Merseburg and Weissenfels. Since some of these comrades were employed in the Leuna works, they managed to create a third group. With the help of comrade Bohn, who had moved back to Halle in 1946, groups were formed in the Mansfeld copper mining district which received their political material from us. I worked with the Merseburg and Weissenfels groups on occasions, while Emil Bohn looked after Mansfeld; representatives of these groups only came together for meetings in Halle.

On 9 September 1948, I spoke at a big conference in Berlin of officials of the ÖTV (Öffentliche Dienst, Transport und Verkehr, Public Service and Transport Workers' Trade Union), in the East Berlin district of Friedrichshain.

At this meeting I argued against the slogan: 'Our children shall live tomorrow as we work today,' and also against the thesis that the German people bore a collective guilt in the war. At this time neither the SPD nor the SED were campaigning for socialism. By contrast, I said: 'The anaemic democracy of the Weimar period, which brought Fascism to power, should not be allowed to reappear. The fight for socialism should be on the agenda, since a democracy without socialism is incapable of leading the fight against capitalism successfully.'

At the request of the audience, and despite the opposition of the SED, my speaking time was doubled. (At that time only twenty minutes were allowed for each speech — and we as a Trotskyist group were far too weak by ourselves to apply for an extension of our speaking time.) The Russian control officer told a comrade in the SED, who was one of our sympathisers: 'Listen to what this man is saying — that is just how our Trotskyists speak!' Despite this we were able to continue our discussion after the close of the meeting, outside the hall and then on the way back to Alexander Platz, without the Soviet military administration doing anything to stop me. Two days later, I again travelled to Halle to attend a meeting and to take some political material along.

On this journey, as on others, I obeyed all the rules of underground work: I found a train which left Berlin at around eight o'clock in the morning; I went to my work beforehand, and my daughter brought all my things to the station in Friedrich Strasse; in Halle, I got on the tram at the last moment, to make sure that no one got on after me and that there were no cars following; I did the same when I changed to another tram.

Once more, things went well, and some comrades were already in the apartment when I arrived. Among those present was a branch secretary of the SED from the Bitterfeld coalfield — once a member of the KAP — who turned out to be the traitor, as Emil Bohn told me after I had been released from prison.

On the following morning, I left my friend Emil Bohn's house only when the tram was in sight — it could be seen from the window. Just as I was boarding, a man behind me said: 'Lovely weather today' and seized my rucksack. He was a Russian. My attempts to shake him off failed, for at the same moment several more men arrived, and together they dragged me down from the tram and bundled me into a car which drove us to Luisen Strasse, the headquarters of the NKVD in Halle. I had to wait a long time there before anyone bothered about me. Then I was taken to be interrogated by a Russian officer. I was accused of having entered the Soviet-occupied Zone illegally. After all my personal belongings had been taken away, I was locked in a cell in the basement.

The room was large, but gloomy. In the middle stood a plank bed with a straw mattress, but no blankets. I had to spend three weeks there and then was taken to an isolation cell on the second floor.

I stayed in Halle for six weeks. On the second day I was taken up for interrogation. The interrogator, also an officer, informed me that I had been arrested for 'anti-Soviet activity' and 'forming illegal groups'. I rejected the accusation, saying that I was unaware of any anti-Soviet activity or the formation of any illegal groups. My political activity made little impression on him — I had already pointed out that I had fought for the resistance against Fascism and had been imprisoned because of it.

The same interrogations took place every day, from morning until night, always the same questions. Sometimes I was given a pencil and paper to write down my personal details and those of my parents and to describe my activity before and after 1945. Again and again I wrote these down. My interrogator was changed three times, again and again it was the same thing. Torture was not used at this stage.

One day I came up for interrogation again; this was now with my third officer, who, in contrast to his predecessors, earned some respect from me. I had to consider my answers very carefully with him. When I gave him back what I had written, which agreed with my earlier statements, he leapt from behind his desk in a rage and begin to swear at me. At that moment I lost all my respect for him: this man, who had been so impressive behind his desk, now stood in front of me like a little gnome with legs that were far too short and, quite involuntarily, I had to laugh.

That was my last day of interrogation in Halle. On the following morning I was summoned to the head of the NKVD and told that, if I did not make a statement, he would send me to Berlin; there, he assured me, I would talk. I told him that I would talk neither here nor in Berlin, since everything political that I had done since May 1945 had been in accordance with the treaties of Tehran, Yalta and Potsdam and that I therefore had nothing to confess.

A few hours later I was taken from my cell. My things, which had been taken away on the first day, were now returned to me, as well as the food which I had got from my sister. I was taken back to Berlin, driving up the autobahn in a big Mercedes in the company of three officers, my hands cuffed together. Somewhere near Wittenberg the car had to stop since the dynamo had broken. Both the transport officers stood next to the mechanic who was doing the repair, leaving only the driver in the car. I wondered whether I should attempt an escape; it was clear how I was going to 'thrive' in Berlin. There was forest all around, but having my hands in handcuffs prevented me from escaping.

On the journey we had several discussions. During a conversation with Russian officers in 1945, when the anti-Hitler coalition still existed, I had criticised Churchill and his reactionary attitude towards liberal tendencies and the Marxist workers' movement; for this I was not only cursed, but also called an 'anti-democrat' and a 'Hitler supporter'. This time my officers branded me an 'agent of American imperialism'. The driver of the car, also an officer, seemed to be transformed when we were alone during the repairs. Before, he had joined in the criticisms, but now he talked to me in a friendly manner and gave me something to eat and drink. It all changed again as soon as the other two reappeared.

When we arrived in Berlin, at Hohenschönhausen, I was taken to a cell on the ground floor. I was in no doubt that I was not going to be released in the near future. I was still considering which tactics to adopt — I did not yet know that they had incriminating material about me — when the door opened. The guard addressed me with the words 'kak familiya' — 'what is your name?' I did not understand; I only knew a little Russian at that time. I wore the badge of the VVN, the League of those Persecuted by the Nazi Regime (Vereinigung der Verfolgten des Naziregimes); he tore it off my lapel and swore endlessly at me. He cursed horribly on the way to the basement.

The building had been put up by the Nazis, and the SS had used it for their interrogations and tortures of resistance fighters. When we got downstairs, I was put in a windowless cell with a fixed plank bed that stretched from one wall to the other. Apart from a bucket for the calls of nature, there was nothing in the cell, neither a straw mattress nor a cotton mattress, nor any blankets. Nothing else happened that day, and I could even get some sleep.

On the following day — I do not know what time it was, since you lose all sense of time and space in a basement like that — I was taken upstairs by a guard. It must have been quite late, since there were already street lamps shining outside. In the room to which I was led there sat a whole row of officers, including a lieutenant-colonel who was later to be my interrogator. Apart from a conversation between myself and this officer, nothing at all happened that evening.

We sat at a large table, just like at a 'round table conference'. Not a word was spoken about the reasons for my arrest; rather, we discussed the history of the Russian Revolution, the Communist Party of the Soviet Union, Lenin and the International. In the course of the conversation, a guard came in with a large tray covered with sandwiches, and another brought glasses of tea. I had not even seen tasty things like that for quite some time, let alone eaten them. Again and again they told me to help myself.

I was ready for anything, but not for a welcome like this. For three days in succession, always in the evening, I was taken up to this room and each time the same thing happened — food and conversation.

On the fourth day things changed and I was rudely brought back into cold reality. The same officers sat around the table again, not to discuss political problems with me and drink tea, but — as they said — to talk about my criminal activity. There were two bundles of documents on the table. They said that my criminal activity was all contained in them; and encouraged me to make a full confession. I told them that I had not acted in a criminal fashion, but rather that my activity since May 1945, and during the fight against Fascism before that, was directed towards the realisation of democracy and socialism.

There now began in Hohenschönhausen the same nonsense as in Halle: alternating interrogations and written statements. The only difference was that in Halle this never went on for more than eight hours at a time, while in Hohenschönhausen it went on every day for twelve to sixteen hours, for seven long months and mostly at night.

As a rule, the interrogations of other prisoners were finished by midnight, whereas I only got back to my cell at 3.30 or 4.30 in the morning. Sleep was almost out of the question under those circumstances, for reveille was at six o'clock and no one was allowed to lie on their beds after that time. My nerves were so stretched that I could never get to sleep in the short time before six. If I really did try to stretch out on the bed, the guard was there immediately, dragging me to my feet again.

Six cells were guarded by one man who spent his time going from spyhole to spyhole. The SS, in their time, had built a system of lights, just like traffic lights, with green and red so that the prisoners could never meet in the corridors. The system usually worked, but if two prisoners did manage to pass each other, the guards swore terribly, for if the 'cellar-major' — the commandant of the basement — ever found out, the guards would be punished.

The same rules applied whenever I was taken out for exercise, which lasted for twenty to thirty minutes. It was not unusual for there to be no exercise at all on some days. At the back of the main building they had built a number of small courtyards, four or five metres square, surrounded by walls four to five metres high, so that no unauthorised person could see into them. Only the occupant of a single cell could enter one of these yards at any one time. The cells, which were only occupied by one person at a time, had to exercise entirely on their own; there was not even a guard there, since the yards were locked.

Again and again I went upstairs for interrogation. Weeks had passed, but nothing had changed: always the same answers, always the exhortation to make a full confession. My statement that I had been in the anti-Fascist resistance from the first day to the last made no impression on them at all — the interrogator brought his fist angrily down on the bundles of documents: 'Here is the proof of your criminal activity!' In reply I demanded that, if the proof of my guilt was so weighty, they should sentence me. He replied: 'We want the men behind you.'

In Halle, I was never manhandled or beaten, and for the first two weeks nothing happened here either. But then began the reprisals.

At first it was not my interrogating officer, Chernikov, who carried them out, but the head of the whole place, Danilov. (I do not know whether these were their real names. The interpreter was a young lieutenant named Brussilov.) At the start of my stay in Hohenschönhausen, I was interrogated by a first lieutenant. He always said to me: 'Hippe, it will be bad for you if you do not make a statement.' Sometimes he was alone with me.

We talked about many things, except the crime of which I was accused. I received cigarettes from him, not in the interrogation room, but downstairs in my cell. I do not know whether there was some kind of method in these gifts of large numbers of cigarettes — since the food we got was so bad, smoking was like taking poison. For a whole year I, like all the other prisoners in Hohenschönhausen, had to eat a stew of pickled cabbage. Sometimes there were also potatoes in it, sometimes even a couple of threads of meat; occasionally there was a quarter-herring; but always there was pickled cabbage, thin or not so thin, for a whole year. A ration of bread went with it, 350 grammes, and in the morning a soup which consisted mostly of bran.

With food like that, scarcely any sleep and long periods of interrogation, it was no wonder that I got thinner. I entered the place weighing 160 lbs, and after fifteen months, at the end of investigative custody, I weighed only 94 lbs.

I had been in custody for over a year, when I could not believe my eyes on seeing the midday meal. We got Russian kasch, a meat dish which was stewed with cabbage — one layer of cabbage, one of meat, alternating. This delight only lasted for three days, however, and then we were back to pickled cabbage and then sometimes millet gruel or barley broth. No one knew why. Had a new boss arrived? But Danilov was still there.

This Danilov appeared more and more frequently in the interrogation room, and more and more frequently I got to feel his fists. With Lieutenant-Colonel Chernikov I had less to suffer, although he was no softy. There was a stool at the door to the room, fastened to a chain, and I had to sit on that while the officer conducting the interrogation sat at the other end of the room behind the desk. Colonel Danilov was also in the room. The discussion which followed concerned Stalinism and Trotskyism and which of the two really defended Marxist-Leninist ideas. Danilov intervened.

One blow threw me from one end of the room to the other, and I came to under a wash-hand basin. When this night was over, I went back to my cell quite exhausted. These excesses were quite often repeated.

Many weeks had gone by in the meantime, and it was still just like the first day. One evening — I was usually taken upstairs in the evening shortly before ten o'clock, sometimes when I had just lain down on my bed — the door opened and the guard shouted the usual 'kak familiya'. We were hastened upstairs with the command 'poshol'. This time the interrogation did not last very long; after a short time the officer informed me that he had the means to force a statement from me. He sent me to a cell which was situated right beside the boiler-room. With the temperature here, the sweat burst out of my pores.

I had to stay there for three days, but my will to resist was not broken. When I went upstairs again on the fourth day, Lieutenant-Colonel Chernikov asked me whether I was now ready to make a confession. As before, I refused and told him that I was not guilty of anything. In a rage, he brought his fist down on the documents. Apart from Chernikov, both Colonel Danilov and the head of the recording section were also present.

They cross-examined me and tried, with blows and bright lights, to break my resistance. I held firm until late into the morning when they took me back down, but not before Lieutenant-Colonel Chernikov called after me that, if he could speak German better, he would make me confess. I sat in my cell for a long time, despite the guard's insistence that I lie down.

On the following morning, the interrogator 'discovered' that my shoes were completely through. The soles had ripped from the thread, the leather uppers were completely worn through. Nor could we wash; we were taken for a bath once a week. That morning, along with my beating I received a new pair of shoes; sometimes it seemed as if the interrogators also had their human side.

There was a Russian woman doctor in the basement; she was known as the 'Angel of Hohenschönhausen' by all those who consulted her. I too had to have treatment. The nails on my toes had grown in; I had not had a chance for many months to cut either my finger- or toenails. She took my shoes off herself, cleaned my feet and began to cut the nails out very carefully. While she did this, she always told me (she spoke perfect German) how brutal people were and that it was time to create truly human relationships. I took the opportunity to tell her that I was a Marxist and that was the reason why I was in here. She was also a Marxist and admired Lenin. This day was of tremendous importance for me: for months I had only known brutality and arbitrariness all around me; but here I had met a person full of humanity and sympathy. That day gave me renewed strength to resist.

My health had deteriorated greatly, but my spirit remained unbroken. To punish me for my stubbornness, I was moved underneath the basement cells into a narrow 'dungeon', which was situated under a staircase. You could not stand upright in it, and there was neither a bucket for the calls of nature nor anything else in it. There was an infernal stench; the cell was completely soiled, so that you could hardly sit down on the floor. I stayed there for three days, without getting anything to eat. Only once a day was there anything to drink.

This form of isolation was the worst that I had experienced until then. When I was taken upstairs that night, Danilov was present again. I prepared myself for more excesses; but nothing happened apart from the usual questions.

Then came the decisive session. There was a whole row of officers in addition to Danilov and Chernikov, along with four young people in civilian clothes. They conversed amongst themselves, but did not speak to me. It was as if some secret was floating around the room. A long time passed, and then suddenly the colonel took four pistols out of the desk, gave them to the young people and turned to me: 'Hippe, if you refuse to make a statement, then we will bring your wife and daughter here tomorrow — we have everything ready.' That was not an empty threat, since the Stalinists had used methods like that in the past. I could not sleep that night.

The guard at the door urged me to lie down; I swore at him angrily. One thing was sure: under no circumstances could my wife and daughter be brought here. But how could I prevent it? There was only one alternative — either make a statement, or commit suicide. I considered this for a long time, and at first I reached no conclusion. The guard kept appearing at the door telling me to go to sleep. I paid no attention to him, for the thought kept going round and round in my head: 'Whatever happens, I must prevent Gertrud and Renate from being brought here.'

I began to tear my shirt into strips and to twist them into a rope. The four walls were made of concrete, with no nails and no ledge to attach the rope to. The only possibility was the door — the lamp in its niche there was protected from the inside by some wire-netting. I dragged the bucket to the door, climbed on top to attach the rope to the netting. Just as I was putting the rope around my neck, the door flew open and I was pulled from the bucket with a terrible din.

The major in charge of the basement also turned up immediately to curse me; but I let it all pass over me, only regretting that my suicide had not succeeded.

They took me to a cell which already contained two people. The two of them were utterly destroyed — I could not get a word out of them for days; only gradually did they manage to return to normal thoughts and speech. Hans Lehmann was in this cell — he had been a representative of the Eastern Bureau of the SPD. (I was acquainted with Hans Lehmann for a long time after we were released — he went to Frankfurt and wrote to me that he found work there as a functionary.)

I had been alone for many months; now the inmates of the cells were constantly being moved: it was a principle of the guards not to leave prisoners too long together. There were continual cell searches: they made very sure that not a single scrap of paper was left with the prisoners, nor any newspapers printed in Russian. Since we had neither toilet-paper nor any other sort of paper, everyone tried to get hold of newspapers. You could not hang on to them for more than two days, since they were taken off you during a search.

In these cellars, the word 'hygiene' was written in very small letters indeed. One day a new prisoner turned up, and he began to curse the SED and the Russian occupying power fearfully. Both his hands were bandaged — he told us that he had tried to commit suicide. Then he also started cursing the victims of and fighters against Fascism, and to call them criminals. When I demanded that he provide some evidence for his assertions or else to retract them, he replied with even worse outbursts.

This man was either mad or a provocateur — I assumed the latter and told him what he was. There was a fight, during which I beat him up. (When we were in Bautzen we discovered that he had been a stool-pigeon there.) The Russians had greatly refined the system of stool-pigeons, and there were always people to betray their fellow-sufferers for a couple of cigarettes and better food. The spy was removed from our cell on the following day; I was not even asked why I had hit him.

When I next went upstairs after my attempted suicide, neither my wife nor my daughter were there: the whole thing had simply been a bluff. My interrogators did not mention my attempted suicide. They tried to shatter my resistance. Those were bad days, but I was determined to continue to stand firm. Bouncing the bundle of documents on my head did not do them any good either. One evening an officer appeared who led me through various corridors to another room. He did not interrogate me. First of all he busied himself with the documents; from time to time he looked up at me, but without ever saying anything. All of a sudden he pulled a pistol out of the desk and loaded a magazine. He then aimed the pistol at me, and also at other objects in the room. Although it scared me at first, it began to get ridiculous.

I do not know how long I was in that room with this officer, but I reckon that it was longer than two hours. Only when we had returned by the same route that we had come did the questions begin. As so often, Colonel Danilov was present. Shortly before they took me back to my cell, they opened one of the bundles of documents to show me something.

Tomorrow, said my interrogator, we will talk about this some more.

Only a few hours later, they fetched me again; in the meantime I had been thinking how to deal with the change in the situation. I had seen copies of our paper, the *Marxist*, and of *Solidarität* and the *Internationale* in that bundle. I could no longer make some general statement that I had participated in the building of democracy and socialism; the argument was now Trotskyism versus Stalinism, and I was determined to defend the position of Trotsky and the Internationalists, come what may.

They again accused me of anti-Soviet activity and illegal formation of groups. I now confirmed this accusation and justified it with our fight to protect the Red October against the Stalinist doctrines, before 1933 and up to 1945. I particularly condemned the Stalinists for dissolving the Third International in 1943 at the request of the Western Allies. So then they introduced a new accusation, not against me, but against my organisation, the Fourth International. I was to confess to them that it was an American spy organisation.

I told them that they could make whatever statements they liked about me as an individual, but that I would rather die than sign any transcript which stated that the Fourth International was an American spy organisation. Once more I was transferred to another cell, this time moving from the basement to the upper floor where there were several cells for so-called state officials. In my new cell there sat a good-looking man who introduced himself as Roger. It was one of my principles that, whenever I was put in a new cell, I would talk about anything except politics.

In contrast to the basement there was good food here, although I could not eat any of it for the first few days since my stomach was so dried up. After we had been together for a few days, Roger really did try to establish my political position, but I did not let him find out where I stood. He later confessed to me that he had done espionage for the Americans. During the war he had been in the General Staff, Foreign Armies West (Counter Intelligence). One day he came back from his interrogation and spoke openly: he had been given the task of sounding me out, but he had told the Russians that he was no longer able to do that.

On the following day I went back down to the basement. I never heard anything more about Roger, nor did he turn up in Bautzen. I must suppose that he was taken off to the Soviet Union. In the meantime I had found out what was in both bundles of documents. Apart from the newspapers they also had our leaflets. There was a report of every meeting at which I had given a talk or led the discussion. Nothing was missing from my activities of the past three years.

I knew that there were groups in the Berlin FDGB who prepared reports not only on trade union meetings but also on meetings of the political parties. The leader of one of these groups was a certain Fritz Meyer. Once, when I asked him why head office also needed these detailed reports from the meetings of political parties, he replied that they were only done to keep an eye on subversive activity. Now, in prison, I found out that they were used to keep an eye on political and trade union officials who were not trusted, and that, without exception, they were handed over to the Soviet occupying power.

During one of these interrogation sessions, which no longer took place daily, I learned that comrade Walter Haas, with whom I had been tried and sentenced for 'preparation for high treason' under the Nazis, was also in prison. They also asked me about Paula Wünsche. When I said that I knew Paula Wünsche, but that she had never worked politically with us, the interrogators changed the subject: 'Well, let's leave that.' I only learned of the arrest of the third comrade — Leo Silberstein — when I was arraigned.

Now it was no longer a question of material which incriminated me — I had provided enough of that in the discussion about Stalinism and Trotskyism. What they wanted to find out from me now was the structure of our German and international organisation. They repeatedly suggested that I was at least 'the moving spirit' of the IKD. Since my arrest, the *Marxist* had stopped publication, but it seemed that the organisation had also stopped functioning. After my arrest my comrades had in fact decided to stop publishing the paper because they thought that it would help me. But they achieved the exact opposite. I refused to make any statements about the structure of the organisation, nor was there any pressure on me to make any such statement.

Weeks later, I was fetched from my cell and taken to a prison vehicle. There I met both Walter Haas and Leo Silberstein — for the first time in over a year. I think our trial took place in the prison in Magdalene Strasse in Lichtenberg. It started early in the morning and lasted until late in the evening. We did not receive any written accusation. The Soviet military court accused us of 'anti-Soviet propaganda' and 'illegal formation of groups'. According to the Soviet Special Law, Article 58, the penalty for anti-Soviet propaganda was between four months and 25 years and for the illegal formation of groups it was between six months and 25 years.

The basis for the trial was formed by the files of documents, accompanied by a short report by the investigating magistrate. The incriminating material against Leo Silberstein consisted of two years' editions of the magazine *Der Untermensch*. This anti-semitic journal was published by Stürmer Press during the Nazi period. Leo Silberstein, who was Jewish, had only collected these pamphlets; when he was arrested, they were confiscated and considered to be 'especially incriminating'. We only had to point out to the court that none of the editions was dated later than 1945 and that it was a Fascist publication.

It was not easy to argue with them, for all three officers of the court spoke bad German. When they had understood, they were somewhat embarrassed; they put the file aside without any further discussion, and the trial continued. We did not have much opportunity to defend ourselves. Whenever we wanted to correct something, they cut us off short. Then we asked for legal representation. This time the presiding officer reacted positively. He suspended the trial to discuss the application. Afterwards he told us that it was impossible at that time to give us any legal representation, since there were no lawyers available. So the trial continued where it had left off, but with the difference that they now listened to us occasionally. But the whole proceedings did not seem serious.

In the evening the president of the court passed judgment after a 'deliberation': each one of us received 25 years for each crime, the terms to run concurrently since the Soviet Special Law, Article 58, did not provide for a longer punishment. The sentence did not surprise me, for I knew that, in the past, the opposition in the Soviet Union had been destroyed by sentences of decades in prison. In the summary which justified the sentences, the court particularly stressed that the Trotskyist opposition had supposedly murdered Comrade Kirov, the leading official of the party in Leningrad. Even at this time it was no secret that Stalin had ordered this murder.

Immediately after the trial we were taken to the transit cell. There we received the first warm food of the day. There were already several other prisoners in the transport cell who had been sentenced the previous day, among them Ernst Gering, a police officer and SPD man. He had been arrested later than myself and was able to tell me that the trade unions and humanitarian organisations were campaigning for my release. Days passed and the cell filled up. Every prisoner without exception had received a sentence of 25 years.

Outside it was a cold November day, with sleet. While all the others walked round and round — it was a large cell — I did my exercises, as I had done in the Nazi prisons and in the NKVD cellar or during the exercise-hour. All of a sudden there was a thunderous knock on the door. I wanted to stop my exercises, but my colleagues reassured me and told me that it was not me that was being warned, but themselves because they had talked too loudly. So I continued; suddenly the door burst open with a tremendous crash and I was dragged out.

The guard took me to a 'swill-cell', where the pails were usually emptied. The window could not be closed and the door was left open. I was ordered to strip to the waist and to make myself wet; then I had to sit on a stool below the window. In a draught like that you could get pneumonia. The only thing I could do was to rub my torso to keep from getting too cold. By chance, the guard caught me doing this. So I had to soak myself again. This time I kept a better lookout; after a certain time he returned and led me back to the cell. On the way he addressed me as 'Kamerad', and asked why I had been doing exercises. Once back in the cell, a fellow-prisoner gave me a pullover and I managed to get warm again. I was lucky — there were no after-effects apart from a runny nose.

We stayed at Magdalene Strasse for a few more days. No one could say with certainty where the transport was headed. Some bet on the Soviet Union, others again said that only convicted spies were still sent to the Soviet Union, while all others stayed in the Soviet-occupied Zone. One morning we were taken in a prison van to the Lichtenberg railway station and loaded into prison-carriages on a train. Since the glass panes of the windows had been replaced with metal shutters, it was difficult to see anything of the country through which we passed, although some claimed that we were on the line to Frankfurt on the Oder — that is, on our way to the Soviet Union.

Hours passed, and then we arrived at the town of Bautzen. We were taken from the station to the prison, and were initially placed in quarantine in Building III of the cell-block. Three men had to stand outside each cell door. We managed to get Walter Haas, Leo Silberstein and myself in front of the same door. A Russian officer gave directions on how we were to behave for the next 30 days. In that period we could not leave the cells, for security reasons. Apart from meals, which were very basic, the cell doors would not be opened, although the guard would enter the cell in the evening to pull up and secure the shutters on the windows. The guards, in contrast to their superiors, did not treat us as criminals, but as equals. But if they were given specific instructions, they carried them out to the letter; we found that out after we had been moved from quarantine into the basement room.

As for the accommodation, there was no difference between Nazi imprisonment and Russian imprisonment. Then, as now, three men were kept in cells measuring eight square metres. Only the food was much worse; this we could understand, since the Nazis had surpluses of food available to them, whereas now the daily allowances were rationed. We had been fed from the 'starvation menu' during investigative detention, which meant that some of the food remained attached to those employed in the kitchen and the food store. When 30 days had elapsed we were released from quarantine and taken to the basement room, which was only 2.10 metres high and held 185 prisoners in a space ten metres by eighteen metres. There were a number of prisoners in this room who had been sentenced for their activity in the Eastern Bureau of the SPD, including Willy Irmler from Dresden, who was later to play an infamous role when we were handed back to the German authorities. Only the smallest minority of the prisoners were those who had really acted out of conviction.

At that time, January 1950, two-thirds of the inmates in Bautzen were one-time members of the Nazi party: 'war economy'-leaders, SS and SA people, so-called 'Golden Pheasants' — that is, party officials. No more than about fifteen per cent had acted from political conviction. The other twenty per cent were people who had worked in the administrative offices and had somehow come into conflict with the Russian military administration, or they were food-transporters who had diverted some of their load for their own use and had been condemned to 25 years for economic sabotage.

We also had a few young people in the basement room who had received the same punishment for 'Werewolf' activity. In the last weeks of their rule, the Nazis had provided enough evidence to show that they were quite prepared to sacrifice the German youth in their insane plans. In these cases I made every effort to talk to the prisoners, and managed to gain their trust. They convinced me that they had found stockpiles of weapons and ammunition in the woods around Halle, and had gone around shooting it off; this was simply a case of young people of sixteen.

None of the prisoners could gain any recognition for his political convictions: for the Russian military administration, just as it would be later for the 'Volkspolizei' (People's Police of East Germany) when they took over, there were only criminals.

Our residence in the basement room lasted right to the end of 1950. We were left to ourselves in this room. The guards only came in if they had to remove a prisoner — either to an ambulance or to the sickroom or the governor's office. There was absolutely no provision for culture. Most of the inmates sat or lay on the bunks; only a minority occupied itself with card games or chess. Chess was still permitted. The figures had been made by the prisoners by compressing pieces of bread from the meagre rations; the board was drawn on cardboard. Pieces of pencil five millimetres long could be bought for a ration of bread. Anyone caught in possession of a pencil-end was arrested.

There were guards patrolling outside the windows and they kept an eye on the card games. The prisoners were forced to sit near the windows to get just a little light to play by. Comrades who were caught playing 'skat' were locked up for 21 days. Despite our poor rations, we managed to keep them supplied with food, for they only received a warm meal every three days. And despite these repressive measures, there were always contraventions against the 'house rules', since survival was otherwise simply not possible.

In April 1950, the prison was handed over to the Volkspolizei. One morning some Russian and German officers turned up. They told us in a short address that, now that the German Democratic Republic had been founded, the prison was under German jurisdiction, and that all arrangements would be made by German authorities. During this address, Chief Commissar Schulze (we called him 'Hound-dog Schulze' since he was always accompanied by an alsatian when he passed through the cells and rooms) greeted the prisoner Willy Irmler with a handshake.

Both had participated in the spring of 1946 in the merger of the KPD and SPD into the SED. Schulze had become a loyal errand-boy while Willy Irmler attempted to engage in the 'double strategy' and had thus got caught in the wheels of the Russian occupying power. One of the first changes which took place after the handover was that the Volkspolizei introduced a certain amount of self-management for the prisoners. 'Elders' were to be elected for each room and each floor, and all requests and complaints were to be channelled through them.

By chance, two prisoners who had just come back from the sickroom overheard a conversation between Willy Irmler and Chief Commissar Schulze. They agreed that Willy Irmler should get himself elected as elder of our room. Together with Walter Haas and Ernst Gering, we confronted Willy Irmler; we demanded that, under these circumstances, he should withdraw his candidacy for elder. He agreed. Two days later, at the election, Irmler declared that he did wish to stand after all and he was proposed by his friends from the Eastern Bureau.

I then stood up on my bed and spoke to my fellow-prisoners, telling them of the conversation which had been overheard; Irmler could not deny it. I also pointed out how important these elections were: if the Volkspolizei thought that they could settle everything with this system, then the elders from each room and floor should function as the shop stewards of the prisoners and not those of the Volkspolizei. This argument convinced them, and Ernst Gering was elected as elder for our room, with only a few votes against.

Only a little while later Chief Commissar Schulze appeared and demanded of myself and Walter Haas that we withdraw our accusation that he had made an agreement with Irmler, or that I tell him who my informants were; I refused. On the very same day, Walter Haas and I were put into solitary confinement in Block I. My reply was to go on hunger-strike. I refused all food for almost eleven days, and for six days I refused to drink, which was tremendously difficult to bear.

Every day they brought food to my cell — both soup and a midday meal — and they even laid my daily ration of bread on the table. On the first two days I tried by force to prevent the meals being put into my cell. Since they then threatened to institute more proceedings against me, I did not try again. Much worse than the temptation of food was the daily visit from other prisoners. The sick-bay lay on the same floor, and the prisoners from all over Block I used this as an excuse to come to my cell.

I never heard any encouragement, but rather phrases like: 'Just keep starving. When you die, at least we will have more to eat.' On the fifth day the agonising hunger was not so bad, but my desire for water grew all the more. So on the following day I began to drink again.

On the eleventh day two Russian officers came and asked me why I had begun this strike. I told them the story. They gave their word as officers that they would investigate the case, but only if I stopped my hunger-strike; I agreed to do that on condition that they really did investigate. And indeed, on the following day, a member of the Volkspolizei came and took a statement. He appeared a second time, but then I heard nothing more from either the policeman or the Russian officers.

I remained in solitary for quite a lot longer, but I did not regret the time — all the cells were occupied by three men, the rooms were overflowing and breeding grounds for tuberculosis. In that prison, before we arrived, many hundreds had died of the disease, which flourished because of the bad food and overcrowding. Fortunately for the prisoners, the doctors in the GDR had developed a medicament which successfully combatted tuberculosis. Later, this same drug was dissolved in the water supply, and the success rate was even greater.

There were only a few people with tuberculosis now, though hunger was still rife. I had settled into my cell, which was on the top storey. I had a wonderful view out of the window across the countryside. The only things missing were books and materials for writing; the only book that was permitted was the Bible — and even that came with conditions attached. One day the blow fell: a member of the Volkspolizei ordered me to get my things together, and I was moved. My protests did not help. I was moved to Block III, to a room containing 386 prisoners — in a space twelve by 25 metres.

The room elder showed me a place to sleep. Luckily this was on the side where the windows were, and the air was fresher than on the other side of the room. The room was arranged during the Nazi period in exactly the same way as now. There were no beds, only bunks, one above the other. Three men lay in each bunk; it was so narrow that you could only turn over together, as a group. The food was just as bad as before: in the morning three-quarters of a litre of soup, as thick as paperhangers' paste. It consisted mostly of bran and did not taste nice, but at least it contained some vitamins.

Before the soup arrived in the room in the morning, there was a regular concert of curses. In the afternoon there was coffee substitute and the daily ration of 350 grammes of bread which was baked from the same stuff that was in the soup. When this swede-drink had been doled out, the trusties would shout out: 'Anyone for more — step forward!' The burnt swedes still floated about in the wooden pots, and these were served up as 'seconds'. Two lieutenants who had been sentenced for being 'war economy' organisers marched to the front to get another helping, though these substitutes had absolutely no nutritional value. Every worker soon realised that it would only damage your health; but our 'men from the General Staff' still marched to the front every day.

What things hunger drove us to — in the expectation that the most rational utilisation of the bread would somehow still the pangs! Thus, bread was kneaded into pellets, since someone had suggested that this would provide the most calories. Some only used to eat the bread if there was nobody else there; others kept the bread until the following day, but they often had it stolen from them in the interim.

During the course of 1950, the Volkspolizei permitted every prisoner to receive a packet weighing three kilos from his relatives each month. As a rule, some good things were sent, and many prisoners consumed the entire package in three days and then down the toilet it went. Gradually, the packages got heavier and heavier, and in one case the weight was eighteen kilos. Then the administration started to send back any packet over the limit.

There was one guard who supervised the opening of the parcels — we called him 'spinnaker-ear' — who cut the sausage and cheese into slices. Perhaps they were simply jealous, for even the guards went around with hollow cheeks during those months. The packets were a great help to us, and it was only at this time that I managed to recover a little.

In our room there was a schoolteacher named Haustein, who stood up on his bed every day and fulminated against the regime; on the other hand, this same Haustein — so said one of the guards — had volunteered to write an article to justify the Oder-Neisse Line as the eastern frontier of Germany.

One day a group of young people manufactured a banner — written in black on a sheet: 'We protest against our imprisonment and demand the release of all prisoners.' For several hours this banner remained hanging on the outer wall of the room, until a unit of the Volkspolizei appeared and pulled it back in. Their attempts to find those responsible failed.

Very few people had any work in the prison. Anyone who had work in the bakery, the butcher's, the clothes store, kitchen or the sickroom would count himself lucky, for work was like a medicine. Those in protective custody — these were members of the NSDAP and related organisations — occupied a special position. When we arrived at Bautzen, they were moved to an outside camp. They had better conditions than us, even some cultural activity. There was a theatre group, a singing club and a large orchestra. In addition, they had complete freedom of movement inside their camp. The reason for this differential treatment was that the one-time Nazis were still under the control of the Soviet power. Only in 1952 were they put in prison at Waldheim, where they were sentenced.

I had been in Bautzen for almost a year, and still had had no communication with my family. In the spring of 1950 we were permitted to write for the first time, having arrived in Bautzen in December 1949: we had to use a card without any envelope, and it had to be a sentence that was dictated to us. I did not follow this instruction with the result that the card did not get sent, but ended up in my file. I had written that I was imprisoned in Bautzen, condemned by a Soviet court to two terms of 25 years, and could hardly think of survival under these conditions.

In the next letter, I discussed the GDR, so far as space permitted — how far it was justifiable, since the GDR had not even existed when I was first imprisoned — and this letter also ended up in my file. Only the third letter reached my wife, though this time I described the reason for my imprisonment and the length of my sentence.

My wife took this news to my previous place of employment and managed to get my dismissal rescinded. In November 1948, when I was arrested by the Soviet Military Administration — SMAD — the SED had spread the rumour that I had not been arrested for political reasons, but for being a speculator dealing in foodstuffs. The Social-Democratic town councillors sacked me immediately because I had culpably not turned up for work, despite the fact that, when I had not returned in good time, my wife had reported both to the police and to the personnel office in the District Council of Charlottenburg that I had not returned from a trip into the Soviet Zone. Even the shop steward at the district council gave his permission for my dismissal. It took two years for the district council to yield to public pressure and decide that my dismissal was illegal.

In 1952, the food got better. At first there were plenty of potatoes, and later the bread ration was increased as well. By the end of the year you could get as much bread as you wanted; only fat and sausage products remained on ration. At that time they also created work for the prisoners, who were then employed within the prison by nationalised firms. Thus, the Görlitz carriage works ran a large workshop which made seats for railway carriages. There was also a textile works operating in Bautzen, and later even a factory producing lorries.

All those employed were paid at the same rates as workers outside, the only difference being that large deductions were made for board and lodging. From the money that remained, a third could be used for purchases in the state-owned Trade Organisation (Handelsorganisation — HO), while the rest went towards supporting dependants, or was paid on release. Apart from the manufacturing shops, there was also a so-called Translations Section, in which the wages were many times higher. The prisoners employed there went home with suits, coats and shoes which they had bought from the money they had earned.

More than 90 per cent of those prisoners capable of work were already employed. I was amongst the few who were not. Work was at a premium in Bautzen. Anyone who was employed could count himself lucky. Not only did the employees have quite a lot of freedom of movement, but they could also buy cigarettes and subscribe to a newspaper, while the unemployed were excluded from any privileges. The reason for my lack of work was that I was always at odds with the administration about my imprisonment.

I told the head of the governor's office that the GDR had no right to keep me in prison, since there had simply been no GDR when I was arrested by the Soviet occupying power. And my wife was not allowed to visit me, the reason given being that she lived in West Berlin, though it could be proved that other prisoners were allowed visitors who travelled from that part of the city.

Only two sisters of mine, who lived in the GDR, received permission to visit me for half an hour every month, though all visits were forbidden later as a result of some violation of prison discipline.

My superintending officer was always the same one. He had been with the Nazis in the concentration camps; he hated anything in prisoners' clothing. Because of his strong glasses, the prisoners called him 'the eye of democracy'. Once when a visit was due, my sister Martha turned up. She was very pious. The first thing she said to me after our greeting was: 'Oskar, I pray for you continually so that you will be released.' I replied:

'Praying won't help. If you want me to get my freedom back, then you must fight with other weapons.' That was the signal for the visit to be terminated; after two minutes, despite my protests, I had to leave the visitors' room.

The 'tug', who escorted the prisoners from their rooms and cells, cursed me. On the way back to the cell-block, he threatened to hit me. I warned him that if he touched me I would defend myself, because I was not prepared to be punched without resistance, as I had in the Nazi period. He immediately took me to the governor's office. I had to stand in the 'glasshouse' in the main building for a long time, until I was taken to the head of the governor's office. This man, a tramdriver, belonged to the old guard of the Leipzig KPD — he had fought in Spain and later was put in one of Hitler's concentration camps. The incident in the gatehouse and the premature termination of the visit had no consequences.

After a few weeks the governor's office had new personnel; the new chief warder was a one-time Hitler Youth leader, and we called him 'the little Napoleon'. This 'little Napoleon' was also the one who picked me out as I returned from a walk, when I was talking with a fellow-prisoner on the cell-block stairs, and locked me up in the 'cage'. His word alone was sufficient, and the 'officials' themselves were allowed to impose a punishment of up to three days in the cage without having to give any justification to the governor's office.

On the fourth floor two cells were knocked together into one. One of the doorways was sealed off from inside and part of the doorspace was bricked off. As a punishment, a prisoner was made to stand in the remaining space and the door would be closed. They shut me in here and locked the door from the outside — it was as if nails were being driven into my chest. This torture lasted two hours.

Again and again, people were locked in there for the least transgression. I was sent to the cage a second time. Once more, the man who handed out the punishment had been a leader of the Hitler Youth — we called him 'Shortjaws' because of his receding chin. The reason for this punishment? — my wife had not had any post from me for three months and was now asking why.

I reported to the governor's office. When we looked in my personal file, it transpired that my letters had been confiscated because I had taken the liberty of making a few remarks about my stay in prison. 'Shortjaws' then declared: 'Instead of criticising us, you should help us build the socialist republic, and not carry on counter-revolutionary propaganda as you do now.'

I could not resist telling him that I had fought for three decades for socialism, and that included the period when he was strutting around under the flag with the swastika. That got me two hours in the cage, with immediate effect. You could hardly breathe, and you certainly could not move. When the door was opened after two hours I fell out in a faint.

In 1952 the former officials of the NSDAP, who had been living outside in the camp for more than two years, were transported from Bautzen to Waldheim. At the same time, there was a reorganisation in the prison. All men over 50 were taken out of the rooms and cells and put in the camp: this was a great relief for us. For one thing, the rooms were not so full out there as in the permanent buildings, and for another we had more free time; there was no employment at all in the camp. Only once was there some work — sorting out waste paper and tinfoil. When we were doing this we discovered among the paper an old copy of the Prison Regulations of the Kingdom of Saxony, which bore many resemblances to current regulations, which I took the opportunity to mention to the governor's office.

In the camp I met up with comrade Alfred Schmidt again, having been in Block III with him before. This was a great relief to me, for I had been able to discuss all kinds of political problems with him. Alfred Schmidt was an old KPD man, had belonged to the leadership cadre in Thuringia, but had later come into conflict with the party bosses because of his membership of the Communist Party Opposition and because he had defended the position of the opposition. He too had also been sentenced to 25 years by a Soviet court. Even if there were heated arguments in the course of our discussions, it was still the best time that I spent in Bautzen. With most of the prisoners it was simply impossible to conduct any kind of political discussion, because they were consumed with hatred for anyone who confessed himself to be a socialist. The Social Democrats on the other hand were simply incapable, and unwilling, to make any distinction between the various groups in the communist camp. Their main priority was to work out how much compensation they would receive when they were released and could go over to the Federal Republic.

One small group busied itself with developing a system to rob the bank at Monte Carlo and getting rich. During the hunger period, they discussed the possibility that the SED regime was consciously attempting to starve us all to death. When the rations improved, and packages really did turn up, their propaganda was changed to: 'They will get rid of us through the chimneys.' Even when the government of Federal Chancellor Adenauer was conducting negotiations in Moscow which touched on the subject of the release of all people imprisoned by the Soviet and GDR regimes, only a few could believe in our release.

Only when the first prisoners got out in the early summer did everyone start to dream of being one of the first out. Those in Soviet prisons were released first, and then those in GDR prisons who had been sentenced for crimes committed in the Nazi period. The very last to get out were those who had worked against the political regime in the GDR after 1945. On 17 June 1953, we heard on the radio news programme 'Tägliche Rundschau' about strikes and demonstrations taking place in the GDR. No one could get a clear picture of it all, since the reports were one-sided and the events were portrayed as counter-revolutionary. Only later, when the first prisoners arrived — at first into isolation cells — did we find out more. Most of them were accommodated in basement cells in Block I.

By then, the prisoners were able to do their work and move about anywhere almost without any supervision; by contrast, the 'new ones' were all 'supervised' by members of the Volkspolizei. They had no free time and were not permitted to leave their cells at all. Later there was a rumour that the prisoners of 17 June could only eat their meals while on their knees. When the isolation period was finished after a few months, and the prisoners were distributed around various areas, it emerged that they really had been treated that way for some of the time. Among them were people who had looted and burned along Unter den Linden in Berlin, and on the Potsdamer Platz and Leipziger Platz; the FDGB trade unionists distanced themselves from those people, among whom were SED members.

We were able to speak to shop stewards from Magdeburg who had stood firmly beside their protesting members because they were not prepared to swallow the increase in the workload without putting up some resistance. They told us that in the days around 17 June they had not only distanced themselves from the murkier elements, but had even taken up the fight against them. The whole thing had primarily been to guarantee the right of the workers to co-manage in the factories, so that orders sent down from the ministries could only be enforced with the agreement of the factory committees and the shop stewards; only later had it been a case of improving the conditions of the working population.

In 1954, all the prisoners who still came under the jurisdiction of the Soviet military administration were handed over the the GDR authorities as German citizens. From that day on I reported to the governor's office every week and demanded that I be released, giving as my reason the fact that the GDR did not exist at the time of my arrest, that indeed I had been arrested by the NKVD in September 1948 and had also been condemned by a Soviet military court to two terms of 25 years. Now that I was supposed to be in the hands of the GDR, they had a duty to release me. Apart from that, I had been sentenced to a work camp and not to a prison.

One day, after I had reported to the governor's office a few times and had continually 'preached' to them that I should be released, I was transferred. In one section of the camp, there was a workshop run by a firm from Bautzen or Görlitz — we could not find out exactly — which painted and waxed lorries and fitted bonnets. All of a sudden I was employed in this section, although they had found no work at all for me in the preceding years. Despite this change, I continued to badger the administration to get released, naturally without any success. I was quite aware that the GDR authorities would take no decision without consulting the Soviet military authorities. Undeterred, however, I did not give the GDR authorities any peace.

More than six months had passed when, at the end of July or the beginning of August 1955, a messenger appeared at my work one day. I was to report to the main building right away. At that time all prisoners could move about without any supervision, but they had to wait at every gate until it was opened by a guard with keys. When I eventually arrived at the main building, they were raging because I was so late. I told them that if they had given me a key, then I would naturally have turned up earlier. We were off at the double to the main offices and the personnel office, where I picked up my few possessions.

Down in the yard there was a van for transporting prisoners, which was already loaded — they were only waiting for me. While all the other prisoners were put together in one cell, I was handcuffed and put in a single cell. No one knew where we were going. Just as had happened after our trials, there now began a guessing game to see where we ended up.

When we got on to the autobahn and determined that we were travelling northwards, it became clear that we were headed for Berlin. After about an hour, we reached Berlin and it was not too long before we arrived at a large camp. As we later discovered, this was the work camp at Hohenschönhausen, which was looked after by the state security people. After our personal possessions had been checked, we were taken to our various sections. The vehicle and construction sections were the biggest, while all the others were quite small. I was 'introduced' to the heating section, which was led by an engineer who was also a prisoner. Before the evening meal we were taken to our quarters. Unlike Bautzen, the dormitories were occupied by twenty to 25 people, and the meals were taken in a large dining hall. During the day the prisoners could all move freely about the camp, for it was very 'liberal' here. Only the camp commandant had to be saluted when you met him on the paths.

The inmates of the camp were mostly people who, in their factories, had come into conflict with factory management or party leadership, for reasons of discipline, but often for political or even trade union reasons. That was also the reason why there was such a very good atmosphere among the prisoners.

In most cases the leaders of the sections were one-time Nazis, including the engineer in the heating section. In the first few months I got on very well with him, until he realised where my political allegiances lay. From then on he treated me with a certain distrust. I had good relationships with the comrades — that is what the prisoners called each other. There were various ways that I could discuss the differences between ourselves in the KPD and Stalinism, and I could even find agreement for my viewpoint, although their sympathies now lay overwhelmingly with the SPD.

Unlike Bautzen, there was no payment for the work done here. But the food was at least 100 per cent better, and you received cigarettes according to the amount of work you did. Anyone who had enough private means for an account could buy things at the Trade Organisation (HO), including, on special occasions, beer in small amounts. Before we arrived there was no limit on purchases of beer, but then it was closely controlled because many inmates got themselves tanked up and abused the guards. We were looked after better than the workers outside in the nationalised factories. In the vehicle section they repaired all the cars belonging to the party, trade unions, the Volkspolizei and similar 'firms' in Berlin and district, while the construction section put up blocks of apartments outside the camp for the members of the state security service. The whole area was out of bounds for anyone else.

At the start of 1956, Wilhelm Pieck decreed that those sentenced to 25 years by the Soviet military courts should have their sentences cut to fifteen years. I wrote a letter to my wife telling her that I did not consider this 'act of mercy' as merciful but as a second death sentence. This letter did not leave the camp, and I was summoned to the administration office where they tried to get me to rewrite my monthly letter. I refused. I told the boss that I had already been in prison for seven and a half years. I probably would not survive another seven and a half. That is why I could not write the letter any differently. So once more my wife did not get a letter from me.

In the meantime I had already been around eight months in the camp when the head of the heating section told me one day that I was to relieve the heating engineer in Magdalene Strasse, since the man there — a 'serious student of the Bible' — was no longer capable of carrying out the work. I refused and said that if he did not have any more work for me, then he should have me sent me back to Bautzen; working as a heating engineer, always on night shift, was not something I could do. But he declared that there was nothing to be done about the work allocation, it was already being cleared by the security officer.

A colleague who looked after the water and sanitation section told me that the 'Bible student' was not the reason for it at all, but rather their desire to get me and my Marxist ideas out of the camp. So now I went to see the security officer. I told him I was prepared to return to Bautzen, today if necessary, but not to be shunted down a siding. He promised me he would sort things out. But first I would have to carry out the heating work, and in ten to fourteen days I would be back in camp. And in fact I was back in camp after fourteen days. The security officer offered me the job as head of the heating section. I turned it down, because I was not prepared to take on any supervisory work at the camp.

Shortly after I had been summoned to administration because of the letter, I had to go once more. This time I was presented to two men who introduced themselves as 'representatives of the public prosecutor'. When I heard the word 'public prosecutor', my ears pricked up, for it was well-known that the people from the public prosecutor's office were not allowed into camps administered by the Soviet authorities.

They said they had come to find out about the working and living conditions for the prisoners. I told them that the working day lasted more than ten hours and that there were no wages for work done as had been the case in Bautzen. But the board and lodging was extraordinarily good, and in my opinion we were looked after better than workers in the nationalised industries outside. On top of that we received between five and twenty cigarettes according to our work.

'Now don't make such a song and dance,' said one of the men.

I replied: 'If you have come from the public prosecutor's office, then you will be familiar with my file, and you would know that I have always fought for my political principles. The thing that displeases me about this camp is that there are dogs on long chains running around the inner walls, making such a noise with their barking that it is difficult to sleep. And if you want to know something else that I don't like: I have only had one visit from my wife until now, shortly before I was transferred here. All the other people from West Berlin get regular visits from their families.'

He acted very astonished and told me that he would get that changed immediately.

Some fourteen days had passed when I was summoned to the Visits Office. Our usual dress was made of dyed police uniforms, with broad stripes on the back, sleeves and legs. But if there was a visit we received ordinary blue suits. The visits did not take place in the camp but in the prison at Rummelsburg, to which we were driven. That same morning I travelled there with other prisoners and was taken to my wife after a short time. In contrast to the visiting days at Bautzen, things were quite 'liberal' here. One prison officer supervised three sets of people and we could talk undisturbed.

Gertrud told me later that she was taken to a special room after the end of the visit. There the same officials who had questioned me two weeks previously told her that I would be released immediately if she would help them get their hands on two known Trotskyists in Berlin. These were Liselotte Beck and Franz Schrodt. My wife replied that they should have come six or seven years ago. After such a long time she was used to being alone; besides, she would not do anything without her husband's agreement.

I do not know how long it was before I was taken for another visit, but it was not long. I was taken to a large room where my wife and the two state security men were already sitting. After exchanging greetings they gave me to understand that they would retire so that I could discuss 'private matters' with my wife. Naturally Gertrud also told me what the two of them wanted. After some time they came back and addressed me as 'thou' and as 'comrade'. I replied that they should not forget that I was not only a socialist but also a prisoner of the Soviet government and that the GDR was also involved in this question.

Again they offered me my freedom if my wife could ensure that Liselotte Beck and Franz Schrodt fell into their hands. They appealed to my 'Marxist solidarity', and said it was my 'duty' to 'destroy counter-revolutionaries'. I answered that I knew neither Liselotte Beck nor Franz Schrodt personally and so did not know how they had worked against the GDR. It should be no secret to them that I had been arrested and sentenced in 1948 as a 'counter-revolutionary American agent'.

'I know that I still have seven and a half years of prison ahead of me. But even if I have to count on not surviving these years, I will not be turned into some small-time informer. Spare yourselves the effort. I will never turn traitor, precisely because of my Marxist principles, and especially not under the present circumstances.'

That was the last visit I received from my wife.

In the meantime, those who had been sentenced by Soviet courts began to be released from our camp. This was a time of great tension. No one knew whether he would be next. I often asked myself the question whether I could even think about being released. Stalin had died in 1953, but the Stalinist bureaucracy stayed on, and you had to reckon on them taking revenge for my refusal to act on their behalf.

Those who had been condemned for Nazi crimes were the first to be released. Even SS people who had been guards in the concentration camp at Sachsenhausen got out, although, as I found out after my release, they had been taken to the Soviet Union after intervention by the Red Army.

Weeks passed, and only a few were left in the camp who might have been released. One day I was taken in a car to Magdalene Strasse. All releases took place from this prison. When I arrived, the governor of the place welcomed me and told me that he was empowered to show me to a special cell and to ask what I required. They even put a double cell at my disposal, with a real bed in it, a table and chair, and a picture from the workers' movement on the wall.

If I had any special requests, especially in the matter of food, then I should just let him know via my 'attendant' — his name for the jailer — and he would see to it. It was immediately obvious to me that there was some dirty business lurking behind this friendliness. Twice a day I had recreation, one hour in the morning and half an hour in the afternoon. There was reading material: apart from the newspaper *Neues Deutschland* and some other journals, there were also books, Marx and Engels as well as a few novels by modern GDR authors.

Reading material, which had been withheld from me for eight years both by the Soviet occupying power and the authorities of the GDR, now lay in piles on the table, so much that I would not have been able to read them in weeks. I busied myself with Marx and Engels and with Lenin's *State and Revolution*. *Neues Deutschland* interested me only marginally, since you would hardly expect it to inform you about the real situation in the two parts of Germany. The food which I received did not come from the prison kitchens; the three meals could compete with any hotel food. I received as many cigarettes as I wanted. Three days had passed, and nothing had happened about my release. I gradually got worried. On the fourth day my two 'acquaintances' from Hohenschönhausen appeared. They apologised for the fact that I was still here, but said that nothing more stood in the way of my release. But these state security men still wanted to know about my political ideas. They were especially interested in my position on the SPD.

When I told them that the SPD had become a petty-bourgeois party and had ceased being a workers' party, they protested and said that the SPD still got votes from millions of workers. That, I replied, fell far short of being proof that it was a workers' party. There was certainly a Marxist wing of the party, but this had no influence in deciding domestic or foreign policies. The political programme of the SPD was decided by people who had packed their bags in 1933 and returned in 1945 with ideas formed in Britain or America, or by people like Wehner who had unconditionally defended Stalinist doctrine in the Weimar period and had played a major role in the expulsion of the left.

The comrades of the SAPD, who had meanwhile returned to the arms of the 'mother party', took a minor part in the SPD, as did those who had drawn up the Prague Manifesto in 1934. The only thing they were permitted to do was to unite in a working group.

I made no pretence about my rejection of Stalinism on the other hand: Stalinism had led the German and international working class to defeat, and me to the correction houses and prisons of the Hitler regime and the Soviet occupying power. If I, like many others, was now close to being released, then that was only due to the recognition by the present leadership of the Soviet party that the strategy and tactics of Stalinism had been unsuccessful. Despite my openness, they still addressed me as 'thou' and 'comrade'. I refused to use these terms.

The state security men let me know that my release, like all the others, would be effected from Luckau prison. A short time later both my 'friends' informed me that there was transport going to Luckau on the following day or the day after and that I would be released directly from there. But if I was going to arrive home with nothing, then they would give me 300 Western Deutschmarks to tide me over the first few days. I knew immediately that they were not moved by selflessness to support me, and I refused. They insisted that I take the money; since I would not have to sign anything, I need not worry.

But I continued to refuse, noting that I would not be released directly from here, but from Luckau. Since prison transports from one institution to another were always searched both on departure and on arrival, someone would be sure to find the money on me. So now they suggested that, since I was travelling via Berlin, I should meet them on the Frankfurt Bridge and they would hand the money over there. In order to avoid any more discussion, I agreed. However, I was certain that I would not be at the meeting place.

On the next morning but one, the head of the institution appeared to accompany me in person to the prison van. I was not sure whether this was all a sham or whether he really did not know what was going on here. There were already three fellow-sufferers in the van. As it turned out, all three of them belonged to the SPD. They had had connections with the Eastern Bureau of the SPD and had been sentenced to 25 years because of it. When we arrived at Luckau, we went first to the clothing store. Our few utensils were taken away from us straight away. Then we had to undress completely.

We stood there pale and naked. Now I understood: this is where the money was supposed to be discovered, in the presence of my Social-Democratic fellow-prisoners. They wanted to make my position in politics impossible. Having failed to get me to betray two comrades, they wanted to try to compromise me with 300 West German marks! How petty and ugly these people were, thinking that they could get anything they wanted with money because times were hard.

I had to stay in Luckau for almost a week; there were four of us in a cell. If our treatment had been generous and 'liberal' in Hohenschönhausen, we were now straight back onto the treadmill. Treatment and food were both far worse than in Bautzen. In the evening, when we were locked in, all our possessions had to be folded and placed in a neat square pile in front of the door. All four of us had then to stand under the window, and the elder had to stand to attention and report the cell number and number of occupants. When we first arrived, I had been designated as elder. So when the evening roll-call came, I reported at the door: 'Cell occupied by four persons.' I refused to stand to attention, and every time there was a fuss. They threatened us with 21 days punishment.

My colleagues told me fearfully that I really should report in the prescribed fashion, otherwise I would endanger our release. But I had meanwhile gained some experience of prison life and calmed them down, telling them that neither the screws nor the prison governor could decide on our release, but that it was solely a matter for the Soviet authorities and that such a trifling matter would not jeopardise our release.

Two days later I was taken for interrogation once more. Sitting opposite me was a member of the Soviet occupying power, and once more he wanted to discuss my political stance. I answered him in the same way that I had done in Magdalene Strasse in Berlin. When he asked why I was going to West Berlin and would not stay in the GDR, I told him that there were two reasons: firstly, because my family was in West Berlin; secondly, because in the eight years of imprisonment I had never had the feeling that I was in the prison of a socialist state.

Finally the time arrived. On the morning of the following day, we were taken to the administration block to await our release in the release cell. We were called into the office singly to receive our release papers. Apart from personal details, this document stated only that I had been provided for up until 26 July 1956, that it was valid until 29 July 1956 and that it authorised me for one journey to Berlin-Charlottenburg (in the Western Sector). There was no official stamp apart from an illegible signature of some chief commissar, and no indication as to the length of my imprisonment.

After waiting for hours, an officer from the governor's office came in the early evening and told us that we would not be released that day, since there was still a signature missing; we had to return to the cell-block. I protested and said that we would not return to the cell-block under any circumstances, since we already had our release papers in our pockets; we might as well spend the night here. He asked us not to make difficulties for him — it was not his fault.

My colleagues were prepared to return to the cell-block. The officer was relieved. He took us back personally to the place we had left that morning, and handed us over to the warders. These were the same people with whom I had had a difference of opinion over roll-call a few days before. When the door opened at lock-up time, there was no response on our side. 'Don't you know the rules?' I told him that we had already been released and so were no longer bound by prison regulations.

This time he did not threaten me with 21 days, and he closed the door, swearing. It was a disturbed night since my colleagues were still wondering whether we would really be released on the morrow. I did not take part in the discussion and waited for morning.

I lay thinking how, almost exactly twenty years previously in the same prison, I had found myself in an almost identical situation. Back then I had sat in a cell with Walter Cholleck waiting for our release, when the head-guard had arrived and had taken comrade Cholleck back up to his cell because he was of Jewish extraction.

Early the next morning we were taken to the administration block again, received breakfast there and a ticket. All three of my colleagues went to West Germany; I was the only one who travelled to West Berlin which was an island in East Germany.

14.

ON THE LEFT WING OF THE SPD

By early afternoon I was already in Berlin. I took the S-Bahn to Charlottenburg Station and a few minutes later I was home again. My wife was not there because she had gone to a friend's house with her two foster-children. Instead, my sister was in the house. For a moment I was somewhat disappointed, but I soon got over it and I waited for Gertrud to return home.

Hours went by, and then all of a sudden the janitor's wife appeared at the door and shouted excitedly that my wife was lying downstairs in her apartment. She had fainted on learning that I was home. I no longer know how quickly I got downstairs. My wife had regained consciousness in the meantime: 'Oskar, you are here at last!' She had been hoping for my return but, after such a long time, it was so unexpected and overwhelming that her circulation had broken down. On top of that, her imprisonment by the Nazis and the torture had weakened her heart.

I had envisaged our reunion as being somewhat different. For hours we were not alone. Only late in the evening did we have the chance of talking about the many things that concerned only the two of us. Gertrud had always been optimistic when it came to the matter of my release. She had never doubted that I would be home again in the foreseeable future, while I had always thought that I would have to serve at least the 15 years to which Wilhelm Pieck's decree had reduced my sentence.

Many marriages had gone under during a period of imprisonment. I kept hearing about fellow-sufferers who had received letters from their wives saying that they had applied for a divorce since they could no longer bear to live alone. The number of such cases certainly went into hundreds.

In order not to be alone and in order to help one of her friends, my wife had taken her friend's grandchildren under her wing. Since her financial situation had not been good during my period in prison, she had been forced to sublet one of the two rooms in her apartment. Her present tenant was a young girl, a student by the name of Rosemarie, with whom she had built up a friendly relationship.

Gertrud had agreed with her friend (the grandmother of the two little girls) that the youngest child would have to return to her mother when I came home, but Petra, the older child, could stay on as part of our household. Shortly after my return, the mother, who had meanwhile got married, took her youngest daughter back. Petra stayed on with us. I had got used to the child and grown fond of her. When Petra was seven years old, her parents — now living in West Germany — applied through the youth welfare office to regain custody. It was clear to us then why the parents wanted Petra back: it was not out of love for their child, but rather that, at seven years of age, Petra was now old enough to be able to act as nursemaid in her parents' home. So I went to the district youth welfare office to see if Petra could stay with us.

All our arguments — that Petra and my wife were good friends and that she would receive a good upbringing with us, that all avenues of education would be open to her, whereas she would simply be a 'Cinderella' with her own parents — all these had no effect. It seemed that the parents now had the greater right than the foster-parents. When I told the district youth welfare officer that I would not hand Petra over willingly since I could not take responsibility for what might become of her, she told me that the police would come and take her away instead. That being the case, we gave up the fight for Petra and handed her over to her fate. When she had to leave us she sobbed, 'No one wants me any more'.

Six weeks later the same youth welfare officer turned up and asked my wife if she was willing to adopt the newly-born child of a student couple, since she had been such a good mother. When we asked what guarantee she could give us that the child would stay with us, she said that there was no such guarantee in the law. So we turned down the offer. Petra left her parents twice to return to her Nan in Berlin; she had been forbidden to even speak of her Nan in Berlin, and she was always beaten if the word 'Nan' escaped her lips.

The eight years of prison had not only been years of separation for my wife and myself, but also years of struggle. Gertrud had stood firm against all hardships, while I had not only had to defend myself against the attacks of the penal authorities of East German justice but had also laid myself open to the suspicions of most of my fellow-prisoners who had regarded me as a collaborator of the SED regime.

For them, anyone who defended socialism had to be either an open or closet sympathiser of the SED or the Russians. On the three occasions that I had seen my wife during these eight years, I had been quite uplifted to see that she still retained the old fighting spirit. Thus, on the last two visits, she had told the officials from state security quite unequivocally that the penal system in the GDR had nothing whatsoever to do with the principles of a socialist society. What was happening here, she said, was motivated by revenge and not by the desire to resocialise, which ought to be the founding principle of a truly socialist party. 'Our fight is against a system that despises humanity — capitalism — but not against individuals, as yours is' — that is what she told them.

What my wife had suffered from most during my imprisonment was the lack of moral assistance from our organisation. Although comrades often came to Berlin, even from abroad, they never once visited my wife. It was different with the Berlin comrades — especially comrades Klemz and Herbert Heumos, who stood at my wife's side through it all. She also found great strength in the young student, Rosemarie Riemer, who lodged with her and gave her the courage to go on.

After I was sentenced, I had written to my wife — she only received the letter after I had been in prison for two years — and told her to rearrange her life as if I no longer existed. It was unlikely that I would survive 25 years in prison under such harsh conditions. But in all the letters which I received from her, she assured me that she would stick by me whatever happened. These letters were worth more to me than the monthly parcel which always arrived punctually.

During the first years of my sentence, Gertrud found it hard going, for she had to rely on public assistance. Only after she found out after two years that I was imprisoned by the Soviet authorities could she then claim — with the help of some friends — the money which all the political prisoners there were entitled to. Despite this, she had only limited funds available. Some friends had helped her gain recognition for herself and me as anti-Fascist resistance fighters, but for me she could only get compensation for my time in prison under the Nazis.

She did not touch a penny of the money which she had received on my behalf. When I asked her, she said it did not belong to her. Her own compensation was not paid, since they claimed that she had not been in prison long enough. And this was in spite of the fact that she could prove she had been in prison for nine months and had been released a cripple: in the Nazi prison she had had her spine shattered. The senator responsible had indeed given her the official certificate as a resistance fighter, but the compensation board still refused to consider her case. Only when I had been able to clarify the situation during a discussion with the official responsible did my wife receive full recognition as an invalid and a resistance fighter.

Everything was quite different in my case. While I did receive recognition from the compensation board, and my wife received the money as compensation for my time in prison, the person responsible at the senator's office was not prepared to give me a certificate as a resistance fighter. When I asked why, the woman in charge — she was a member of the SPD, as I later found out — told me that I had worked against democracy in 1919 and so had a criminal record.

This 'criminal record' related to the episode, in 1919, when I and many other comrades had liberated the chair of the Querfurt District Workers' Council from the hands of the 'Orgesch' organisation. The workers' and soldiers' councils at that time had been organs of the provisional government. Only after I had spoken to the head of the department, comrade Löffler, and had told him that I would go to court on this one did he agree that everything was in order and that his colleague had made a mistake. I found out later that there were two lawyers employed in that office who had previously belonged to the NSDAP.

When I had been arrested in September 1948 by the Soviet military police in Halle, there had been a group of 52 comrades in Berlin, all active in the trade unions and factories. When I returned in 1956, the group practically no longer existed. On the basis of a decision by the Fourth International, the comrades had entered the SPD in order to build a socialist wing along with the lefts in the party. In so doing they had entirely forgotten to develop the contacts of the organisation, or to look after the organisational unity of the group or recruit new members to the group. This was necessary, for it is only possible to create a revolutionary cadre in an independent organisation, and to educate them for the coming confrontation with capitalist forces.

Not all the comrades had gone along with the move into the SPD. Some had tried to build a new left in the 'Pro and Contra Group', but after only a short time they had to admit that there was no way of campaigning for revolutionary policies in such a tightly-knit group.

Basically, the step taken by the comrades to work within the SPD was the correct one, for in a period of revolutionary downturn it is not possible to work directly on the construction of a revolutionary party. But if the price of such a step is the abandonment of an independent organisation, then it can have devastating effects.

In the spring of 1956, friends in Zurich had invited me, through my wife, to come with her on a holiday trip to Switzerland after my release from prison. We spent the whole of October there. We spent most of our stay in Zurich, and then twelve days in Caviliagno, a town in the Italian part of Switzerland where we were put up in a workers' holiday home belonging to the Swiss trade unions and where we had a good rest. Before that, I had made a trip to Cologne.

Friends in Berlin had told me that Cologne was the headquarters of the German Section of the Fourth International, led by a comrade whom I knew from the Weimar period. This was comrade Georg Jungclas from Hamburg. I had several discussions with him and other leading comrades about the decision to enter the SPD. There too I saw the same results as in the Berlin organisation. I pointed out that our organisation's activity could not consist simply in joining with the left-wing social-democrats in criticising the policies of the SPD leadership.

Our job was rather to stamp our authority on the the left-wing movement. But even more important was to turn our organisation into a revolutionary cadre and not, as had happened, to neglect the organisation. Comrade Jungclas confirmed to me that the organisation was in bad shape and said it would be good if I could reorganise things from Berlin. When I pointed out that there were two problems with this — firstly that I would need time to get my health back, and secondly that anti-communist feeling was running very high in Berlin and so we could not even consider leading a reorganisation from there — they did not want to know.

Since I stood by my guns, the question remained undecided. On the afternoon of the same day, comrade Jungclas introduced me to comrade Hans-Jürgen Wischnewski, who later became an SPD minister and Secretary of State in Bonn. He was presented to me as a Trotskyist. A few years later, when the Algerian revolution was in full swing, Wischnewski was quite often in Algeria doing solidarity work, or so I was told by comrade Otto Freitag, whom I got to know later.

In 1953 the Fourth International had split. In a number of countries — but not the Federal German Republic — there were now two Trotskyist organisations; one was led by the International Secretariat (Pablo, Frank, Mandel, Maitan) and the other by the International Committee (the SWP in the USA, Lambert, Healy). I asked comrade Jungclas if he could supply me with the documents on the split so that I could consider the matter; but he refused. I later had an opportunity, through my friends in Zurich, to see all the documents and study them at home.

I found one pamphlet by Pablo particularly problematic, the one entitled *Where are we going?* This pamphlet, and its perspective of '200 years of Stalinism' was crucial in my decision to cease cooperation with the International Secretariat and to work for the International Committee. I considered it wrong that Pablo and his organisation should reckon on another 200 years of Stalinist rule and direct their organisation accordingly.

Shortly before I left Cologne, I found out that there were a whole number of pamphlets in comrade Jungclas's apartment which had been written by Trotsky and published before 1933 by Anton Grylevicz's Energia Press. As I have already said, I saved these pamphlets in the spring of 1933 and preserved them through dangerous times. While I was sitting in Bautzen, Berlin comrades had managed to get most of them to Cologne. When I asked comrade Jungclas if he could give me some of the pamphlets, he refused to give me even one.

Back in Berlin I tried to sort out my trade union membership again. To that end, I went to the headquarters of the Public Service and Transport Workers' Union (ÖTV). Of course, my arrest had partly been due to my opposition after 1945 to the policies of the occupying powers, who wanted to control the trade unions. I had expected them to make a note in my membership card to the effect that I had been in a Russian prison for eight years because of my trade union activity: this was a great mistake on my part.

They sent me to brother Girnatus; I think he was the organisational secretary at that time. He told me that I was no longer a member of the ÖTV. The rules forbade any exceptions. It is not without interest that Girnatus had been a member of the NSDAP until the collapse in 1945.

Brother Meike, then the chairman of the ÖTV in Berlin, to whom I then turned, was in no position or was unwilling to contradict the decision made by Girnatus. He suggested that I speak to brother Adolph Kummernuss, the chair of the Federation, in Stuttgart. I did so. And only after a short time the decision came back that brother Hippe was to be readmitted, and that in future no one should place any obstacles in the way of similar cases. Despite this, I had to catch up on the arrears for the whole time I was in prison.

Although the rules of the ÖTV provide for financial support in such cases, I never heard anything about it and I made no move to apply. They also made no attempt to let me take an active part in trade union life. I had intended to shift the bulk of my political work into trade union activity. But since there was no pensioners' branch in the ÖTV, any work inside the trade union was practically impossible for me.

I considered for a long time whether I should follow my comrades and enter the SPD. I knew the difficulties of defending revolutionary policies based on Marxism inside a party which was turning away from even the last traces of its reformism. But there were still possibilities. Inside the SPD there were officially-recognised 'Marxist Working Groups' (Marxistischer Arbeitskreis, MAK), whose members were amongst the very few in West

Berlin — apart from the SED — who based themselves on Marx and Engels and the principles of scientific socialism.

Some of my friends, who had worked with the Trotskyist group earlier, were active there. One of them, comrade Kurt Raabe, was also on the executive of the MAK. I had some discussions with him as to whether it would be possible to work with the MAK without being tied organisationally to the SPD. He told me that it was possible to introduce me as a guest; but that to work actively with them I would have to become a member of the SPD. After three months I took the decision, in order to be able to pursue my political work inside the MAK.

Branch 11, the residents' organisation of the Charlottenburg SPD, had many workers as members, despite being located in a petty-bourgeois residential area. Comrade Georg Kunz, whom I had known during the Weimar period — he had then belonged to the SAPD — advised me simply to make an application to join and he would take care of the rest. In November 1956 I attended my first meeting, and thereby gained the right to become active in the MAK. Branch 11 was regarded as left-wing in the party. I soon became an official and was elected as district delegate at the next elections. I was able, in my contributions both in the branch and in the district delegate meetings, to continue my work along socialist lines, basing myself on Marx and Engels — since the Heidelberg Programme of 1925 permitted such a position. We were still three years away from the Godesberg conference.

Amongst the members of the left-wing faction, whose meetings I regularly attended, I was known by some comrades as 'the socialist conscience'. Indeed, Harry Ristock shouted after I had been fiercely attacked by the right wing: 'There is the permanent socialist conscience!'

I met Harry Ristock in 1957 at a Berlin aggregate conference for party officials. At that time he was regarded as a Marxist and revolutionary in the party — indeed many regarded him as a communist resistance fighter. He did not attend the meetings as an individual, but rather marched in at the head of his group of leaders of the Falken (left-wing youth organisation) and Jusos (Young Socialists). At one of these meetings he was denounced as a 'communist' by the right wing after he had contributed to the discussion. Ristock answered:

'If you are calling me a communist because of my contribution, then I must tell you this: if what I have said makes me a communist, then I am proud to be called a communist.' He then left the meeting early, along with his officials. I only ever saw him like that one other time. In the years when I worked with him inside the SPD, I found out that he became more and more of an opportunist and pragmatist.

At the end of February 1957, a messenger arrived from East Berlin with a letter and a small package which he handed to my wife at the door. When she asked him to come in and talk to her husband, he replied that he was in a great hurry and had to be on his way. When we opened the package, all became clear. It came from the same people who had appeared at Hohenschönhausen four months before my release and had tried to get their hands on two comrades with the help of my wife.

Their letter, dated 27 February 1957, addressed me as 'Dear comrade Oskar'. They were trying once more to recruit me as their spy. The package contained 25 cigars. At the start of May 1957 I received a second letter, in which they expressed their disappointment that I had not replied to their first letter. 'Unfortunately we have not heard from you; but you must gradually realise who your political opponents are.' After that I heard nothing more from 'Gerhard' and 'Eduard', as the two called themselves. It was not until after the agreement on visits, which was signed between the ruling bodies of the GDR and West Berlin in 1964, that I paid a visit to friends in East Berlin, and only then after I had checked with the appropriate authorities in the West that I could go across without danger.

The first visit passed without incident. But just before the second visit, my friends asked me not to come since the state security people had been asking after me. So my wife travelled alone, and in the late afternoon, the self-same state security man turned up at my friend's apartment and seemed disappointed not to find me there. He said I should just have come along; nothing would have happened to me, he only wanted to chat over a few things with me. I never went back to East Berlin until the Berlin Agreement was signed.

On various occasions the Berlin party leadership of the SPD tried to snuff out the Marxist Working Group, but without success. The fact that it finally 'died' in the 1960s was not due to the 'efforts' of the party leadership, but could be traced back to the ineffectiveness of the then leader of the group, who was unwilling to hand over the leadership to younger people.

At the beginning of 1958 Alfred Weiland came to see me. He had previously been a member of the KAP and a leader of the Socialist Working Group. At the end of 1950 he had been kidnapped from West Berlin and sentenced to fifteen years' jail in the GDR. He was released early, in 1957, and joined the SPD. Weiland asked me if I would work with him to smash the Marxist Working Group. I asked him where he had got this ridiculous idea from — of destroying the only left-wing group that functioned in Berlin at that time. He replied that this tiny group was damaging the construction of a free West Berlin.

At the next meeting, he stood up by himself and began to slander the leader of the group in a most provocative way. I made a contribution in which I reported to the meeting how he had come to see me and what he had said. Comrades who had worked with him during the Berlin railway-workers' strike accused him of being an agent of the American occupying power. I challenged the comrades to provide proof of that, or else not to repeat such an accusation. I will leave it up to the readers to judge for themselves what happened a short time later. But on that day it was impossible to continue the discussion and the meeting broke up early. The argument between Weiland and a few other comrades continued outside the meeting place, the latter repeating their accusations. Alfred Weiland caught the same No.19 bus as me. He threatened to take legal action against all those who had accused him of being an agent. 'If you have a clean nose,' I said, 'then it is your perfect right to turn to the bourgeois courts.'

Weeks went by and no one in the group thought any more about the incident. Then several comrades received summonses to Branch 1A of the Political Police at the Tempelhof Police Headquarters, myself included. All of us were interviewed about the events in the Marxist Working Group, without the police being able to complete their preliminary investigation. Two members, comrade Klemz — who had not even been in the room during the incident — and comrade Bernd Kleinert — who had been unable to attend the meeting since, as he could prove, he had been in West Germany — were accused by Weiland of being the leaders of the conspiracy against him.

At the beginning of my interview, the events at the group meeting were only discussed as a side issue. The official was far more concerned with events in the work camp at Hohenschönhausen and in the penal institute at Magdalene Strasse in East Berlin. He wanted to know what the two state security men wanted in their discussions with me. After I had given him a brief and truthful resume of the conversations, I asked him what this had to do with the events in the group and the accusations made by Weiland.

I told him that directly after my release I had informed several close friends, as well as Liselotte Beck and Franz Schrodt, that the state security office had an interest in them. I had later told Alfred Weiland about the incident as well. I told my interviewer straight that he could only have known about it through Weiland. The official did not deny it. Comrade Bohn, who had once been a friend of Weiland and had also belonged to the Communist Workers' Party in the Weimar period and had also been condemned by the GDR authorities for 'subversive activity', then told me that Weiland had already being working with the most right-wing elements in the prison at Bötzow.

Through left-wing comrades in the SPD I made contact with three Falken youth groups: the Spartacus Group in Schöneberg, with its chairman Wolfgang Hohmann; the Rosa Luxemburg Group in Wilmersdorf; and another in the Kreuzberg district. Even the names they chose expressed the fact that they wanted to stand in the revolutionary tradition of the workers' movement. After my first political discussions with comrade Hohmann and his friends it became clear that their basic conceptions of socialism almost completely agreed with mine.

There were continual discussions, particularly with the Schöneberg Falken group, about the fundamentals of scientific socialism and our further work in the SPD. These were soon followed up by talks which I gave on the conflicts inside the Communist Party during the Weimar period, and about the role played by the subjective factor in the fight against capitalism. These talks were usually given at youth centres in the Schöneberg district, or in the 'White Rose' youth centre, and were also attended by members of the Wilmsersdorf and Kreuzberg groups.

I also remember a group of young Zionists from Israel, who had been invited by the Berlin Senate and were now being wheeled around the youth groups of the SPD and the Falken, in order that they might be admired for their fight for Greater Israel. They were enraged to find that the Schöneberg Falken group had no sympathy for their aggressive stance towards the Arabs in general and the Palestinians in particular. They had to endure being told by the young comrades that their repressive policy bore many resemblances to the methods of the Fascists.

My political work with the Falken, whose central organisation was the Falken group Spartacus in the Schöneberg district, did not prevent me from also furthering my political activities within the left wing of the SPD. During the first years of our collaboration I had a good healthy relationship with the comrades in the left-wing group. At that time the district organisation was dominated by the right-wing group led by the senator in charge of Construction, Schwedler. The chairman of the Charlottenburg district was comrade Lothar Löffler, the son of a resistance fighter. Lothar Löffler was one of those members of the SPD with whom you could have a proper rational discussion.

It was quite different with Schwedler and Neubauer, who were in fact not members of the district organisation, but spoke out against the left in a defamatory fashion both in the branches and in district conferences. Neubauer remained a member and chairman of the Friedrichshain district (East Berlin) right up until the construction of the Wall, even though the

SPD did not officially exist there any more: the East Berlin Social Democrats still met in trusted company; some of their meetings took place in West Berlin.

Neubauer had long since transferred his field of activity into West Berlin. The right wing were keen on the Charlottenburg district because Kreuzberg, Schöneberg and Tiergarten were already controlled by the left. Since branches 2, 5 and 11 of the Charlottenburg district were now sending left-wing delegates to the district delegate meetings, and in other branches the left constituted a considerable minority, the right wing wanted to make sure they held on to Charlottenburg.

Harry Ristock was the spokesperson and leading light of the left wing, not only in Charlottenburg, but in the whole of West Berlin. At that time he and the whole left wing were defending a Marxist position against the aspirations of the 'Navvies' (Kanalarbeiter) to throw Marxist principles overboard and to become a 'people's party'. Willy Brandt in particular, who was then chair of the Berlin SPD, was campaigning for a new programme which would make the SPD a 'party of the people'.

At one conference of Berlin party officials in Kliems Rooms, where I opposed Brandt's arguments along with comrade Köhler, he had only this to say to support his position: 'You should find yourselves somewhere else to go! Anyone who defends positions like yours has no place in the ranks of the SPD.'

Harry Ristock finally succeeded in becoming the chair of the district. He immediately started pointing his nose in the direction of the mayor's office for the district. The right wing under Schwedler and Neubauer, Wolf Tuchel and Gerd Löffler protested against this at a district delegate meeting, pointing out that Ristock could not become mayor since he had a criminal record. (Ristock had been sentenced by a court because it was claimed that he had misused funds from the Falken organisation.)

So Ristock now started extending his influence in the town hall by different means. If the right wing had prevented him from becoming district mayor, then they had nothing against him being nominated and elected as councillor responsible for Social Services. His friends Dieter Masteit and Arved Rogall were elected to the council, Dieter Masteit in charge of Youth and Sport, and Arved Rogall in charge of Education. This election was preceded by a long struggle inside the left-wing faction. Kurt Neubauer and Wolf Tuchel had protested in vain against the two being elected to the council. The SPD group meeting voted to reject the protests.

Schwedler now mobilised the Social-Democratic faction of the city council. The councillors, who as we know answer only to their own consciences and do not feel bound by any petitions or instructions, declared succinctly that they would not think of obeying the recommendations of a general management committee. So the faction voted by eighteen to six against disowning Masteit and Rogall.

In addition, Klaus-Peter Schulz polemicised against Harry Ristock in Branch No. 8. He accused him of pursuing power politics. The Ristock Group, as he called the left, was 'trying to block the way to a people's party and trying to turn back the wheel of history.' In the meantime, the regional executive and the regional committee were examining the situation. The regional committee authorised the three leaders — Mattick, Neubauer and Thiele — to negotiate with Ristock and the SPD faction on the council. Only then would the postponed district delegate meeting take place. Masteit was dropped; they sacrificed him so that Ristock and Rogall could keep their positions.

From that time onwards, the left in the Charlottenburg district had the upper hand and never lost the leadership of the district. Unlike before, Ristock and his supporters no longer wanted to conquer the party, but tried to creep in by the back door. One of the most decisive arguments which took place in the Social Democratic Party revolved around the struggle over the Godesberg Programme in 1959. At that time, the left was still determined to do everything in its power to oppose any attempt to abandon a programme which was centred around the working class.

Although the then chair of the SPD, Erich Ollenhauer, had declared at a party congress that the development of democracy after 1945 simply meant that we now had a presidential democracy in the state, with all the power in the hands of the Federal Chancellor, he was still one of the most zealous proponents of the Godesberg Programme. The right wing, to which Willy Brandt also belonged, argued that, as a social-democratic party, they needed the support of the whole population.

In all of this, Ollenhauer, Brandt and Wehner had 'forgotten' that the SPD was a workers' party, which should represent the interests of the workforce in a determined manner, and had also 'forgotten' that 80 per cent of the population were working. The SPD were primarily concerned to underpin in theory the policy which they had already pursued in the Weimar period: the policy of collaboration with the bourgeois parties.

In the Autumn of 1959, Jesko von Puttkammer wrote in Number 46 of *Vorwärts*, the party journal of the SPD: 'The democratic state is not just a fruitful ground for socialism; it is in fact the only form of the state in which socialism can be developed. That is the foundation stone for the new draft of the programme, upon which we can develop the individual theses which, in their turn, would be unthinkable without the tradition and ideals of social democracy.'

The left in the SPD then fought enthusiastically against the programme which betrayed the interests of the working population. In those days you could still talk about a left wing in the SPD. The one-time SAPD members, who had re-entered the party in 1945, fought for their own — centrist — programme. A few years after Godesberg, there was no longer any trace of them. Comrades had left the party or had been expelled, while those who remained in the social-democratic movement were resigned to the situation.

From then on, it was no longer possible to talk of a left wing in the SPD. One result of the Godesberg Programme was the 'Incompatibility Clause', which was accepted by the SPD party leadership on 6 November 1961 without any justification at all: 'Membership of the association known as the "National Association of the Socialist Sponsorship Society of the Friends, Sponsors and former Members of the Socialist German Students' Union" is incompatible with membership of the Social Democratic Party of Germany; equally incompatible is membership of the SDS (Socialist German Student Union) with the Social Democratic Party of Germany'.

This clause on 'incompatibility' was supposed to show the other bourgeois parties that the SPD was serious about its Godesberg doctrine: any students who refused to leave the SDS were automatically expelled from the SPD. In 1963 the lefts in the Berlin SPD met officially for the last time. They gathered at the youth centre known as 'The White Rose'. I attended this meeting, and Ristock and Karnatz were the speakers on the subject 'The situation in the SPD'. The party leadership had made new decisions about cooperation in the groups and the districts.

Amongst other things, they said that groups in the branches and districts could only meet if they had the permission of the appropriate higher leadership. In his speech, Ristock submitted to this ban on factions, but then declared that the 'left' would take over the party within five years. In my contribution to the discussion I said that the SPD could not simply be taken over; that would depend on a strong socialist faction inside the party and on defending the interests of the working class both inside and outside. What was now happening in the SPD, I went on, was a repeat of what we had experienced at the end of the 1920s as a result of the Stalinisation of the KPD, even if the situation was now different.

The SPD could no longer be taken over: what was now required was to prevent the party leadership from acting in the interests of the ruling class and placing itself at the head of the anti-communist movement. Even a bourgeois writer like Thomas Mann had had to admit that anti-communism was the underlying stupidity of our century. Together with the trade unions and the bourgeois parties, the SPD was organising the fight against communism, and now no longer differentiated between the Stalinist forces and the oppositional communists, as it had still done in the years 1945 to 1948. Today, their fight was against the left wing, and the social-democratic 'left' remained silent.

Just how the 'left' performed is shown by the Kressmann affair: during a speech made in the Kreuzberg district on May Day, the district mayor Kressmann accused Willy Brandt and Ernst Lemmer of being protagonists of the Cold War. The bourgeois press demanded severe reprisals to be taken against him for such a statement. Kressmann retracted it but was still reprimanded by the SPD and received an official warning. Then the regional executive of the SPD went one step further: it apologised to the CDU for the behaviour of mayor Kressmann. The CDU were not satisfied with Kressmann's retraction; nor was the apology from the regional executive enough for them. At a closed SPD meeting in Steglitz, Kressmann had stated that there was common ground between social democracy and communism. The CDU protested again. When summoned before the party leadership, Kressmann gave in again and declared: 'As a democratic socialist I can find no common ground with communism.'

Despite this, Kressmann was reprimanded once more and they told him that any political intervention would be unwelcome. On paper at least, Kressmann belonged to the Marxist Working Group, but he was never active there in the years that I belonged to it. He only turned up when he needed some support in his differences with the regional executive; otherwise he was never to be seen. Kressmann accepted the second reprimand that was handed out and kept well in the background during public events.

During these conflicts on the party line, I got to know Horst Mahler; he was a district delegate and belonged to Branch No.2. Additionally, he was a member of the Socialist Students' Union (SDS). His contributions to discussions at district delegate meetings aroused not only my interest; other comrades were interested in the clarity of his ideas, which were based on the principles of Marx and Engels. Whenever there was a chance, he campaigned in the party not only so that the demands of the SDS would receive attention, but also for support for the principle of equality, which the university students were demanding — that is, to be permitted to participate in deciding the curriculum. Neither Horst Mahler nor the other members of the SDS who were also members of the SPD received any such support from the party executive. On the contrary, they were always being told by the party executive that they should not meddle with the party's education policy, which should be left to the leadership.

Inside the SPD, the SDS then proceeded to discuss these questions in their own factional meetings. There was close cooperation in the Charlottenburg district between the Socialist Students' Union and the Young Socialists (Jusos). At one of these meetings, on 31 August 1961, the topic was 'The tasks of the Social-Democratic party within bourgeois democracy'; I gave the main talk.

In my contribution, for tactical reasons I referred to the Godesberg Programme of the SPD which had not yet abandoned the claim to be building democratic socialism. In the introduction to the Programme, where the destructive forces of two world wars were discussed and the dangers of the atomic age spotlighted, the authors of this Programme stated that humanity could only open the path to its own liberation by constructing a better social order.

Such a new and better social order was the one sought by democratic socialism. And in the section entitled 'Principles of socialism' it said: 'The socialists are striving for a society in which everyone can develop his or her personality in freedom and can, as a useful member of society, participate responsibly in the political, economic and cultural life of humanity.' And in the section headed 'Basic demands for a humanitarian society', it said: 'Socialism will only be realised through democracy, and democracy will be fulfilled by socialism.'

I built my arguments on these formal statements of principle. I pointed out particularly that we lived in a highly-industrialised society, in which 80 per cent of the population was employed and was still oppressed and exploited by the ruling class. Even in a parliamentary democracy it was still possible for the majority of working people not to participate in political decisions. Only once every four years was the voter permitted to put his cross on the voting slips. But the very next day he was disenfranchised again, for the law says that those elected are only responsible to their consciences and not to those who voted for them.

'It is far worse when the working man enters his place of work and the gates shut behind him. For then he is simply a recruit; for there he can only stand with his thumbs against his trouser seams and obey the orders of his employer or employer's representatives. The task of the party must be to unite theory and practice and fight for the realisation of democratic socialism.'

Two members of the right wing of the party were present at this meeting as observers — Heinz Wendland and Gerd Löffler, who was later to lead the Berlin SPD. Soon afterwards, on 6 September, I received a letter which had been agreed by the district executive at its meeting of 5 September 1961: 'On account of incidents of which you are aware, a party procedure has been started against you according to paragraph 27 of the rules.'

This letter had been written at the instigation of Gerd Löffler without anyone hearing my side of the story beforehand. I had given the chair of the arbitration commission on 29 September the names of those who would sit on the committee on my behalf; after that, I heard nothing more about the party investigation until the end of May in the following year.

In September 1961 I had expressed my readiness to suspend my party functions in the interests of a swift conclusion to the proceedings. Finally, on 10 June 1962, I wrote to the district executive, for the attention of Gerd Löffler, that I was not prepared to consider suspending my party functions any longer if the proceedings against me were not concluded as soon as possible. I received no answer to this letter. At the next meeting of party officials, I proposed that a discussion of the party proceedings against me be put on the agenda.

When this point was discussed, the officials unanimously declared that I should become active again; the next branch meeting also passed such a motion. The district executive did not prevent me taking up my activities again, not even in my function as district delegate. The party proceedings against me were never concluded, although Gerd Löffler had declared at a meeting of the district delegates that he would not rest until I had been expelled. I belonged to the SPD up until 1968; that year I announced my resignation from the party when Emergency Laws were passed with the support of the parliamentary faction of the SPD.

This affair had some significance in student circles, since Horst Mahler and his friends were also subject to similar proceedings. The proceedings against comrade Mahler were resolved by the invocation of the incompatibility clause; he fought with other comrades for reacceptance into the SPD. These comrades distributed leaflets and organised demonstrations in an attempt to make the party membership realise that it was not in the interests of democracy to expel members because of their criticisms of the party.

In November 1961, Horst Mahler distributed leaflets on the incompatibility clause in front of the Charlottenburg town hall during a district delegates' meeting. All the comrades took a leaflet from him, and I was just arriving when Neubauer, the future Senator responsible for Internal Affairs, attacked him. He struck him in the side several times with his fists, snatched the leaflets from his hands and trampled them underfoot.

Horst Mahler, although he could have acted in self-defence, did not resist. Directly afterwards I commented on Neubauer's attack during my contribution to the discussion. I attacked him sharply and declared the political differences were not to be resolved by violence but by political argument. Mahler then brought a court case against Neubauer for grievous bodily harm. When the case came up, Neubauer was already Senator

Oskar Hippe at the beginning of the 1970s

responsible for Internal Affairs in Berlin. He was found not guilty, even though I, as the only witness, gave evidence against him.

Since the days of our united struggle inside the SPD, apart from sharing common ideas on the scientific basis of socialism, Horst Mahler and I had been bound together by a close friendship. This was not only manifested when we backed each other up in party meetings, but also when we defended the same Marxist conception in the left-wing faction. I was often at his apartment, where three of us — his wife was also in the socialist movement — held discussions. Horst Mahler and his friends were always quite sure, and were always stating, that no successful fight could be conducted without or against the majority of the working class. In the mid-1960s, Horst Mahler completed his studies and set up in practice as a lawyer.

We did not meet quite so often in that period. But when we did meet up, I discovered that his basic ideas had not changed. Only the impatience of his youth caused him to make leaps in thought which went out far ahead of reality. Thus, he thought that state violence had to be met by individual counter-violence. One could not wait until the majority of the working class had been persuaded; one had to light a torch which would shine out and show the workers the way forward.

I objected that state violence could only be met by counter-violence if the majority of the working class had already been won over, and warned against undertaking anything in the current situation which did not strengthen either the young left or the working class. I advised all the comrades to read Lenin's *State and Revolution* and *'Left-wing' Communism: an Infantile Disorder*.

In November 1968 we had the events surrounding the so-called 'battle' in Tegeler Weg: Horst Mahler had to appear before a 'court of honour' of lawyers to answer for his political activities. The leading public prosecutor for the Berlin area had demanded that the city's society of lawyers hold this disciplinary hearing against the young lawyer who had defended numerous students and demonstrators in the courts since the mid-1960s. The charge against Horst Mahler was that the manner of his defences, as well as his own political activities, was scarcely compatible with the 'code of honour' and 'responsibilities of the profession' of a lawyer or indeed with the fundamental tenets of our 'free democratic constitution'. Because he had brought the legal profession into disrepute, he should now be stripped of the right to act as a lawyer.

Various political groups demonstrated against these proceedings. The police attempted to break up the demonstration right in front of the high court building, but they failed because the demonstrators defended themselves. Here, at least, one could say that state violence was met with counter-violence. The police had to retreat and there was jubilation in the ranks of the young left. For the first time they seemed to have succeeded in resisting the police.

I told those who joined in a discussion at the Republican Club that there was no cause for celebration. The police, although they had been beaten this time, would return tomorrow with reinforcements and make up for their failure. As long as progressive forces were as weak as they were now, the police would always win the day. What was now necessary was a broadening of the political basis of the movement. But comrade Mahler burned all his bridges behind him and became a founder member of the Red Army Faction (RAF). The bourgeois state reacted to this challenge to its power with exemplary punishments; at the time of writing Horst Mahler still sits in prison.

It was obvious that the 'left' under the leadership of Ristock, who now led the Charlottenburg district, was now putting forward ideas which were opposed to those of the Federal and Area executives, but which did not base themselves on Marxism as was the case in the 1950s. Thus, they left open the question which the Social Democrats had occupied themselves with between 1945 and 1963 as to who had fought most consistently against Fascism before and after 1933.

It was said that the people involved in the 20 July plot had been the real resistance fighters. Apart from Leuschner and Leber, former trade union leaders, the other participants in the 20 July plot had been right-wing politicians, members of the German National Party, or former high-ranking officers (Field-Marshal von Witzleben etc.) who had stood by Hitler through thick and thin until Stalingrad.

In an article in the July-August 1959 edition of *Solidarity*, the information bulletin of the Charlottenburg SPD, Ristock wrote as district chairman:

'The 20 July plot stands as a symbol of the resistance against the National Socialist regime. This resistance is indivisible. From Carl von Ossietsky, who had already been thrown in prison during the last days of the Weimar Republic, through to the men of 20 July, we have an unbroken chain of people whom we should really honour as heroes of our nation.'

Ristock did not even have the courage to stand up in the SPD and state that, apart from the people of 20 July, who included fighters from both bourgeois and social-democratic camps, the main strength of the resistance came from the communists. The comrades of Branch No.11 and other branches now spoke out unanimously against any idea that 20 July people should be regarded as the core of the resistance against Fascism.

With the slogan 'Against tyranny! Against bourgeois falsification of history!', comrades Georg Kunz, Herbert Haufschild and myself were commissioned to produce a leaflet attacking the position of the Federal and Area executive on this question. Here is an extract:

'The article presents the plotters of 20 July as the centre of the resistance against Fascism within Germany and the attempt on Hitler as the only visible evidence of this resistance. So the people who are recorded in history as the handservants of National Socialism, who participated in the suppression of the real resistance, that is, the resistance of the proletariat, and who saw in National Socialism the saviour from proletarian revolution, who themselves acted as the gravediggers of freedom and democracy — these are now the people whom we are supposed to regard as liberating heroes of the nation and exemplary democrats.

'To be sure, the resistance of the proletariat is not to be found in bourgeois histories. To be sure, we find nothing or very little to show that this resistance was active even in the concentration camps and prisons filled with workers, members of the Jewish bourgeoisie and left-wing intellectuals, and was not to be broken by horrific acts of terror, and that this took place not just after 1944. There has been a deliberate silence about it because, despite the later differences, they still agreed with Hitler that the proletarian organisations had to be smashed if they themselves were to survive.

'The smashing of the proletarian organisations met with the wholehearted approval of Western democracies which now describe themselves as "the free world", although in the event of a serious threat to their own claims to power they would take at least the same steps, as the case of France shows today. The declaration that there is a "collective guilt" in the German people also belongs to this struggle against the proletariat, since from the outset they want to discriminate against the proletariat, the overwhelming majority of the people. They want to drive home the idea that their failure was due to their inferiority, and to explain once and for all that the proletariat is incapable of taking a grip on its own fate and revolutionising society.

'The men of 20 July, especially the officers and with few exceptions, saw in Hitler the real representative of their interests. They served him loyally and unconditionally until they began to fear being dragged down with the collapse of the regime (this is what our writer calls the "unmasking" of National Socialism) and tried to save their own necks and in particular their own social system — that is, their positions of power — by sacrificing those who had until then been their idols.

'After the writer of this bourgeois falsification of history, which condescends to allow a few resistance fighters among the proletariat even before 1944, indeed even admits of a few warnings from them before 1933 — after he has thus presented it all as the most valuable and most sacred inheritance of the German spirit of freedom and of German democracy, he comes to the true meaning and purpose of his article, which is already quite clear from the motto: that is, the communist threat.

'He compares 20 July 1944 with our present-day situation and suggests that if we do not learn from the dilemma of these people of 20 July, who had different political persuasions and whose plot only failed in the final analysis because of inner conflicts, then we ourselves will fall prey to communism.

'The first thing to be said about the plotters of 20 July is that they did not fail because of the wide spectrum of their political ideas, but rather because of their political naivety and intellectual backwardness in wanting to turn the wheel of history not forwards, but backwards. Unfortunately, when they went down, they took with them some major leaders of the proletariat who, from a sense of political responsibility and recognition of their duty as true resistance fighters, had to seize on any opening to change the domestic situation in Germany. It was not their fault that the attempted coup failed.

'A comparison of the situation of 20 July with today is not possible. Any such comparison completely ignores historical fact and tries to fool the proletariat into thinking that they must defend bourgeois democracy alongside the bourgeoisie as part of the punishment for the defeat. The freedom of the bourgeoisie, the freedom of the ruling class is, however, not the freedom of the proletariat. Real freedom and democracy can only be realised through socialism. They will only exist if they are built on socialist foundations and if we, as today's socialists, emulate those men who, before and after 30 January 1933, right through to the month of May 1945, held high the banner of humanity, of democracy and of socialism.'

Two thousand copies of this leaflet were printed by Branch No.11, so that it could circulate beyond the Charlottenburg membership. In the branches which were led by the right wing, our comrades were forbidden to distribute this leaflet. And there were also 'lefts' like comrade Rogall who did not want to distribute the leaflet.

After they had won the Charlottenburg district, the 'left' led by Harry Ristock increasingly resorted to policies of half-measures. They justified this by saying that they should not antagonise comrades who had adopted a conciliatory attitude towards them. Ristock was of the opinion that the 'left' would conquer the party within five years. I still worked with the faction, although Ristock and the majority of the faction had quite different ideas from me. Again and again the comrades demanded that I maintain discipline and preserve the unity of the 'left'. I replied that as long as Harry Ristock continued to 'dance on eggs' and as long as his policies were neither fish nor fowl, I would not think of supporting the present policies of the 'left'. Neither before 1933 nor now would the SPD be won over to policies which worked primarily in the interests of the workers. The SPD had ceased to be a workers' party, and with the Godesberg Programme it had become a petty-bourgeois liberal party.

From then on I was no longer invited to meetings of the faction. At the next elections Ristock and his followers ensured that I did not remain a delegate for the district. But in Branch No.7, which was what No.11 became after the party reforms, I continued to have the support of 29 comrades. Branch No.7 had something over 300 members, between 70 and 80 of whom were active; only at the annual meeting, when district delegates and branch officials were elected, were the remaining 'card-carrying corpses' wheeled on.

I often asked myself whether it still made sense to carry on as a member of the SPD. But comrades Haufschild and Kunz still tried to convince me that it was better to work in the main organisation than to resign from the party and remain outside. I told them that it was certainly not my intention to resign, but that the work in the main organisation was not sufficient to create a socialist consciousness inside the party.

Although the Charlottenburg left had become as meek as lambs, the struggle with the district leadership continued. The right wing tried everything they could to regain Charlottenburg. Although I was no longer a district delegate, I still attended the district delegate meetings as a guest. Even among the guests there were comrades with whom it was worth having a discussion.

At one such meeting, in the summer of 1966, at which the opposed ideas of both wings collided, comrade Rumprecht took part in the discussion. Rumprecht stood on the right wing, and along with Schwedler and Neubauer he was one of the 'whips' for the 'Navvies'. I have already mentioned the episode in April 1945 when Rumprecht and I lived in the same building at 12 Spielhagen Strasse. Rumprecht was then still a Hitler man. During a discussion at his future in-laws apartment there had been a conversation about the outcome of the war. I had said that no reasonable person could ignore the fact that the war was lost, and Rumprecht had jumped up and said that, if he was not in the house of his parents-in-law, he would have me arrested.

At this meeting, as always, Rumprecht did not pull his punches against the left. In the course of his statements, he said: 'I am only small fry.' I could not resist interrupting with 'You were always small fry'. I immediately received a warning from Willy Haberland, who was chairing the meeting. He told me I should be ashamed of myself — comrade Rumprecht had only one arm and did not deserve being run down in this way. I demanded to be allowed to speak and give a short explanation; I received permission and told them that Rumprecht had not lost his arm in the socialist cause but in the service of Hitler. I then received a second warning; at the same time Haberland told me to leave the room. I defended myself by saying that the constitution allowed me to speak the truth.

Haberland then replied: 'I refuse to let the meeting continue until you have left the room.' To the applause of the right wing — even Ristock applauded — I left the room.

I had the impression that both Willy Haberland and Harry Ristock, who had after all only recently been elected town councillors, were trying to prove to their right-wing friends that they could work together in future in the same way. I remained a member of the SPD for another two years. But I no longer had any opportunity to campaign for my ideas, except in the branch.

I had entered the SPD a decade previously in order to influence the party and the working class alongside the then left. But it was not the right wing who put me out of the party with the aid of the party constitution, but rather it was the 'left' who drove me out with the help of their intrigues. It was not the right-wing group who, in 1961, applied to have me expelled from the party after proceedings had been instituted against me; it was the hatred of a petty-bourgeois gone wild, who had come to the SPD after the reconstruction of the political parties.

Even Kurt Neubauer, one of the most right-wing people in the SPD, who had been designated to chair the arbitration commission by the area executive, had still not completed the proceedings against me when I left the party in 1968. I can only suppose that he did not feel quite right having to conduct a disciplinary action against a comrade with my history.

At the turn of the year 1964-1965 there began the policy of 'little steps', or 'change through rapprochement', a policy which did not arise in the heads of Egon Bahr and Willy Brandt. The Americans must have seen that the 'roll-back' policies of Dulles and Adenauer had not been successful. They now tried for their part to find ways of ending the Cold War and coming to an arrangement with the Soviet Union.

It was Egon Bahr who first took steps in this direction and impressed upon Willy Brandt the necessity of taking social democracy in a new direction. Harry Ristock, who had shown a flair for accommodation since he had moved into the party bureaucracy, wrote in *Solidarity* of March 1965, the SPD bulletin for Charlottenburg:

'Even in the West today, and without any of that piety engendered by the Cold War, they are demanding a German answer to the German question. For us as Social Democrats, now — or at the very latest on the day after the elections to the Federal Parliament — now is the time to embark on a great programme which will shatter illusions, for that is the only way we can begin to formulate a German *policy*.

'Its aims: The construction and development of a completely new relationship with the entire eastern European bloc.

'The establishment of diplomatic relations with Poland, Czechoslovakia, Hungary, Rumania and Bulgaria, the strengthening and reorientation of our relations with the USSR. This would be the German contribution to the defusion of world tensions: the division of Germany is only partly a cause of this tension, but is primarily its outcome.

'The establishment of full diplomatic relations with the state of Israel. Here the policies of Willy Brandt and the Berlin Senate point the way.

'The "little steps" policy is certainly no substitute for the reunification of Germany. It sets up unalterable preconditions to combat the ever-deepening division, to make the Wall transparent and to really help the people on the other side of the Wall and on this side of the River Elbe.'

I do not reproach Harry Ristock for campaigning for an end to the Cold War. It goes without saying that any workers' party which claims to fight for a socialist society must distance itself from the chauvinistic bourgeoisie and cooperate with those forces who have emblazoned their banners with the words of peace and social stability. What I did reproach him for was that he threw himself into the arms of the executive members of the SPD who used the occasion of the twentieth anniversary of the ending of the war to describe any celebration of 8 May, 'Liberation Day', as 'a national indignity'. One could not, after all, celebrate one's own 'defeat'.

He was not the Harry Ristock of fifteen years ago. He had developed from being an upstanding fighter for the socialist cause into an opportunist and will end as one. Harry Ristock and his 'left faction' sought rapprochement with the policies of the party executive at a time when the Federal government was preparing a new battery of legislation, the Emergency Laws, and a group within the SPD (led by Erler) was campaigning for these laws. In the fight against the Emergency Laws, the West German workers and their trade unions, together with university teachers and students, scored major successes at first. In a broad protest movement involving trade unionists, there were many rallies against the Emergency Laws in West German towns. This was not confined to the trade unions — among SPD members there was also great unrest, and here you also found a will to fight the Emergency Laws.

Because of the protests and the excitement among the workforce, the Federal government did not think it wise to put the law to the vote for the time being. Similarly, Erler's group delayed their propaganda within the parliamentary faction for acceptance of the law. But when the draft was again presented two years later and was put to the vote in the Federal Parliament, the SPD faction voted by a large majority for the Emergency Laws. In the course of two years they had succeeded in reassuring large parts of the FDGB (West German Trade Union Federation) executive and many in their own ranks as well. Without the support of the SPD faction the Emergency Laws would never have been passed, since a two-thirds majority was required. In the two years leading up to 1968 I had been continually toying with the idea of leaving the SPD, since there was little opportunity for me to discuss my political thoughts.

When the Emergency Laws were passed, the SPD abandoned the principles of the rule of law. I took that as the occasion to resign from the party, addressing at the same time a statement to both the district executive and the branch.

My resignation from the SPD was not a sign of resignedness. On the contrary, wherever I had the chance of putting forward my point of view, I did so. But I no longer wished to be tied to one party or group, since I saw no possibility of finding a home in the divided groups of the left.

For 52 years I had been active politically. I had begun my struggle in 1916 in the Spartacus League and continued it in the Communist Party, from which I was expelled in 1929. With comrades and friends, I had conducted a fight against Stalinism, had come into contact with the Left Opposition (Bolshevik-Leninists) via the Lenin League, in which, with others, I had taken up the struggle against Fascism, whilst still continuing to fight against Stalinism.

When I returned from Bautzen in 1956, there was nothing left of anything which I had built up with a few other comrades. In joining the SPD I had believed that I could continue the struggle for socialist principles with the lefts, and was disappointed. I now concentrated my main activity on the conflicts within the SDS and the student movement which had been torn apart by ideological differences since 1968 and had split into several small organisations.

Together with the KJO-Spartakus (Communist Youth Organisation -Spartacus), which had been formed by the progressive elements of the Falken Group, with whom I had worked earlier, I tried to direct activity towards the construction of a revolutionary party. KJO-Spartakus, among whose members was Peter Brandt, the son of the Federal Chancellor, had consciously broken with the traditions of social democracy and had committed itself to revolutionary socialism. It stood openly in the tradition of Lenin and Trotsky. In the street demonstrations they formed a considerable bloc — young workers and school students, apprentices and students, trade unionists, former and sympathising members of the Falken.

Our hope that large groups of students would join Spartacus came to nothing. At that time, most of them saw their salvation in Mao Zedong and the 'People's War' and in Stalin they had their ancestor. The strongest

Maoist group called itself the Communist Party of Germany (KPD) and took up the ultra-left policies of the KPD in the final phase of the Weimar Republic, and defended the line of the RGO and the theory of social fascism. According to them, the Soviet Union was a Fascist state which had to be fought with all available means, even in alliance with their own bourgeoisie, as they were later to explain. Just how little the young intellectuals of the 1960s concerned themselves with Marx and Lenin is evident in the route that the 'Maoist' party took.

The KJO-Spartakus group finally collapsed when they tried to put their aims into practice. Although they accepted Trotsky's *Transitional Programme* as their most important platform, they had not realised that there was a long period of struggle before them. The young comrades were impatient: the work was as hectic as if the 'world revolution' was going to break out at the weekend.

Many of them became over-stretched, over-worked, burned out and sucked dry, because they had approached their tasks in the false expectation of rapid success. At the time, I told the young comrades that the crucial thing was to strengthen their cadre organisation from within, to develop their consciousness and to make clear to their members the preconditions for conducting a successful struggle against capitalism. Millions of workers in the Federal Republic of Germany believed in the democracy represented by party and chancellor, even when they recognised the authoritarian nature of the democracy.

But what happened was not the same problem as of old, of allowing members to tire themselves out and wear out their strength in the struggle for single-issue demands. When these comrades saw that they were getting no immediate results, they gave up.

At the end of these memoirs, I would like to set out a couple of sentences from a talk that I gave during the 'organisational phase' of the student movement. They seem to me to retain their validity and actuality:

'We have the advantage that we do not have to find "brand new" paths. For a century now, workers in many lands have fought under the tried and tested banner of Marxism. Marx and Engels laid down the foundations for successful struggle. In several countries the working class allied to the peasantry has been victorious. The Stalinists in the Soviet Union have made something different of it all. It is the duty of the working class to ensure that, on the international arena, the imperialist powers of the world do not have their way. On the other hand, it is equally important that the bureaucracy are restrained so that the forces of revolution are no longer tied down.'

15.

REVIEW AND PROSPECTS

At the turn of the year 1942-1943, there occurred what the Left Opposition of the KPD had always predicted. In 1931-1932 the Left Opposition within the German Communist Party had said that Hitler would take the power if we did not succeed in our struggle to create a workers' united front between the two workers' parties, the KPD and the SPD. Then he would pitch Germany into the inferno of a war from which the German working class could not escape by its own efforts. Fascism would only collapse as a result of a war with the great powers.

The collapse began at the end of 1942. When the German Sixth Army under Field-Marshall General Paulus had to surrender at Stalingrad in January 1943 it was plain that Hitler and his General Staff were going to lose the war. In tremendous battles of encirclement across the whole eastern front, the Red Army drove the German troops back. First the southern part of the Soviet Union and the Ukraine was liberated, then Soviet and Polish troops penetrated far into Poland, so that now even the Western Allies saw themselves forced to open up their long-promised front and begin the invasion.

In the summer of 1944, the united British and American units in Normandy began the invasion. Strong American forces had landed in Italy from the south. The German General Staff was now forced to fight on three fronts. In an editorial in the weekly journal, *Das Reich*, which was published by the National Ministry of Propaganda under Goebbels, the Hitler government tried to prove that the British and Americans had submitted to the demands of the Soviets by recognising the Lublin government:

'This is Britain's Polish "test case" in its true colours, the test case which permits the Soviet power to infiltrate Europe with the blessing of the democratic powers of the West. "The fact that Europe permits communism to be forced in this way on countries who have fought it like the plague is a sign of a sad dereliction of duty" — this is the moral which our own *Voz* newspaper drew from the development in the policies pursued by Britain and America in eastern and southern Europe, and stigmatises the abandonment of Europe by the western democracies.

'The conclusion is thus even more clear: since it is not prepared to abdicate in favour of either the Soviets or the British and Americans, Europe must place itself under the leadership of Germany in order to extricate itself from a situation where its very existence is under threat: a fight to the very end and with a firm resolve to fend off and overcome the deadly threat from east and west . . .

'We as a people hold the view that if the British, Americans and Soviets declare with monotonous regularity that, in the event of victory, they intend to uproot us, to lay waste our country, destroy our economy and transport our working population to the Siberian tundra, then that has always been known to be the plan of the enemies of the German people . . . There can now be no other task for the German people than for every individual among us to dedicate himself tirelessly and hour for hour to the war and his overriding duties, and not to hold back until victory is ours.' (*Das Reich*, 10 September 1944)

If Goebbels was still talking of peace through victory in September 1944, then it was quite clear to him in January 1945 that large sections of the German people no longer believed in peace through victory and were no longer prepared to commit themselves to such a thing. So this opportunist now remembered the points on the programme which were supposed to make up the platform of 'National Socialism', but which had been sacrificed to the interests of capitalism no later than June 1934 in the so-called Röhm putsch.

In that month he wrote:

'The age of plutocracy has now finally ended, even in the states which have been built and governed on the classical model. Throughout the world nations are marching towards a socialist society. Such a society will burst through with a mighty force after the war in all countries, especially in those whose leaders have oppressed the people for longest. We shall then have no more to say; after all, we entered this war to protect all those ideals which are slowly but surely rising up through all the bloody battles.

'We will be not only the military victors but also the spiritual victors of this battle of nations. That is because we do not wish to conquer philosophy but to to defend a single philosophy. We are several steps ahead of the rest of the world.' (*Das Reich*, 14 January 1945)

But only a few weeks later — the demagogic call to defend 'socialism' had not lit any fires, the Russian troops were at the River Oder, the capital of the German Reich was under threat and the Western Allies had advanced far across the Rhine — Goebbels appealed in an editorial to the bourgeoisie of Europe to consider their position and to halt the advance of Bolshevism:

'The political bourgeoisie of Europe, including Britain, has taken on its shoulders a heavy historical burden of guilt. In a time of the greatest economic and social crisis, which are the signs for a complete change and reconstitution of the state, they have abandoned the foundation stones of national life and have approached or even thrown themselves into the arms of starry-eyed, but for that reason all the more deceitful and terrible, ideas and conceptions.

'Such ideas, in the final analysis, lead to the overthrow of the traditional order of the state and dissolve in economic and political anarchy: from this, anyone with some knowledge of social relations will recognise that they can only be regarded as the first stage of Bolshevism . . .

'Bolshevism will never be strong enough to attain its goals by its own strength alone; it will always hobble on crutches to power, crutches which are supplied and offered by the political bourgeoisie, even today . . . It would be no problem for us to deal with the problem on our own, let alone if all peoples of our continent recognised the acute threat to the most basic principles of their political, economic and social life and defended themselves against it with united forces.' (*Das Reich*, 4 February 1945)

But all these appeals had no effect; the defeat was sealed. In the first days of May 1945, the fighting in Berlin was finished. The German forces had capitulated unconditionally. Millions of German soldiers were captured, the troops were disarmed. Since the officers still had the power of command, it quite often happened that the German courts martial still passed judgement and sentenced soldiers even after the surrender, as happened in the Filbinger affair.

Even at that time, there were tensions between the Western Allies and the Soviet Union. Negotiations took place in Potsdam. In Germany, all the political power lay in the hands of the occupying powers. Germany was divided into four occupation zones, and Berlin into four sectors. Political life first re-emerged in Berlin and the Russian-occupied Zone.

Political parties and trade unions were set up to fulfil the role of auxiliary organs of the military government. The trade unions in particular were directed politically by the so-called trade union officers, who not only controlled the construction of the organisation but also gave each official in the district committees a thorough examination.

In the British-occupied Zone, these officers took the thing very seriously and were closely informed about the political past of the officials. All political events, whether they were in the trade unions, the political parties or vestigial administration bodies, were subject to decree, as indeed most of the democratic renewal was conducted by command and decree.

The occupying powers took little notice of the fighters in the resistance movement against Fascism who had been active in Germany to the very end. In the Soviet Zone — this included Berlin in the first months — the Soviet military government, with the help of the Ulbricht group, had slotted into the administration, the judiciary and the police apparatus comrades returning from prisons and concentration camps. But with the growing tension between the Western Allies and the Russian occupying power, the contradictions soon broke through.

In the Western sectors — especially in the American sector, and more particularly among the police there — all those who were members of the SED or were close to it were removed from their posts and replaced by people who only yesterday had been members of the SS. On the basis of the Decartelisation Laws, those businesses in the Soviet Zone which had operated in the service of Hitler or had supplied armaments were expropriated.

In West Berlin the owners of the factories left the city in droves and moved to the Western Zones, even if they were not covered by the Decartelisation Laws. The trade unions in Berlin took over responsibility for the factories. Trade union officials soon began to restart the factories affected with the aid of engineers and skilled workers. In the course of this it rapidly became apparent that the factories operated just as well as before — indeed in many cases much better.

Now the works committees not only represented the social interests of their colleagues in the factory, but also had a seat and a vote on the 'production committees'. While the political parties in the Soviet-occupied Zone, under the direction of the Soviet military government, tried to reawaken political interest, in the Western-occupied Zones there were at first only tentative moves towards political parties, and the construction of trade union organisations only came later. In the Soviet-occupied Zone the organisations all adhered strictly to the decisions of Yalta, Tehran and Potsdam.

The political parties which had been banned by Hitler were legalised again. At first only the two workers' parties, the KPD and SPD, were able to rebuild their organisation; the CDU (Christian Democrats) and finally the LDP (Liberal Democrats) followed on. If there had been a broad, divided spectrum of bourgeois parties during the Weimar Republic, now they regrouped in a concentrated form. In central and north Germany they grouped as the CDU, in Bavaria as the CSU. Former National Socialists also flocked en masse to these parties. In the De-Nazification process, which classified the vast majority of former NSDAP members simply as 'fellow travellers', these people now regained a political footing in the new parties. Overnight the enthusiasts for a totalitarian state had been transformed into honest democrats — at least in the eyes of the representatives of the occupying powers. The FDP (Free Democrats), who also provided a political home for many former National Socialists, tried to organise earlier liberal politicians in its ranks. In contrast to the members of the two workers' parties, the circle of liberal politicians who had resisted Fascism was miniscule.

To make up for it, large numbers of former members of the German National Party, who had been allies of Hitler in the Harzburg Front, now found their liberal soul. All parties without exception — even the two workers' parties — submitted to the orders and directives of the occupying powers. It was announced both in the Allied Control Commission and at the conferences of Yalta and Potsdam that Germany alone bore the responsibility for the war.

The only people who spoke out against this lie of war guilt were the representatives of the International Communists of Germany (IKD) who put forward their position particularly inside the trade unions. If the Left Opposition in Germany had already led the fight against Stalinism during the Weimar period and fought in illegality during the Fascist period under Hitler, then now, as the IKD, it was not prepared to submit to the orders and directives of the Allied Control Commission.

The following call was published in our then (unauthorised) organ in 1946, and found support among our comrades in the Western countries:

'*International solidarity with the German proletariat!*

'Hitler's Fascism now lies in the dust, shattered by the force of weapons, and a sigh of relief can pass the lips of humanity. At last, at last, the German working people above all can breathe again after twelve years of the most frightful oppression and after five terrible years of war full of blood and tears and can look forward to a better future.

'But that may not happen. The Goebbels propaganda machine spouted falsely for years that Hitler and the German people were as one; this has now become the official reason for the treatment of that people by the victorious Allies. Vansittart from Britain, Morgenthau from America and Ehrenburg from Russia all preach in the same hate-filled way that the entire German population was guilty of all the crimes of Hitler.

'The division of the country, the annexation of further territories, the enforced cultivation of the land, the removal of machinery from factories, all kinds of requisitions, military contributions, deportations, the expulsion of millions of people from their homelands, starvation blockades, reparations which are said to run into billions — that is the "peace" which is imposed on the "collectively guilty German people".

'German workers in town and country! In this situation we, the International Communists, feel obliged to stand by you with all the strength and conviction of our class solidarity. Let it be known that we are not Social Democrats who support the declaration on collective guilt because of their cowardly opportunism and who act as agents of Anglo-American or French imperialism in Western Germany.

'Let it be known also that we are not Stalin Communists who also declare the German people to be collectively guilty because the Russians have ordered them to and who welcome the annexations in the East by this same Stalin who once refused to place a single foot on foreign soil in defence of the Soviet Union. Rather, we are communists in the spirit of Lenin and in the tradition of the forever glorious Russian October Revolution.

'We can only defend the foundations of that revolution if we take up positions against any imperialist exploitation or rape, whoever commits it and against whomsoever it is directed.

'Today it is you, the German proletariat, you, the proletariat of Karl Liebknecht and Rosa Luxemburg, who have most need of the solidarity of the proletariat of other countries. For you, the German proletariat which has stood by its comrades in a hundred class battles, which has bled from a thousand wounds, which has lost tens of thousands of its best people in the concentration camps, we, the International Communists want to stand witness.

'We do so although we know for sure that we will be spat upon and slandered as "Hitler Trotskyists" by the ravening pack of journalists and a corrupt band of party bigwigs. Just let them attack us! Solidarity is solidarity. And truth remains, despite everything, the truth.

'This truth commands us to state publicly before the world proletariat that Hitler-Fascism was not an *all*-German affair, but was, on the contrary, a full-blown dictatorship by German monopoly capitalism over the German working population. Hitler first unleashed a war against the German proletariat before he began the World War.

'The destruction of the German workers' organisations and the uprooting of the German workers' officials were the prerequisites for Hitler to be able to build up his war machine undisturbed and commit his war crimes. As long as Hitler acted only as the hangman of the German proletariat he was met with the applause of foreign capitalists. It was they who encouraged him and signed agreements with him.

'The collective guilt of international capitalism with Hitler's Fascism can only be emphasised when these self-same international capitalists today spread the lie of the collective guilt of the German people in order to squeeze billions in reparations from them.

'The truth also commands us to declare that the Second World War was an attempt by Hitler to redistribute the markets and spheres of influence of the world to the advantage of German monopoly capitalism. If Hitler really was the antagonist when he acted as representative of a German imperialism which had arrived late on the world market, then the other imperialists cannot be classified as peace-loving democrats simply because they were defending imperialist thefts which took place earlier.

'They are in fact even less innocent when, with their imperialist competitor Hitler only just defeated in battle, they arrange themselves around the new imperialist contradictions and organise new power blocks and plot new wars. And these imperialist contradictions are fought out today particularly on the backs of the German proletariat.

'We International Communists therefore denounce the capitalist system, from which Fascism and wars are born, as the main accused. We say to the international proletariat and the German proletariat that world peace is not ensured by the fall of Hitler's Fascism alone, but that it also requires the successful struggle for socialism and the Union of Socialist Nations.

'But if we are to find those responsible from a proletarian standpoint, then we must point first at the past leadership of the German proletariat.

'From the murder of Liebknecht, through Noske, Severing and the whole policy of coalition and affirmation of the state by Social Democracy, there runs an unbroken line of development which leads to Hitler. On the other hand, the Communist Party leadership with its blinkered methods of "social fascism" also made a decisive contribution to Hitler's victory over a German proletariat whose class strength was already broken.

'However, the German proletariat itself fought heroically despite the failure of its leadership. The thousands and thousands of bloodied witnesses in its ranks prove that the theory of collective guilt is a slander on the flower of the German proletariat. Right to the very end, when the Allied planes were saturation bombing the workers' districts and so contributing to the crippling of any serious resistance to Hitler, German revolutionary workers fought against Fascism with strikes and demonstrations.

'German deserters and foreign workers rose up against the SS. In many places the workers boldly rose up even before the arrival of the Allied armies and seized power. These same military forces which now accuse the German people of not toppling Hitler have done everything they could to liquidate and conceal this proletarian revolt. For, in the final analysis, the victorious imperialists and the defeated Fascists of Hitler and the German bourgeoisie who mock at democracy today are all agreed that their common enemy is the proletarian revolution.

'The very treatment of the German people on the principle of collective guilt opens up new possibilities for the disguised Fascists to fish in the muddy nationalist waters. All the more because logically the portion of guilt borne by the truly guilty Nazis has been lessened and they have the prospect of escaping their just punishment if the whole German people is guilty.

'In view of this situation we warn the German proletariat not to trust a bourgeoisie that now declares itself to be democratic. In reality these new "Anti-Fascists" belong to the very capitalist circles which are already working on their connections with international monopoly capitalism, organising their class front against the German proletariat and trying to conclude a pact with the foreign imperialists to throw the whole weight of the reparations demanded of Germany on to the backs of the working population.

'We International Communists from the so-called victorious nations therefore regard you German workers and peasants as victims whom we feel obliged to help. We are ready, in the spirit of Lenin, to fight alongside you for your liberation from the imperialist yoke. We protest alongside you against the dividing up of Germany, against the military contributions, the requisitions and the burden of billions in reparations.

'We welcome every fraternisation between the soldiers of the occupying powers and the German proletarians and at the same time we encourage these soldiers not to be used for imperialist and reactionary purposes against the German proletariat.

'We demand trade union rights, reasonable wages, humane accommodation and enough food for all German workers employed in the reconstruction.

'We demand, with you, the treatment of prisoners of war according to the humanitarian guidelines of the Red Cross and their release as soon as possible.

'We are against the expulsion of millions of workers from their home territories and we are for the smashing of the starvation blockade which is strangling the German proletariat — especially its children — and threatening the world with epidemics.

'We are for fraternal, reciprocal aid.

'We are for the right of self-determination for the German people.

'We, the International Communists everywhere, wherever we stand, will fight for these demands. For this struggle we will endeavour to organise the proletariat of all countries. We owe that to the memory of Liebknecht, Luxemburg and the thousands of martyrs of the German proletarian revolution.

'And that is why we call to the world proletariat: Solidarity with the German proletariat! Help it to shake off the imperialist yoke!

'German class comrades! We do not doubt that you for your part will take up the task of building your organisations with renewed strength. Build strong, militant and united class trade unions.

'Keep your workers' movement free from all those who wish to haggle with the bourgeoisie and imperialists for coalitions. The liberation of the working class is a task for the workers themselves. The independence and the autonomy of the German workers' movement are of the most decisive importance in this hour of imperialist enslavement.

'Only by this class autonomy, only in the straight fight for class goals will the international character of the workers' movement be formed. Just as Lenin formed the Communist International after the collapse of the Second International, so today the Fourth International exists after the Communist International disintegrated and finally dissolved itself.

'This Fourth International has inherited the mantle of Marx and Lenin. The German section of this International must evolve into a party that is capable of leading the German working class to victory in the coming struggles. That is the greatest task facing the German proletariat.

'We know how difficult your fight will be in the harsh conditions of occupation. Freedom of association, freedom to meet and to demonstrate, freedom of a workers' press and freedom to strike — these are the democratic rights which you must wrest by mass action.

'In order to overcome the lack of housing, to control the distribution of food, to monitor prices, to organise the reconstruction and to reopen the factories you should come together in committees and councils of all working people.

'Do not accept that only those Nazis who are war criminals in the eyes of the Allies should be punished; all those who played a role as informers and executioners of the German proletariat should also be brought to justice. Only a revolutionary workers' tribunal is in a position to sentence them. Be aware that only you as a united and determined proletariat can utterly uproot Fascism. Be aware that "Anti-Fascism" means nothing on its own: Fascism and imperialism can only be destroyed by the overthrow of capitalism and the victory of international socialism.

'Long live the German proletarian revolution!

'Long live the Union of Socialist Nations!'

A leading member of the Brandler Group, August Thalheimer, who led the Communist Party with Brandler between 1921 and 1923 and who supported the domestic policies of the USSR for a long time, wrote a pamphlet in September 1945 with the title: *The Potsdam Agreement: a Marxist investigation into the policies of the major powers towards Germany after the Second World War*.

This pamphlet led to Thalheimer and his friends being called 'paid agents' of American monopoly capitalism by the KPD and SED. What was the reason for this? Thalheimer had written:

'No real revolutionary can place himself at the disposal of the offices of government and administration in the service of the occupying powers . . . The Potsdam Agreement was the product of a temporary alliance between the imperialist Western powers and the Soviet Union. The honeymoon of this marriage has long since passed, and the frost of unconquerable enmity has destroyed the bouquets.

'At no time can a real communist party build its policies on a compromise agreement between the USSR and the capitalist states. The USSR may be forced to sign such agreements. But this agreement should never become the basis for struggle of the German proletariat. The German proletarians cannot be mobilised for the implementation of the Potsdam Agreement, but only for their own class interests. In the fight for these interests the unity of the working class East and West will be forged again, as will the unity of Germany on a socialist foundation.'

Just as the workers' parties had refused to cooperate with the NSDAP, it should now have been their duty after 1945 to refuse to help the military apparatus of the victors. The decisions of Yalta and Potsdam had been reached by secret diplomacy and decree. The task there should have been to turn to the organisations of the international working class and with them take up the fight for the democratisation of society on socialist principles.

Under those conditions, it would not have been possible for Adenauer to place anti-communism at the centre of his government policy. This anti-communism among the bourgeois parties and the imperialist powers was in reality a fight against socialism as such, and right from the start it included the division of Germany. In the decisions of Potsdam all four Allies had determined that Germany had to be democratised.

In Nuremberg they had set up an international court martial and there they sentenced a few politicians and generals to death or life imprisonment. Just as they had 'sacrificed' the monarchy to the masses at the end of the First World War, now a few political, economic and military leaders had to lose their lives; otherwise, everything remained as before.

In West Germany no one even thought of changing the basis of the bourgeois social order, although broad layers of the German people had already fought against the monopolies during the Weimar Republic, and even after 1945 the majority of the working population wanted a change in society. Even the CDU was obliged to talk about nationalisation in its Ahlen Programme of 1947. Various regional parliaments had enacted laws on 'socialisation'. In Hesse, however, the American occupying power had annulled this law.

In West Germany, capitalism was restored, even if only by the grace of the capitalist occupying powers; for the German bourgeoisie it was limited to the economic and political realms which these powers saw fit to allow.

In the Soviet-occupied Zone, the occupying power proceeded, with the help of the Business Decartelisation Law and the support of the KPD (later the SED and the trade union federation, the FDGB) to place property relationships on a new footing. But it did not do so by handing responsibility to the workers in the factories, but by creating a new bureaucratic apparatus, whose leadership had its headquarters in the 'House of Ministries' in Leipziger Strasse.

If the KPD had regarded the Western occupying powers for three years as guarantors and helpers in the de-Nazification, democratisation and demilitarisation of Germany — that is, for as long as the Anti-Hitler Coalition existed — they now 'discovered' at the start of the Cold War in 1948 that these people were violating agreements and going against the treaties of Yalta and Potsdam.

The Soviet Union and the KPD discovered this violation when the monopoly capitalists failed to be expropriated, as if anyone could seriously have expected the Western powers to put their democratic phrases into practice. In the 'democratic renewal' of Germany, the Western occupying powers were not concerned with putting an end to authoritarian ways of thought — for then they would have had to call on the really democratic forces who had had to pass through the Fascist concentration camps and prisons — but rather they were concerned with the restoration of capitalism.

But for that they needed both the bourgeoisie itself as well as the forces who had supported capitalism during the Weimar Republic and the twelve years of Hitler's rule. This also explains why tens of thousands of members of the NSDAP were able to join the so-called democratic parties. In this way, people like Globke — co-author of the laws concerning Jews — were able to become Secretary of State in the Adenauer cabinet, and Kiesinger — a former responsible collaborator of Goebbels in the Ministry of Propaganda — could become Federal Chancellor.

Hundreds of prominent names could be listed of those who had held leading positions in the state apparatus during the Third Reich and who returned to leading positions after the war in the so-called democratic parties, the administration, the judiciary and the state apparatus. This democracy which developed in West Germany was exactly as it had been before: the disguised form of capitalist rule.

It is unimportant in this context that the capitalists had exercised their rule autonomously before, whereas now they were primarily a tool in the hands of international capitalist power groups. The first government to be formed after the foundation of the Federal Republic of Germany, the Adenauer government, was — as the chair of the SPD, Schumacher, described it — 'the government of the Allies'.

And indeed, Adenauer and his party, the CDU, found themselves in complete agreement with the intention of the Americans, which was to push the Russians back to their own frontiers. The US Foreign Minister Dulles and Federal Chancellor Adenauer were the crusaders in this fight. With their so-called 'roll-back' policy they tried to bring central Europe and large areas of the Balkans back under the control of the Western world. In contrast to later years, Social Democracy at first still tried to pursue an independent policy, although even Schumacher was a fervent anti-communist.

After its defeat in 1933, the SPD had still declared in its Prague Manifesto of 1934:

'The revolutionary struggle demands a revolutionary organisation. The old form, the old apparatus, no longer exists, and any attempt to revive it will be insufficient for the new conditions of struggle. New organisational forms must arise, with fighters prepared to sacrifice themselves . . .

'The regime of the Kaiser was not brought down by the organised, prepared, desired and revolutionary struggle of the working class, but by defeat on the battlefields. Social Democracy, as the only organised force remaining intact took over the leadership of the state without meeting any resistance by sharing the power from the very start with the bourgeois parties, the old bureaucracy, indeed even with the reorganised military apparatus.

'That they took over an almost unchanged state apparatus was a grave historical mistake committed by the workers' movement as a result of the disorientation during the war.'

Such confessions and principles no longer had any role to play after the collapse of the 'thousand-year Reich'. Like so many other principles of old Social-Democratic policies, it was forgotten; the Prague Manifesto rotted away in the archives. As in 1918, Social Democracy formed another 'united front' with the bourgeois parties. This time it was not German generals with whom they conducted an anti-communist crusade, but British and American officers.

At the start of the 1950s there were lively discussions on principles in the SPD, in which both former SAPD people and former members of the KPD took part. The left put forward the view that, in the coming struggles, you had to base yourself on the principles and knowledge of Karl Marx. The Schumacher leadership, and then Ollenhauer and Willy Brandt, was opposed to this and considered that in modern times social-democratic policies had to be developed against Marx. Yet a third group said: not against, but without Marx. The 'Navvies', as the anti-Marxists called themselves, gradually got the upper hand. Thus, as early as 1957 there appeared a draft which was eventually accepted as the basic programme at the Godesberg Party Congress (13 to 15 November 1959). In the section entitled 'Basic values of socialism' there was this passage which made no mention of social classes at all:

'The socialists want a society in which every individual can develop his personality in freedom and participate responsibly in the political, economic and cultural life of humanity as a serving member of the community.'

And on the order of the state:

'The Social Democratic Party of Germany lives and works among the whole of the German people. It stands by the constitution of the Federal Republic of Germany. In the spirit of the constitution it strives for the unity of Germany in freedom and security.'

With this programme, the SPD had finally found its place in bourgeois society, standing alongside parties in whose ranks there were many members who yesterday had defended the totalitarian state. It had not only ceased to be a socialist party, but had ceased to be any kind of representative of the interests of the working class. It had undergone a metamorphosis into a petty-bourgeois liberal party.

Meanwhile, as the German Social-Democratic Party accommodated itself more and more to the ideas of the Western occupying powers after 1945, the second workers' party, the Communist Party, collaborated closely with the powers of the Soviet-occupied Zone. The basis for this friendship was the fact that in the Soviet Zone the power of the bourgeoisie and the land owners had been broken.

But neither the 'anti-fascist, democratic' phrases nor the 'democratic-bloc politics' nor the policies at the level of the regional parliaments could substitute for a revolutionary policy which the German working class would have had to conduct after the collapse of Fascism. The bureaucratic methods and the submissive behaviour of the KPD towards Moscow guaranteed anything but the rights of workers.

It could never be the duty of a party calling itself revolutionary to defend the dismantling of machinery and the exploitation of an entire people. Equally it could equally never be the duty of communists to take positions of responsibility in bourgeois governments in the Western Zones which only existed by the grace of the Western occupying powers.

A list of terrible names like Buchenwald, Sachsenhausen, Dachau, Mauthausen, Ravensbrück, Belsen etc., speak another language. There the flower of the German working class suffered, was tortured, murdered. The German working class did not deserve to be stripped of all political rights by the Western victors, and even less by the Red Army.

The attempt by the Communist Party in 1946 to recreate the unity of the German working class in a single party was doomed to failure, because the KPD could never regain the trust which it had lost among the social-democratic workers even before Hitler, with its theory of social fascism, and then again after the war with its policy of relying on the Soviet military administration.

In the Soviet-occupied Zone it was of course possible to unite the SPD and KPD by administrative means into the SED. Most members of the SPD at that time quickly left again after the unification. Hundreds of members of the KPD in Berlin, who had defended the policies of the party right up to the invasion by the Soviet troops, refused to continue, sobered by the measures which the Red Army were taking, and tried to prevent the dismantling of factories.

When they felt the practical effects of Stalinist politics on their own persons, they stood aside, disillusioned, or else they joined the Social Democrats. In the entire Soviet-occupied Zone, including East Berlin, leading posts could only be attained by comrades who had unconditionally supported all the old policies in the past.

Comrades who had fought for a time with the Fischer-Maslow group during the conflicts inside the party, and who had then returned to the party line after their capitulation, were considered unworthy of filling responsible posts. Even those who had lived in exile in the West had considerable difficulties. The founding principle of the legal Communist Party — that only those who unconditionally recognised the leadership of the Soviet party could become party officials — was transferred over to the Socialist Unity Party (SED) when it was formed.

All attempts by the rank and file to breathe life into the development of democracy were stifled from inception by the party apparatus and the occupying powers. Only what was decreed by the occupying power, and

Oskar Hippe

later the party leadership, had validity in the development of democracy.

The Federal Republic of Germany was the historical inheritor of Fascism. If at first democracy (at least in words) was writ large, then the democrats at the head of the new state very quickly showed themselves for what they really were. The first Federal President was Theodor Heuss, a man who had capitulated to Hitler, whose party — the liberal State Party — had dissolved itself and abandoned any resistance from day one. Its second President, Heinrich Lübke, had built the huts in the concentration camps; he was a man who had shown no liberal tendencies even in the Weimar Republic.

It was only the SPD-Liberal coalition which gave us, in the Social Democrat Gustav Heinemann, a Federal President who had always opposed the Nazis, had fought against them in the Weimar Republic, had not hidden his opposition to the 'Thousand Year Reich' and after 1945 had tried to build the foundations of democracy. During his period of office as Federal President, he was the only leading statesman who concerned himself with democracy and social equality.

The people in the CDU and CSU were continually putting spokes in his wheels; indeed there were rumours that members of his own party used to cause difficulties for him, to such an extent that he was not prepared to stand for office a second time. After Adenauer and Erhard, this Federal Republic finally managed to select a Chancellor, Kiesinger, who had occupied a leading position in Goebbels' Propaganda Ministry.

Leading politicians in West Germany had served their Führer loyally until the eleventh hour (and some for longer than that) and had only become honest democrats at the behest of the Western occupying powers. Tens of thousands of people who had a seat and a vote in the so-called democratic parties had carried their National Socialist theoretical baggage with them into the newly-founded state. The first government, which was formed by Adenauer, was not only the 'government of the Allies', but also the government of the ruling class.

In their fight against communism they had found unexpected Allies in the SPD and the trade unions. In the Cold War, which was not simply directed against the Soviet Union but against all the deformed workers' states in the Eastern Block and against the workers' organisations in the capitalist countries, the Social Democrats outdid even the bourgeois parties on many points.

Even May Day, which had been the day of struggle of the international working class for over eight decades, had been turned into a farce with 'freedom rallies'. Social Democracy in this period refused to implement the demands of its own programme, and thereby succeeded in dulling the consciousness of the workers; the mass of the working population was no longer prepared to fight for its own class interests and fell prey to the bourgeois-capitalist parties.

Bourgeois-democratic society followed a similar course of development. The aim of any bureaucracy is this: the maximum amount of bureaucracy with the minimum of democratic awareness. In this established democracy, led by bourgeois parties and tolerated by the SPD, an ever more centralised society developed, with increased bureaucracy which, in many cases, especially in the police and the judiciary, came close to using methods of the police state.

Such a development had to call forth resistance among the progressive forces in the youth. The younger generation which had made itself available for the reconstruction — in the political sense as well — after 1945, but which regarded the older generation with a certain scepticism, directed this mistrust against the two workers' parties in particular, since they had capitulated to Fascism in 1933 without putting up a fight.

The intellectuals of this generation in particular demanded of the democratic parties that they too should be given direct responsibility. They remembered the demands which had been put forward as early as the bourgeois revolution of 1848, but which had been satisfied neither then nor later in the November Revolution of 1918. Even the SPD, which still regarded these demands as their own in the Weimar Republic, was not prepared to satisfy them when the Socialist German Students' League (Sozialistische Deutsche Studentenbund, SDS) demanded the right of co-determination in the universities.

This refusal of justified demands led, among other things, to a politicisation of the SDS which soon gripped the entire student body. The SPD, instead of discussing with the younger generation the questions which it had posed, had no other response than to declare that simultaneous membership of the SDS and the SPD was incompatible.

If the party leadership thought that it could bring the members of the SDS under control, it was wrong. In Berlin and across the entire country, the students launched a movement which also involved small sections of workers and apprentices. The state apparatus hoped to smash this movement by brutal police methods, but the younger generation managed to gain control of the streets in the course of battles with the police.

This was a hopeful beginning for the socialist opposition both inside and outside the SPD: perhaps a bridge could be built between the movement of the young intellectuals and the factory workers, which could then create the common political representation needed by the working class in its fight against capitalism. Unfortunately these hopes came to nothing.

Inside the SDS there were splits into diverse groups which moved in opposed political directions. Some of them saw in Stalinism the true embodiment of Marxist principles, applauded the example of the Chinese revolution and regarded its leader Mao Zedong as the new Lenin.

Another group tended in the direction of the GDR and the Eastern Block and organised themselves in MSB-Spartakus (Marxist Student League-Spartacus) which was close to the West German Communist Party (DKP-SEW).

A third tendency united with the Red Army Faction (RAF), saying that you had to oppose the violence of the state with direct counter-violence. At first they contented themselves with meeting police terror with the counter-violence of demonstrators, in the belief that they were lighting a torch for the oppressed masses; then they turned to individual terror, still in the hope that they were showing the way for the working population.

Politics such as this had to fail because experience has shown time and again that only mass movements are capable of toppling a ruling regime. Our established parties, which regard an ordained democracy as a healthy world and anyone who refuses to recognise the constitution as a criminal, now had to admit that they were no longer able to clear up their problems with the help of the police and judiciary. Every day the same forces who play down the Fascist danger are mobilising the entire press corps, the radio and television stations to announce that our security is threatened by terrorism. Both in the Federal Republic and in West Berlin, the RAF together with its sympathisers comprises only a few hundred people. An organisation like that, isolated from the masses, will never be in a position to shake a state like the Federal Republic, let alone smash it.

Those in the ranks of the CDU-CSU who scream for the laws to be tightened up know quite well that terrorism only gives them pin pricks. They really only need a tightening up of the law in order to suppress the organised workforce when it is no longer willing to submit to the repressive policies of the employers.

As long as real Marxists are unable to build a mass movement independent of the bureaucratised workers' parties, and as long as the state apparatus can think of nothing other than branding people as criminals, then there will always be the danger that young people will try to fight the state with individual terror and so become a brake on the fight to liberate the workers from capitalist exploitation.

The Federal Republic has not become more democratic in its 30 years of existence. The ruling force in this country is, despite the SPD-Liberal coalition, the capitalists. Anyone who has observed the development of the Federal Republic will know that Fascism exists not merely in the tiny gangs of thugs belonging to neo-Fascist organisations, but also has roots in certain groups in the established parties. Such arch-conservatives as Dregger, Carstens, Strauss, Zimmermann and all the rest of them, would be ready tomorrow to replace democracy with an authoritarian state.

Together with Social Democracy, and assisted by the policies of Stalinism, it was possible for them to turn the communist mass movement into a sect after 1945. Today the same people who call themselves democrats are directing their fire against the SPD, accusing them of being agents of Moscow, of being a party which threatens freedom and democracy and of wanting to turn the whole of Germany into a 'trade union state'.

As for Social Democracy, it made its own contribution after 1945 to the destruction of the class consciousness of German workers, by continually declaring that the teeth of capitalism had been drawn, so that it could still growl but could no longer bite. In the SPD-Liberal coalition they ensured that taxes were diverted to support capitalism in its sickness.

They did not undertake anything serious when the spirit of Fascism kept cropping up in the Federal Army, or when the judiciary struck mercilessly against the left wing, while the right wing were given the full clemency of the law — even though the Minister of Justice is a Social Democrat. Rudolf Wissel's statement in January 1919 at the SPD Party Congress still applies to Social Democracy:

'Despite the revolution, the people find their expectations disappointed. What the people expected from the government has not happened. We have further extended formal political democracy. Certainly! But we have really done nothing more than continue the programme which was begun by the Imperial German government of Prince Max von Baden. (Cries of "Hear, hear!") We have prepared the constitution without involving the people. (Shout: "Give them something to eat!") We have been unable to overcome the dull rancour felt by the masses, because we have no real programme . . .

'In essence, we have governed according to the old forms of the state. We have only been able to breathe a little new life into these forms. We have not been able to influence the revolution in such a way that Germany appears filled with a new spirit. The inner life of German culture, social life, appears to be changed very little. Certainly not for the better. (Loud applause) And the people believe that the conquests of the revolution only have a negative quality, that in the place of a military and bureaucratic rule by individuals we simply have another whose maxims of government are not essentially different from those of the old regime . . . '

As for the DKP (West German Communist Party), it is certainly not the class party of the workers. The DKP was set up after 1945 and placed itself unconditionally under Stalinist leadership: at that time it slandered the Marxist opposition which criticised the removal of machinery and the exploitation of the German people, calling them 'Werewolves' and neo-Nazis (see *Einheit*, the theoretical organ of the SED, April 1947).

The left communists were then the only ones who unmasked the intentions and aims of the Anglo-American armies, which consisted not only in gaining an economic footing for themselves but also in gaining political influence to repress the German proletariat. The KPD, on the other hand, wrote about the Potsdam Conference in their lecture notes Nos.5-7, 1945:

'This shows that the Allies are not interested in dividing Germany into three or four sectors, but that the unity of Germany is to remain, so that we can look forward confidently to the future in this respect as well . . . With the principle that Germany is to be regarded as a truly united country, we see clearly the honest desire of the three major democratic powers to smooth the path into the future for the German people . . . This settlement of the problem of reparations gives the German people a clear and hopeful perspective. After the reparations are paid, and the monopolies have been shaken off, a healthy economy can be built up which will satisfy the people's peaceful needs.'

A party which, like the DKP, unconditionally supports the policies of the SED in East Germany, although the working class there plays no leading role, and which defends the bureaucratic conditions there as real socialism, has no right to present itself as the vanguard and it has no chance of becoming the vanguard.

In West Berlin and the Federal Republic it was not possible to push the movement of young intellectuals on to truly Marxist roads. The KJO-Spartakus, the youth movement, was not capable of bringing to bear the experiences of the German workers' movement in general and the experiences of the Marxist Opposition in particular. On the contrary: in the course of the splits of the young left, they themselves were sucked into this whirlpool of inner conflict.

Despite this, the Trotskyist tendency still exists, even if badly split. It is to be hoped that the 'quarrelling brothers' today will recognise their historic task and overcome their differences in a united organisation.

It is their historic task to build a party in the Federal Republic and internationally, which will enable the working class to lead the fight against capitalism and replace bourgeois-capitalist society with socialist society.

When I returned home in 1956 from Russian imprisonment at Bautzen, it was not so easy for me to pick up contact again with people of the same political persuasion. The political friends with whom I had worked in illegality and with whom I had rebuilt our group after 1945 no longer worked as a group. On the basis of a decision of the Fourth International the overwhelming majority of the comrades had entered the SPD.

When I got in contact with friends in Switzerland and France, they advised me to write my memoirs and publish them in book form. However, I refused, because at that time the conditions were not right for the reception of such a book. My political friends in Berlin also urged me to set down on paper my experiences in Nazi imprisonment and in Bautzen.

Again I repeated my refusal and told them that no publishing house would accept a work like that. It would only have been possible to find a publisher if I had made concessions to the established parties, and that I was not prepared to do. That would have meant that the book would have formed another link in the chain of the fight against communism.

The only thing which I did in this period was to make a few notes, in order to keep my experiences alive. After I had decided in November 1956 to enter the SPD, I came in contact with the then district chair of the SPD, Max Gantschow, at the Charlottenburg district delegate meetings; Gantschow suggested to me that I give a talk about my experiences in Hohenschönhausen, Bautzen and Luckau on Radio Free Berlin.

Again I refused and told him that, as a Marxist, I could only give a talk on the radio if they gave me the opportunity of speaking about our struggle in the Communist Party, about the causes of the 1933 defeat, and about the petty-bourgeois liberal politics of the SPD in the Weimar Republic and later. Max Gantschow replied that I would have to restrict myself to the twelve years of Nazi rule and the time in Bautzen. This being so, I turned down his offer, and he never repeated it.

When I was involved with the Marxist Working Group, and when in the 1960s a Marxist group crystallised out of the Berlin Falken organisation, later to become the KJO-Spartakus group, my political activities were concentrated on them and on the student movement (SDS). At that time, this seemed more important to me than writing my memoirs.

Only in 1975, when my friends in Switzerland urged me once again, did I promise them to write not only about my political experiences in the Weimar period but about my whole political life. So I sat down in the summer of 1975 to begin the first chapters.

In the autumn of 1975 my wife was very ill and everything was shelved. For a whole year I did not write a single word; only when my wife was better did I return to the work.

At the turn of the year 1978-1979 everything was virtually complete. I had great support from my friends in Berlin — I do not know if I could have done the book in the same way without them. I had much help especially from Inga Reissner. I would like to thank every one of them.

At a time when a critical younger generation is studying the October Revolution and critically examining what came after, I believe that this book can help the process of clarification in the sense of true Marxism and Leninism. If that is the case, then my work has not been in vain.

Oskar Hippe
Berlin, May 1979

GLOSSARY OF PARTIES AND ORGANISATIONS

AAU. Allgemeine Arbeiter Union (General Workers' Union): Trade union organisation formed and led by the KAP in 1920.

ADGB. Allgemeine Deutsche Gewerkschaftsbund (General German Trade Union Federation): Trade union organisation led by the reformist SPD until 1933.

APO. Ausser-parlamentarische Opposition (Extra-parliamentary Opposition): Loose confederation of independent radical and left-wing groups in West Germany in 1960s and 1970s.

Brown Shirts. see SA

CDU. Christlich-Demokratische Union (Christian Democrats): Main West German right-wing party (see also CSU)

Centre Party: Bougeois party representing Catholic interests before 1933.

Communist Party of Germany. see KPD

Communist Party Opposition. see KPO

Communist Workers' Party. see KAP

Communist Youth League. see KJV

Communist Youth Organisation. see KJO-Spartakus

CSU. Christlich-Soziale Union (Christian Socialists): Conservative party in West Germany, with main power base in Bavaria.

DDP. Deutsche Demokratische Partei (German Democratic Party): Active in the 1920s and early 1930s; also known as the State Party.

DGB. Deutsche Gewerkschaftsbund (German Trade Union Federation): West German trade union organisation linked to the SPD after 1945.

DKP. Deutsche Kommunistische Partei (German Communist Party): West German Stalinist party set up following the banning of the Communist Party in West Germany in the 1950s. Linked to the SEW in West Berlin.

DMV. Deutscher Metallarbeiter Verein (German Metalworkers' Union): Engineering workers' trade union of 1920s and 1930s.

DNP. Deutsche Nationalpartei. (German National Party): Right-wing party of 1920s.

DVP. Deutsche Volkspartei (German People's Party): Centre-right party of 1920s.

Extra-Parliamentary Opposition. see APO

Falken (Falcons): Left-wing youth organisation within the West German SPD of 1960s and 1970s.

FDGB. Freie Deutsche Gewerkschaftsbund (Free German Trade Union Federation): East German trade union organisation, organised and dominated by Stalinists after 1945.

FDP. Frei-Demokratische Partei (Free Democrats): Small centre (liberal) party in West Germany.

Freikorps: Right-wing militias of the early 1920s; examples in this book are the Lützkow Freikorps, the Maercker Freikorps and the Ehrhardt Brigade.

General German Trade Union Federation. see ADGB

General Workers' Union. see AAU

German Communist Party. see DKP

German Democratic Party see. DDP

German National Party. see DNP

German People's Party. see DVP

Government of People's Representatives (Regierung der Volksdelegierten): Provisional government of Germany formed by the SPD and USPD during the military collapse of 1918.

IKD. Internationale Kommunisten Deutschlands (International Communists of Germany): Following Hitler's seizure of power in January 1933, this was the name of the German section of the International Left Opposition and then of the Fourth International. Worked illegally in Germany and in exile.

Independent Social-Democratic Party. see USPD

Independent Trade Union Opposition. see UGO

International Secretariat of the Fourth International (ISFI): Set up in Europe after the Second World War to lead the Fourth International. Led by Michel Raptis (Pablo) and Ernest Mandel (Germain). By the early 1950s this leadership had succumbed to the view that Stalinism could play a revolutionary role. The ISFI and its successor, the United Secretariat of the Fourth International (USFI) has become a source of more and more open attacks on the theory and practice of Bolshevism.

International Committee of the Fourth International (ICFI): Founded in the 1950s to combat the liquidationism of the International Secretariat. Main participants in its creation were the Socialist Workers Party of the United States, the French Parti Communiste Internationaliste and the small 'Club' of Trotskyists in Britain. The British and French sections split in 1971. The ICFI succumbed to some degree to the same political pressures as the ISFI and it collapsed in 1985, opening a new chapter

in the struggle for the Fourth International.
Jusos. Jungsozialisten (Young Socialists): Generally left-wing youth movement of the West German SPD.
KAJ. Kommunistische Arbeiterjugend (Young Communist Workers): Syndicalist youth movement of 1920-1921..K analarbeiter. see 'Navvies'
KAP. Kommunistische Arbeiterpartei Deutschlands. (Communist Workers' Party of Germany): Emerged from a faction expelled from the KPD in 1920 because of their determination not to recognise existing trade unions, but to organise their own trade union bodies. The AAU of the early 1920s was led politically by the KAP.
KJO or KJO-Spartakus. Kommunistische Jugend Organisation (Communist Youth Organisation): Trotskyist youth organisation formed by left-wingers of the Falken movement in the late 1960s.
KJV. Kommunistische Jugendverein. (Communist Youth League): Youth section of the KPD in the early 1920s.
KPO. Kommunistische Partei Opposition (Communist Party Opposition): Opposition group which emerged from within the KPD of the late 1920s, led by former KPD chair Heinrich Brandler.
KPD. Kommunistische Partei Deutschlands (Communist Party of Germany): Founded by Rosa Luxemburg and Karl Liebknecht as a development of the Spartacus League in 1918. A major party in the Comintern, this party became Stalinised in the 1920s. After 1945, the KPD was briefly resurrected, before becoming the SED in East Germany and the DKP in West Germany. The West German Maoists of the 1960s formed an organisation also known as the KPD.
LDP. Liberal Demokratische Partei (Liberal Democrats): Short-lived centre party in West Germany after 1945.
Left Opposition (Bolshevik-Leninists). see VLO-BL
Lenin League (Leninbund): Formed in 1928 after wholesale expulsions of oppositionists from the KPD. Later developed into various other groups, including the IKD.
MAK. Marxistischer Arbeitskreis (Marxist Working Group): Discussion groups within the SPD of the 1950s, where Marxists and Trotskyists could organise and discuss.
MSB-Spartakus. Marxistischer Studentbund- Spartakus. (Marxist Student League-Spartacus): Student political organisation close to the West German Stalinists in the late 1960s and 1970s.
National Socialists. see NSDAP
Navvies (Kanalarbeiter): Right-wing tendency within the West German SPD of the 1950s.

'New Beginning' Group. see SAG

NKVD: Soviet secret police, forerunner of GPU, in 1920s and 1930s.

NSBO. National-Sozialistische Berufsorganisation (National Socialist Professional Organisation): Trade union body set up and organised by the Nazis.

NSDAP: German Fascist party.

OdF. Organisation der Opfer des Faschismus (Organisation of the Victims of Fascism): Postwar organisation set up to assist members of the SPD and KPD imprisoned or punished by the German Fascists.

Orgesch: Right-wing militia in early 1920s.

ÖTV. Öffentliche Dienst, Transport und Verkehr (Public Service and Transport Workers' Union): Public service trade union in West Germany after 1945; part of the DGB.

People's Marine Division. Volksmarine: Militia of left-wing conscripted sailors during and after the military collapse of 1918.

RAF. Rote Armee Fraktion (Red Army Faction): Small, ultra-left 'direct action' group operating in West Germany in 1970s and 1980s. Also known as the 'Baader-Meinhof' group, after its leaders Andreas Baader and Ulrike Meinhof.

Red Aid (Rote Hilfe): Workers' first-aid organisation of 1920s and 1930s.

Red Front League of Fighters. see RFB

Red Women's and Girls League: Women's organisation, led by KPD in 1920s.

Red Youth Front: Youth organisation led by KPD in 1920s.

Reichsbanner. Full title: 'Schwarz-Rot-Gold — der Reichsbanner' (Black-Red-Gold — the Standard of the Nation): Founded in 1924 by leading members of the SPD, the Centre Party and the DDP, to combat the rise of the right-wing militias.

Revolutionary Trade Union Opposition. see RGO

RFB. Rote Front Kämpferbund (Red Front League of Fighters): Workers' militia founded and led by KPD in 1920s and 1930s, with a membership of tens of thousands.

RGO. Revolutionäre Gewerkschaftsopposition (Revolutionary Trade Union Opposition): Trade union organisation founded by the KPD during its ultra-left phase of the late 1920s.

Russian Social Democratic Workers' Party: Socialist party in Russia from which the Bolsheviks and Mensheviks emerged in 1903.

SA. Stürmerabteilung (Storm Troop): Fascist militia of 1930s.

SAPD. Sozialistische Arbeiterpartei Deutschlands (Socialist Workers' Party of Germany): A left-wing split from the KPD in 1931.

SAG. Sozialistische Arbeiter-Gemeinschaft (Socialist Working Group):

Also named 'Neues Beginnen' (New Beginning). Left-wing organisation in occupied Berlin in 1945.

Scholem-Rosenberg Group: Left-wing opposition group within the KPD of the early 1920s, from which the Lenin League drew some of its founder members. Rosenberg went on to co-found the SAPD.

SDAP. Sozial-Demokratische Arbeiterpartei (Social-Democratic Workers Party): Left-wing organisation of 1920s.

SDS. Sozialistische Deutsche Studentenbund (Socialist German Students' League): Left-wing West German students' union of 1960s.

SED. Sozialistische Einheitspartei Deutschlands (Socialist Unity Party of Germany): Stalinist party of East Germany founded in 1945.

SMAD. Soviet Military Administration: Governing body in Soviet-occupied Zone of Germany (East Berlin and East Germany) after 1945.

Social-Democratic Party of Germany. see SPD

Social-Democratic Workers' Party. see SDAP

Socialist German Students' League. see SDS

Socialist Unity Party. see SED

Socialist Working Group. see SAG

Socialist Workers' Party of Germany. see SAPD

Spartakusbund (Spartacus League): Precursor to the KPD, a Marxist party founded by Rosa Luxemburg and Karl Liebknecht in 1914.

SPD. Sozial-Demokratische Partei Deutschlands. (Social-Democrats): Originally socialist party which supported its own imperialist government in First World War; revived as completely reformist party in Germany from 1919 to 1933, and in West Germany after 1945.

SS: Fascist secret police.

Stahlhelm (Steel Helmet): Right-wing militia in early 1920s.

State Party. see DDP

Storm Troops. see SA

SWP. Socialist Workers Party (USA): Trotskyist party in USA during and after 1930s.

UGO. Unabhängige Gewerkschaftsopposition (Independent Trade Union Opposition): Trade Union organisation founded in 1945 in Western-occupied Zones by Social Democrats and right wingers.

United Left Opposition. see VLO-BL

Union of Hand and Head Workers (Union der Hand- und Kopf-Arbeiter): Trade union organisation founded by members of the KPD in 1920 in opposition to the 'official', reformist ADGB.

USPD. Unabhängige Sozial-Demokratische Partei Deutschlands (Independent Social-Democratic Party of Germany): Left-wing party founded in April 1917 by members of the SPD, gaining mass support

in the next few years, and eventually merging in 1920 with the KPD.
VKPD. Vereinigte Kommunistische Partei Deutschlands (Unified Communist Party of Germany): Mass organisation created by the merging of the KPD and USPD in November 1920.
VLO-BL. Vereinte Links-Opposition (Bolschevisten-Leninisten) (United Left Opposition (Bolsheviks-Leninists)): Group founded in 1930 by Trotskyists in the Lenin League still attempting to correct the policies of the Stalinised KPD.
Vopos. Volkspolizei (People's Police): East German state police.
VVN. Vereinigung der Verfolgten des Naziregimes (League of those Persecuted by the Nazis): Set up after 1945 to assist resistance fighters who had been active during the Nazi period.
Workers' Samaritan League: Workers' organisation concerned with providing first aid and social assistance in late 1920s and early 1930s.
Werewolves: Fascist militia formed by fanatical Nazis, composed mostly of youth, to continue fighting in the last days of the war in 1945.
Young Communist Workers. see KAJ
Young Socialists. see Jusos

GLOSSARY OF NAMES

ACKERKNECHT, Erwin (Eugen Bauer): leader of the Trotskyist movement in Germany. Born 1906. A doctor, he joined the Young Communists in 1926 and the KPD in 1928. Exiled in Paris, part of the International Secretariat, 1933-1934. Left the movement in 1934 and worked in the SAPD.
ADENAUER, Konrad (1876-1967): first Chancellor of West Germany 1949-1963; CDU member.
ALBRECHT, Erich: born 1902; locksmith. KPD member who joined the Left Opposition; arrested by the Nazis in 1934.
BAUER, Gustav-Adolf (1870-1944): right-wing Social Democrat who led the coalition government after Scheidemann, from 1929.

BELLEVILLE, Fritz: born 1903. Studied law; supported Korsch. Joined Young Communists in 1919 and KPD in 1920s, from which he was expelled in 1926. Helped form Lenin League; subsequently a leader of the Trotskyist movement based in Basel, Switzerland.

BIBACH, Bruno: born 1904; engraver.

BÖTTCHER, Paul: born 1891. Printer; member of SPD, later USPD and KPD. Editor of KPD paper the *Rote Fahne*. Expelled 1929; founded the KPO with Brandler.

BRANDLER, Heinrich (1881-1967): builder; SPD member 1901, expelled for internationalism in 1915. Joined Spartacus League and KPD. President of KPD 1921; went often to Moscow. Expelled in 1929 and formed right-wing KPO as supporter of Bukharin's right opposition.

BRANDT, Willy (1913-): leading member of SPD; mayor of Berlin 1957-1966; Chancellor 1969-1974; president of Second International.

BREITSCHEID, Rudolf (1874-1944): founder of USPD; Reichstag deputy from 1920. Joined SPD 1922. Escaped to France in 1933 but was handed over to the Gestapo and killed.

BRÜNING, Heinrich (1885-1970): leader of the Catholic Centre Party. Chancellor 1930-1932; ruled by decree, repressing the rights of unions and the press. Represented capitalist interests opposed to Hitler.

BURNHAM, James: leader with Schachtman and Abern of the petty-bourgeois opposition within the American SWP, 1939-1940; subscribed to theory that USSR was 'state capitalist'.

CHAMBERLAIN, Arthur Neville (1869-1940): Conservative prime minister of Britain 1937-1940.

CHKHEÏDZÉ, Nikolai (1864-1926): Menshevik leader and first president of the Petrograd soviet.

CHOLLECK, Walter: born 1907, a white-collar worker.

CUNO, Wilhelm (1876-1933): banker and businessman. Formed right-wing government in 1922 but ousted by general strike in 1923.

DÄUMIG, Ernst (1866-1922): president of the USPD in 1919 who fought for fusion with KPD. Joint president of the KPD after the merger.

DITTMANN, Wilhelm (1871-1925): right-wing USPD leader and opponent of the 1920 fusion with KPD; joined the SPD in 1922.

EASTMAN, Max (1883-1969): edited *The Masses* in United States in First World War; early supporter of the Left Opposition and translator of Trotsky's works into English, later anti-communist.

EBERT, Friedrich (1871-1925): saddlemaker; right-wing SPD leader; president of the republic from 1919 until his death. Presided over the crushing of the 1918 revolution and the murder of Liebknecht and Luxemburg.

EICHHORN, Emil (1863-1925): former glassworker, headed SPD press bureau in 1881 and subsequently that of USPD. Joined KPD; communist deputy in the Reichstag. His dismissal as chief of police in Berlin provoked the January 1919 uprising.

ENDERLE, August (1887-1959): mechanic; SPD member in 1905, later in USPD and KPD. Oganised in metalworkers' union. Delegate to congress of red unions in Moscow in 1922-1923. Expelled 1928, joined KPO and later SAPD.

FEUERBACH, Ludwig (1804-1872): German philosopher whose attempts to formulate a materialist philosophy formed a vital step between Hegel and Marx.

FISCHER, Ruth (born Elfriede Eisler) (1895-1961): founder member of the Austrian Communist Party who later led the German party. Delegate at the fourth congress of the Third International; in the Reichstag from 1924-1928. Led the left wing against Brandler, and led the 'Bolshevisation' of the party after 1924. In Moscow 1925-1926, but then replaced by Thälmann; expelled with Maslow and Urbahns in 1926, formed the Lenin League. Worked with Trotskyists in Paris in the 1930s, but died an anti-communist in exile.

FRANK, Pierre (1905-): Trotsky's secretary in Turkey 1932-1933. Interned in England during the Second World War. Pabloite leader in France.

FRÖLICH, Paul (1884-1953): became a journalist. Joined SPD in 1902; an internationalist who was detained as a psychiatric patient when he opposed the First World War; released by the 1918 revolution. Elected to the Reichstag as a communist in 1921. Became a Brandlerite; expelled from KPD 1928; joined KPO and afterwards SAPD. Biographer of Rosa Luxemburg.

GESCHKE, Ottomar (1882-1957): joined SPD in 1910, later the Spartacus League and KPD. Elected to the central committee in 1921. Led the 'Bolshevisation' of the party. Later allied with Thälmann. Imprisoned by the Nazis in 1933.

GOEBBELS, Joseph (1897-1945): Hitler's propaganda chief.

GROSSMANN, Oskar: born 1912. Trotskyist who worked clandestinely in Nazi Germany. Arrested December 1933; tried at same time as Hippe but subsequent fate unknown.

GRYLEWICZ, Anton: born in 1885. Joined the SPD in 1912, later the USPD and the KPD. Berlin district secretary and left-wing leader. Expelled in 1927. Leading Trotskyist and publisher of Trotskyist newspapers and pamphlets. Exiled in Paris, later Cuba; returned to Berlin in 1955.

HAAS, Walter: born 1912. Young Communist who joined Trotskyist opposition in 1932. Worked underground in Nazi Germany; arrested December 1933 and sentenced November 1934.

HEALY, Gerry (1913-1989): a founder and leader of the International Committee of the Fourth International; expelled 1985 for sexual abuse of women members, slander and physical attacks on party members.

HECKERT, Fritz (1884-1936): builder; joined SPD in 1902; sympathiser of Spartacists who joined KPD. Central committee member 1921; member of political committee and praesidium of Third International in 1928.

HEGEL, Georg Wilhelm Friedrich (1770-1831): German 'objective idealist' philosopher whose work was crucial in the formation of the ideas of Marx and Engels.

HESSE, Max (1895-1964): mechanic; founder member of KPD, a leader of the Charlottenburg district. On executive of Third International from 1924 to 1926, but expelled from the party in 1927. Joined the Lenin League. Imprisoned at Orianenburg by the Nazis, but escaped.

HEYM, Guido (1882-1945): metallurgist; member of the SPD in 1901, the USPD in 1917 and the KPD in 1920. Elected to the Reichstag in 1924. On the left wing of the party, he was expelled in 1927 and the following year he joined the SPD. Shot by the SS in 1945.

HILFERDING, Rudolf (1877-1944): leader of the SPD and founder member of the USPD in 1917. A right-wing opponent of its fusion with the KPD, subsequently rejoined the SPD. Known as a writer on economics and author of *Finance Capital*; Minister of Finance in Stresemann's government (1923). Escaped from the Nazis to France but was handed over to the Gestapo by the French police in 1942 and died in Buchenwald in 1944.

HINDENBERG, Paul von (1847-1934): Prussian commander of German army before and during First World War. Elected president of republic in 1925, succeeding Ebert, and re-elected in 1932. Appointed Hitler Chancellor in 1933.

HITLER, Adolf (1889-1945): founder of the NSDAP (Nazis); Chancellor from January 1933.

HOELZ, Max (1889-1933): former metalworker, in the USPD and KPD; organised the workers who fought against the Kapp putsch in 1920 and led the armed struggle in Mansfeld in 1921. Sentenced to life imprisonment, he was released in 1928 and went to Moscow, where he died in an accident.

HÖRSING, Otto (1874-1937): Social Democrat, and president of Saxony; founder of Reichsbanner.

HUGENBERG, Alfred (1865-1951): banker and right winger, opponent of the Weimar republic, head of the Nationalist Party in 1928. Supported Hitler but dismissed by the Nazis soon after Hitler came to power.

JOGICHES, Leo (1867-1919): Polish socialist who, alongside Rosa Luxemburg, led the Spartacus League and the KPD in its early years. Murdered by the Freikorps in prison on 10 March 1919.

KAMENEV, Lev Borisovich (1883-1936): leading Bolshevik, who supported Stalin against Trotsky until 1925, then joined Opposition. He was readmitted to the Communist Party of the Soviet Union in 1928, but was later shot after the first of Stalin's Moscow Trials.

KAPP, Wolfgang (1858-1922): Prussian nationalist whose name is associated with the putsch in 1920 which attempted to re-establish the monarchy and a military dictatorship.

KATZ, Ivan (1889-1956): Joined the SPD before 1914, later the USPD and the KPD. On the political committee of the KPD in 1924, and sent to Moscow. Expelled 1926.

KAUTSKY, Karl (1854-1938): SPD leader and theoretician; Engels' collaborator, he was regarded as an orthodox Marxist before 1914, but a pacifist during the First World War whose opposition to Bolshevism provoked replies from Lenin and Trotsky. He was for a short time in the USPD but rejoined the SPD in 1919.

KAYSER, Paul (1885-1950): trade unionist and socialist who was successively in the SPD, USPD and KPD. Led the communist building workers' union in 1923. Expelled from KPD 1924.

KOENEN, Bernhard (1889-1964): KPD delegate to the third congress of the Third International. Seriously wounded by the Nazis in 1933, he emigrated to the USSR and capitulated to Stalin.

KOENEN, Wilhelm (1886-1963): member of the central committee of the KPD and Reichstag deputy. Delegate to the third congress of the Third International. Went to western Europe in 1933; returned to Germany in 1945 and became a leading member of the SED.

KOHN, Joseph (Joko): Left Opposition leader; editor of the *Permanente Revolution*. Returned to KPD after expulsion for urging others to rejoin it, the line advocated by the Stalinist agents Well and Senin.

KORSCH, Karl (1886-1961): law professor who joined the USPD in 1917 and the KPD in 1920. Reichstag deputy in 1924. Expelled from KPD as a left-winger in 1926. A writer on Marxism.

KRUPSKAYA, Nadezhda (1869-1939): old Bolshevik and Lenin's wife. Joined the Left Opposition briefly in 1926 but left fearing a split in the party. Virtual prisoner of Stalin for the last years of her life.

LAMBERT, Pierre: a founder of the ICFI; leader of the Parti Communiste Internationaliste in France. Abandoned the fight to rebuild the Fourth International and split with Healy in 1971.

LASHEVICH, M: old Bolshevik and Red Army commander.

LEDEBOUR, Georg (1850-1947): founder member of the USPD; opposed the Spartacus League; founded the Socialist League. In 1931 he joined the SAPD. Fled to Switzerland in 1933.

LEGIEN, Karl (1861-1920): trade union leader, president of the ADGB federation of trade unions. Hostile to Marxism.

LEIPART, Theodor (1867-1947): conservative trade union leader who led ADGB after Legien.

LEOW, Willy (1887-1937): carpenter; SPD member in 1904. Joined Spartacus League during the First World War. Led the RFB in 1924. A Reichstag deputy in 1928. Went to the USSR and disappeared, a victim of Stalin.

LEVI, Paul (1883-1930): lawyer, leader of the Spartacus League with Rosa Luxemburg. President of the KPD but after being expelled in 1921 he joined the SPD.

LIEBKNECHT, Karl (1871-1919): Leader of the Spartacus League; imprisoned for his internationalist opposition to the war after he refused to vote for war credits in the Reichstag. Murdered in January 1919 by order of Noske, minister in the Social Democratic Ebert-Scheidemann government.

LUDENDORFF, Erich von (1865-1937): general who participated in the Kapp putsch in 1920 and the Beer Hall putsch to restore monarchy in 1923; supported Hitler; created theory of 'war of annihilation'.

LÜTTWITZ, Walther von: General, commandant of Berlin, who led the 1920 putsch with Kapp. Subsequently released from prison.

LUXEMBURG, Rosa (1871-1919): active in the Polish socialist movement, and in the German social democratic movement from 1897. Imprisoned during the First World War, she led the Spartacus League and helped form the KPD; she edited *Rote Fahne* (*Red Flag*) and led the KPD until her murder, with Karl Liebknecht, in January 1919.

MAITAN, Livio: Italian Pabloite; a leader of the ISFI.

MAO ZEDONG (1893-1976): Chinese Communist Party leader and first leader of the People's Republic of China, 1949.

MASLOW, Arkadi (Max) (1893-1941): a Russian Jew whose family came to Germany in 1899. Joined the KPD in 1919 and led the party with Ruth Fischer and Urbahns from 1924. Opposed Trotsky from 1923 to 1925, then briefly supported Left Opposition. Expelled from KPD 1926 and formed Lenin League. Died in Cuba.

MEYER, Ernst (1887-1930): member of SPD in 1908, later with Rosa Luxemburg in Spartacus League; in leadership of KPD 1918-1922. Worked on the KPD paper *Rote Fahne (Red Flag)*. A central committee member in the centre of the party, against 'ultra-leftism', in 1929.

MÜLLER, Alexander (Sascha): born 1892 in Moscow; a white-collar worker and member of the KPD from 1918 to 1929. A leading member of the national leadership of the German Left opposition, responsible for administration of *Permanente Revolution*. In June 1931 with Kurt Landau he left the Left Opposition and founded group around journal *Kommunist*. Worked illegally in Berlin until arrested in January 1934. Annegrete Schüle (*Trotzkismus in Deutschland bis 1933*) says he may have given Oskar Hippe's name to the police under torture.

MÜLLER, Richard: leader of the metalworkers and president of the workers' councils in 1918.

MUSSOLINI, Benito (1883-1945): fascist dictator of Italy from 1922.

NEUMANN, Heinz (1902-1937): joined the KPD as a young intellectual in 1920; sent to Moscow in 1925, and from there to China, where he led the Canton insurrection in 1927. He became Stalin's man, and edited the *Rote Fahne*. Allied with Thälmann. Came into opposition after 1932; arrested and presumably executed in Moscow in 1937.

NOSKE, Gustav (1868-1946): from a working-class family; Social Democrat leader and army minister who put down the German revolution in January 1919. Resigned after the Kapp putsch.

PABLO, Michel (Raptis): secretary of the Fourth International after Second World War; gave his name to tendency called Pabloism.

PAPEN, Franz von (1878-1969): landowner, aristocrat, military attaché in USA during First World War. Chancellor in 1932, he helped Hitler to power and was tried as a war criminal.

PFEMFERT, Franz (1879-1954): writer; founder member of the KPD, a member of the KAP after 1920. Editor of the magazine *Der Aktion*. He made contact with Trotsky and the Left Opposition, publishing many of Trotsky's writings in German. Went into exile after 1933.

PIECK, Wilhelm (1876-1960): originally a carpenter; joined the SPD in 1895 and the Spartacus League during the First World War, when he was imprisoned several times. An ally of Karl Liebknecht in 1918. Central committee member of the KPD from its formation and on the executive of the Third International in 1928. President of the KPD and later the SED; president of the GDR until his death.

PREOBRAZHENSKY, Evgenii Alexeyevich (1886-1937): Bolshevik and writer on economics associated with Bukharin. Supported Left Opposition until 1929, but eventually a victim of Stalin.

RADEK, Karl (Sobelson) (1885-1939): Polish revolutionary. Associated with Rosa Luxemburg and Leo Jogiches in 1905, he later chose the opposing side in the split in the Social-Democratic Party of Poland and Lithuania. Worked on left-wing Social-Democratic publications in Germany before First World War. Worked closely with Lenin during war. Sent to Germany by Bolsheviks in 1918, he played an important role in the early years of the KPD, occasionally from a prison cell. Left Oppositionist until 1929, then capitulated to Stalin but subsequently tried and imprisoned by Stalin.

RAKOVSKY, Christian (1873-1941): a leading figure in the revolutionary movement in the Balkans. Chair of the Ukrainian Soviet 1918, later Soviet ambassador to Britain and France. A leader of the Left Opposition; deported to Siberia in 1928. He capitulated to Stalin in 1934. One of the main defendants in the third Moscow trial in 1938; sentenced to 20 years' hard labour.

REMMELE, Hermann (1880-1939?): metallurgist; in the SPD in 1897, later in the USPD and the KPD. Allied with Thälmann after 1926. One of the leaders of the KPD and on the praesidium of the Third International. Tried with Neumann to replace Thälmann in 1932. Went to Moscow in 1933; arrested in 1937, he disappeared.

ROSENBERG, Arthur (1889-1945): university professor, USPD member in 1918 and KPD member from 1920. On the central committee and political committee from 1924 to 1925. Joined Thälmann in 1926, and left the party in 1927. Wrote a history of the Weimar republic.

ROSENFELD, Kurt (1877-1943): lawyer in SPD in Berlin in 1909. A founder member of the USPD in 1917 and USPD deputy in the Reichstag in 1920. Rosa Luxemburg's lawyer. Minister of Justice in Prussia in 1918. He opposed the fusion with the KPD and consequently rejoined the SPD, from which he was expelled in 1931. Formed the SAPD with Seydewitz, but left it in 1933 and went to the USA.

RÜHLE, Otto (1874-1943): professor; member of SPD in 1900. Reichstag deputy in 1912, refused in 1914 with Leibknecht to vote for war credits. Joined Spartacus League and KPD. Helped form KAP and was then expelled from it; returned to SPD. Emigrated to Mexico and served on Dewey Commission into Stalin's Moscow Trials.

SCHEIDEMANN, Philipp (1865-1939): printer; right-wing Social Democrat and first president of the government of the Weimar Republic. Suppressed the 1918 revolution and responsible with Noske and Ebert for the murder of the Spartacist leaders. In the Reichstag until 1933, when he went to Denmark.

SCHLECHT, Paul (1882-1950): metallurgist; member of SPD in 1900, later USPD and KPD. On the central committee and political committee in 1924. A Reichstag deputy.

SCHLEICHER, Kurt von (1882-1934): German army leader; Chancellor in 1932 until replaced by Hitler. Murdered by the Nazis.

SCHMIDT, Alfred: born in 1891, entered SPD in 1909 and later the Spartacus League and the KPD. Expelled in 1928, he went into the KPO and fought against the Nazis. Spent many years in prisons and concentration camps. In the SED after the war; expelled in 1947 and sentenced to death in 1948, commuted to 25 years. Freed from Bautzen in 1956, he went to West Germany.

SCHNEEWEISS, Helmut: born in 1903 in Berlin; joined the Young Communists and led the unemployed workers' committees and proletarian militia at Orianenburg. Popular worker' leader in KPD who brought many workers with him into the Left Opposition after he was expelled for inviting Urbahns to a KPD public meeting. Organised armed workers' self-defence groups. Fled abroad from the Nazis in 1933; became expert forger of official papers during war.

SCHNELLER, Ernst (1890-1944): joined KPD from the SPD in 1920. Responsible for defence. Opposed Trotskyism and 'Luxemburgism'.

SCHOLEM, Werner (1895-1940): in the SPD from 1913. Imprisoned in 1917 for opposing the war. Joined USPD and then KPD. On the central committee with Ruth Fischer until 1925. Joined the Lenin League and contributed to its press and that of the Trotskyists. Arrested 1933, he died in Buchenwald in 1940.

SCHUMACHER, Wilhelm: in the SPD in 1910, then joined the USPD and the KPD before the fusion; led the garment workers' union. Expelled 1924.

SCHWARZ, Ernst (1886-1958): joined SPD in 1918, then USPD and KPD. Reichstag deputy in 1924. Sympathetic to Left Opposition and expelled from KPD 1926.

SEDOV, Leon (1905-1938): son of Trotsky and Natalia Sedova; a close collaborator with Trotsky in the Russian Left Opposition; expelled from CPSU in 1927. Following Trotsky's exile to Turkey, became main leader of International Left Opposition. From 1919 he edited the *Bulletin of the Opposition*. In 1931 he went to Berlin and with Eugen Bauer (Ackerknecht) ran the Secretariat of the International Left Opposition. Left Germany on Trotsky's instructions in March 1933; worked on *Bulletin* from Paris, where he wrote the *Red Book on the Moscow Trials* and was subsequently murdered on Stalin's orders.

SEIPOLD, Oskar (1889-1966): Polish-born, Russian-raised. In the SPD in 1909, later the USPD and KPD. Nationalised German in 1919. In prison from 1924-1927. In the Left Opposition; put Trotskyist position in Prussian Landtag. Prisoner of the Nazis.

SENIN (Abraham Sobolevicius): Stalinist agent in the Trotskyist movement.

SEYDEWITZ, Max: born 1892. In the SPD in 1910, and on its left wing; edited various SPD journals. Expelled in 1931, he founded the SAPD, which he left in 1933. Became a Stalinist functionary in the GDR.

SCHACHTMAN, Max: leader of SWP petty-bourgeois opposition with Burnham and Abern in 1939-1940.

SOMMER, Michael (1896-1938): miner, member of the USPD in 1918 and the KPD in 1920. Leader of the red unions in Berlin. Sent to Moscow, where he became a victim of Stalin.

STERNBERG, Benno (also Barois or Benno Sarel): in the French section of the Fourth International during Nazi occupation. Left in 1952. Schachtmanite.

STRAUSS, Franz Josef (1915-1988): right-wing leader of Bavarian CSU in the 1960s and 1970s; held various ministerial posts from 1953.

STRESEMANN, Gustav: leader of Deutsche Volkspartei. Member of coalition government with SPD in 1923.

THÄLMANN, Ernst (1886-1944): in the SPD from 1909, later in the USPD and the KPD. In the Reichstag in 1923. On the central committee, and selected by Stalin to lead the party after the Fischer-Maslow leadership was expelled in 1926. Arrested by the Nazis in 1937; executed in Buchenwald in 1944.

THALHEIMER, August (1884-1948): joined SPD in 1904, Spartacus League during the First World War, and then the KPD. With Brandler, led the right wing of the party into the KPO.

THOREZ, Maurice (1900-1964): French Communist Party member from its formation in 1920; Stalin's main representative in French party.

ULBRICHT, Walter: born 1893; carpenter; joined SPD in 1912, and later the KPD. Worked for 'Bolshevisation' of the party and represented the party in Moscow. Succeeded Thälmann after his arrest. In the USSR after 1937; returned with the Red Army in 1945. For many years leader of the GDR.

URBAHNS, Hugo (1890-1947): A Spartacist in 1918, and a KPD leader in the Hamburg area. Imprisoned after leading 1923 uprising. A key figure in the left-wing opposition with Fischer and Maslow, he was expelled in 1926 and with them formed the Leninbund. Briefly associated with the Left Opposition, he expelled Trotskyists from the Leninbund in 1930. Went to Sweden in 1933.

UTZELMANN (Kempin), Franz Peter: born in 1894; member of the

Volksmarine (People's Marine Division) in 1918. Member of the KPD and of the left-wing KAP. Sentenced to life imprisonment in 1921 but released in 1923.

WALCHER, Jakob: born in 1887, in the SPD from 1906; sympathetic to Spartacists and a founder member of the KPD. In Moscow 1924-1926. Expelled from the party in 1928 he joined the KPO and later the SAPD. Functionary in the GDR.

WEBER, Hans: born 1895. In the USPD from 1917 and later a KPD district secretary. On the left wing of the party, he was at the fifth congress of the Third International. He was associated with the 'Bolshevik-Leninist' opposition.

WEHNER, Herbert: leader of the KPD, implicated in the liquidation of Remmele in Moscow. In the SPD after Second World War; in the Bonn parliament.

WELL, Roman (Sobolevicius, Ruvin, alias Robert Soblen) (1901-1962): joined the KPD in 1927 and with Eugen Bauer (Ackerknecht) built one of the first Trotskyist groups in Germany. By 1930, with Kurt Landau, one of the leaders of the German Left Opposition. Factional struggles resulted in Landau and his supporters leaving. It is not clear at what point Well became a Stalinist agent with his brother Abraham (see Senin). In 1933 produced a fake issue of the *Permanente Revolution* which pretended the majority of the Left Opposition favoured returning to the KPD.

WELS, Otto (1873-1939): right-wing leader of the SPD until 1933; military commissar in Berlin in 1918 who suppressed the revolutionary movement.

WEYER, Paul (1887-1943): locksmith; in the SPD from 1910, the USPD from 1917 and then the KPD. A leader of the metalworkers' union in 1923, he was expelled from the KPD in 1924.

ZEIGNER, Erich (1886-1961): in the SPD 1919; argued for fusion with the KPD. Led government in Saxony in 1923; invited communists into government in October; subsequently thrown out by the Reichswehr and imprisoned.

ZÖRGIEBEL, Karl: born 1878; Social Democrat commissioner of police in Berlin.